ADULT EDUCATION
IN THE CHURCH

Edited by

Roy B. Zuck

and

Gene A. Getz

MOODY PRESS
CHICAGO

Copyright © 1970 by
THE MOODY BIBLE INSTITUTE
OF CHICAGO

Library of Congress Catalog Card Number: 79-123154

ISBN 0-8024-0468-5

12 13 14 15 16 17 Printing/BB/Year 87 86 85 84

Printed in the United States of America

CONTENTS

Part II—HELPING FAMILIES

PREFACE

As Christian education has developed over the last several decades, much emphasis has been placed on the children and youth ministries of the church. This has not been a wrong emphasis, except that several false implications have seemingly grown out of the fervor with which these areas of the educational program of the church have been promoted. One such notion is that the way to reach adults is to reach children and youth first—but particularly children. Another is that since few adults can and will be saved, we must reach children and youth. And another—and perhaps the most unfortunate—is that, to be effective, Christian education *must* take place in the church.

All would agree that adults have been reached for Christ by first reaching a child (through the cradle roll department, for example), and that it is seemingly easier to get *more* decisions from children and youth than adults, and that a well-functioning educational program in the local church for children and youth is a must in our present culture with all of its secular and antichristian influences. However, a long view also reveals —regretfully—that if a child is reached for Christ, he is very frequently lost to the church in his adolescent years if his parents are not eventually reached with the gospel and encouraged to cooperate in his Christian nurture. Furthermore, it has been demonstrated, particularly in recent years, that adults can be reached for Christ if properly approached. (Campus Crusade for Christ has demonstrated this in a remarkable way through their Adult-Lay Institutes of Evangelism.) And it is also becoming increasingly obvious that church leaders, no matter how dedicated and effective, cannot be substitutes for nonchristian parents, nor even for Christian parents. There is something inherently educational about the twenty-four-hour-a-day, seven-day-a-week environment of the home. In addition, home nurture is a very important foundational experience for an effective educational experience at the church level.

It is time to refocus the biblical principles of Christian education. Several very significant questions need to be faced: Who were those who were reached for Christ when the New Testament church came into being, and who formed its nucleus—children, youth or adults? How were those adults reached—through their children and youth or by direct confrontation with the gospel? Who throughout the scriptural record (in both the Old and New Testaments) were basically responsible for the spiritual nurture of children and youth—the church or parents?

The biblical pattern is unusually clear. Christian education in the Bible focused on adults who in turn were responsible to educate their children. Those first saved were *adults,* and those first trained and equipped to serve Christ were *adults.* The implication is clear: an adult reached for Christ and built up in the faith resulted in entire families being reached for Christ and taught in Him.

This in no way negates the importance of an up-to-date and well-functioning educational program of the church for *all* age levels. The home—Christian though it be—cannot carry the burden of Christian education alone. Our society and culture is far too sophisticated, complex and demanding to attempt to reproduce the complete biblical pattern— just as parents do not bear the responsibility per se of the general education of the young as they did in certain periods of biblical history.

Though we cannot reproduce the biblical pattern because of cultural differences, we can refocus the biblical principles: The New Testament church placed primary emphasis on adult education, *and* the home was foundational in the education of the young.

Part I of this book deals with the church's teaching ministry with adults, and Part II considers the home's responsibility in its Christian educational ministry to children and youth. It is our belief that to omit either of these emphases or to consider them as secondary will lead to a weak program of Christian education. It is our hope that this volume will contribute to a reevaluation of the adult program of the church and, consequently, a new application of biblical principles resulting in a greater ministry of Christian discipleship and outreach.

GENE A. GETZ, PH.D.
ROY B. ZUCK, TH.D.

Part I
TEACHING ADULTS

1

THE CHALLENGE OF ADULT CHRISTIAN EDUCATION

John T. Sisemore

Adult education in the work of a church is as old as Christianity itself. In fact, it antedates the church. Ever since God began to reveal Himself to man, there has been an unfolding educational movement directed toward adults.

Throughout the biblical record there is a close correlation between the education of adults and the unfolding revelation of God.

> In the early patriarchal period all education was *oral* and religious truth was transmitted by word of mouth. *Written* forms of education were introduced by Moses in the giving of the Law . . . . Under the prophets, *preaching* became a part of the educational process. The rabbis introduced *formal teaching* as a vehicle of education. Jesus brought the education process to its apex by the *sharing of Himself* as a Teacher.[1]

The education of adults was carried out vigorously by the early church. In fact, the education of adults, along with the attendant activities growing out of education, largely constituted the church's program. In subsequent years the success of local churches has ebbed and flowed with the degree of effectiveness obtained in educating adults in Christian living and service.

The vital relationship between church progress and the quality of education provided for its adults is obvious. A church is essentially, though not entirely, an adult institution. It was originated by an adult, it was organized with adults, it was given a mission that requires the reaching of adults, and it was assigned an educational function which is to be beamed toward adults.

JOHN T. SISEMORE is the Adult Field Services Unit Supervisor for the Sunday School Department of the Southern Baptist Sunday School Board, Nashville, Tennessee.

Three times in history there has been a veritable surge of adult religious education. Each time there has been an accompanying religious awakening. In early Hebrew history both the priest and the prophet majored on adult education.

The second surge of religious education for adults came as the early Christians "that were scattered abroad went every where preaching the word" (Ac 8:4). It is noteworthy that this surge had a very strong evangelistic flavor. The result of this approach was a winning of much of the then-known world to Christ in less than three centuries.

In the course of history, there came a decline of interest in adult Christian education. The attendant "Dark Ages" were routed only by the Reformation which once again brought into prominence the educating of adults. The results of this renewal of interest in adult Christian education were so outstanding that the Roman Catholic parochial school system was established to offset the advances made by Protestant adult education.

The world is waiting for and may now be witnessing the early stages of a fourth great surge in the religious education of adults. Interestingly, this new thrust correlates with an unusual development in adult education generally.

THE CHALLENGE OF THE ADULT EDUCATION MOVEMENT

Never before in history has the interest in education been as intense as it presently is. The significance of this statement is amplified by the fact that "adult education is the largest and fastest growing segment of American education."[2] Just as the education of the child consumed the interests of educators in the first half of the twentieth century, the education of adults is increasingly the major concern of the last half of the century.

Actually what has happened is not so much a change in *interest* as it is a change in *concept*. Because it has become quite clear that persons continue to develop and change all through life, educators have concluded that individuals must be educated throughout adulthood. The far-reaching consequences of this concept constitute a new educational challenge of unprecedented magnitude.

The real challenge of the adult-education movement is intertwined with the future, but it is best understood when viewed from its historical perspective. Concern for the education of adults in the United States has come to the forefront in recent years, but it is by no means a new interest. As far back as 1607 the Jamestown colonists developed an adult-education program. Although their activities were primarily vocational and religious in nature, those functions were nevertheless the beginning of the present-day adult-education movement.

Six years after the Puritans landed in Massachusetts, they had established Harvard College; in another eleven years they had passed a law that laid the foundations for the public school system.

> More formally organized programs of adult education date from the end of the eighteenth century. In Philadelphia, Benjamin Franklin had his Junto Discussion Clubs before the Revolution, and in 1785 the Philadelphia Society for Promoting Agriculture was formed, including George Washington, Noah Webster, and Benjamin Franklin among its members.[3]

In addition to these agricultural studies, schools, and discussion clubs, interest in educating adults led to the development of the public library. By the end of the eighteenth century, subscription libraries, specialty libraries and free public libraries were being utilized. Many of these libraries carried on organized programs of education in addition to their book-loaning services.

The growing demand for more practical information gave rise to the lyceum as an adult-education tool. By the middle of the nineteenth century, giving and listening to lectures had become a national pastime, if not a way of life.

Following the Civil War, the Chautauqua Movement, which really began as an assembly for Sunday school teachers, played an extensive role in the Christian education of adults. Although the Chautauqua Movement died out in the early part of the twentieth century, it gave birth to the leadership-training programs now followed by most churches.

As the twentieth century dawned, both the Sunday school movement for adults and the formalizing of adult-education agencies occurred. As early as 1913 at least one major denomination had established an organized program for adults in Sunday school. In 1926 the American Association for Adult Education was formed, and in 1951 the Adult Education Association of the U.S.A. was organized.

In the intervening years both the scope and purpose of continuing adult education programs have been delineated. The objectives of secular adult education are now generally accepted to be as follows:

1. To make adults aware of their civic responsibilities to one another and to the community, the nation, and the world
2. To make them economically more efficient
3. To develop a sense of responsibility and a knowledge of how to proceed in making personal adjustments to home life and family relationships
4. To promote health and physical fitness
5. To provide the means for encouraging cultural development and an appreciation of the arts
6. To supplement and broaden educational backgrounds

7. To provide for the development of avocational interests through opportunities for self-expression[4]

At the present time approximately one in every three adults in the United States is involved annually in one or more types of educational activity. In spite of this achievement, the adult-education movement has not yet been thoroughly unified and established, but it offers a growing challenge to the adult world and the church.

History teaches that *if there is to be any vital Christian influence in the world, churches must be dynamically concerned with and singularly engaged in the education of adults.* Such an engagement at this time would constitute an unprecedented challenge that defies description.

THE CHALLENGE OF TODAY'S ADULT GENERATION

One of the most dramatic changes in the contemporary religious milieu is the attitude toward adults. What was once an attitude of unconcern, if not antagonism, has now become one of great concern and action. More and more church leaders are recognizing that a program of adult education is a key factor in any significant advance in church programs.

Adulthood may be described as the "promised land" toward which children and youth are advancing. It is truly, as Robert Browning has written, the period of life "for which the first was made." Adulthood is the longest period of life, and it is also an ever increasing span as life expectancy is extended.

Adulthood is reached when an individual becomes personally accountable for himself and accepts adult responsibilities. This stage of life is sometimes reached in a dramatic or sudden manner, as when a person marries or enters a vocation. At other times, adulthood follows a transitional period or "twilight zone" between youth and adulthood.

Various definitions and delineations of age-ranges are used to pinpoint the arrival at adulthood. Because of the extremely individualistic development of persons, it has become the general practice in religious education to set an arbitrary age-range to classify persons as adults. Generally, adulthood has been reached by age twenty-five, and this age is usually considered the appropriate beginning point for classifying persons as adults for purposes of education. However, those who advocate this age-range for adults generally acknowledge that some persons reach adulthood before this time (and some may reach it after twenty-five, if ever at all). Other Christian educators suggest that adulthood begins with age eighteen or twenty-one.[*]

[*]*Young adults* is therefore a term difficult to define. For some it means college-age youth from ages 18 to 21, for others it suggests a wider range from ages 18 to 25, but for still others it suggests ages 21 to 40 or 25 to 40. For more on this subject, see chap. 3, "The Nature and Needs of Young Adults."

Adults constitute the largest and most divergent age-group. Adulthood includes several distinctive stages of development. Adults in all stages should be educated at the church, in the home, or in other appropriate places.

Adults, as persons, are unique and special individuals. Although there are many obvious similarities, each adult is essentially different from all those who have preceded him or will follow him. These differences grow out of heredity, environment, endowment, age, sex, schooling and experience.

In addition to these factors, adults face perennial pressures, treacherous temptations, perplexing problems and relentless responsibilities. Because of these complex forces, which constantly exert far-reaching influences on adults, a personal concern for individual adults is an especially important challenge to churches.

Another important facet of the challenge of today's adults is the very large and growing number of adults who are untouched by the churches. Counting as adults only those persons who are twenty-five years of age or over, there are more than ninety million adults in the United States who are not enrolled in Sunday school. In fact, many churches have more adult church members *not* enrolled in Sunday school than they have in their total adult Sunday school membership. Added to these tragic situations is the probability that the unchurched adult population may well continue to increase by about one million persons per year. Undoubtedly the numerical challenge of today's adults is unparalleled in history.

THE CHALLENGE OF A NEW EDUCATIONAL STANCE

Somehow in the modern preoccupation with the education of children and youth, churches have inadvertently overlooked the necessity of educating adults.

Such a situation seems incongruous when it is recalled that in ancient times most of the education was addressed to adults. Socrates, Aristotle, Plato, the Hebrew prophets, the teachers of the Sanhedrin, and Jesus Christ Himself addressed themselves not so much to the young as to mature persons. All the great social movements of the sixteenth, seventeenth and eighteenth centuries were directed toward adults.

In this enlightened day it would be unforgivable for churches to overlook or neglect the giving of paramount attention to adult education. The significance of adult-education programs cannot be overestimated. Their impact is a fact of history.

> Great periods of religious rebirth have not emerged as a result of child nurture . . . for the religion of the child will usually be a relatively pale

edition of the faith of the older generation. This means that unless the faith comes alive in the soul of some mature individual or group, religious vitality may be expected to continue to decline in modern culture.[5]

No amount of Christian education gained in childhood, or even in youth, can last a person throughout life. The massive problems confronting adults today as a result of rapid social and technological changes demand that Christian education of men and women be continuous and lifelong.

It is well known that churches in the past two centuries have focused their educational attention on their children and youth. A number of Christian leaders, however, are challenging this approach by asserting that, whereas the Christian education of children and youth is extremely important, educating adults is equally significant, if not more so.

This new stance in education, which spotlights adults, seems to have a twofold basis: first, the premise that the family is a most effective educational agency; and second, and even more important, the desperate need of adults for basic Christian education so that they can fulfill their roles in the home, church and society.

The extent to which this educational stance will move more favorably toward adults is presently unknown. However, some very salient concepts are becoming popular. Among them is this one: It is adults who shape attitudes, create the spiritual tone, determine the policies, set the pace, furnish the leadership, provide the finances, influence the young, spearhead Sunday school advance, and determine church destiny.

In spite of the developing new stance, the educational program in many churches is still weakest where it should be strongest. Frequently the adult program gets weaker leaders, more inadequate space, poorer equipment, less consideration and more criticism than any other program.

This deplorable condition exists in part because it has been assumed that adults are already educated from their childhood instruction. However, there are several other evident reasons for this neglect of adult education. Chief among them is a philosophy peculiar to America. Whereas almost all other nations revere and respect their adults, this nation tends to elevate childhood and youth to such a degree that adulthood is often unconsciously depreciated.

Churches have justified their neglect of adults by proclaiming that the children are the church of tomorrow. To be sure, this concept is true; but it is only a part of a larger truth. The full truth is this: The children are the hope of *the day after tomorrow*, the youth are the hope of *tomorrow*, but adults are the only hope for *today*. Lose the children, and the church will die in *two* generations; lose the youth, and the church will die in *one* generation; lose the adults, and the church may very well die in *this* generation! Who could deny that the current moral, social and theological conflicts are largely, if not totally, the result of the failure to meaningfully reach adults for Christ and adequately involve them in Christian education?

On the other hand, the need for reaching and teaching children and young people dare not be underestimated. In recent years educators, psychologists and sociologists have been unanimous in stating that the first few years of a child's life are his most formative years. Even before a child enters public school, his entire bent of personality is set and his character traits are formed almost irrevocably. Furthermore, a person's attitudes toward Christ, the Bible and the church are greatly influenced in his childhood years. Also children are remarkably responsive to the gospel and tenderly sensitive to spiritual truths.

Young people, too, constitute a tremendous challenge to the church. They have great spiritual needs which can be met only by a vigorous evangelistic and teaching ministry. Many youth are wonderfully receptive to the gospel and openly responsive to challenges to serve Christ and the church. Their relentless energy, their ability to think deeply about spiritual matters, their idealistic altruistic concern for the needs of others, their emotional fluctuations and problems of social adjustment— all these characteristics make adolescents a generation of people that the church *must* reach. Admittedly many adults are difficult to win to Christ and to enlist in the work of the church because they were not adequately ministered to in their childhood and/or youth. But it must also be admitted that if the church reaches children and youth without reaching the parents as well, it frequently loses many of the children and youth as they grow older. A strong church program without the support of the home often fails to do the ultimate job of Christian education.

Undoubtedly churches must continue to make adequate provision for the Christian education of the children and youth, but they can no longer stop with these groups. A church's Christian-education program is complete only when it provides adequately for all three major age-divisions— children, youth and adults. Churches must assiduously face up to the fact that they cannot make appreciable and lasting gain in their work until they begin to give at least as much attention to adults as they do to the younger segments of their constituency.

Education is a process that requires a philosophical strategy. If churches are to achieve their essential mission, they must have the leadership, resources and influence that adults alone can provide. Therefore any successful strategy for Christian education must, because of the very nature of a church, place adults in the front line of opportunity and emphasis.

Because of their need, and because of their importance to the church, all adult church members need to be enlisted and actively involved in the church's educational ministry. Those adults who are not presently involved should be the prime object of concern and compassion. And this attitude toward and concern for adults is indeed a new and challenging stance in contemporary religious education.

THE CHALLENGE OF RETHINKING BASIC OBJECTIVES

At the present time, most evangelical denominations and many individual churches are rethinking and restating their educational goals and objectives. This renewed concern about goals has both grown out of and is responsible for another very serious evaluation—that of reexamining the nature and mission of the local church. The net result is the growing conviction that Christian education is inherently essential to the ministry of the church.

After accepting the idea that the education of adults is essential to its life and work, a church would do well to consider what it is trying to achieve in its adult-educational program. Several important questions relate to the problem of determining objectives:

1. What are God's purposes for adults?
2. How does the Bible relate to the needs of adults?
3. What needs of adults can and should be met by a program of Christian education?
4. What specific areas of the Christian life should be included in the goals for Christian education?
5. How should adult goals be stated? In terms of organizational structure, church functions or developmental tasks?
6. Do theology, educational philosophy and church history have any bearing on adult-education goals?
7. How may the goals for adults reflect the differences between secular and Christian education?
8. How may adult goals be specific while at the same time broad enough to allow for individual differences?
9. How may the work of the Holy Spirit be reflected in Christian-education goals for adults?

These questions are in no way incidental or academic. They are at the very heart of the current problems in the enlistment and education of the contemporary adult generation.

Any church that is thoroughly sincere about its adult program could profitably spend a prolonged period of time in coming to satisfactory answers to these questions. The scope of this chapter does not include the theory behind such questions, but it does recognize the need for churches to make such studies.

Recognizing that it would be unwise, even if it were possible, for a church to follow a stereotyped set of goals, the following statements are suggested as a beginning point in formulating goals for an adult Christian-education program:

1. *Christian conversion*—Our aim is to lead each unsaved adult to a genuine experience of the forgiving and saving grace of God through Jesus Christ.
2. *Church membership*—Our aim is to guide each Christian adult into intelligent, active and devoted membership in a New Testament church.
3. *Christian worship*—Our aim is to help each adult to make Christian worship a vital and constant part of his expanding experience.
4. *Christian knowledge and conviction*—Our aim is to help each adult to grow toward mature Christian knowledge, understanding and conviction.
5. *Christian attitudes and appreciations*—Our aim is to assist each adult in developing such Christian attitudes and appreciations that he will have a Christian approach to all of life.
6. *Christian living*—Our aim is to guide each adult in developing habits and skills which promote spiritual growth and in applying Christian standards of conduct in every area of life.
7. *Christian service*—Our aim is to lead each adult to invest his talents and skills in Christian service.[6]

THE CHALLENGE OF MAKING ADULT EDUCATION EFFECTIVE

Making the adult-education programs effective is the underlying thesis of this book. Therefore the purpose at this point is best served by simply pointing out some of the significant aspects of the challenge to make education effective.

Making adult education effective is a stimulating challenge to Christian workers—a challenge (1) to locate and enlist the adults for which a church bears the responsibility, (2) to provide organization and leadership equal to the adult opportunity, (3) to project a Christian fellowship that attracts an unbelieving public, (4) to gear Bible teaching and training to the desperate needs of adults, (5) to refocus the evangelistic thrust of the churches, and (6) to call to commitment a generation that is uncommitted.

Because Bible study and other Christian-education activities motivate adults to be and do what God desires of them, the challenge of making the educational program effective is one of immense proportions.

As churches improve the quality of their educational ministry to adults, they will reap many benefits. The children will be blest, the home will be reinforced, the community will be uplifted, the church will be revitalized, and the Lord will be honored. Surely today is the day for an unrelenting effort to provide meaningful Christian education for adults. When this provision has been made, the results will be the same as in New Testament days: "And believers were the more added to the Lord, multitudes both of men and women" (Ac 5:14).

NOTES

1. John T. Sisemore, *Vital Principles in Religious Education* (Nashville: Broadman, 1966), p. 18.
2. Malcolm S. Knowles, *Handbook of Adult Education in the United States* (Chicago: Adult Education Assn. of the USA, 1960), p. 5.
3. Paul B. Maves, *Understanding Ourselves as Adults* (New York: Abingdon, 1959), p. 21.
4. Jayne and Spence Sheats, *Adult Education* (New York: Bryden, 1953), p. 5.
5. H. Shelton Smith, *Faith and Nurture* (New York: Scribner, 1941), pp. 102-4.
6. Curriculum Committee, *The Curriculum Guide, 1963-64* (Nashville: Convention, 1960-61), pp. 29-33.

FOR FURTHER READING

Bergevin, Paul. *A Philosophy for Adult Education.* Greenwich, Conn.: Seaburg, 1967.

Burns, Hobert W., ed. *Sociological Backgrounds of Adult Education.* Brookline, Mass.: Center for the Study of Liberal Education for Adults, 1964.

Ernsberger, David J. *A Philosophy of Adult Christian Education.* Philadelphia: Westminster, 1959.

Fry, John R. *A Hard Look at Adult Christian Education.* Philadelphia: Westminster, 1961.

Grattan, C. Hartley. *In Quest of Knowledge.* New York: Association, 1955.

Hurlock, Elizabeth B. *Developmental Psychology.* New York: McGraw-Hill, 1959.

Kempfer, Homer. *Adult Education.* New York: McGraw-Hill, 1955.

Knowles, Malcolm S. *Handbook of Adult Education in the United States.* Chicago: Adult Education Assn. of the USA, 1960.

Little, Lawrence C., ed. *The Future Course of Christian Adult Education.* Pittsburgh: U. Pittsburgh, 1959.

———, ed. *Wider Horizons in Christian Adult Education.* Pittsburgh: U. Pittsburgh, 1962.

Loessner, Ernest J. *Adults Continuing to Learn.* Nashville: Broadman, 1967.

Sisemore, John T. *The Sunday School Ministry to Adults.* Nashville: Convention, 1959.

———, ed. *Vital Principles in Religious Education.* Nashville: Broadman, 1966.

Wyckoff, D. Campbell. *Theory and Design of Christian Education Curriculum.* Philadelphia: Westminster, 1961.

2

THEOLOGICAL FOUNDATIONS OF ADULT CHRISTIAN EDUCATION

Edward L. Hayes

The renewal of interest in adult education among Evangelicals is one of the significant developments of our times. Undoubtedly the rise of adult participation in church-educational endeavors is a reflection of awakening community action in adult education. Increasing demands for skills brought about by an accelerating technology coupled with new opportunities spawned by expanding leisure time have provided the impetus for adults to go back to the classroom. Riding the crest of a revival in community and world culture, increasing numbers of adults are delving into subjects ranging from Plato to painting, music appreciation to mass communications. A wide range of learning opportunities is afforded by community colleges, universities, high schools, religious and cultural groups for the new wave of adult learners.

Within the sphere of local church education a stirring among adults is taking place which indicates a growing restlessness and dissatisfaction with traditional approaches to adult education. Lay renewal, evidenced in many segments of Christendom, is forcing a new look at educational programs and the power structure of church life. Recent developments in community life have brought an uneasiness among adults. Questions being raised about change, crisis and conflict demand theological answers. In this last third of the twentieth century, evangelical church education may be facing its greatest crisis. The good will and relatively high level of participation among adults in Christian education, enjoyed since the evangelical resurgence of the forties and fifties, may not prevail unless continuous attempts are made to upgrade adult education and to meet the basic issues of our times with authentic theological concern.

EDWARD L. HAYES, Ph.D., is Professor of Christian Education, Conservative Baptist Theological Seminary, Denver, Colorado.

A PERSPECTIVE

Only a relatively few decades ago church attendance was at an all-time low. The meteoric rise of the Sunday school burned itself out amid the apathy of the early years of the twentieth century. Born in eighteenth century England to meet a social crisis among children subjected to unfair labor practices, the Sunday school became a useful instrument on the American frontier for evangelism. Late in the nineteenth century some of the Sunday schools boasted large adult classes. According to some observers of the scene, these adult groups possessed qualities of a formidable movement. The revivalist tradition was front and center in American church life at the peak of the Sunday schools' success.

Theological winds blowing late in the nineteenth century were bearing portents of a shift in American Christianity. An overly optimistic view of man and a concept of the church devoid of a mission were two prevailing foundation stones of a theology which crumbled in the decades of the dawning utopia of the twentieth century.

The roots of the religious-education movement may be traced to the dual developments of liberal theology and educational pragmatism. Amid the awakening conscience of churchmen toward education was a predisposition to follow the developments of the new education rather than to critically adopt a theological base for religious education. The early years of the religious-education movement were marked by a more careful attention to progressive education than an attempt to reconstruct an impotent theology. While on the one hand assuming the stance of a liberal theology, religious education took its methodological cue from John Dewey.

Recently there has been a shift back to theological concern among liberal religious educators. The works of Miller, Munro, Smart, Sara Little, the Cullys and others have served as partial correctives to a religious education suffering from theological malnutrition.

Within evangelical circles, theological concern has been slower in coming. Midpoint in the decade of the sixties an editorial appeared in *Christianity Today* which analyzed the liabilities of American Christianity. Carl Henry's critique was equally applicable to liberalism and conservatism when he wrote:

> The liabilities of American Christianity include . . . an absence of authentic theological concern and interest in churches, colleges, and even seminaries that has impoverished the sources of great preaching. In too many American churches and schools, theology has been displaced by psychology and sociology.[1]

In the mid-fifties church attendance reached a new high, and adult education, which suffered during the long night of the Sunday school decline during the early part of the twentieth century, was again showing signs of virility. The emphasis on the total church program brought a return to family and adult participation in local church life. However, the resurgency of interest was mainly program-centered, and theological concerns remained peripheral. Evangelism and missions, signs of a virile and legitimate activism, were foremost in the renewal of evangelical church life. But theological concern was eclipsed by budgets, buildings and bus routes.

Then came the sixties with its succession of crises. Growing fomentation among nearly all segments of society has brought traditional evangelical church programming into question. Marked as the "Establishment," many churches are being called into question by adults who are asking serious questions but are not receiving theological answers. As never before in recent history, a theology for adult education and participation in the life of the church is needed—a theology which stands the tests, equips for crisis, and faces the tough questions of our times.

THE RELEVANCY SYNDROME

Critics level the charge of irrelevancy against churches. According to the dissidents, churches have lost touch with the times; and an almost cultic appeal goes out to abandon the ship and join the action wherever it is. This action, we are told, may have little or no relationship to current church life. The irrelevancy charge has enough truth in it to give considerable credence to the current pro-God but antichurch sentiment. Many churches have lost touch with their communities, and Christians end up speaking to themselves rather than serving Christ in the world. Many congregations do suffer from a "four walls" mentality and have concluded that the significant action is not in the marketplace but in the church building. Much preaching and teaching does suffer from opaqueness and obscurity. The blunt, plain speech of the prophet touching the nerve center of life is indeed missing. In the process of rejecting the defective ministries of some local churches, it is often concluded that theology is suspect and must change.

How relevant is Christian theology for today? Does orthodox Christian thought still retain its grip on man in society? The answers to these questions are not simple, but we must constantly differentiate between truth held in creed or formulated in doctrinal statements, and truth espoused in action. However, the disparity between these two often leads to the critics' barbs. As for theology losing its grip on man's thoughts, it may safely be asserted that Christianity has always been a minority faith even though the influence of its ethic has gone beyond its personal acceptance.

The term *relevance* suffers from lack of specific definition at any given point in time. An adequate theology will not be a "theology of reaction" or of concensus molded by contradictory assessments of a particular period of history. The real question is whether or not man and institutions shall stand in judgment before divine truth. Thus it seems more accurate to refer to "adequacy" of theology rather than "relevancy." Does the truth fit? Does it say anything to the painful, contemporary problems?

The problems facing our society are complex. Rapid social change, loss of community, alienation between generations and between ethnic groups, and fermenting revolution mark our times. Following the death of Robert Kennedy the question was raised, "Is there a sick society in the United States?" And it was Senator William Fulbright who ventured that the "great society has become a sick society." Internal problems unparalleled in our history call for solutions and remedies. The question of the sickness of a society calls for a theological answer.

When rapid social change takes place, it becomes easy to ask if theology must change. Escalation of technology, violent social upheavals, and an advancing culture have led to "fadism" in theological circles. "We are on the way in a time of great concern with crucial problems," claims Gunther Bornkamm, New Testament scholar at Heidelberg. "But we do not have final answers, and I am unsure what is at the end of this theological road."[2] On the contemporary scene, theologians often outlive the influences of their own theologies. The realm of systematic theology suffers from confusion because there is not yet a new binding concept. Barth's star has been sinking, and now Bultmann's is sinking too. The death-of-God issue is practically "dead," its short-lived life spanning less than a decade. In the face of theological uncertainty we are called to the certitude of an adequate theology forged squarely from the Bible and relevant to daily life.

An adequate theology must stand the tests of rapid social change, it must equip adults for the crises of life, and it must face the tough questions of man's destiny. An openness in confronting modern problems will not dilute the Word of God. There is a certain liberating quality in giving the Word of God free course. Its timeless essence speaks to all generations and to basic problems. In short, it fits life.

THEOLOGICAL FOUNDATIONS

Several basic revelational postulates serve as underpinnings of a theory of adult education. Understandably these are not unique to adult education, but a restatement of basic theological assumptions may provide a focus for continued study and action. It should be noted that this is a discussion of theological *foundations* for adult education; in no way should this be construed as a full-orbed theology of adult education—if indeed one is possible. Nor is the discussion designed as a theology *for* adult laymen. Rather, certain imperatives emerge which may provide a normative statement useful in forging out new frontiers in adult learning.

THE CENTRALITY OF THE BIBLE IN ADULT EDUCATION

One does not have to look far to document the slippage of the Bible from the center of Christian educational concern. At best it has been relegated to the "resource" category in much of the curricula currently in use in main-line denominations, or to the role of a "special book" in the ongoing progress of revelation.

Without the authority of the Scriptures (*Sola Scriptura* to the Protestant Reformers), Protestantism may soon become merely an echo of a decadent society. Conservative evangelical scholars assert that Christians are not in pursuit of truth; rather, they are in possession of the truth. The centrality of the Bible is a major plank in the platform of evangelical education. The Scriptures are profitable "for teaching the faith and correcting error, for resetting the direction of a man's life and training him in good living" (2 Ti 3:16, Phillips). All of this is in order that the man of God may be perfectly fit and thoroughly equipped for every good work. Christian adult education conceived in this tradition is not speculative, tentative or exploratory. It is rooted in the truth that God's Word is authoritative.

The Bible is the primary source of truth and the only inerrant criterion of truth. The primary source of our theological and educational commitments is Scripture. For the Evangelical, all opinions on faith and practice are tested by their adherence to the inspired writings. To what source can Evangelicals go to find renewal of thought and action—"to what source but the Holy Scriptures?" asks Lois LeBar.[3]

Such a position of traditional conservatism has naturally given rise to objections. Does this not lead to a narrow, bigoted authoritarianism? Does this not lead to indoctrination of the highest order? Christian adult learning based on authoritative Scriptures, however, need not be a caricature of learning, a subtle brainwashing, a matter of running an intelligible cookie cutter which stamps out the same stereotype on plastic minds. Evangelicals believe that it is possible to be committed to revelational dogma without closing the mind. Theodore Brameld, a leading educational philosopher, espouses a position of "defensible partiality" to help meet the dilemma created by the tension between dogma and relativism.

> What we learn is defensible simply insofar as the ends we support and the means we utilize are able to stand up against exposure to open, unrestricted criticism and comparison. What we learn is partial insofar as

these ends and means still remain definite and positive to their majority advocates after the defense occurs.[4]

Brameld defends education based upon an authoritative stance. He rejects indoctrination which allows for no "open, unrestricted criticism and comparison." In this light he is not far from the Christian position of authority. While he rejects the existence of absolute truth, a position central to Christian thought, he does espouse a defensible position at the operational level of education. Christian adult education, while holding to a position of authoritative truth, rejects an authoritarian method. Looking at the issue in brief, it is useful to work out the dilemma created by the tension between dogma and relativism by holding to authoritative truth and rejecting unwarranted dogmatism.

Christian adult education commits itself to reflective commitment. Adults need not be subjected to one-way indoctrination. Rather, they should be encouraged to explore, to discover for themselves and to subject their convictions to critical, scrupulous comparison with alternative doctrines. Truth is welcomed from any quarter, but the Scriptures are normative. Profoundly convinced that all truth leads back to God, the Christian educator gratefully endorses the emphasis of John Calvin:

> If we believe that the spirit of God is the only foundation of truth, we shall neither reject nor despise the truth where ever it shall appear. . . . They are superstitious who dare not borrow anything from profane writers. All truth is from God, and consequently, if wicked men have said anything that is true and just, we ought not to reject it; for it has come from God.[5]

Adult education can become a process through which learners are guided to a free acceptance of truth—of biblical truth that liberates. A theology derived from Scripture is consistent with truth about God's world, and highly adequate to the issues men face today.

A CHRISTOLOGICAL IMPERATIVE

Truth is inherent in Jesus Christ because He is the supreme revelation of God. He is "full of grace and truth" (Jn 1:14). Propositional truths in the Scriptures are for the purpose of facilitating personal encounter and fellowship with Jesus Christ. Thus the function of Scripture is instrumental—it is the means of bringing men face to face with Christ. All men are called on to repent, turn from their man-made ways to God through faith in Jesus Christ.

Bible study for adults involves both an understanding of the truth and an application of it. Education that is Christian must be totally absorbed with Jesus Christ, as revealed in the Scriptures, and with leading men to spiritual maturity through Him. "Him we proclaim, warning every man and teaching every man in all wisdom, that we may present every man mature in Christ" (Col 1:28, RSV).

THE HUMAN FACTOR

A Christian view of man is essential if we are to discover how the revelation of Jesus Christ through the Scriptures impinges upon the affairs of mankind. The Scriptures function as an undistorted mirror by which we may see our own distortion. Christian theology posits man as created in the image of God, possessing a responsible and responsive will, and capable of spiritual fellowship with the Creator. In the Genesis passage dealing with man's first failure, we possess the account of the original fall—the entrance of sin into the world. This cataclysmic event marred the human scene, separating sinful man from the holy God. That man is a sinner is an affirmation that does not lack empirical verification. But behavioral analysis of man fails to comprehend the depth of the biblical understanding of man. The apostle Paul, describing the human backdrop of the history of redemption, wrote:

> To you, who were spiritually dead all the time that you drifted along on the stream of this world's ideas of living, and obeyed its unseen ruler (who is still operating in those who do not respond to the truth of God), to you Christ has given life! (Eph 2:1-2, Phillips).

Man caught in the web of pride, spiritual rebellion, and separation from God is, nevertheless, able to respond by faith to divine love. Total depravity is man's incapacity of achieving wholeness and holiness apart from divine intervention.

Through Christ's death on the cross He provided a way whereby man could be reconciled to Himself. Faith, man's response to God's act of grace and mercy, makes men new creations in Jesus Christ. God commands all men everywhere to repent, turn from their wicked ways and be converted.

The implications of a proper understanding of man to Christian adult education are many:

1. It means that education is concerned with relationships—the relationship between man and Jesus Christ and the relationship of man to his neighbor.
2. It means, furthermore, that Christian educators will be concerned with leading adult men and women to Christ for salvation from sin.
3. It also suggests that educators will seek to understand the spiritual nature of man, the meaning of the image of God in man, and the learning capacities which God has given man.

4. In addition, it implies that Christian education will build on the human responses of belief and lead men to full maturity in Christ. Christian adult education will not confuse "childlike" faith with "easy believism" but will rather seek to establish adults in the faith, grounded and settled and not moved from the hope of the gospel (Eph 4:15; Col 1:23; 1 Pe 5:10).

5. Above all, the Christian doctrine of man means that only in Jesus Christ can the full potential of man be realized. As the historic confession puts it, man's chief end is to glorify God and enjoy Him forever.

THE CORPORATE MISSION AND MINISTRY OF ·THE CHURCH

One of the first tasks of theology is to expose confusion and uncertainty of the church concerning itself. Involved in this task is inquiring how the church can adequately fulfill its mission. Every Evangelical ought to be occupied in the renewal of church ministry. Of particular importance is a reaffirmation of the nature of the ministry itself and its relationship to lay mobilization.

By definition, the church of Jesus Christ is a called-out body of disciples devoted to fulfilling a ministry of the Word in the world. Transcending geographic locale and span of generations, the church is a corporate entity whose Head is the Lord Jesus Christ. Wherever the Spirit of God has worked in human lives, local expressions of the "body of Christ" have come into existence. Thus the church may be referred to in a universal and visible, a translocal and a local sense. The imagery depicting the church may be varied, but the ideal of a corporate unity is real. This radically new humanity touched by God's sovereign grace is a group that has little in common but Christ.

What the church of Jesus Christ is determines what it does. The church carries out its role as a worshiping, edifying community of believers, proclaiming the gospel of redemption, seeking to observe all things Jesus has commanded. A particular church seeking to embody the essential quality of the nature and mission of the larger corporate body should not be content to become ingrown and encased with useless custom and tradition. Rather, a church modeled after biblical guidelines will become a ministering body serving actively and meaningfully in a crisis-ridden world and bearing witness to the resurrected Christ. The only corrective to a lifeless institutionalized church is active obedience to the command of Christ to disciple all nations (Mt 28:19-20).

Christian adult education in this context is designed to help people mature within the sphere of the church. Church education, rightly conceived and properly instituted, is education for Christian discipleship.

The teaching focus of a church should be designed to assist every believer in becoming all that Jesus Christ intended for His church. Christian men and women who live and share in the context of a true community of faith seek to mutually edify one another and share their salvation in the world.

Central to Christian ecclesiology is an adequate understanding of the ministry. More than a nurturing, edifying body, the church is a ministering body following Jesus Christ, whose example provides the norm for all Christian service. In the New Testament the ideal of "servantship" is ever present. Two words, *diakonos* and *doulos,* provide the focal point for a doctrine of ministry. Both are used by Jesus Christ. "Whosoever will be great among you, let him be your minister [diakonos]; and whosoever will be chief among you, let him be your servant [doulos]" (Mt 20:26-27).

The John 13 account of Christ washing the disciples' feet teaches us not to lust after power and position but after ministry. *Diakonos* is used in the New Testament both in a general way to indicate the nature of the service to be rendered by every Christian and in a technical way referring to an "order" of ministry—that of the deacons. The idea of lowly service, as implied in the term *doulos* as well, is the fundamental idea in all Christian ministry. In Philippians 2:7 Jesus is spoken of as a slave or bond-servant, wherein He set the pattern for us all.

A special order of deacons seems to be implied in Acts 6. Neglected widows prompted the selection of special ministers, in the proper use of the term, whose shared function with that of the apostles complemented the ministry of the Word. In no way is a hierarchy inferred by the differentiation of function. The ministry was the ministry of the whole church; rather than being mere supporters of the ministry, deacons were active participants in the life of the church.

One of the partially misoriented understandings of the church is the false division between clergy and laity. Since the days of the sixteenth century Reformation, theologians have addressed themselves to the function and status of the ministry, that is to say, the ordained clergy. This subsidiary treatment, notes Kraemer, is an inexcusable lack.[6] As a result, the distinct role of the whole people of God has been eclipsed by a preoccupation with the "ministry" as a special class of individuals. No less an authority than Hans Küng, a spokesman for a new breed of Catholic theologians, observes that a distinction between clergy and laity was unknown until the third century. In his monumental and important work, *The Church,* Küng set forth a position usually associated with reformed theology:

> The word [*laos*] in the New Testament, as also in the Old Testament,

indicates no distinction *within* the community as between priests ('clerics') and people ('laity'). It indicates rather the fellowship of all in a single community.[7]

In the New Testament the church was never understood as being led by the clergy, with the laity as second-class members. The layman in the church is only a layman in the sense that he has neither the formal ordination to minister as an undershepherd of a congregation nor the special gift and training to fulfill that function. The only authentic difference is one of function and divine gift, providing for divisions of labor in the church. There are some who, of necessity, must give full-time service in the church. But this makes them no more ministers in terms of quality or kind than the so-called laymen. The really essential element about the New Testament view of the ministry, according to Leon Morris, is the one basic ministry of Christ Himself. Our ministry is but a continuation of His.[8]

Another important dimension to a theology of the church which has direct bearing on adult education is the biblical teaching on spiritual gifts. The New Testament does not recognize any ministry carried out apart from spiritual God-given abilities. In 1 Corinthians 12:7 the manifestation of the Spirit is given to every believer. These grace gifts are divided by the Holy Spirit "to every man severally as he will" (1 Co 12:11). Some indication of the full scope of participation in church ministries is given in 1 Corinthians 14:26. And the apostle Peter articulated similar teaching when he wrote, "As every man hath received the gift, even so minister the same one to another, as good stewards of the manifold grace of God" (1 Pe 4:10).

The concept of gifts appears to refer to function rather than office, although there were special gifts singled out. But the tremendous variety of exercised gifts indicates that there was no predictable human pattern. Granted, God is a God of order, and the exhortation was given to do all things decently and in order, but the unique pattern of church ministry was the divine exercise of spiritual gifts "for the work of the ministry" (Eph 4:12).

A final facet of inquiry into a Christian ecclesiology with relevance to adult involvement is evidenced by the important New Testament teaching regarding the priesthood of all believers. We recall Martin Luther's famous dictum that all Christians are truly priests.[9]

The priesthood of believers means direct access to God (Ro 5:2; Eph 3:12; Heb 10:22), the right and privilege to offer spiritual sacrifices (Ro 12:1; Phil 2:17; 4:18; 1 Pe 2:5), and the responsibility of witness in the world (1 Pe 2:9; 3:15). It is God who creates this priesthood.

Significant pronouncements which have come from the Second Vatican

Council indicate a crack in the creedal position of conservative Catholicism.

> . . . the apostolate of the spoken word, which in certain situations is the required one, enables lay people to announce Christ, to explain his teaching, to spread it in a measure fitted to each one's ability and circumstance, and to profess it faithfully.[10]

Küng carries this pronouncement further and denies the whole priestly order in the Roman Catholic Church.

The idea of the priesthood of all believers is foundational to a renewed church. Yet it must be more than a teaching to commend Protestantism. It must be a transforming vital principle. More than a flag to march under, it must become a biblical idea that transforms.

Perhaps there is need for a new "article of faith" which asserts the role of laymen in specific terms. Such a statement should acknowledge the interdependence and interexistence of all members of the body of Christ. A corrective to sterile inaction by congregations who are little more than passive audiences is the implementation of a theology of the church which accounts for the total discipleship of the people of God. Only then will the church become what Schweizer describes as "a group to which Jesus' words and deeds have struck home."[11]

One disturbing factor remains. Laymen do not generally conceive of themselves as ministers of the gospel and as servants of Christ. Primarily they think of themselves as helpers of the pastors. A reversal of this general attitude is extremely important for two basic reasons.

First, the ground swell of reaction within congregations appears to be rooted in a dissatisfaction with this passive role. At least the guilt level is rising among increasing numbers. One layman expressed it bluntly when he said that "there must be more to my Christianity than going down to the church and laying linoleum in the church kitchen." The simple fact that laymen are discovering significant ministries elsewhere than through organized churches indicates that church leaders may lack creative skills in mobilizing congregations in meaningful service. It may also mean that church leaders lack a theological understanding of the place and exercise of spiritual gifts by *all* church members.

Another reason laymen need to see themselves as ministers, not merely pastoral helpers, is that the missionary and witnessing enterprise demands it. Years ago John R. Mott, writing of his commitment to discipleship, saw laymen as an expression of the church and its calling and function in the world:

> The most vital and fruitful periods in the history of the Christian Church have been those in which laymen have most vividly realized and

most earnestly sought to discharge their responsibility to propagate the Christian faith.[12]

How can Christianity make its greatest impact on the world in the last third of the twentieth century? Only through total involvement by the people of God, the entire body of Christ—an involvement that is more than emotionalism prompted by guilt, an involvement rooted in Christian discipleship sharpened by knowledge of the Scriptures and Christian theology, an involvement that is more than a reaction to clericalism, an involvement that joins pastors and congregations into a formidable force for propagating the gospel of Jesus Christ.

THE HOLY SPIRIT AND CHRISTIAN ADULT EDUCATION

Christian education is basically different from general education, writes Rachel Henderlite.[13] Discovering the difference can transform adult education from much of its current drabness and ineffectiveness to a revitalized education. In order that we might be able to make proper distinctions, certain aspects of the Holy Spirit are to be seen in relationship to the educative process.

As the divine Teacher in Christian education, the Holy Spirit instructs (Jn 14:26), reminds (Jn 14:26), guides (Jn 16:13), declares (Jn 16:13-15), and reveals (1 Co 2:9-10). The Holy Spirit is the Agent who illumines the mind and heart of man, enabling him to apprehend and appropriate the revealed truth of God.[14]

It must be emphasized that the ministry of the Holy Spirit as Educator is linked closely to the Scriptures. Only by the Holy Spirit can eternal truth be correctly understood, interpreted and personalized. He works on the written Word to internalize it in the students' lives.

Such a work of the Spirit is too restrictive to Nels Ferré. While he quite correctly views God as Educator in the broad sense of the term, he fails to link the work of the Spirit to Scripture. To Ferré the educative work of the Spirit is not in shedding light on the inscripturated truth but in creating new truth for a new age.[15] However, Ferré's theology is without objective norms. Those who jettison the concept of totally trustworthy and authoritative Scripture, revealed by the Holy Spirit, must exchange the rational notion of faith as walking in the light of God for what James Packer calls "the irrational existential idea of faith as a leap in the dark."[16]

Discovering the relationship between the inner work of the Spirit and the educative process is one of the great tasks of the Christian educator. A basic principle of evangelical Christian education is that the inner change and modification of behavior in the learner is dependent on the

Spirit of God working through the Word of God. Jahsmann describes the relationship between the Holy Spirit and the learning process as follows:

> The understanding of the Word requires something more than verbal, intellectual definitions, explanations, and instructions. Though these are needed too, spiritual meanings of the Word must be *experienced* through the experience of the *Spirit* of the Word.[17]

The impingement of God's Word on human experience is carried out by the Spirit. Educational methods which call for discovery, insight and thinking are best used in creating the proper climate for the Spirit to do His work. The Christian adult teacher who seeks to lead adults into the riches of God's truth will acknowledge the fact that the Holy Spirit is the Teacher of divine truth and, at best, the human teacher is but an associate. However, because human teachers are partners with the Holy Spirit in the educative process, they "should seek to be under the full employment of the Spirit as clean and capable instruments. Effective Christian teaching takes place to the extent that teachers allow the Holy Spirit to speak through them and use them."[18]

THEOLOGY AND THE INNOVATIVE PROCESS

How can the church of Jesus Christ truly be the church? This question still calls for an answer, and each generation of believers will have to ask it again and again. It may appear rather odd that a discussion of theological foundations should take a turn toward innovation and reformation. Let it be clearly understood, however, that this does not imply tampering with God's revealed truth. The fixed norms of God's self-disclosure through the Bible still provide the compass for charting a course of change in our times. But change is essential for the life of the churches.

The rationale for change in the church is rooted to the nature of the Holy Spirit. The Holy Spirit is the Spirit of liberty. It is inconceivable that there should be a fixed methodology in adult ministries of church education. In reality the Bible gives us no fixed methodology, no once-for-all technique. The genius of the Christian advance in the world has been linked to freedom in the Spirit to innovate in communicating the gospel and in creating educational settings for Christian nurture. Without abandonment to irresponsible disorder in church programming, churches can nevertheless bring about change in the educative process. Without abandoning Christian truth to a "process theology," churches can exercise a certain methodological elasticity. Important issues confront adults in our generation, and these call for theological answers learned and discovered in church settings that maximize the latent power of Christians who live and learn in the Spirit.

CONCLUSION

The limitations of such a brief treatment are obvious. No attempt was made to treat all the major doctrines. Some may question the basis for the selection of only a few themes—the Scriptures, Christ, man, the church, and the Holy Spirit. There was no particular reason for neglecting other areas except for the limitations of the chapter. If Christian educators and theologians feel provoked to explore the full sweep of Christian theology in the educational context, the author's purpose will in part have been fulfilled.

Albert Einstein once said that we live in an age of perfected means but confused ends. This may be true in the world of technology and of science. It may also be true in theological circles. Carl Henry has astutely observed that contemporary Christianity is face-to-face with a major transition time in theology. This, he asserts, "affords evangelicals a providential moment for earnest engagement."[19] We are committed to bringing men to salvation, wholeness and maturity in Jesus Christ, but we may not be using the best means to accomplish these goals. At this point we all need the humility to admit that evangelical church education needs theological direction and that freedom is needed to explore ways to carry on creative adult education in the church.

NOTES

1. Carl F. H. Henry, "Perspective on American Christianity," *Christianity Today* 9 (Apr. 23, 1965):29.
2. Quoted in Carl F. H. Henry, *Frontiers in Modern Theology* (Chicago: Moody, 1966), p. 83.
3. Lois E. LeBar, *Education That Is Christian* (Westwood, N.J.: Revell, 1958), p. 50.
4. Theodore Brameld, *Ends and Means in Education; A Midcentury Appraisal* (New York: Harper, 1952), pp. 92-93.
5. John Calvin, *Commentaries on the Epistles to Timothy, Titus, and Philemon* (Grand Rapids: Eerdmans, 1959), pp. 300-1. Calvin also discusses the nature of general truth in his *Institutes*, Book II, chap. 2, para. 15.
6. Hendrik Kraemer, *A Theology of the Laity* (Philadelphia: Westminster, 1958), p. 9.
7. Hans Küng, *The Church* (New York: Sheed & Ward, 1968), pp. 125-26.
8. Leon Morris, *Ministers of God* (London: Inter-Varsity, 1964), p. 25.
9. Ewald M. Plass, comp., *What Luther Says* (St. Louis: Concordia, 1959), 3:1139.
10. *Teachings of the Second Vatican Council, Complete Texts of the Constitutions, Decrees, and Declarations* (Westminster, Md.: Newman, 1966), pp. 328-29.
11. See Eduard Schweizer, *Church Order in the New Testament* (London: SCM, 1961) for a careful treatment of the entire subject of ministry in the New Testament.
12. John R. Mott, *Liberating the Lay Forces of Christianity* (New York: Macmillan, 1932), p. 1.
13. Rachel Henderlite, *The Holy Spirit in Christian Education* (Philadelphia: Westminster, 1964), p. 15.

14. Roy B. Zuck, *The Holy Spirit in Your Teaching* (Wheaton: Scripture Press, 1963), pp. 44-50.
15. Nels Ferré, *A Theology for Christian Education* (Philadelphia: Westminster, 1967), p. 107.
16. James I. Packer, "The Necessity of the Revealed Word" in *The Bible—The Living Word of Revelation*, Merrill C. Tenney, ed. (Grand Rapids: Zondervan, 1968), p. 49.
17. Allan Hart Jahsmann, *Power Beyond Words* (St. Louis: Concordia, 1969), p. 113.
18. Zuck, p. 76.
19. Henry, *Frontiers* . . . , p. 142.

FOR FURTHER READING

Clark, Gordon H. *A Christian Philosophy of Education.* Grand Rapids: Eerdmans, 1946.

Ferré, Nels F. S. *A Theology for Christian Education.* Philadelphia: Westminster, 1967.

Fuller, Edmund, ed. *The Christian Idea of Education.* New Haven: Yale U., 1957.

Gaebelein, Frank. *Christian Education in a Democracy.* New York: Oxford U., 1951.

LeBar, Lois E. *Education That Is Christian.* Westwood, N.J.: Revell, 1958.

Little, Lawrence C. *Foundations for a Philosophy of Christian Education.* Nashville: Abingdon, 1962.

Little, Sara. *The Role of the Bible in Contemporary Christian Education.* Richmond, Va.: John Knox, 1961.

Lynn, Robert W. *Protestant Strategies in Education.* New York: Association, 1964.

Ramm, Bernard. *The Pattern of Religious Authority.* Grand Rapids: Eerdmans, 1959.

Roddy, Clarence S., ed. *Things Most Surely Believed.* Westwood, N.J.: Revell, 1963.

Schreyer, George M. *Christian Education in Theological Focus.* Philadelphia: Christian Education Press, 1962.

Waterink, Jan. *Basic Concepts in Christian Pedagogy.* Grand Rapids: Eerdmans, 1954.

Wyckoff, D. Campbell. *The Gospel and Christian Education.* Philadelphia: Westminster, 1959.

Zuck, Roy B. *The Holy Spirit in Your Teaching.* Wheaton, Ill.: Scripture Press, 1963.

3

THE NATURE AND NEEDS OF YOUNG ADULTS

Clifford V. Anderson

Barbara is a talented young adult. The major amount of her leisure time is devoted to a drama group in which she is a leading actress. She is not attending church. "I was emotionally exploited as a child and teen in my church. . . . When my child is a little older, I'll take her to Sunday school and church, but it won't be the same kind of church."

Bill and Norma have stopped attending church. They were outstanding workers in the educational ministry of an alert, active church just a few years ago. Now they are looking for a church that costs less, that doesn't demand involvement. A new home, furnishings, a car and travel are claiming their energies.

George really "lived it up" in high school and college. Then he changed. The Christianity he had been taught in his home and church popped into focus, and he discovered Christ in a personal way. Now his goal in life is to help others discover the reality of Christ.

A wealthy young man seemingly had everything he needed. Yet he was searching for deeper meaning in life. When challenged to fully commit himself to a ministry of service to God and others, he turned away sorrowfully.

The lonely girl from the small town upstate couldn't find friends at work and was the odd person in the apartment she shared with three other girls. She is looking for true friendship and something to live for.

These word sketches stimulate the memory to recall other young adults: the school dropout or the young man who entered military service and never went back; the couple who married in their teens, had several children in swift succession, and are finding it difficult to live on their low income; the young unemployed member of a minority group, leaning up against a building and seemingly waiting for something to happen.

CLIFFORD V. ANDERSON, Ed.D., is Associate Professor of Education and Dean of Students, Bethel Theological Seminary, St. Paul, Minnesota.

In this chapter we explore the nature and needs of young adults and offer general suggestions for ministering to them.

YOUNG ADULTS AS A GROUP

Unlike children and youth, the period of life known as early adulthood is not easily defined. Specific age designations are not universally accepted. Some include as young adults all post-high school-age persons through age forty, whereas many prefer ages twenty-one to forty or twenty-five to forty. Older youth, a designation currently in use, applies to persons between the ages of eighteen and twenty-one or twenty-five.

It is increasingly recognized that age alone is not an adequate criterion for defining adulthood or its divisions into young, middle, and older adults. J. Gordon Chamberlin, in an earlier work on this subject, has pointed out that "young adults have only one characteristic in common— they are young at the business of being adults."[1]

Another student of adult Christian education suggests seven experiences as the identifying criteria of young adulthood. "These are (1) marriage, (2) permanently leaving home, (3) the completion of formal schooling, (4) self-support, (5) reaching one's political majority, (6) military service, and (7) chronological age."[2]

There is also some interest in merging the older youth and young adult groups into one group called young adult.* This grows out of the recognition that many persons presently called older youth have accepted adult responsibilities and share the interests and needs of adults rather than those of persons in an earlier dependent period of life.

The young-adult group is a growing group in our society due to the post-World War II baby boom. Estimates suggest that this group numbers more than thirty million persons in the United States. In 1966, Moore cited the expectation that in the decade of the sixties there would be a 64 percent increase in persons between the ages of eighteen and twenty-four, compared with the total population which was predicted to have grown 17 percent.[3]

"It is estimated that 75 to 80 percent of this young-adult generation lives in urban areas. Approximately 14 percent of the population of a given city is young adult."[4] In some small-apartment areas of cities the concentration of young adults reaches one-third and more of the immediate population, as the search for employment, training, adventure and independence beckons them to these urban areas.

*This recommendation was made to the Methodist Church by their Older Youth/ Young Adult Project. The report warned against using age as the only determining factor but pointed out that persons in their late teens and twenties will constitute the general constituency. *Directions for a Young Adult Ministry* (Nashville: Div. of the Local Church, General Board of Educ. of the Methodist Church, 1966), p. 83.

Cities vary, but not substantially, in the percentage of young adults in their total population. San Francisco's young-adult population (nineteen- to twenty-nine-year-olds) is 13.15 percent of their total. Washington's percentage is 15.07. Other examples are Atlanta, 14.54; Dallas, 13.35; Wilmington, 16.42; Chicago, 12.60; Minneapolis, 14.90; Denver, 12.78; Anchorage, 16.84; and Honolulu, 14.90 percent.[5]

CONCERNS OF YOUNG ADULTS

The period of young adulthood is a time of transition between adolescence and adulthood. The young adults described at the beginning of this chapter are all different. They are different because of heredity, environment and personal reaction to their nature and their nurture. Felt and unfelt needs, interests, personality differences, abilities and situations all contribute to these differences. So immense is the potential for individuality among human beings that great caution must be exercised in making assumptions and generalizations about characteristics and needs of young adults. Gordon W. Allport, in discussing the dilemma of uniqueness, expressed it this way, "I venture the opinion that all of the animals in the world are psychologically less distinct from one another than one man is from other men."[6]

The matter is further complicated by the realization that there are subcultures within the young adult group. Students of college life recognize four subcultures.[7] The *collegiate* subculture flourishes on the busy round of social activities found on college campuses. Football, social organizations, fun and dating are dominant aspects of this subculture. The *vocational* subculture represents students who are concerned with getting a diploma and improving their chances of finding a better job than they could otherwise expect. The *academic* subculture refers to the group of serious students, who identify with the intellectual concerns of an education and are in pursuit of knowledge rather than fun or job-oriented skills and a diploma. They are to be found in libraries, laboratories and advanced seminars. The other major subculture in college is the *nonconformist*. The nonconforming student may exhibit a critical detachment from the college. Sometimes these students are deeply concerned with ideas that are expressed outside the halls of learning. Rebellion against current conditions of life in the wider adult society may be evidenced in word and action. A distinctive style of life is exhibited in language, appearance and attitude.*

---

*For more information on college youth the reader is referred to Paul Fromer, "The Nature and Needs of College-Age Youth," *Youth and the Church*, Roy G. Irving and Roy B. Zuck, eds. (Chicago: Moody, 1968); Paul E. Little, "Reaching Youth in College," *Youth and the Church*; and Henrietta Mears, "Teaching College-Age Youth," *An Introduction to Evangelical Christian Education*, J. Edward Hakes, ed. (Chicago: Moody, 1964).

It is difficult, of course, to insist on pure types of subcultures. Blending of elements of various types occurs, and a given individual may change his dominant orientation from one type to another.

The young adult culture may also be differentiated under the category of employment. There are the unemployed, the underemployed and the employed. In each of these groups there are attitudes of apathy and ambition and varieties of skills and resources.

When interpersonal relationships are reviewed, young adults may be seen as "joiners" or "isolates." They may be searching for companionship in appropriate and inappropriate ways, or they may withdraw from contacts with others. In terms of sex-based associations, there are single and satisfied; single and searching; homosexual; married; married with children; married who are separated through discord, divorce or death; and extramarital relationship types. Other subgroups can be found when the military, socioeconomic, racial, cultural and other categories where persons differ are studied.

Young adults also differ in their attitudes toward religion. Some are religious but do not attend church faithfully. Others are not basically religious but do retain certain habits of the religious life. Complacent church attenders, concerned critics and committed persons are also found among young adults.

But despite the complexities arising from these individual differences and subcultures, students of human behavior still find it possible to report characteristics that apply to most young adults in our culture. For example, Robert Havighurst has popularized the concept of developmental tasks as they relate to the growth of individuals in our society. By developmental tasks he means those learnings necessary for satisfactory growth.

> A developmental task is a task which arises at or about a certain period in the life of the individual, successful achievement of which leads to his happiness and to success with later tasks, while failure leads to unhappiness in the individual, disapproval by the society, and difficulty with later tasks.[8]

Efforts in education should be timed to coincide with teachable moments. Clues to these arise from the study of human development.

In Havighurst's discussion of the tasks of early adulthood, he points out that this period of life "is the fullest of teachable moments and the emptiest of efforts to teach."[9] The tasks given here refer to the period of life from eighteen to thirty: (1) completing or continuing education, (2) selecting a mate, (3) learning to live with a marriage partner, (4) starting a family, (5) rearing children, (6) managing a home, (7) getting started in an occupation, (8) taking on civic responsibility, and (9) finding a congenial social group.

These tasks constitute major expectations of society for this age-group, but not all young adults work at these in the same way. Some will be hard at work in the beginning stages of these tasks in adolescence. Developing a philosophy of life, viewed as an adolescent task, may be a continuing matter of concern for some young adults. While not all young adults will develop associations with members of the opposite sex that lead to marriage, these expectations of society form a significant part of their thoughts and activities.

Erik H. Erikson speaks of "central crises of growth" in his theory of human development.[10] He proposes eight psychosocial crises in the life span from birth to old age. The central crisis of young adulthood is *interpersonal intimacy* while the counterpart of intimacy is *repudiation* or *isolation*. The psychosocial crisis of adolescence is *identity*. Failure to resolve this crisis leads to identity diffusion and this can disturb the development of interpersonal intimacy as the individual moves from adolescence to young adult years.

Young adults are constantly faced with the challenge of forming true and mutually satisfying relationships with others. This suggests more than sexual intimacy, although this is part of the psychological intimacy of husband and wife. "Intimacy is really the ability to fuse your identity with somebody else's without fear that you're going to lose something yourself."[11]

Lewis Joseph Sherrill sees the central task of young adulthood as making the basic identifications around which life as a mature adult can be developed. He suggests that the temptation in this period of life is to "get as much as you can, and give as little in return as you can get away with."[12] This is particularly apparent in economic relationships and responsibilities. Similar temptations to shrink back from responsibility are found in the social, intellectual and religious realms.

THE CHURCH AND YOUNG ADULTS

In many churches there is a serious attrition among persons of eighteen to twenty-five years of age (as well as among teens between thirteen and seventeen).

If the church is to minister effectively to young adults, it must strive to understand them and the world in which they live.[*] It must view them as individuals who are *liberated, skeptical* and *searching*. Certainly

[*]Donald N. Michael, *The Next Generation*, calls attention to trends and circumstances likely to appear over the next twenty years that will affect the youth of today and tomorrow. Unprecedented opportunities and demands confront the young adult in the present and immediate future.

they are *liberated* for they are urban and mobile. The cords that bound them to home, school, church and customs have been loosened in the flight to the city and to independence. The taboos of home and church are questioned as the circle of experience expands. They find it easy to drop out of activities in the crowded but impersonal relationships of the city where they experience anonymity.

Young adults are *skeptical*. They are reacting to adult values and patterns of behavior, and they are very much aware that the problems of our world have not been solved by the talk or action of the adult community. Atomic power, massive retaliation, nuclear fallout, cold and hot wars, spiraling populations, impending food shortages, demands for accelerated education, job insecurity, hostility within and between racial groups, an era of material abundance promised by cybernetics with greatly expanded leisure, increased crime and delinquency, urban sprawl and decay, waste of natural resources, air and water pollution, and grinding poverty around the world and around the corner stand out in bold relief as unsolved problems. There has always been a natural gap between generations in the sense of tension between adolescents and adults, but today these young adults are actually wary of the adult world. They are very reluctant to join its institutions or adopt its customs. They do join, however, groups and movements of their own making or persuasion.

This general skepticism also extends to the church. Young adults grow weary of form without function, and of piety and dogma without relevance and power in life. Those who do cling to the church too often conform to the ways of their elders in separating the sacred from the secular, and faith from daily life.

Young adults are *searching*. The quest is for self. What kind of person am I? What kind of person ought I be? And in their freedom they experiment with themselves.

The quest is for others, perhaps *an*other, and for some, *the* Other. They want to make friends and be where friends can be made, as indicated by the current phenomenon of computerized dating.

The quest is for meaning in life. Our anxious age produces anxious persons. There is a despair that pervades the life of the person without orientation. Viktor Frankl has suggested that a will to meaning exists in the human psyche, and many see his hypothesis as being especially relevant today.*

The quest is for a style of life in a modern world. How can one direct

---

*Viktor Frankl, *Man's Search for Meaning*. The emptiness and anxiety of modern man may be the best clue for evangelism in a secular society. See Leighton Ford, *The Christian Persuader*, chap. 10, for a good treatment of the relevance of evangelism today.

his energy and influence to enrich self, loved ones, and the near and distant neighbor?

While many suggestions for ministering to young adults are found elsewhere in this book, here are several that grow out of this study of the characteristics of young adults in today's society:

A MINISTRY TO YOUNG ADULTS WILL BE PRIMARILY URBAN

While we dare not neglect young adults who live, work and worship in town and country areas, it is clear that the church must focus on the city if it is to win the young adult. Already 70 percent of our population is urban and the percentage will grow still larger.[13] In contrast, 70 percent of the churches of fourteen major Protestant denominations are found in town and country areas.[14] The city is the port of entry to the promised good life for many young adults, but they do not find the church there in power. In a period of some fifteen years New York City lost more than 300 churches; Chicago, 150; and Cleveland, 72.[15]

Christian young adults are needed in the church and in the world. Sherrill concludes,

> Young adulthood is a peculiarly strategic time for the undiluted moral demands of a holy God to confront the human soul, especially in the case of those who are mature enough to understand their meaning but not yet so deeply encrusted with convention that they dare not obey.[16]

How will they hear without a preacher, without the presence of the church? We must follow them to their school, the armed forces, the city, and the apartment. We may follow them through correspondence, referrals, personal contacts, and specialized ministries. Several organizations penetrate the academic and military communities, but what of the other places where young adults are found?

A MINISTRY TO YOUNG ADULTS WILL BE BASED ON THEIR NEEDS

Whenever we speak of meeting the needs of persons, we recognize the importance of variety and flexibility in approach. Many churches offer a program that is directed especially to the needs of families with children. However, single young adults and those who are married but have no children are not in mind and often not in sight. The time has come to ask young adults how the church can help them and to listen and respond to the suggestions that are given.

Certainly one need which is obvious without asking is to provide a setting where friendships can be made. A careful study of young adults revealed that, while nine out of ten of those questioned claimed church membership, "less than 10 percent, either single or married mentioned the church as a place to meet with friends."[17] Bennett suggests greater use of homes as the locale for young adults and the interests of participants as the basis for meaningful programs for them.

Gibbs offers seven basic topics for argument and decision as the kind of tough training necessary for lively adult Christians:

> (1) What is authority in our daily lives? (2) What is "commitment"? (3) In what sense is the world "good," . . . and in what sense is it "wicked"? (4) Sex, of course. (5) Making the most of what we've got (stewardship). (6) Who is my neighbor anyway? (7) What on earth does prayer and worship mean to ordinary lay people?[18]

Other topics such as the church and social issues come to mind. In all of these the Scriptures are the essential source of guidance. Young adults are capable of selecting topics for study and of teaching themselves, if given a chance. It is better to have an interested group explore a topic with the assistance of a helpful discussion leader than a well-prepared resource person on a topic having no relevance to the group.

A YOUNG-ADULT MINISTRY SHOULD BE BROADER THAN THE INSTITUTIONAL CONCERNS OF A LOCAL CHURCH

Not all churches can or will have effective ministries with young adults. Some are not located where there are young adults. Others cannot offer the kind of opportunities in worship, teaching and fellowship that young adults desire. Cooperative programs that bring young adults together from various churches are helpful. Insistence on local church organization smacks of institutional self-survival rather than ministering to needs.

> The church that is to win the attention of these young adults and minister to them must be their servant. This means that it must not expect young adults to serve the institution's need for new members, committee workers, and financial contributions. Instead the church must become aware that young adults have needs of their own which must be served by the church before they are ready to become church members.[19]

Admittedly it is difficult to place ministry to persons above the continuance of an institution. But is it not likely that institutions that meet needs of people will endure?

A MINISTRY TO YOUNG ADULTS MUST BE PILOTED BY YOUNG ADULTS

It will not do for the church to make all the arrangements and set up the agenda. Young adults want to work through their problems in *their* way and to seek the advice of older adults when they feel the need to do so. Beyond this, election of young adults to key boards and committees of the church and willingness to listen to their views are signs of a church that cares for them in a mature way.

Of course it is recognized that a young-adult group with evangelical objectives will be functioning within the framework of scriptural authority. Those who minister to and work with young adults need to adopt a non-authoritarian approach without compromising the absolutes of our authoritative message—the Bible.

CONTINUED EMPHASIS ON THE ESSENTIALS OF CHRISTIANITY IS IMPORTANT TO
     YOUNG ADULTS

Some churches are biblical only in a narrow sense. Certain selected themes of the Scriptures are emphasized while other important matters are neglected. The following experiences should be a part of a ministry to young adults and can provide the context for the communication of the essentials of our faith:

1. Proclamation and teaching about the method and content of God's revelation to man, which includes the *bad news* of man's sinful estrangement from God, others and self, and the *good news* of reconciliation to God, others and self
2. Encouragement in responding to the love and claims of Christ is vital
3. Teaching about Christian vocation involving service to God and man
4. Equipment in the skill of Bible study together with the opening of the life to the Spirit of God and the needs of others in order to discern the will and way of God in the world
5. Meaningful worship that leads to honest encounter and fellowship with God, worship in both the corporate and private realms of life, which is necessary for spiritual growth
6. Sharing in the life of the church and in the lives of Christian persons at a depth of fellowship and mutuality which can satisfy the intense hunger for affiliation and association that young adults have
7. Opportunities for witness and service—the outer-directed dimension to the Christian life, requiring the involvement of every Christian*

A MINISTRY TO YOUNG ADULTS SHOULD RESPECT THEIR FREEDOM TO UNDERTAKE AND STRUCTURE THEIR SEARCH FOR REALITY IN THEIR OWN WAY

Freedom to differ and to come to one's own conclusions requires patience and less defensiveness by church leaders, parents and friends.[20] The church needs the ideas and strength of young adults to pursue its mission

---

*A useful outline of the general goals of Christian education for adults is found in *Correlated Christian Education in the Local Church* (Chicago: Harvest, 1962).

in the world. Taking them seriously means to take their problems, questions and viewpoints seriously, and to hear them out and to work together with them for solutions. Dialogues between young adults and pastors and other church leaders, reading material to help serious students grapple with their questions, and special periods of time given over to consider significant problems and themes are among suggestions for strengthening a church's ministry to young adults.

NOTES

1. J. Gordon Chamberlin, *The Church and Its Young Adults* (New York: Abingdon-Cokesbury, 1943), p. 15.
2. Joseph John Hanson, *Our Church Plans for Adults* (Valley Forge, Pa.: Judson, 1962), pp. 14-15.
3. Allen J. Moore, "The Church's Young Adult Ministry" in *An Introduction to Christian Education*, Marvin J. Taylor, ed. (Nashville: Abingdon, 1966), p. 196.
4. *Directions for a Young Adult Ministry* (Nashville: Div. of the Local Church, General Board of Educ. of the Methodist Church, 1966), p. ix.
5. Ibid., p. 43.
6. Gordon W. Allport, *Becoming: Basic Considerations for a Psychology of Personality* (New Haven: Yale U., paperback ed., 1960), p. 23.
7. Burton R. Clark, *Educating the Expert Society* (San Francisco: Chandler, 1962), chap. 6.
8. Robert J. Havighurst, *Human Development and Education* (New York: McKay, 1953), p. 2.
9. Ibid., p. 257.
10. See Erik H. Erikson, *Childhood and Society* (New York: Norton, 1950); idem, "Identity and the Life Cycle," *Psychological Issues* 1 (1959).
11. Richard I. Evans, *Dialogue with Erik Erikson* (New York: Harper & Row, 1967), p. 48.
12. Lewis Joseph Sherrill, *The Struggle of the Soul* (New York: Macmillan, paperback ed., 1963), p. 125.
13. Robert C. Weaver, *The Urban Complex* (Garden City, N.Y.: Doubleday Anchor Book, 1966), p. 1. Also see U.S. Bureau of the Census, *Statistical Abstract of the United States: 1967*, 88th ed. (Washington D.C., 1967), p. 16.
14. C. R. McBride, *Protestant Churchmanship for Rural America* (Valley Forge, Pa.: Judson, 1962), p. 40.
15. Ted Kimmel and Ward Kaiser, *Focus: The Changing City* (New York: Friendship Press, 1963), p. 7.
16. Sherrill, p. 146.
17. Thomas R. Bennett, "A Profile of the Young Adult," *International Journal of Religious Education* 42:9 (December, 1965).
18. Mark Gibbs, "Training for Adult Christian Freedom," *Christian Comment*, no. 58 (November-December, 1964). Mark Gibbs and T. Ralph Morton authored *God's Frozen People* (Philadelphia: Westminster, 1965), a significant contribution to the literature on the laity.
19. Ronald W. Johnson, "A Ministry to Young Adults in the City," *International Journal of Religious Education*, 43:18 (September, 1966).
20. See John R. Jamison, "Freedom Within the Church," *Report from the Capitol* 22:4-5 (December, 1967).

FOR FURTHER READING

Allport, Gordon W. *Becoming: Basic Considerations of a Psychology of Personality.* New Haven: Yale U., 1960.

———. *The Individual and His Religion.* New York: Macmillan, 1960.

Bennett, Thomas R. "A Profile of the Young Adult." *International Journal of Religious Education* 42 (Dec., 1965): 8-9.

Chamberlin, J. Gordon. *The Church and Its Young Adults.* New York: Abingdon-Cokesbury, 1943.

Clemmons, Robert S. *Single Young Adults in the Church.* New York: Association, 1952.

———. *Young Adults in the Church.* New York: Abingdon, 1959.

Directions for a Young Adult Ministry. Nashville: Division of the Local Church, General Board of Education of The Methodist Church, 1966.

Doniger, Simon, ed. *Becoming the Complete Adult.* New York: Association, 1962.

Franklin, Lottie M. *So You Work with Young Adults.* Anderson, Ind.: Warner, 1960.

Havighurst, Robert J. *Human Development and Education.* New York: McKay, 1953.

Haynes, Joseph M. "Meeting Special Needs of Married Young People." *The Sunday School Builder* 49 (May, 1968): 8.

Maves, Paul B. "The Christian Education of Adults" in *Religious Education: A Comprehensive Survey.* Marvin J. Taylor, ed. New York: Abingdon, 1960.

Moore, Allen J. "The Church's Young Adult Ministry" in *An Introduction to Christian Education.* Marvin J. Taylor, ed. New York: Abingdon, 1966.

———. *The Young Adult Generation.* Nashville: Abingdon, 1969.

Mowry, Charles E. and Willford, Earl R. "The Christian Response to a Young Adult Culture," *Baptist Leader,* 30 (Nov., 1968): 32-35.

Saffen, Wayne. *Young Married Couples in the Church.* St. Louis: Concordia, 1963.

Sherrill, Lewis Joseph. *The Struggle of the Soul.* New York: Macmillan, 1963.

Towns, Elmer. *The Single Adult and the Church.* Glendale, Calif.: Regal, 1967.

Wise, F. Franklyn. "Reaching Young Adults," *The Sunday School Times and Gospel Herald,* 57 (May 15, 1969): 9-11.

Ziegler, Earl F. *Christian Education of Adults.* Philadelphia: Westminster, 1958.

4

THE NATURE AND NEEDS OF
MIDDLE ADULTS

H. Norman Wright

Middle adulthood has been termed the "forgotten age"—both by society and those who are a part of this ever increasing age-group. This period of life has been designated the "awkward age," the time when men and women are no longer young and not yet old. Others have labeled it "man's second adolescence," suggesting that it can be another time of storm, stress and transition.

Next to old age, middle age is the most dreaded time in the life span of many. It is *the* period of life most adults do not want to admit they have reached. People resist accepting the fact that they are now middle-aged. Desmond has stated, "Americans slump into middle age grudgingly, sadly and with a tinge of fear."[1] Unfavorable stereotypes and the false belief that this is an unproductive time of life, coupled with the over-indulgent emphasis and importance given to youth in the American culture, have caused adults to look unfavorably on themselves as they reach this period of life.

Much attention has been given in our society to the impressionable years of childhood. Organizations, books, studies and programs have arisen to assist in the development of children. Then with the ever expanding group of youth, who in their tumultuous searching during the period of adolescence cause bewilderment and consternation to adults, we again find an abundance of resources to help both those who work with youth and the youth themselves. More recently, a greater emphasis has been placed on the study of programs for assisting retired or aged persons. Meaningful activities and programs now abound in the attempt to make a place for them and to provide for them.

But the in-between group, the middle-aged, have generally been passed

---

H. NORMAN WRIGHT, M.R.E., M.A., is Assistant Professor of Religious Education, Talbot Theological Seminary, La Mirada, California.

by. Tizzard and Guntrip wrote the following graphic description of middle age:

> Many people are, in fact, afraid of getting to this time of life. Some have always been afraid of moving on from one stage of life to another. That is largely the fear of the unknown. Some of us have always been apprehensive of the unknown ever since as children we peopled the dark with the fearful shapes of our own imagining. And the middle years are still pretty much unexplored territory. There are numberless books about youth and the early years of marriage. The country has been mapped and charted again and again, every inch of it. But the maps to guide the traveller into middle age are rather of the primitive, unscientific "here-be-dragons" sort.[2]

How many churches can state, "We recognize the uniqueness of middle-aged adults and have developed a program of education specifically for them?" The boast, "This is a youth-centered church" is much more frequent. Evangelical churches must see the need to minister to *each* age-group and every person equally.

WHAT IS MIDDLE AGE?

Middle age is generally thought of as extending from age thirty-five to sixty, or forty to sixty-five. Entrance into this period is gained not so much by passing the milestone of a particular birthday, but by events which indicate to a person that he is no longer a young adult. Gray hairs, baldness, bifocals, menopause—these are some indications that a new time of life has been entered.

This is a period of life characterized, for many, by *accomplishment*. In middle age, many persons reach a peak of experience and reap the benefits of years of preparation and diligent work. It is a time when occupational and vocational goals are being reached and when financial and social prestige goals are attained. Warner stressed,

> At forty years of age, normal persons should have had sufficient experience through education and human inter-relationships to have developed sound judgment or values about social relationships. At this age, they should have a high degree of understanding and be mellow and tolerant toward the weaknesses, frailties, and personal peculiarities of their fellow men. Their financial and social positions should be established, and they should at least begin to have a clear vision of the future and the goal which they wish to attain. If these accomplishments are complemented by good health, then life can begin at forty.[3]

Not only is this the age of accomplishment, it is also the age of *responsibility*. The full brunt of life's responsibilities is upon middle adults. Many parents in middle age have heavy financial responsibilities, including helping their young people gain a college education. Griffen emphasizes this responsibility by stating,

> The thirty-fifth year, or thereabouts, brings the greatest economic responsibility. The child draws a baby bonus. Grandfather gets the old age pension. But what of the man in between? He pays the taxes for both. To middle age belongs the responsibility for children and old people, the paying of bills, the feeling of exhaustion, the nervous breakdowns and coronary attacks.[4]

Economic responsibilities are great, but income can be at its peak stage, and thus a balance is achieved. Even though many adults have achieved prominence in their vocational and social life, challenges and pressures continue to occur. The pressure to achieve for one's own self-esteem is very noticeable at this point.

Middle adulthood is also a time of *accountability*. An adult of middle age comes to realize that his life values have been valid, or he realizes that they are invalid and that to hold onto them would be fruitless. Either he has achieved most of his material or vocational goals, or he will not reach them. His job will become more secure because of his skill and experience, or more insecure as his skill becomes obsolete and work is more difficult to find and to hold. Either his children are close to adulthood or he will not have any children. Youth, and perhaps even his own offspring, consider him "old" and part of "the establishment" which must be rebelled against. Educational goals are either completed or they will not be attained. If a middle adult faces unfulfilled goals with little hope of accomplishing them, he must either seek new goals and interests that can be achieved, or remain frustrated and defeated.

These years are also a time of *adjustment*. If a middle adult has realized his goals, will he be content to rest on these achievements and allow boredom to invade his life? His values must reach further and deeper, and he must seek richer relationships and involvement. Loneliness is also an experience to which adults must adjust. Many of them experience the loss of relatives or friends, and many face the adjustment of being "just husband and wife" with the children out on their own establishing their own life and home.

Adjustments are called for in the lives of many middle adults when their children become teenagers and when those teens, a few years later, leave home for college or military service. As Ziegler explains, "This is the era in married life when the teen-ager . . . gives his parents the most frustrating experiences of their lives."[5] Ziegler continues:

> If there are three or four children in the household, one or more of them is getting married before the parents are out of their forties or fifties.

New anxieties arise about in-laws, buying homes, vocational advancement of the married couple, and then—the "threat" of being grandparents. Some welcome this experience with grateful thanks to God; some dread the new status that brings them dangerously near to being "oldsters."[6]

CHARACTERISTICS OF MIDDLE-AGED ADULTS

BIOLOGICAL CHANGES

Quite often the changes in the biological or physical realm cause the greatest amount of concern to the individual entering middle age. These changes are inescapable. The body experiences less strength and energy, and there is a waning of sexual power and ability. The manner of aging varies as much as individuals do, and much of aging is psychological as well as physical. Middle adults have a tendency to gain weight, to acquire the "middle-age spread," and to gain a receding hairline or graying hair. Also the texture of the skin tends to grow coarser and wrinkles appear.

There is a noted difference in the decline of sexual functions between man and woman. The woman enters the menopause and loses her reproductive function in the middle forties or early fifties, whereas the man's slow decline in sexual power and desire does not alter his reproductive functions. Also many of the glands that function to rid the body of wastes become sluggish.

In the latter part of middle age the physical senses decline in acuity. Vision can become impaired, hearing may be affected, and even touch and taste can diminish in intensity. This group of adults is more prone to illnesses and diseases than earlier adults. Many adults in their fifties and sixties have been hospitalized for surgery or illnesses common to that age-group.

Many men who feel the drain of their strength go to extremes to maintain or assure themselves that they are still physically capable of accomplishing what younger men can do. This in turn can cause serious injury if done in excess, for the motor skills and powers are now less adept. Women, too, tend to spend more time grooming themselves in order to escape the oncoming changes in physical appearance.

SOCIAL CHARACTERISTICS

In the social realm a variety of changes occur in middle adulthood. Within family life itself there are adjustments. With the children leaving home and establishing their own families, the home may seem empty, and some couples must learn to adjust to one another. Loneliness may set in and the companionship of the other mate may seem insufficient to compensate for the loss. The difference in the time of the physical change process of man and woman may cause strain between them. The prospect of becoming grandparents requires adjustment. And for many middle adults, their aging parents present another problem.

During this period, the problem of singleness must be faced. There are those who have never married and have by this time adjusted to this pattern of life and are reasonably happy. Many such single persons tend in middle adulthood to plunge into their work. But for the once-married individual who now, either through divorce or the death of his spouse is once again single, there are major adjustments. A man has more opportunity for remarriage and fewer adjustments to make. A woman may find herself having to seek employment for the first time in her life, and altering her total life routine may be difficult. Her chances for remarriage are less than that of the male.*

Vocation looms with importance at this time. Some adults find themselves in a position of prominence and seek to remain there or even forge ahead. Devotion to work can assume overwhelming proportions, as this is a creative outlet that brings great satisfaction for many. Others experience stagnation and dissatisfaction as they find themselves blocked from further advancement. They may even desire a change of vocation. Because of shorter work weeks and automation it is not uncommon for adults to feel less useful. Compulsory and early retirement faces this group in a few years, and they must consider the implications of this new status.

Because of more time available for leisure and recreation, men and women can now devote more attention to that which they enjoy. However, some tend to cling to old interests instead of seeking new ones. They may change if they find their old interests no longer satisfying or impossible to pursue because of changes in their lives. Many who have had a broad range of interests narrow these down during middle adulthood. They select those that give the greatest pleasure and concentrate upon them. Interests will also be narrowed to those which are *less strenuous* and more solitary in form than before. There is a shift of interest from large-group activity to smaller groups of a few friends. Hobbies and collections may take precedence over other forms of recreation.

The middle-aged adult now begins to prefer quieter events such as reading and parties, in comparison to strenuous sports or picnics. This can be a very creative time of social life, as couples may have the freedom they earlier lacked for an active social life. Dinner parties, study groups, adult-education classes, travel and leisure outings are just a few of the events that are characteristic of this age-group.†

Studies of social participation have shown that membership in formal

*For more on single adults, see chap. 6, "The Nature and Needs of Single Adults."
†See chap. 16, "Church Recreation for Adults."

community, church and business groups is low during early adulthood but reaches a peak in the late forties or early fifties before it begins to decline.[7] Middle age is the age for service. More time can now be given to volunteer work, service projects, and board and committee activities.† The freedom that comes with fewer family members, establishment in vocation, increase of leisure time, the need to feel useful and creative and to have a clear purpose in life all contribute to this opportunity for service. Church workers will recognize that among older adults there is a wide range of interests and needs because of the extensive age span of approximately twenty-five years, and because of their involvements in so many areas of life.

MENTAL AND INTELLECTUAL CHARACTERISTICS

Stereotypes abound when the learning or intellectual ability of middle-age adults is discussed. The belief of severe mental decline and lessening of learning ability is rooted in fables and myths, which unfortunately are taken seriously by some. Studies indicate that after the early twenties adults experience a small steady decline in learning or intellectual speed, but this varies considerably from one individual to another. The decline is so gradual that one may not even notice a change. Even early in this century there was optimism concerning the learning ability of the middle-aged person. In 1928 Thorndike stated,

> In general, nobody under 45 should restrain himself from trying to learn something because of a belief or fear that he is too old to be able to learn it. Nor should he use that fear as an excuse for not learning anything which he ought to learn. If he fails in learning it, inability due directly to age will rarely, if ever, be the reason. . . . Teachers of adults of age 25-45 should expect them to learn at nearly the same rate and in nearly the same manner as they would have learned the same thing at 15-20.[8]

Later research has shown even more positive results in the ability of adults to learn. It may take an older person longer to learn, but the learning capacity remains. Many adults who have been out of a learning context for years and are either unaccustomed to the academic type of learning structure or are out of practice, still rise to the challenge to learn.*

EMOTIONAL CHARACTERISTICS

A consideration of the emotional characteristics is essential and in many ways pivotal, because the attitudes and perspectives that are focused on other areas of life stem from the emotions. This is especially true in regard to adults between ages thirty-five and sixty, who have experienced much of

†See chap. 15, "Service Projects for Adults."
*Also see chap. 8, "The Learning Process for Adults."

life and felt the gamut of emotional experiences, ranging from sorrow and despair to joy and elation. One's psychological or emotional outlook on his physical changes is just as important as the biological changes themselves. As aging continues, it is easy to slide into a process of deterioration, especially with the loss of sensory props. How the person has viewed and prepared for this stage of life is involved in the reaction that occurs. Insecurity can arise, depression is common (especially with women and their physical changes), and self-abasement may occur as uselessness (whether real or imagined) is felt.

An adequate level of emotional or psychological stability and maturity includes the following capacities and abilities:

1. "Continual flexibility" is a necessary capacity for adjustment throughout life, and particularly in middle age. This is the ability to invest strong, meaningful emotions in new activities, experiences and relationships. This means that the adult does not neurotically cling to old attachments which are no longer possible to maintain. When a significant loss occurs, whether the death of a near relative or a loss of position, he does not feel that life is meaningless. This "emotional flexibility" is the ability to shift attachments from one person to another or from some activity to another. This is a stage that requires new learning for some and expansion for others who have already practiced this in early life. A person in this period of life can suffer an impoverished emotional life if he is unable to invest in other substitutes as the persons and objects he holds dear disappear. Along with emotional flexibility, "mental flexibility" is also necessary. This is the ability to use past experience and learning as guides to new learning rather than to adhere to fixed, inflexible rules. It implies a degree of openmindedness, a concern to avoid becoming set and narrow. It is the capacity to appreciate what is new and to try new patterns of behaviors and organization.

2. "Wide self-involvement" is another desirable goal. This is the ability to enjoy a varied set of activities in life and to avoid putting too much dependence on a single role such as one's profession.

3. "Body transcendence" is the ability to have a good feeling about oneself, to feel worthwhile and contented without basing this on physical health or bodily comfort and satisfaction. If one can maintain warm human relationships and meaning to life in the midst of pain and suffering, he has made a good adjustment.

4. "Self-transcendence" is the ability to find satisfaction in fulfilling the needs of other individuals. It is being concerned with others rather than being preoccupied with self. This idea of "self-extension" is a mark of true maturity at any age.

5. "Body satisfaction" is the acceptance of one's own body along with the increased sensitivity to physical changes that occur. The mature adult values wisdom now more than physical might and ability.

6. "Sexual integration" is the capacity to integrate one's sexual desires with other aspects of life. The sexuality of young adulthood must now give way more to sociality with deepening and new friendships. He must replace those friends which he has lost with new ones, thus compensating in order to avoid becoming impoverished in his personal relations.[9]

The basis for meeting any change in life is a maturing faith that continually deepens and grows. A childish faith does not suffice for the problems of adulthood. But a faith and commitment to the purpose of life that God has ordained are best built well in advance of this life period. The church must assist adults in planning for middle adulthood by boldly anticipating and becoming increasingly aware of what to expect and how to derive the most from it.

In teaching middle adults, certain characteristics of their learning state must be considered:

1. Many of these adults do not come to a learning environment with a learner's attitude. For most of the week they are involved in producing, but now they sit and absorb.

2. They have more definite and concrete ideas than others, even to the extent of rigidity.

3. They come with a backlog of experiences from life, which enables them to contribute more to a learning experience and to assimilate new information and experiences more effectively and readily.

4. They are used to an immediate application of information. They want to know, "How is *this* relevant to my life right now?"

THE CHURCH'S MINISTRY TO MIDDLE-AGED ADULTS

In sheer numbers the middle-aged comprise the bulk of the membership in many if not most local churches. They are also "the church's backbone in . . . leadership, experiences, and potentialities."[10] For these reasons and because the range of interests and needs of middle adults is so wide, the church's educational program for this age-group is highly significant.

The following general suggestions are given as basic guidelines for a church educational ministry to middle adults, based on their characteristics and needs discussed in this chapter.

TEACH THE BIBLE CREATIVELY AND RELEVANTLY

Make Bible study enjoyable. Bible teaching that interests adults is varied in methodology, is given out of thorough preparation, is related to adult needs, and gives maximum opportunity for interaction and involvement. Meaningful Bible study for middle adults enables them to discover the truths of the Word and to explore their implications through involvement in the class sessions rather than through mere listening-to-the-teacher sessions.*

The Bible should be taught to adults in such a way that their biblical illiteracy is being transformed into an articulate comprehension of God's Word. As Ernsberger states, "The biblical and theological illiteracy of the average adult today constitutes an enormous challenge to educators in the church."[11]

PROVIDE INSTRUCTION AND GUIDANCE ON POTENTIAL ISSUES OF ADULT LIFE

Middle adults face numerous difficulties in many areas of life. Many of them are looking to the church for tangible help on questions such as these: How can I train my children to have genuine spiritual interests and values? How can I understand and communicate with my teens? How can I get along better with my husband/wife? How can I find fulfillment and meaning in our confused world? How can I witness effectively for Christ in our secular, we-don't-need-God society? How can I make a meaningful contribution to our church program? How can I avoid being caught up in a materialistic web and a breathless schedule in our jet age? How can I be a wise steward of my money? How can I adjust to changes at work, at home, at church, in our community?

Churches would do well to consider Ernsberger's comments on the pragmatic concerns of today's adults:

> Pragmatism is deeply ingrained in adult folkways and attitudes. Adult interest in learning generally begins (and all too often ends) with the words "how to . . . ." Adults are far more interested in learning efficient techniques for meeting problems or fulfilling duties or for some other sharply definable purpose than they are in acquiring knowledge whose utility is not immediately evident. Thus almost invariably far more adults will attend training sessions for church school teachers, financial canvassers, evangelistic callers, new members, and parents of children to be baptized than will attend learning groups whose purposes are less utilitarian. The educator in the church must keep in mind that training sessions, for all their obvious limitations, nevertheless command the attention and the energies of a considerably higher proportion of adults than do more generalized study groups.[12]

OFFER INSTRUCTION AND COUNSEL ON HOW MIDDLE ADULTS CAN ADJUST TO
  DIFFICULT CIRCUMSTANCES OF LIFE

As stated earlier in this chapter, middle adults face numerous problems that demand solutions—and many that call for drastic adjustments, such

---

*For ways to do this, see chap. 9, "Instructional Methodology for Adults."

as death; illness; pain; loss of employment; transfer of the family to another city; departure of children for college, military service or employment; marriage of children; menopause. Personal counseling as well as class instruction on how to adjust to these problems can be very meaningful to adults. Bible lessons and sermons that focus on God's answer to loneliness, discouragement, depression and bitterness are welcomed by middle adults facing difficulties.

ENCOURAGE ADULTS TO PLAN AND PARTICIPATE IN ADULT-SIZE SOCIAL AND
    RECREATIONAL ACTIVITIES

Bowling leagues, socials, hobbies, men's and women's fellowships, and numerous other possibilities give adults an escape from loneliness, boredom, and hectic restless schedules.*

PROVIDE MEANINGFUL AND CHURCH-RELATED SERVICE OPPORTUNITIES

Adults' need for and interest in Christian service can be channeled into significant work for the Lord. Many middle adults have unlimited abilities and experience in specific and sometimes highly technical and specialized areas. Each talent God has given laymen vocationally may be a possibility for a ministry within the local church.† As a church utilizes these abilities of its adults, it gives them a new sense of personal worth and usefulness.

EVANGELIZE ADULTS THROUGH PERSONAL WITNESS, VISITATION, AND NEIGHBOR-
    HOOD AND BUSINESS BIBLE CLASSES

As discussed elsewhere in this book,‡ Bible classes for the unsaved are being used in marvelous ways to bring adults—many of them in middle adulthood—to Jesus Christ. The church that encourages this kind of evangelistic-educational outreach is helping many adults find the answer to their search for meaning and purpose in life—through salvation in Christ.

LEAD ADULTS IN GENUINE WORSHIPFUL EXPERIENCES

Christian middle-aged adults need to experience the spiritual refreshing of adoration of the Lord in church group worship and in personal devotions. The characteristics and needs of middle adults suggest that churches help them grow in their relationship with Christ through a deepening prayer life and meaningful group worship.

NOTES

1. T. C. Desmond, "America's Unknown Middle Agers," *New York Times*, (July 29, 1956).

*See chap. 15, "Church Recreation for Adults."
†Also see chap. 14, "Adults in Service Projects."
‡Chap. 7, "Reaching and Winning Adults."

2. Leslie J. Tizzard and Harry J. S. Guntrip, *Middle Age* (New York: Channel, 1958), p. 47.
3. A. A. Warner, "Sex Behavior and Problems of the Climacteric," *Successful Marriage*, M. Fishbein and E. W. Burgess, eds. (Garden City, N.Y.: Doubleday, 1955), pp. 475-90.
4. Leonard Griffen, *What Is a Christian?* (Nashville: Abingdon, 1962), p. 84.
5. Earl F. Ziegler, *Christian Education of Adults* (Philadelphia: Westminster, 1958), p. 103.
6. Ibid.
7. Elizabeth B. Hurlock, *Developmental Psychology* (New York: McGraw-Hill, 1959), pp. 487-97.
8. E. L. Thorndike, *Adult Learning* (New York: Macmillan, 1928), pp. 177-78.
9. Bernice L. Neugarten, et al., *Personality in Middle and Late Life* (New York: Atherton, 1964), pp. 16-20.
10. Ziegler, p. 114.
11. David J. Ernsberger, "Adults" in *The Westminster Dictionary of Christian Education*, Kendig Brubaker Cully, ed. (Philadelphia: Westminster, 1963), p. 12.
12. Ibid., pp. 10-11.

FOR FURTHER READING

Bergler, Edmund. *The Revolt of the Middle-Aged Man.* New York: Grossett, 1954.

"Best Years of Our Lives?" *Newsweek* (February 19, 1968), p. 88.

Funk, Otto D. "Those Neglected Middle-Agers," *Eternity* (June, 1967), p. 26.

Howe, Reuel L. *The Creative Years.* Greenwich, Conn.: Seabury, 1964.

Hurlock, Elizabeth B. *Developmental Psychology.* New York: McGraw-Hill, 1959.

Kuhlen, Raymond G. "Trends in Religious Behavior During the Adult Years" in *Wider Horizons in Christian Adult Education*, Lawrence C. Little, ed. Pittsburgh: U. Pittsburgh, 1962.

Maves, Paul B. *The Best Is Yet to Be.* Philadelphia: Westminster, 1951.

Milt, Harry. *Middle Age—Threat or Promise.* New York: Public Affairs Committee, n.d.

Neugarten, Bernice L., et al. *Personality in Middle and Late Life.* New York: Atherton, 1964.

Nystrom, Gertrude. *Middle Age: The Challenging Years.* Chicago: Moody, 1956.

Peterson, James A. *Married Love in the Middle Years.* New York: Association, 1968.

Raber, Chester A. *Middle Age: A Test of Time.* Scottdale, Pa.: Herald, 1966.

Talbot, Gordon. "The Middle Years," *The Sunday School Times and Gospel Herald*, 66 (Nov. 15, 1968): 26-27.

Tibbitts, Clark and Donahue, Wilma. *Aging in Today's Society.* Englewood Cliffs, N.J.: Prentice-Hall, 1962.

Tizzard, Leslie J. and Guntrip, Harry J. S. *Middle Age.* New York: Channel, 1958.

Ziegler, Earl F. *Christian Education of Adults.* Philadelphia: Westminster, 1958.

Filmstrip: *Middle Age—Making the Most of It.* Hollywood, Calif.: Family Filmstrips. Color, 33⅓ rpm record, and discussion guide.

5

THE NATURE AND NEEDS OF OLDER ADULTS

David O. Moberg

A personal goal of most people is to live a long life; yet our society treats old age and the process of aging as a social problem. This paradox is at the very center of the nature and needs of older adults. It will be recognized by all who are interested in Christian education for this age level.

The alternative to attaining old age is to die during childhood, youth or the middle years of life. The great advances in longevity which are characteristic of the present century reflect the conquering of many causes of death at those earlier stages of the life cycle. Enabling people to survive the perils of infancy and the infectious diseases of childhood and youth has greatly increased life expectancy at birth, but it has had relatively little impact on the life expectancy of those who have reached the age of 60. An American male reaching age 60 in 1781 could expect on the average to live to 74.8 years, and one reaching 60 in 1958 could expect to live to the age of 75.6 years. Comparable figures for females reaching age 60 were 76.1 in 1781 and 79 years in 1958.[1]

As a result of the world's population explosion and recent gains in longevity, it has been plausibly guessed that half of all people who ever lived to the age of 65 are still living today. While we have no way of conclusively determining the validity of that estimate, it does serve to dramatize the fact that we are living in a totally new situation in the world's history.[2] Old age once was a prize grasped by few; now it is enjoyed by multitudes. Since the value of any phenomenon tends to vary inversely with its abundance, old age has rapidly changed from a prize to be sought to a condition taken for granted.

DAVID O. MOBERG, Ph.D., is Chairman of the Department of Sociology and Anthropology, Marquette University, Milwaukee, Wisconsin.

In the days of classic Greece and Rome [life expectancy] was 25 years. By the year 1800 in the United States it had reached 35 years; by 1850 it was 40 years; by 1900, some 48 years. It is now 70 years. It has increased 22 years since 1900. While the population of the United States has doubled since 1900, the population over age 65 has quadrupled; the proportion over 65 was then about 4 percent; it is now over 8 percent.[3]

As of July 1, 1966, there were approximately 18,457,000 people aged sixty-five and over in the United States and nearly eight million additional persons aged sixty to sixty-four. In other words, almost one-tenth of the national population has passed the age of sixty-five, and 13.4 percent are aged sixty and over.[4] In many local communities the proportions are substantially higher. Numerous Midwestern villages are almost like retirement communities because of their heavy concentrations of elderly people. The net increase of the population past age sixty-five is 820 per day. By 1985, they are expected to total more than 25,000,000.[5]

NEW DIMENSIONS OF OLD AGE

There is a strong tendency for Christian educators, like others, to assume that characteristics and conditions of the elderly are like those that prevailed in the past and to project the situation of the present into plans for the future without considering the possibility that radical changes may occur. Have our church programs considered the fact that soon 60 percent of all retired people will have an older parent or relative for whose care they will be at least partly responsible? The multigeneration family of four or five generations is already common, and its prevalence is increasing. "What preparation are we making to help two persons of retirement years know how to live together in happiness? Also, what is being done to help adult sons and daughters care for their own children and provide for their needs and their parents as well?"[6] Surely this is a major task for adult Christian education.

There have been both quantitative and qualitative changes in grandparent-grandchild relationships since as recently as the beginning of this century.[7] Except for the postwar baby boom that has clearly been subsiding since 1959, birth rates have sharply declined at the same time as death rates have been reduced. Children today are much more likely to have living grandparents, while the grandparent has many fewer grandchildren upon whom to bestow his or her affection.

Potentially there is therefore a basis for much closer grandparent-grandchild relationships than in the past, but there also are paradoxical counteracting tendencies. The great mobility of the population, with one-fifth of all families living in a different residence from the one of twelve months earlier, makes it more likely that they do not live in the same community and that they see each other only on visits. The rapid rate of social change contributes to misunderstanding, for each generation is the product of greatly divergent social and technological conditions. Communication becomes difficult across the barriers of the generational gap as children tend to consider their grandparents outmoded relics of an "ancient" past, and the latter tend to evaluate their descendants in terms of customs and standards totally alien to youth. Indeed, this problem is frequently evident even in relationships between the parents and grandparents of the child, for each living generation has been shaped by societal conditions different from those of the others, tends to have its distinctive life styles, and interprets its own set of values as the ideal by which others ought to live. Conflicts between the age-groups on the normative level of "right" and "wrong," "good" and "bad," and even "Christlike" and "worldly" are much more the result of cultural influences on moral interpretations than of the strictly theological matters of accepting or rejecting the Bible to which such variations are often attributed.

SOCIAL ISOLATION AND LONELINESS

The coming of Social Security, Medicare and other governmental provisions for some of the needs of the aging has produced important changes in their status. Now most of their material needs can be met, even if poorly, without direct dependence on children or other younger relatives. This has reduced the potentiality for and the reality of many interpersonal stresses and has also made it less likely that they will live in the same household as younger generations. Social isolation is common among the elderly as a result, yet it may not be as widespread as many people think. A national sample survey in 1962 found 45.3 percent of 2,442 noninstitutional people aged sixty-five and over were either single, widowed or divorced (23.7 percent of the men and 62.4 percent of the women). Less than a majority (47.6 percent), however, of even these unmarried people lived alone. If social isolation is defined as having no visitors and doing no visiting either in person or by telephone on the day before interviewing, only about 6 percent of the total older population may be considered "socially isolated."[8] Yet the quality of interpersonal relationships may be more significant than their mere presence or absence.

New patterns of housing for older adults that have developed in recent years have contributed to a sense of "loneliness in the crowd" for many. These patterns include high-rise apartments and mobile trailer parks.

Among the institutionalized, however, social isolation from relatives and friends is much more widespread. In one study of 436 patients in twenty-five nursing homes, 20 percent had no living relatives or friends and had no visitors at all. Others were visited only very infrequently and perfunctorily. Thirty-two percent of these patients had only social needs rather than medical or nursing requirements. A large number lacked even companionship with other patients, and numerous deficiencies of the staff and the program added to their problems.[9]

One of the by-products of Operation Medicare Alert, which contacted older persons individually early in 1966 to advise them of their rights under Medicare, was increased insight into their needs. One of the most serious problems reported over and over again was the loneliness of many elderly Americans. From community after community came the report from people of all social and economic levels, "No one has knocked on my doors for six months." Accompanying the desperate loneliness, starving for companionship, and dejection was a debilitating poverty of the spirit.[10]

A survey of 222 persons past age sixty still living in the community of Durham, North Carolina, found that over half were suffering from various psychiatric disorders.[11] Other studies also have found high proportions of the elderly to have such symptoms. Many of them have been relegated to institutions, and increasing numbers are being referred to psychiatric out-patient clinics. Research findings indicate "that the psychiatric problems per se of these patients are only part of the total biological, psychological, and sociological problems involved."[12] Many problems of "senility" and other "mental illness" among the aged might be given other labels if the environmental, social, physiological and other sources of their symptoms were fully understood.

NEW PATTERNS OF DEATH

With changes in health and longevity have come changes in behavior related to death and dying. In the immediate experience of most people, except for an occasional automobile accident casualty, death is almost entirely limited to old people. No longer is it common in childhood, youth and young adulthood. Perhaps that makes it all the more "unreal," for often those who die have already experienced a social withdrawal either of their own choice, or as a result of disabling chronic illness and frailty, or as an outgrowth of social isolation more or less forced on them by younger people. When children do die, the loss is deeply felt because they seem cheated out of a life full of potential contributions to their family and society, but the aged are considered to have had their share of life and to have made their contributions already, so the "social loss" of their death is considered to be much less.

The process of dying has become increasingly institutionalized as more and more families shift responsibility for care of the aged to people outside the family. Over half of all deaths in the United States now occur in hospitals, and many more take place in nursing homes, mental hospitals, homes for the aged, and other institutions. While undergoing gradual physical decline, these patients are "socially if not biologically dead" in facilities that are largely custodial rather than rehabilitative.[13]

There is a sense in which the very process of aging can be interpreted as "the process of dying," and vice versa. Yet, when it is no longer commonplace except among the older generation, it takes on an aura of mystery, and people are not prepared to face it by normal experiences of childhood and youth. Until very recently it has been a "taboo topic" in America, one which even behavioral scientists shunned; but it is receiving considerably more attention now as its significance to the living as well as the dying becomes increasingly clear.

Fear is often associated with death, but there is a great difference between fear of dying and the fear of death. The former, which has to do with the circumstances of death, suffering and inconvenience to others, apparently is stronger and more widespread. Some older people "turn to religion as a refuge from the finality of death. . . . Religion, however, seems to be most comforting and reassuring to those who come to it through faith rather than through fear of death."[14]

LIVING PATTERNS

The style of life, needs and aspirations of people presently past the age of sixty-five may be significantly different from those who just now are attaining that age. The generation born just before 1900 had fewer years of schooling, bore more children, experienced bereavement of the marriage partner much sooner after their last child had left home, were much less likely to have wives working for pay outside the home during middle age, were more likely to enter marriage as virgins, experienced a different pattern of male working careers, and were somewhat more likely to be immigrants to the United States. Events of historical significance (World War I, women's suffrage, prohibition, the great depression, World War II, etc.) occurred at different stages of their life cycles and may therefore have had differential impacts upon them. In contrast, those born from 1900 to 1909 have not had to be on the battlelines fighting a war, may have fared better than any other age-group during the depression of the 1930s, filled the lucrative defense jobs of World War II, had fewer children to educate, received more double paychecks (both father and mother working) than any other generation of the aged to date, and have ridden the crest of the lengthy postwar period of prosperity, which may be the longest one in national history. Therefore the characteristics of those who are now old are not necessarily a valid basis for planning public policies and church programs in the future.[15]

Since 1890 there has been a pronounced decline (from 68.3 to 26.9 percent in 1966) in the proportion of men past age sixty-five still participating in the labor force, but the proportion of elderly working women has increased from 7.6 to 9.6 percent. Even in the forty-five-to-sixty-four age category of the "older worker" there has been a decline among males from 92.0 to 90.6 percent, while female employment has risen from 12.1 in 1890 to 47.4 percent in 1966. A substantial proportion of the workers past age sixty-five (37.0 percent of the men and 48.7 percent of the women) were working only part time. Once an older worker is unemployed, he typically remains unemployed longer and finds it harder to secure reemployment than younger workers.[16]

Early retirement is characteristic of the present labor force. Only in relatively recent times has it become necessary to set arbitrary, compulsory retirement ages, for most people died relatively young or could continue working on the farm. Since work is central to the self-concept and sense of worth of the typical American male, this has profound implications for personal and social adjustment. Indeed, a "gospel of work" is often an implicit part of Protestantism, partly as a result of explicit statements in Scripture, among which 2 Thessalonians 3:10 and certain of the proverbs are outstanding. When one no longer has a steady job, he tends to feel that he is no longer contributing to society, that he has lost his sense of worth, that he is "just retired" (a reaction carrying an emotional loading similar to the sigh of regret of many a frustrated woman who is "just a housewife"), and that he is caught in a retirement trap and unable to cope with leisure because all he knows by experience and mental orientation is how to work.[17]

Attitudes of rejection, indifference, and minimizing of capacities of the aging are common in churches as well as elsewhere in society. This undermines the self-esteem of the older person and "places him in double jeopardy, since by aging he is threatened from within by loss of previous sources of strength, and because he is a part of the community and is affected by its attitudes."[18]

THE CURSE OF STEREOTYPING

Stereotyped perspectives of the aging process, the aged patient, and the therapeutic process are widespread among people in the healing and helping professions;[19] so it is no surprise that they are common in the remainder of the population. Indeed, there is such diversity among the aged that any generalization about them can find its examples, thus "proving" to the satisfaction of the stereotype-wielder that his sweeping statement is correct. The fallacy lies in the fact that the illustration may be characteristic of only one or two cases in a hundred. A systematic attempt should be made to discover negative as well as positive evidence before statements of broad applicability are made.

Many stereotypes about older adults contribute indirectly to their problems. They are considered to be living in the past, beyond the age of usefulness, desirous only of a life at ease in their rocking chair, anxious to be free of all responsibility, cantankerous and disagreeable, no longer able to learn, impossible to change, and on the shelf if not the scrap heap of society. They are seen as *old* rather than as *people*, each of whom is different from all others.

In fact, however, there is, if anything, an even greater range of individual differences among the elderly than among younger people.[20] Yet when these differences are deemphasized, many older people themselves are prone to accept the generalizations made about them. Expecting themselves to become worthless, they indeed become worthless, dependent on others, and a burden to those who care for them, for the self-fulfilling prophecy is a potent force in human behavior.

The self-defeating attitude is especially obvious in connection with adult education. Arguing that "You can't teach an old dog new tricks," many aging persons will refuse to study, memorize scriptures and engage in other educational activities. They forget that people are not dogs, and they fail to realize that learning is practiced continually as they adjust to new circumstances of their own life and to changes in society.

The attitudes of youth toward the aged, the problems middle-aged people anticipate in their own later years, and the publicity given to various aspects of "the problem of old age" combine to produce subtle feelings of inadequacy and insecurity among the elderly. Social values and norms tend to become internalized and personal during the continual process of personality development, so that what occurs in society at large has profound implications for its individual members. Even the terms used to refer to the older generation and the subtle overtones and nuances of expression accompanying them impart attitudes toward old age and aged people which may heighten intergenerational conflict, contribute to personal fears of retirement, or reinforce prejudices.[21]

The great variations among the elderly population should be recognized clearly by all who associate with them in any way. The same set of outward circumstances may result in different patterns of emotional reactions, interpersonal relationships, and overall adjustment. Different life experiences may have built up different strengths and vulnerabilities in the person, making the occurrence of certain problem-reactions either more or less likely.[22] Each is a person with his own unique characteristics, regardless of the contrary impression conveyed by popular stereotypes.

OTHER SOCIAL PROBLEMS

Much of the disability among the elderly may be created by society. "A high proportion among those entering state hospitals in old age . . . are the poor, the uneducated of low occupational status. Many may have been well adapted until they lost their resources. . . . Social rejection, the cultural discard of older people in the United States, is a major factor in their unhappiness over growing old."[23]

Feelings of rejection by others lead to feelings of self-rejection, anxiety, even fantasy and delusions. When living a marginal existence, wondering whether inflation will reduce their economic status to an intolerable level, they become easy victims of confidence games, land investment promotions, and other "double your money" schemes. When living in fear of declining health or vigor, they readily succumb to the deceptive claims of modern pitchmen selling worthless machines, unnecessary health foods or food supplements, and exotic medical treatments.[24] While part of these problems are due to the relatively low level of education characteristic of the elderly, part can be attributed also to their despair and feeling of hopelessness resulting from social, physiological and economic conditions.

Much more could be said about the problems confronted by older adults in American society. They account for far more than their proportionate share of the population living in conditions of poverty. They find it difficult to participate in social organizations or are eased out of them at the very time when group participation becomes more important to their well-being than it has been for many decades. Their physical health and vigor gradually decline, or may suddenly be removed by diseases of the heart and circulatory system which leave many in a semi-invalid condition for years before their deaths. Strained marital relationships may result from the retirement of a husband, who suddenly is around home all the time "interfering" with what has previously been the wife's exclusive daytime domain. Emotional and mental problems are common, and many spiritual problems emerge as well. For instance, they may experience a subtle sense of guilt for departures from moral standards they were taught in childhood as they conform to changes in society around them. They may have fears of the future because of uncertainties about the forgiveness of sins or other aspects of their relationship to God. When to these are added the physical and social barriers placed in the way of their participation in church life, the burdens of many seem nearly insurmountable.[25]

A bleak, pessimistic spirit is hence common among the aged. It is present to a greater degree among those who are in poor health, persons of lower socioeconomic status, those who reside in rural areas, and those who are retired, in contrast to the implicit counterpart categories, and it is more common among men than among women.[26]

PROBLEMS IN CHRISTIAN MINISTRIES

The church has great potential for its ministry to the aged. More older people are members of churches than of all other voluntary associations together. Through the centuries comfort and spiritual blessings have flowed through the church to its participants, and that remains true today. Numerous studies have revealed a clear relationship between Christian faith and good personal adjustment during the later years of life as well as between religious activities and good adjustment.[27]

Nevertheless, not all is encouraging. The general problems of working with the aged pertain to Christian education as well. Stereotypes of the elderly distort conceptions of their nature and needs. The false belief that they want to be relieved of all responsibility causes a removal of church-related duties from many of them before they are psychologically and spiritually prepared for the change. Fear of their own old age on the part of clergymen and lay leaders contributes to an unconscious withdrawal from involvement with the elderly except when it becomes absolutely necessary. Unawareness of their real needs contributes to the vague but correct feeling by many older church members that their needs are not being met. This feeling is easily transferred into an interpretation that the church is "departing from the gospel" and "growing cold in its love for Christ."

Church attendance tends to decline during the later years of old age in typical congregations, so some have concluded that people become less "religious" near the conclusion of life. They have failed to consider other indicators of spiritual behavior, including prayer, Bible reading, listening to religious programs on radio and television, expressions of religious beliefs, feelings of devotion to Christ, and certain Christian works related to faith. On the basis of all these other criteria it can be said that in general there is an increase in religious commitment with advancing age, at least among those who have any religious inclinations at all.[28] The decline in church attendance is often not voluntary; it is the result of conditions and circumstances that hinder full participation by many older people.

Some of these hindering conditions are as obvious as the problems of stairs to climb, slippery floors to navigate, restrooms inaccessible to the disabled, poor acoustics that confuse the hard-of-hearing or produce a thunderous roar in their hearing aids, and drafty air circulation. Others are the problems of transportation, the feeling that they cannot afford to give as generously as in the past and hence are not wanted, the inability to contribute their work to conventional types of church service, the belief that their clothes are not good enough to wear to church, the impression that younger adults are pushing them out of positions of authority, personality conflicts, and disagreement about the role of older people in the church, in addition to all of the other types of interpersonal problems that can flare up among people of any age.[29] When intergenerational conflict becomes tangled with any of the other sources of tension, the results can be devastating, whether it results from different standards for moral conduct, divergent patterns of church worship, or contrasting ideas about the basic task of the church.

An additional problem that often is overlooked by church leaders is the matter of timing activities and services for older members. Evening activities discriminate against a relatively high proportion of those whose eyesight is failing, whose step is uncertain and slow, whose hearing is fading, and whose personal habits include an "early to bed, early to rise" regimen. When specialized activities like a club for mature adults, excursions, Bible study groups, or continuing-education programs are intended for them, they should be scheduled around the middle of the day rather than the evening.

Innovations which appear traditional and which seem to hearken back to the days of their youth often will appeal most. The fear that their church is departing from the faith of its founders is common among the aged, for they often fail to realize that adjustments in music, modifications of worship patterns, the use of new Bible translations, changes in the techniques of evangelism, and innovations in lesson plans may be made without any departure from the fundamentals of the faith. How changes are made, the rationale given for them, and even the language patterns used to explain them often mean the difference between continued active support from elderly members and their disillusionment.

CHRISTIAN-EDUCATION MINISTRIES FOR OLDER ADULTS

One-third of the total membership of many church congregations is past the age of sixty-five. Christian education directors rightly give much attention to youth in the congregation and community, but they ought not to neglect the needs of aging members and community residents. Opportunities are great for the congregation that is ready to seize them in a meaningful program of evangelistic-educational-social-recreational-fellowship-service outreach.

Many a non-Christian begins to give serious thought to religion and life beyond the grave only when he is retired and relieved of the pressures of other responsibilities that earlier choked the Word that was sown so that it could not bear fruit. When Christians fail to seek them out through friendship and love in their hour of need, they become the victims of cults established by leaders eager to profit from their unease.[30]

GOALS FOR CHRISTIAN EDUCATION

All the generalized objectives of evangelical Christian education apply to programs for older adults. There are, however, some objectives that may be somewhat unique to the aging.

Time is important to older people, perhaps in a somewhat different respect from its importance to others who must punch a time clock and keep appointments punctually. Some suffering children of God long for death with its release from the trials of this life, so each passing day seems another cross to bear. Others fear the possible agonies of the process of dying and consider each day without it a treasure. Many have "time on their hands," while others wonder how time can fly away so rapidly.

An important goal of Christian education for older adults is *to make that which pertains to time (the secular) of timeless or eternal import.* Numbering one's days so that his heart may be applied to wisdom (Ps 90:12) means much more than merely counting the days and adding up one's age. Instead, it involves making the days count. If Christian educators do not help people of all ages do that, who will?

The reconciliation of youth and their parents to the grandparent generation should be another goal of adult Christian education. Instead of widening the intergenerational gap, as some church-related programs currently tend to do, wise efforts should be exerted to bridge them. This cannot be done unilaterally by action only on the "senior citizen" level. It involves education on all levels, from childhood on up, pertinent to the aging process, how to understand others who are different, and thus how to let the love of Christ govern interpersonal relationships.

Bringing people together into worthwhile action programs and service projects can teach a great deal more than mere words in an isolated Sunday school class. "Adopted Grandparents" and "Adopted Grandchildren" programs might be one technique through which this can be achieved. As each generation by love serves the other, love will grow and the generational gap should become less of a problem. Members of different generations must learn to know each other as persons rather than as representatives of age-categories; only then can the false stereotypes each has about the other be removed.

Action programs help fulfill the implications of the gospel, but they also are a form of proclaiming God's love by deeds. *Love* is a meaningless word to those who have never experienced it. *Father in heaven* reminds many people merely of some ungodly earthly father. Only by demonstrating what *love* is so that men can experience it, can they learn to love Him who first loved them.

Every group in every evangelical church ought to have a service project by which the members learn through experience what it means to help others. Past failures in this regard are evident in the self-centered individualistic religiosity of many older church members who think so little of their fellowmen that they, in effect, pray the prayer our Lord taught us thus: "*My* Father which art in heaven. . . . Give *me* this day *my* daily bread. And forgive *me my* debts. . . ." Service *by* the aging as well as *for* them should be incorporated into every church.*

Another significant goal, perhaps the most sweeping of all, has to do with *basic cultural standards which contradict Christian values on so many levels.* Among these are attitudes toward the aged that help to heap coals of fire upon the hoary head instead of recognizing it as "a crown of glory" (Pr 16:31) and relationships to parents that are like the *Corban* of Mark 7:9-13. Christians should not be conformed to this world's standards; instead they should be the light of the world and the salt of the earth, helping to change society in a God-honoring direction.

An interesting description of worldliness (although not labeled so by her) appears in Dr. Margaret Clark's statements about a mentally ill group of aged Americans. She was struck by the fact that the value-orientations associated with maladjustment were "strikingly similar to values found by a number of observers to be characteristic of American culture generally." The values dominant until at least about twenty-five years ago, hence when her subjects were at the prime of life, included achievement and success, movement, aggressiveness, acquisition of money, activity and work, progress, and orientation toward the future. "Yet, now we find that the individualistic, competitive, aggressive, future-oriented and acquisitive American of 25 years ago—that person who rigidly clings to those values in his old age—is today's best prospect for geriatric psychiatry."[31] To what extent has "Christian education" gilded over antichristian cultural norms with biblical proof-texts and taught these worldly values of society as if they were the oracles of God?

It is also important to build strong Christian "reference groups" for people at every stage of the life cycle. Wholesome group loyalties strengthen commitments and have a healing effect on persons as well as institutions. There is evidence that active social relationships in a compatible group protect the aging individual against stresses of the dramatic discontinuities in the American social system which often militate against smooth transitions into the status of old age.[32] What can serve this need better than an active, loving fellowship of Christians?

PROGRAM SUGGESTIONS

Any successful program of Christian education begins by facing felt needs and practical problems. Every one of the problems mentioned in

*See chap. 14, "Adults in Service Projects."

the first part of this chapter has its implications for Christian educators. Retirement when one's own parents are still living creates special burdens for many. Tense family relationships call for the healing balm of Christian love. The need to face bereavement and death and to plan funerals in a Christ-honoring manner that represents good Christian stewardship and does not glorify the earthly remains is an important challenge in a society that tries to cover up the reality of death in its funeral customs. Intergenerational tensions arising out of different normative standards and divergent moral interpretations call for the very best of teaching in order to relate the Bible to the realities of life in the closing third of the twentieth century. The social and psychological needs of people, which tend to be overlooked when economic and material needs are fulfilled, should be met by the church. Problems of the loss of self-esteem upon retirement should be dealt with openly. Members who have already gone through that crisis can help those who are about to face it.

All of this implies that, under wise leadership and by means of effective pastoral counseling, older adults can help each other. Openness to observing their needs—even when they are not expressed verbally—and openness to hear their opinions—even when one does not fully agree with them—can help produce a response of openness to changes of ideas and behavior on their part. But if some never change, don't be dismayed. One can hardly expect in a few short hours of educational and social contact to counteract the strongly engrained influences of many decades! But can we not love them even if we do not agree with them?

Survey research can help to reveal practical needs of the aged in one's own congregation and community, but it must not be superficial. What lies beneath the readily observable surface, underneath the traditional clichés used in daily communication, may be of greatest significance.

When plans are made to help meet discovered needs, those plans should be made *with* the older adults, not merely *for* them. When the latter is done, a program is foisted on mature people as if they were nursery children. This is devastating to their egos and often is a source of deep unexpressed resentment that is harmful to both individuals and the church.

Retirement today is a status into which many slip quietly, almost as though they were ashamed of it. The high values placed by our culture on work and the identification of a man's worth by his job contribute to that feeling of disgrace. It does not yet have a positive value. "Instead, there is a tendency to look on retirement as a bench mark signifying declining physical and mental prowess and impending death."[33] Perhaps the church could help overcome this problem by recognizing the arrival of retirement ceremonially. This could become a Christian rite of passage comparable to confirmation, marriage, infant dedication, and burial of the dead.[34] It could express appreciation to those who have served man and society long and faithfully, give recognition for past contributions, and acknowledge the new status with its many valuable opportunities for volunteer services in the church and community.[*]

The reason there are so few older adults in the typical evangelical Sunday school deserves exploration. Research perhaps would reveal four main reasons for the failure of older adult church members to attend: Some find the curriculum and teaching irrelevant to their current needs; others find them to be repetitious of what they have "always had" in lessons during previous stages of the life cycle; some face complications of physical health, problems of transportation, or difficulties in sitting through two hours of activities; and some have either drifted from their faith or never truly possessed it.

In the typical community there is need for a wide range of services to older adults. Telephone calls to older adults not only can discover whether they may have emergency needs, they also provide a means of friendly interaction for people who otherwise are relatively isolated, and they can become an "entering wedge" for further testimony. Gospel teams of children or youth can present programs in retirement homes, hospitals, nursing homes, and the rooms of shut-ins. Many of the aged, like current teenagers, are delighted when they hear guitars accompanying gospel singing! Every church should have a functioning home (extension) department that operates as a part of the Sunday school. By this means, older adults who are too ill to attend church, the handicapped and those in rest homes can be made to feel they are still a part of the church community as they are visited, receive Sunday school and other literature, hear tape recordings of Sunday sermons, and engage in worship and instructional activities even though they are unable to attend church.[35]

Volunteer services to supplement professional aid are needed in many community agencies; a wide range of opportunity is present for those who have only modest abilities but have time to share with others.

Above all, any program of Christian education that aims to reach all older men and women for Christ must be diversified. The devotional approach that emphasizes traditional types of Bible study and prayer may meet the needs only of those who already are the most devout and who hence tend to dominate the typical older adult Sunday school class. Some will be attracted only by a program that is clearly oriented to their practical problems in our society and that draws on findings of the social

[*]Churches can also encourage retired persons to join local and national fellowships of older adults, for literature and fellowship. One such organization is the National Association of Retired Persons, 1225 Connecticut Ave., N.W., Washington, D.C. 20035.

and behavioral sciences besides teachings of the Scriptures. Others are in great need of social relationships and can be drawn into Bible study and Christian commitment only through the provision of recreational activities and fellowship with Christians. Still others are in need of pastoral care, perhaps including referral to a medical doctor, social welfare agency, or psychological clinic.

Evangelical Christian education demands being like the apostle Paul, who was willing to become all things to all men in order that he thereby might win some. Recognition of the tremendous variety of human needs and interests among older adults will inevitably lead to diverse patterns and programs of Christian education so that the greatest possible number may be reached for Jesus Christ.

NOTES

1. Herman J. Loether, *Problems of Aging* (Belmont, Calif.: Dickenson, 1967), p. 89.
2. Warren T. Roudebush, "Report from the President's Council on Aging" (talk given at the 41st annual Agricultural Outlook Conference, Washington, D.C., Nov. 20, 1963), p. 1.
3. Jay Elmer Morgan, "The Challenge of Our Times to Adult Education" in *The Future Course of Christian Adult Education*, Lawrence C. Little, ed. (Pittsburgh: U. Pittsburgh, 1959), pp. 6-7.
4. "Estimates of the Population of States, by Age," *Current Population Reports: Population Estimates* (US Bureau of the Census), Series P-25, No. 354 (Dec. 8, 1966).
5. Administration on Aging, *Meeting the Challenge of the Later Years: Guide to Community Action* (Washington, D.C.: US Dept. of Health, Education, and Welfare, 1967), p. 25.
6. Virginia Stafford, "Preparing for the Later Years," in *Religion in the Life of the Aging and Aged* (Indianapolis: Proceedings of the Seventh Annual Conference on Aging, Indiana Commission on the Aging and Aged, 1965), p. 42.
7. Meyer F. Nimkoff, "Changing Family Relationships of Older People in the United States During the Last Forty Years" in *Gerontology: A Book of Readings*, Clyde B. Vedder, ed. (Springfield, Ill.: Thomas, 1963), p. 117.
8. Ethel Shanas, "The Older Person at Home—A Potential Isolate or Participant" in *Research Utilization in Aging* (Bethesda, Md.: National Institute of Mental Health, 1964), pp. 81-86.
9. Mary E. Shaughnessey, "Implications of Research in Geriatric Nursing Home Care" in *Research Utilization in Aging*, pp. 72-75.
10. Subcommittee on Federal, State, and Community Services of the Special Committee on Aging, United States Senate, *Needs for Services Revealed by Operation Medicare Alert* (Washington, D.C.: US Government Printing Office, 1966), pp. 3-4.
11. E. W. Busse, R. H. Dovenmuehle and R. G. Brown, "Psychoneurotic Reactions of the Aged," *Geriatrics* 15 (Feb., 1960):97-105.
12. James M. A. Weiss, "Out-Patient Psychiatric Rehabilitation of Older Persons: Implications of Research Findings," in *Research Utilization in Aging*, p. 58.
13. Anselm L. Strauss, cited in "Problems of Psychological, Social Care of Dying Aged," *Geriatric Focus* 6 (May 1, 1967):1, 6.
14. Loether, p. 94.
15. Leonard D. Cain, Jr., "Age Status and Generational Phenomena: The New Old People in Contemporary America," *The Gerontologist* 7 (June, 1967):83-92.
16. Herman B. Brotman, "The Older Worker in 1966," *Aging* 142 (June, 1967):18-20.
17. Loether, pp. 63-76.
18. Esther C. Stamats, "Role of the Church and Synagogue in Community Programs for the Aging" in *Religion in the Life of the Aging and Aged*, p. 27.

19. Rodney M. Coe, "Professional Perspectives on the Aged," *The Gerontologist* 7 (June, 1967):114-19.
20. D. B. Bromley, *The Psychology of Human Ageing* (Baltimore, Md.: Penguin, 1966), p. 298.
21. H. Lee Jacobs, "Developing a Positive Conception of Aging During the Formative Years" in *Selected Papers, Fifth Annual National Conference of State Executives on Aging* (Washington, D.C.: US Government Printing Office, 1965), pp. 59-64.
22. Marian R. Yarrow, Paul Blank, Olive W. Quinn, E. Grant Youmans and Johanna Stein, "Social Psychological Characteristics of Old Age" in *Human Aging*, James E. Birren, et al., eds. (Bethesda, Md.: National Institute of Mental Health, 1963), pp. 257-79.
23. "In Summary" in *Research Utilization in Aging*, pp. 109-10.
24. Subcommittee on Frauds and Misrepresentations Affecting the Elderly of the Special Committee on Aging, US Senate, *Frauds and Deceptions Affecting the Elderly* (Washington, D.C.: US Government Printing Office, 1965).
25. Robert M. Gray and David O. Moberg, *The Church and the Older Person* (Grand Rapids: Eerdmans, 1962), pp. 19-37.
26. E. Grant Youmans, "Pessimism Among Older Rural and Urban Persons," *Journal of Health and Human Behavior*, 2 (Summer, 1961): 132-37.
27. David O. Moberg, "Some Findings and Insights from My Research on Religion and Aging" in *Religion and Aging*, John E. Cantelon et al., eds. (Los Angeles: Rossmoor-Cortese Institute for the Study of Retirement and Aging, U. Southern California, 1967), pp. 27-45.
28. David O. Moberg, "Religiosity in Old Age," *The Gerontologist*, 5 (June, 1965): 78-87, 111-12.
29. Gray and Moberg, pp. 96-117.
30. Careful research is needed to determine the conditions under which elderly non-Christians feel a need for religion, the extent to which mail-order religions, cults and schismatic sects attract the aged, and the patterns of evangelistic outreach which effectively win commitments to Jesus Christ. Service programs ministering to genuine needs can have a significant evangelistic impact if they are properly planned and administered. See David O. Moberg, *Inasmuch* (Grand Rapids: Eerdmans, 1965).
31. Margaret Clark, "The Anthropology of Aging, A New Area for Studies of Culture and Personality," *The Gerontologist*, 7 (Mar., 1967):61-62.
32. Ibid., pp. 62-63.
33. Loether, p. 68.
34. Stafford, p. 46.
35. For an informative treatment of this department of the Sunday school, see Henry Jacobsen, *The Pastor and His Home Department*, Christian Education Monographs, Pastors' Series No. 6 (Wheaton, Ill.: Scripture Press, 1966); and Henry Jacobsen, *How to Succeed with Your Home Department* (Wheaton, Ill.: Scripture Press, 1956). Also see the filmstrip *Who Else Is There?* (Wheaton, Ill.: Scripture Press; color, with 33⅓ rpm record and discussion guide).

FOR FURTHER READING

Allen, Eugene W. "Ways the Church and the Retired Can Help Each Other," *Leader Guidebook*, 70 (Jan.-Mar., 1969: 23-24.

Bayly, Joseph. *Christian Education Trends*. Elgin, Ill.: David C. Cook, 1970.

Birren, James E.; Butler, Robert N.; Greenhouse, Samuel W.; Sokoloff, Louis; and Yarrow, Marian R., eds. *Human Aging: A Biological and Behavioral Study*. Bethesda, Md.: National Institute of Mental Health, 1963.

Bromley, D. B. *The Psychology of Human Ageing*. Baltimore, Md.: Penguin, 1966.

Cantelon, John E., et al. *Religion and Aging: The Behavioral and Social Sciences Look at Religion and Aging*. Los Angeles: Rossmoor-Cortese Institute for the Study of Retirement and Aging, U. Southern California, 1967.

Chakerian, Charles G., ed. *The Aging and the United Presbyterian Church in the U.S.A.* New York: Div. of Health and Welfare, U. P. Board of National Missions, 1964.

Culver, Elsie Thomas. *New Church Programs with the Aging.* New York: Association, 1961.

Gorer, Geoffrey. *Death, Grief, and Mourning: A Study of Contemporary Society.* Garden City, N.Y.: Doubleday, 1967.

Gray, Robert M. and Moberg, David O. *The Church and the Older Person.* Grand Rapids: Eerdmans, 1962.

Jacobs, H. Lee. *Senior Citizens in the Church and Community.* Iowa City, Ia.: Institute of Gerontology, State U. Iowa, 1960.

Loether, Herman J. *Problems of Aging: Sociological and Social Psychological Perspectives.* Belmont, Calif.: Dickenson, 1967.

Maves, Paul B. and Cedarleaf, J. Lennart. *Older People and the Church.* Nashville: Abingdon-Cokesbury, 1949.

McKinney, John C. and de Vyver, Frank T., eds. *Aging and Social Policy.* New York: Appleton-Century-Crofts, 1966.

Narramore, Clyde M. *The Mature Years.* Grand Rapids: Zondervan, 1961.

Older Members in the Congregation. Minneapolis: Augsburg, n.d.

Peterson, Miriam A. *The Church's Ministry with Senior Adults.* Valley Forge, Pa.: American Baptist Board of Education and Publication, n.d.

Rose, Arnold M. and Peterson, Warren A., eds. *Older People and Their Social World: The Sub-Culture of the Aging.* Philadelphia: Davis, 1965.

Scudder, Delton L., ed. *Organized Religion and the Older Person.* Gainesville, Fla.: U. Florida, 1958.

"Some 'Basic Facts' on Older People." *Information Service,* 42 (Feb. 2, 1963): 1-8.

Stough, Ada Barnett. *Brighter Vistas: The Story of Four Church Programs for Older Adults.* Washington, D.C.: US Dept. of Health, Education, and Welfare, 1965.

The Fulfillment Years in Christian Education. New York: National Council of Churches of Christ in the U.S.A., 1953.

The Nation and Its Older People. Washington, D.C.: US Government Printing Office, 1962.

Tibbitts, Clark, ed. *Handbook of Social Gerontology.* Chicago: U. Chicago, 1960.

Tournier, Paul. *The Seasons of Life.* Richmond, Va.: John Knox, 1963.

Whitman, Virginia. *Around the Corner from Sixty.* Chicago: Moody, 1967.

6

THE NATURE AND NEEDS OF
SINGLE ADULTS

Cyril D. Garrett

This chapter deals with a group of adults who have just one feature in common—they are single. Apart from this common feature they may be classified as unmarried, divorced or widowed. The common characteristic of being single indicates that some common problems may be shared by all single adults. But the fact that adults can be single in a variety of ways—unmarried, divorced or widowed—indicates that adults within these groups face diverse problems in relation to the conditions that make them single. So to speak of single adults is to speak of a very divergent group.

This divergency is further complicated when one adds the age differential. The age at which one is classified as single has a significant effect in determining the kinds of needs he has as a single adult. Thus a common group—single adults—may be a very complex group. Few generalizations can be made about all of them. Therefore each of these groups is discussed in terms of needs specific to each one, and suggestions are made about various ministries which the church may direct toward each group.

UNMARRIED ADULTS

Unmarried adults in 1966 were strongest numerically in the twenty to twenty-nine age-group.[1] At ages twenty-five to twenty-nine, 16.7 percent of the males and 9.7 percent of the females were unmarried. Exactly 12 percent of the males in the thirty to thirty-four age-group were still unmarried, while 5.4 percent of the females in that age-group were unmarried. Age thirty seems to become a rather critical dividing age for unmarrieds, for prior to that age they are usually considered "eligibles." After age thirty the possibilities of marriage for the female are problematic, and society in general is likely to have tagged her as an "old maid."

CYRIL D. GARRETT, Ed.D., is Professor of Christian Education, American Baptist Seminary of the West, Covina Campus, Covina, California.

In 1967 there were about three and one-half million unmarried males thirty years of age and above, and there were almost three million females thirty and above still unmarried.[2] Together, these unmarried people represent six and a half million people. It has been estimated that about one in twelve males above thirty years of age and about one in fourteen females above thirty are unmarried.

For purposes of discussing the church's ministry to the unmarried, the group above age thirty will be considered since those below thirty are potentially marriageable and do not present the same social, psychological and theological problems to be ministered to by churches.

There are many reasons why adults do not get married, and space does not permit a thorough analysis of these reasons. The purpose here is to isolate a few problems of the unmarried which may help churches define ways in which they may minister to this group.

A valuable service has been performed by M. D. Hugen in defining the problems confronted by the church in its ministry to the unmarried.[3] While there may be some aspects of the unmarried's problem for which the church is unprepared to minister, there are others that seem to be closely related to the church's message and mission.

The church can attack the current social attitude which defines the unmarried as a "failure" and seek to correct the tendency to depersonalize the unmarried by referring to them as a group held in a negative stereotype. This is basically a social problem in terms of society's attitudes about the unmarried. Unintentionally, the church may strengthen this negative attitude by failing to provide corrective measures in the light of the gospel message. These corrective efforts could include a theological understanding of the legitimacy of being unmarried and an endeavor to provide spiritual resources for facing the gnawing problem of loneliness and sexual problems.

Some of these problems may be dealt with in special programs; but generally speaking, these are areas of life in which the whole church needs to show a sustaining and confirming attitude of acceptance to the unmarried.

The social and theological attitudes which confront the unmarried are closely related. Satisfactory fulfillment of adult social roles is primarily defined in terms of marriage and family relationships, thus the unmarried is atypical socially in terms of the larger social order. While our society has a general attitude of acceptance toward unmarrieds, they are, nevertheless, put under a heavy social disadvantage. This is particularly true for the unmarried female, who is discussed later. Like society, the church has placed great emphasis on marriage and family relationships as a fulfillment of God's plan for man and woman. Accordingly, the church has often failed to see the unwed state as a viable condition through which one may realize his discipleship to Christ and fulfill his commitment to Christ. Unless the church is able to overcome this failure, it will not likely have to bother with the other problems mentioned above, for it will have pushed its unmarried adults out into the subculture of the unmarried to find subgroup acceptance instead of self-acceptance and God-acceptance.

The unmarried American male enjoys a more favorable social position than the unmarried female. The bachelor above thirty years of age is considered "eligible" for marriage, but the female of the same age-group has often been assigned the negative stereotype of the "old maid." Statistically, her chances of marriage are less favorable than the male's. The bachelor's position is humorously considered an advantageous one, for he was "too smart" to lose his freedom in marriage. But the female's position is far from humorous, for she is considered to have failed to develop the personal qualities for marriage or the skill necessary to "catch" a man. A success-oriented society may quickly judge the unmarried female as unsuccessful though her reasons for remaining unmarried may transcend the general social definitions of success. Society expects marriage and parenthood from women to a degree that it does not expect these from men.

The moral and ethical unfairness of such social attitudes is seen in the fact that the stereotyped feelings toward the unmarried female are not based on her actual experience but are assumed as the counterpart of society's definition of the married family woman. This is clearly demonstrated in Hugen's development of the social problems faced by the older unmarried. He reports:

> After examining the details of society's stereotype of the single woman in the period 1820-1935 and the concept of marriage in that age, and after examining the details of the stereotype in post-1935 society and its concept of marriage, it can be reasonably concluded that the social evaluation of the older unmarried woman is directly linked to the social evaluation of marriage. In both periods the stereotype of the single woman is the inverse of society's concept of the marriageable and the married woman. Wherever society changes its idea of the qualities necessary for marriage or of the personal benefits resulting from marriage, the stereotype of the single woman changes to one which is the inverse of the new qualifications and benefits. When, as in the heritage of many early American settlers, the marriageable and the married woman were thought of as gracious, charming, and dependent, the single woman was stereotyped as masculine, strong, and self-sufficient. Marriage was conceived primarily as a relationship which offered security and protection. Later, in frontier days, the marriageable woman was self-sufficient and adaptable and the single woman was stereotyped as weak, dependent, and mild.

Today, the marriageable and the married woman are seen as sexually attractive, personable, psychically mature and well developed; and the single woman is stereotyped as homely, sexually frustrated, maladjusted and neurotic. The single woman is always seen as lacking the qualities necessary for the pattern of marriage of each age.[4]

This is the crucial issue of the unmarried to which the church must speak. The biblical message of the worth of the individual before God passes judgment on society's way of defining a person's place by default— assigning one the inverse position of those it considers successful in marriage and family. The emphasis that woman fulfills herself most fully in bearing children implies that the woman not experiencing motherhood is somehow inferior before God. In contrast to this view, the New Testament emphasizes (1) that marriage is a temporary state in God's overall purposes; (2) that in Christ, being male or female, married or unmarried, counts for nothing in itself (Gal 3:28); and (3) that the believer, whether wedded or single, is responsible to (and capable of) serving Christ. Hugen has expressed this truth as follows:

> There is no universal, absolute obligation to marry, neither for woman nor for man. Man's highest obligation is to serve Christ in the kingdom. He can and must serve Christ in whatever condition, circumstance, and state he lives. Each individual person has his own peculiar relationships and circumstances, and he need not change them in order to realize his ultimate purpose.[5]

Unless unmarried men and women can understand that they may fulfill their lives in God's purposes, then the basic issue of life—one's relationship to God—becomes a constant source of anxiety and frustration. When they do understand it, the state of unmarriedness is much easier to accept as a role in which to fulfill the will of God. This provides bases for which the church may speak to the questions of loneliness and sexuality. If one accepts singleness as a condition he has chosen and one in which he believes he may fulfill himself before God, then he may deal realistically with other problems. Having accepted his singleness, he does not have to engage in anxious or neurotic behavior to make up for his "lacks." Having accepted his singleness, he recognizes his worth, value and purpose before God. To be able to say with Paul that one is "content," before God, "in whatever state" (Phil 4:11, RSV), opens the way for discipleship that is based not on marriage or singleness, but on a personal acceptance of oneself in relation to Jesus Christ.

Three problems related to the unmarried must be dealt with realistically by the church: aloneness, loneliness and sexuality. Aloneness and loneliness are not the same but may grow out of each other. The "family church" with its emphases on family programs may inadvertently isolate the unmarried. Aloneness may turn to an emotional dejection which results in personal isolation. This means that the individual has interpreted himself as society has been interpreting him. If this happens, the unmarried person may then turn to groups outside the church to find companionship and meaning for his type of life. In such groups or subcultures, one can find many other unmarried people. In these subcultures the unmarried can interpret some areas of life in terms of their goals, values, language, dress and recreation, quite apart from the church and society. If this happens, it frequently may mean that the church has been discarded or considered irrelevant for giving meaning to "my type of life." If the church tries to reach these people, it now has to go where they are, to penetrate their subculture, to approach the unmarried on their terms of recreation, in their ways of thinking, and with their values of life in mind.

The following advertisement taken from the personal section of a daily newspaper shows the market of which the single adult is the object:

Single—Divorced—Widowed
Over 21, Under 65

Need dates, companions? Let us help you spend interesting and happy hours with compatible partners. Low fee, $10. Lack confidence? Personal development course is also available. Psychologist on our staff for personal interviews, if needed. Write or phone Partners by Science.

Tours, trips and treatments are provided by agencies interested in the money of unmarrieds. Some of these agencies may also be very much interested in the personal well-being of the unmarried. How does the church minister to these single adults? Consider this advertisement:

Single—Divorced—Widowed
Over 21, Under 65

Need friends and fellowship with other single adults? Let us help you spend time with other single adults looking for same. No fee. Personal counseling available through our staff or cooperating social agencies. Write or call Single Adults, Cooperating Churches, Main Street, ED 2-4034.

Such a program requires "cooperating churches" and cooperation with professional therapists and social agencies. One church group has sponsored its own recreation and conferences for single adults. At a camp-conference they gathered about 175 people. The therapist who was invited to discuss personal and spiritual problems noted that singleness had produced a kind of "psychological and spiritual tunnel vision." Their concerns and questions on spiritual problems indicated that life had become restricted to a very narrow slice of reality. Some were already receiving professional help.

The single adult who is cut off from church and community often finds housing where other single adults congregate. Thus we have not only subcultures but subcommunities. A recent newspaper article indicated that the tourists visiting a certain "hippie" area were creating so many traffic jams that the hippie way of life was being interrupted. One attitude is to express alarm, regret or censure toward these people, while another is to offer a Saviour with understanding, warmth and reconciliation. In the same area where tourists were causing traffic jams, others were working behind the scenes. This "Mission by Penetration" sought to tackle housing problems, to set up centers for dialogue, to cooperate with social agencies in getting those needing help to the proper resources, to work with sex deviates.[6] In other areas they provided groups for vocational students studying in business centers. One married couple took residence in an apartment complex of eighty units, where they found a large population of single young adults. Through a program called LID (Laymen in Dialogue) these young adults began to hear the church's message again and respond to the gospel in new ways.

In another section of the United States a church was reaching out to single adults through coffee hours, music and recreation, personal and group-therapy sessions, and a Bible-discussion group.[7] One single man, forty-three years of age, said: "My room has four walls and a sink. I've got a good job, and I hate to leave it at the end of the day to go home. Know what I do when I get there? I sit and pray. I pray that the telephone will ring and someone will ask me to go someplace. Any place. I get five weeks vacation every year. Know what I do with that? I get on a bus. For five solid weeks I ride the bus. . . . You see, I hate to stay home."[8] Because a church and a Christian therapist cared, this man and other single adults in his area are experiencing redemption from loneliness and meaninglessness. They are learning what Christ can mean to their life situation.

The leader of this project said, "It takes a long time to win a few lonely, single adults to Christ—a lot longer than it takes to gather in a couple who are bent on bringing up their children in the way of the church. But we've found it can be done."

Aloneness, loneliness and sexuality form a triad of considerable difficulty for the single adult. The prevalence of sex relations outside of marriage was exposed to the general public through the Kinsey Report. In his 1948 report Kinsey stated that of the single men thirty-five years of age whom he studied, 87 percent had heterosexual intercourse.[9] And in his 1953 report, Kinsey stated that 48 percent of the single women of the same age whom he studied had experienced heterosexual intercourse.[10] Some researchers have been unwilling to accept Kinsey's research procedures and his data. However, when the impact of the "new morality" since the Kinsey studies is taken into consideration, it is evident that the moral climate today among many single adults is perhaps as promiscuous or more so.

The church has often discussed sex behavior only from a moralistic standpoint. However, one may be morally upright sexually, and still miss the meaning of true discipleship to Christ. A single adult must see his singleness as his way of fulfilling himself before Christ. Only then can he find grace for dealing with matters of sex. This is true for the divorced and the widowed as well as the unmarried. "Eunuchs for the kingdom of heaven's sake" (Mt 19:12) includes not only those persons who have remained unmarried in order to perform specific service for Christ. It may also refer to those who have remained unmarried for other reasons and are committed to leading lives fully dedicated to Christ. It is within this attitude of wholehearted commitment to Christ that the Christian finds God's grace to be all-sufficient (2 Co 12:9) and finds "escape" and "endurance" through God's faithfulness (1 Co 10:13).

If it is true that sex drives are easier to sublimate than other basic drives, then why is there so much irregularity in sexual behavior?[11] The answer is that in adult behavior sexual intercourse is seldom just a biological response. Sex becomes tied up with success, with competency, with completeness. Sex becomes a means of removing personal doubts, proving oneself, showing that "I'm just as capable of fulfilling the marriage role as others if I choose to follow it." Reaction against moral demands in other areas of life may be expressed through reactionary sexual behavior. But the single person who is successful in adult tasks, who has a feeling of competency in meeting life, and who has accepted his singleness before Christ, will not need to be "proving himself" from time to time.

Irregular sexual behavior is more likely to be a problem when one is having personal or social difficulties. But when these basic human needs are being met, one is less likely to become involved in irregular sexual behavior. This is where the church's role is so important. Accepting one's unmarried state before Christ and finding personal and social acceptance among friends who also accept one's singleness goes a long way toward resolving problems of sexual behavior.

The Christian answer to sexual problems among single adults is not to be found in denying or repressing sexual drives or desires. As Hugen has pointed out, "The gift of God is the control, not the annihilation of the drive."[12] But he hastens to point out that "the gift of God is not given to a man full-blown. It must be developed and grow."[13] Thus, while the church speaks of "grace," it must be concerned with helping single adults follow practical steps toward maturity of self-control. Space does not permit a fuller treatment of inordinate sexual behavior patterns, such as heterosexual intercourse, masturbation, and homosexual relationships. The writer strongly recommends Hugen's treatment of this subject, from which the following summary is taken:

> The choice of the way of self-control is the acceptance of the full responsibility of one's life. This choice must be a conscious, well-considered, freely accepted decision. No other person can accept their responsibility for them, they must accept it themselves. This kind of choice is necessary not only for the voluntarily single but also for the involuntary single, for whom the first alternative, marriage, is not a real possibility. This choice is not an acceptance in the sense of being resigned to my fate or being satisfied with my lot but an active embracing of one's obligation in his particular situation or state. It is not the fate, the lot, the unsatisfied desire that is accepted, but the obligation to serve God in this state. Therefore, there is no irrevocable decision to live a life of sexual self-denial, should the opportunity for marriage later arise. The decision is not to be celibate per se, but in the state of singleness to serve God through celibacy. . . . Both the voluntary single and the involuntary single person must become the voluntary, kingdom-purposed eunuch of whom Jesus spoke in Matthew 19. This is the message of the church to the older unmarried in answer to his sex problem.[14]

DIVORCED

"Divorced"—what a shameful word! You don't think so? Then talk to the divorcé who is getting the cold shoulder from his married friends. Talk to the divorcé who can't get back into that "old gang of mine." Talk to the divorced mother who is trying to keep children fed, clothed, in school, and off the streets. Talk to the divorced man who spends sleepless nights wishing he could play the father role more often. Talk to the divorced man who stamps, with a curse, the envelope carrying his alimony check. Talk to the divorcee who was dropped from the church roll shortly after she was divorced. These people know that while the church and society have become more tolerant of divorce as a legal process, the way of a divorcee is still very hard.

Many people know that the divorce rate in the United States is about one in four marriages. But few are aware that the rate of divorce is about twice as high among farm laborers and farm foremen as it is among professional and technical people. Eight percent of all actors but only one-third of 1 percent of all ministers are divorced. If one lives in the West, his divorce probability is about four times greater than for one who lives in the Northeast. If one is in the lower socioeconomic classes, his chances of divorce are greater than those in the middle and upper-middle classes.[15]

Popular current literature gives the impression that divorce is primarily a problem of younger couples. According to Hunt, the picture is quite different.[16] It is true that divorce rates for teenage males and females are three to four times, respectively, higher than the general population, but this indicates a peak, not a total pattern. Over half the divorcing men and women are between thirty and thirty-five. The general length of a marriage before divorce is a little more than seven years. A second peak of marital breakup comes about the fifteenth year of marriage. In recent years, about 60 percent of the divorces affected about one-half million children.

Recent interpretations of statistics uphold the saying that "the family that prays together stays together." Religiously oriented families experience much less divorce. But this does not necessarily mean they are happier! It does indicate, however, that strong religious practices and beliefs hold down the divorce rate. Hunt characterizes the "world of the formerly married" as "more lower-than middle-class . . . more parental than non-parental, more nearly middle-aged than young; a world not of frivolous, hedonistic, footloose youth, but of earnest, conscientious, somewhat harrassed but hopeful adult Americans."[17]

The problems of the divorced are as numerous as the causes of divorce. Some marriages are broken because of internal factors within the marriage while others are affected by factors external to the marriage. Some are broken because of psychological problems of one or both members, while others admit that they just weren't sufficiently mature for marriage. The fact that almost any remarriage is a greater risk than an original marriage does not seem to deter many divorced people from making the second try. Of those divorced who remarry, only two-thirds find permanence in the second marriage.

Of the many problems the church faces in ministering to the divorced, perhaps none is more important than the attitude it communicates about divorce. In some instances the church has communicated the attitude of judgment rather than forgiveness. In seeking to keep its ideals and standards of marriage and family life high, the church may have failed to be God's agent of redemption in ministering to people in their human situations. The tensions of this problem are not easy to resolve, for the church must be committed to both aspects of it. However, if the church is to minister to the divorced, it seems necessary to assume that where sin abounds, grace must much more abound (Ro 5:20). Since a large percentage of divorced people remarry, the problem of interpreting remarriage is one of the church's biggest responsibilities and most glorious opportunities.

As Emerson has pointed out, churches have often stated divorce and remarriage policies in reaction to certain social phenomena—war, bigamy (Mormonism), depression—but mostly in relation to the effects of war times and their aftermaths.[18] Attitudes and policies regarding divorce and remarriage vary from denomination to denomination and within denominations. Such confusion makes it difficult for the divorced to turn to the church for help in one of their most pressing crises. Added to these variations is the attitude the divorced person takes, rightly or wrongly, toward himself as his interpretation of the church's position—that since he has broken a vow involving a lifetime commitment, he must be under the shame and penalty of this vow for life. The unmarried person often considers himself a failure because he did not assume the social roles expected by society, and the divorced person often considers himself a failure because he could not fulfill the social roles to which he committed himself. In this respect, the unmarried and the divorced both suffer from the stigma of failure, though for different reasons. Unless there is enough grace flowing from Christ, through His church, so that the divorced person can sense the potential of reconciliation and fellowship within the church, he will probably turn to other agencies for help with problems stemming from his divorced status.

The problems related to divorce are often complex, requiring resources and professional skills beyond the resources of a particular church. For this reason some churches have found their most useful role to be a supportive one—supporting a family in its spiritual growth while cooperating with social agencies that deal with financial and social matters. A good procedure is to secure from the city, county or state welfare agency a booklet listing the various private and public agencies dealing with divorce and family problems. A pastor who makes himself available for spiritual counseling will probably have numerous referrals from such agencies. He will also find that families whom he refers to such agencies will receive many benefits from being recommended and supported by the church.

One of the problems resulting from divorce to which the church has justifiably given much attention is that of affected children. However, the church has dealt with this problem more successfully in institutions for children than in homes where children are left with a single parent. These problems are dramatically set forth in Jim and Janet Egleson's *Parents Without Partners*.[19] After reading this book, one can hardly shut off the ideas that come forth on how the church can minister to the single parent and children. The "Parents Without Partners" program and organization is reaching thousands of single adults who are trying to keep a family together after divorce has posed more problems than ever dreamed. A church unable to have such a program on its own may give much support to mothers and children in a helping role by cooperating with such an organization.

One church has developed "sponsors" for children living with one parent. This is particularly helpful in providing male models for children without fathers, which is the usual case. This church decided that the "Big Brother" program could work in the church as well as outside it. Other churches have assisted single parents with custody of children by providing day-care centers, preschool programs, or Christian centers with emphases on education, recreation and spiritual growth. Such programs have made it possible for mothers with young children to work without worry over their child's adequate care. Some financial support to the struggling single parent from the "fellowship offering" or "deacons' fund" may be the encouragement the parent needs to keep the family in the church, growing spiritually and developing resources for other problems they may handle on their own.

One statistical survey pointed out that about one out of every fifteen divorced men who remarried a divorced woman remarried his former spouse.[20] This remarriage of the former spouse probably goes on without much attention from churches. If so, one is encouraged to believe that this percentage may be increased significantly through active interest by churches. This is an area where church involvement through acceptance, reconciliation and spiritual guidance may pay rich dividends. Divorcés who remarry tend to marry divorcees. For personal, social, financial and many other reasons, remarriage does and will continue to take place with or without church guidance or approval. This fact poses a problem to which the church must give very serious reconsideration.

A number of ministers and congregations have approved remarriage under limited circumstances for the "innocent party." Such remarriages are often preceded by thoughtful and considerate counseling. But to base remarriage on the "innocent party" approach is to consider the matter from a legal view rather than the spiritual union which so much concerns the church. While the church has recognized society's stakes in marriage and shown respect for the civil contract, it has viewed marriage as going beyond just a legal and social contract. It is a vow taken before God involving both parties in a spiritual union that transcends the legal and social aspects. It becomes much more difficult to define an "innocent party" from this perspective.

Emerson asserts that the remarriage of divorced persons should not be approached unilaterally.[21] For a minister or church to agree to remarriage for an "innocent party" does not mean that the "innocent party" is necessarily ready for remarriage. An "innocent party" legally qualified to remarry may still possess bitterness and an unforgiving spirit. For this and other reasons, Emerson makes a strong case for "realized forgiveness" as the basic condition for remarriage, and not just for the "innocent party."[22]

WIDOWED

From statistics cited earlier in this chapter, one might assume that the divorced represent the largest numerical group of single adults, but such is not the case. Widows outnumber the divorced females four to one, and widowers outnumber divorced males two to one. Most of these are older than the divorced and about four-fifths of them are women.[23] The average American wife outlives her husband by about seven years. Thus the widowed group is basically female and is largest in number after fifty-five years of age. During and after war our society has had numbers of young widows, but the problem is basically one of older-aged people.

In relation to the divorced, Hunt has characterized the widowed as follows:

> Although both face many of the same problems of loneliness, disruption of habits, and practical difficulties in running their home, psychological make-up of the widowed and their feeling about what has happened to them are profoundly different from those of the formerly married, and each finds in the other much that is suspect, unsympathetic, or even antagonistic.[24]

The unmarried fails to assume the social roles society expects of him; the divorced fails to fulfill the social roles he assumed; but the widowed has his social roles broken by circumstances beyond his control. Thus the widow has been a special concern of the church through all ages, and specific biblical teachings of the care of the widowed have offered suggestions and stated responsibilities toward them. The plight of the widow is often used in Scripture to emphasize trust in and dedication to God, and to prick the conscience of the socially irresponsible. (See Mk 12:42; Lk 4:26; 18:3-5; 1 Ti 5:3-16; Ja 1:27.)

The problems of the widowed are too numerous to detail, but consider the case of one widow:

> When my husband died, the knowledge that I would have to go on alone came as a real blow. How could I manage? I worked frantically from morning to night. Everything had to be the same or better. I had to meet our expenses, run our home, be two parents to my daughter, even take care of the car successfully. It took a long time before I could slow down and be myself, instead of trying to equal or outdo him.[25]

Widows experience many problems similar to the divorced mother. But the divorced person who tries to forget an unhappy marriage with a person who is still living and possibly seeing the children occasionally is quite different from the widowed person who has to face the facts of death and final separation in this life from his or her partner. The children of a divorcee who can see their father on some occasion may have many problems, but the children of a widow have their father removed completely, and often very suddenly. They are faced with the problem of trying to recall and cherish happy memories while planning for a future that does not include the person around whom those memories center.

The above mentioned suggestion that the church play a supportive role in working with social agencies helping divorced people is applicable for efforts in helping the widowed. Widows do have some advantage of aid to their children, but despite this, finance continues to be one of the biggest problems. If the father is left with children, the problems take on a different color, but the background is still financial.

From a theological viewpoint, the church can play a vital role in providing the sympathy, understanding and love needed during bereavement. Beyond that, it may help the family interpret the death of father or mother within the light of the gospel and seek to strengthen their hope in God's goodness despite loss and sadness. More difficult yet is the problem of helping children understand why a parent is missing—the meaning of death from a child's perspective—and to fill the emptiness of that parental role. Recently numerous books have been published to assist pastors, churches and parents in interpreting death to children. They are valuable for a church library.*

In recent years the elderly widowed have become a special concern of the church. Metropolitan living has introduced many problems unknown to our rural setting where the widowed were taken in by children of relatives. Special housing in terms of apartments, group living in centers especially designed for retired or widowed, along with social and recreational clubs and projects, have been developed. While there is still debate on the advisability of separating the elderly single adult from the common stream of social life, these steps have at least explored new kinds of ministry which the church may provide.

Unlike the divorced person who is usually dropped by his married friends, the widowed often finds considerable care expressed by his friends and age-mates. Such friendship and concern is of inestimable value in adjustment. Church groups provide stability and offer guidance through periods of loneliness and financial difficulty. Some recent efforts to rearrange Sunday school classes for adults on interest bases rather than age-grouping have met resistance because older adults depend on friend-

*Much practical advice in helping the widowed and their children is offered in *Parents Without Partners*.

ship groups within the church for considerably more than spiritual instruction. To take them out of groups in which they are accepted, secure and finding strength may pose serious psychological problems for some older widowed adults.

Remarriage for the widowed does not pose the problems presented by the divorced. Studies show that widowed adults who remarry usually marry a widowed person. Perhaps this is because there is greater understanding between them. For younger widowed adults there may be more willingness to combine their children into a new family rather than accept a divorced person whose children belong to someone else.

Moreno, in his treatment of death from a social standpoint, indicates "that death is always among us like birth,"[26] and that death is a social problem before it becomes a physical problem. In older adulthood, death is feared because of the disequilibrium it creates in social relationships. It becomes more and more difficult with age to replace the lost member. This is not true for the young widowed adult but is painfully true for the older widowed adult. While the church cannot take the place of the lost mate, people within it can assume other social roles that make it possible for the widowed to establish new social relationships. This is a big step in helping a person maintain his desire for life, to develop new goals, and to find fruitful use of his time. Some churches have found widowed people ready to take on more active roles in Christian service, such as visitation, administrative responsibilities, carpentry, etc.

When one is beyond the age where the lost mate is replaceable by marriage, one's faith in Christ becomes more essential in facing life. While all efforts should be made to help the widowed become constructively active in Christian discipleship, it is also important to help them understand the Christian hope. To abide in the assurance of the future resurrection and of complete fellowship in Christ's glorious reign is to live life toward its fullest consummation instead of being beset by the vicissitudes of life.

NOTES

1. US Bureau of the Census, *Statistical Abstract of the United States: 1967*, 88th ed. (Washington, D.C.: US Dept. of Commerce, 1967), p. 33.
2. Ibid.
3. M. D. Hugen, *The Church's Ministry to the Older Unmarried* (Grand Rapids: Eerdmans, 1958).
4. Ibid., p. 35.
5. Ibid., p. 52.
6. *Directions for a Young Adult Ministry* (Nashville: Div. of the Local Church, General Board of Educ. of the United Methodist Church, 1966).
7. *Crusader*, 22 (May, 1967):5.
8. Ibid.
9. Alfred C. Kinsey, et al., *Sexual Behavior in the Human Male* (Philadelphia: Saunders, 1948), p. 550.

10. Kinsey, et al., *Sexual Behavior in the Human Female* (Philadelphia: Saunders, 1953), p. 333.
11. Norman L. Mum, *Psychology* (Cambridge: Riverside, 1961), p. 281.
12. Hugen, p. 83.
13. Ibid.
14. Ibid., p. 82.
15. Morton M. Hunt, *The World of the Formerly Married* (New York: McGraw-Hill, 1966), pp. 15-22.
16. Ibid.
17. Ibid., p. 22.
18. James G. Emerson, Jr., *Divorce, The Church, and Remarriage* (Philadelphia: Westminster, 1961), pp. 109-47.
19. Jim Egleson and Janet Frank Egleson, *Parents Without Partners* (New York: Dutton, 1960).
20. Hunt, p. 211.
21. Emerson, p. 164.
22. Ibid., pp. 33-83.
23. *Statistical Abstract of the United States, 1967*, p. 33.
24. Hunt, p. 21.
25. Egleson, p. 120.
26. J. L. Moreno, ed., *The Sociometry Reader* (Glencoe, Ill.: Free Press, 1960), p. 64.

FOR FURTHER READING

Bernard, Jessie. *Remarriage: A Study of Marriage.* New York: Dryden, 1956.

Bontrager, Frances M. *The Church and the Single Person.* Scottdale, Pa.: Herald, 1969.

Champagne, Marian. *Facing Life Alone.* Indianapolis: Bobbs-Merrill, 1964.

"Church and the Single Person." *Christianity Today,* 13 (June 20, 1969): 22-23.

Davis, Kingsley. "Children of Divorced Parents: Sociological and Statistical Analysis," *Law and Contemporary Problems,* 10 (Summer, 1944).

Egleson, Jim and Egleson, Janet F. *Parents Without Partners.* New York: Dutton, 1960.

Emerson, James G., Jr. *Divorce, the Church, and Remarriage.* Philadelphia: Westminster, 1961.

Gleason, George. *Single Young Adults in the Church.* New York: Association, 1952.

Goode, William. *After Divorce.* Glencoe, Ill.: Free Press, 1956.

Hoglund, Gunnar. "Give Young Singles the Attention They Deserve," *The Standard,* 58 (Oct. 21, 1968): 25-26.

Hugen, M. D. *The Church's Ministry to the Older Unmarried.* Grand Rapids: Eerdmans, 1958.

Jacobson, Paul H. *American Marriage and Divorce.* New York: Rinehard, 1959.

Johnson, Mildred. *The Smiles, the Tears.* Westwood, N.J.: Revell, 1969.

Jones, Eve. *Raising Your Child in a Fatherless Home.* New York: Macmillan, 1963.

Langer, Marion. *Learning to Live as a Widow.* New York: Gilbert, 1957.

Lentz, Richard E. "Are Churches Neglecting Single Adults?" *International Journal of Religious Education,* 39 (Dec., 1961): 12-13.

Mehl, Duane. "The Absurdity of Being a Single Young Adult in the Church," *Interaction,* 9 (May, 1968): 19-22.

Narramore, Clyde M. *The Unmarried Woman.* Grand Rapids: Zondervan, 1961.

Popenoe, Paul. "Remarriages of Divorcees to Each Other," *American Sociological Review,* 3 (Oct., 1938).

Quiring, J. H. "Dealing Redemptively with the Divorced and Remarried" (a paper presented to the Conference on Issues Concerning Church and Home, Reedley, Calif., Nov. 23-24, 1967, Winnipeg, Manitoba: Christian Press, 1968).

Read, Nat B., Jr. "Why Are Unmarrieds Unwanted by the Church?" *Dimensions,* 19 (May, 1969): 23-25.

Start, Clarissa. *When You're a Widow.* St. Louis: Concordia, 1969.

"The Pleasures and Pain of the Single Life." *Time,* 92 (Sept. 15, 1967): 26-27.

Towns, Elmer L. "Are Single Adults Moral Dropouts?" *Christian Life,* 29 (Nov., 1967): 80-84.

———. "The Church and the Single Adult," *Eternity,* 19 (Oct., 1968): 18-19.

———. *The Single Adult and the Church.* Glendale, Calif.: Gospel Light, 1967.

Wolf, Anna W. M. and Stein, Lucille. *The One-Parent Family.* New York: Public Affairs Committee, 1959.

7

REACHING AND WINNING ADULTS

Donald S. Aultman

The need to evangelize adults for Christ is urgent, and the opportunity is equally challenging. According to the United States Bureau of Census, more than 50 percent of the population of the United States is now twenty-five years of age or older. Also the United States population grew younger *and* older between 1957 and 1967. The number of youths nineteen years of age and under increased by 17.1 percent (from 22.2 percent as of July 1, 1957, to 39.3 percent as of July 1, 1967). And the adults over sixty-five years old increased by 0.8 percent (from 8.7 percent as of July 1, 1957, to 9.5 percent as of July 1, 1967).[1] In the United States the average life span has increased to more than seventy years so that adulthood now occupies more than fifty years in the life of the average American. And according to some medical and social scientists, the possibility of the average life span extending to one hundred years is not too remote in Western culture.

In the first half of the twentieth century, Evangelicals placed great emphasis on reaching children for Christ. Perhaps the last half of this century will become the day for evangelism of adults. It will be an encouraging sign if a massive effort could be launched toward the reaching and winning of adults without lessening our interest in the reaching and winning of children and young people.

The need to contact and evangelize adults can be summed up in these statements: (1) They are the parents of our coming generation. (2) They are the leaders of our communities. (3) They are the leaders of our churches. (4) They provide the greatest source of finances for church programs. (5) They can provide models for young people to follow. (6) They are the spiritual backbone of the church. (7) They provide the most

DONALD S. AULTMAN, Ed.D., is Vice-president, Lee College, Cleveland, Tennessee.

basic potential for lasting church growth and rapid expansion. (8) They are souls—genuine people—who must be won to Christ.*

REACHING ADULTS

Towns quotes a pastor on the West Coast as follows:

> The church is a spiritual ghetto. . . . Christians are stagnant, and need to get out of the stained glass sanctuaries into the manufacturing plants, suburbia, and inner city where people are. The church has lost its power because it has lost its contact with people.[2]

Many Christian leaders agree that churches need to be reaching out for the lost—where they are. It is not enough to expect the unsaved to attend a church service in order to be saved. Many adults simply will not come to the church; therefore the church must go to them. And is this not the biblical pattern? (See Mk 16:15; Lk 14:23; Jn 17:18; Ro 10:14-15.)

Elton Trueblood underscores this problem:

> The stranger who is visited by a representative of the Church frequently gets the impression that he is being viewed as a prospective customer, a potential addition to the numbers or the income, rather than a person who is approached for his own sake. Part of the shame of the contemporary Church is that it seems to be motivated by self-interest. We need to be reminded that the Church exists for men and not men for the Church.[3]

How, then, can a church reach more adults? What are some effective ways by which the church—and individual Christians—can contact adults and seek to lead them to Jesus Christ? Methods used in reaching adults for the Lord may vary with the size of the congregation, the church's social and economic climate, and the church location (rural, urban, suburban). The following methods represent some of the means being used by various churches in adult outreach and evangelism.

REACHING ADULTS THROUGH THE SUNDAY SCHOOL

The observations of European historian Paulus Scharpff bear out the contentions of American Christian educators regarding the value of adult involvement in Christian education. Reviewing evangelism in the United States, Scharpff writes:

> Another factor in the church's outreach has been the church school or Sunday school. In the United States this organization, which teaches the Bible, has had departments and classes for all age-groups, including adults.
>
> Through this means a large group of lay workers is enlisted. They are

*For more on the challenge of reaching and teaching adults, see chap. 1, "The Challenge of Adult Christian Education."

given some training and the responsibility for a class. They not only teach the Bible to the group but also lead members in enlisting others. When people come they get not only the teaching but also the small-group fellowship. Churches which have continued to reach out to lost people have found the Sunday school helpful.[4]

Commenting on the place of the American Sunday school in evangelism, Scharpff makes this observation:

> It would be difficult to find any organization in America with a greater evangelistic impact than the Sunday school, for here, unlike many other countries, the Sunday school is organized to include everyone, from the youngest to the oldest.[5]

Thus an objective observer concludes that the inclusion of adults in Sunday school has not only been a strength of Bible teaching and outreach, but also a major force in American evangelism.

REACHING ADULTS THROUGH VISITATION

A regular program of visitation is the basis for solid outreach to adults. Such a program must be two-pronged: finding and visiting prospects, and identifying and visiting absentees. In the reaching of both the prospect and the absentee there are two vital steps—locating the person and contacting him.

Finding the prospect is the key to reaching new people for Christ and the church. The following list suggests ways that new adults may be located:

1. Survey your Sunday school enrollment list for relatives of those who do not attend.*
2. Secure the names and addresses of new residents from the community Welcome Wagon or from a public utility company.
3. Have visitation workers ask the persons being visited to suggest the name and address of someone who needs to be in church. This plan has been used in the commercial world with tremendous success. After all, the people who are not in church know those who do not go to church.
4. At each church service encourage visitors to sign a guest register or a visitor's card.
5. Ask church members to hand in names and addresses of families to be visited.

*A study of 200 churches in one denomination revealed a relatively high percentage of conversions among parents who were not enrolled in Sunday school but whose children were enrolled. See R. Othal Feather, "Personal Work in the Educational Program of the Church" (unpublished doctor's dissertation; Fort Worth, Tex.: Southwestern Baptist Theological Seminary, 1956), and R. Othal Feather, *A Manual for Promoting Personal Evangelism through the Sunday School* (Nashville: Convention, 1959).

6. Display highway signs and outdoor bulletin boards.
7. Submit church news stories to local newspapers.
8. Advertise in newspapers. Offer to send a free copy of your denominational magazine or other material to those who write in.
9. Use spot announcements on the radio.
10. Conduct "emergency visitation." Watch the newspapers for announcements of deaths, accidents, etc., in your community, and go offer the services of your church.
11. Conduct a street meeting.
12. Conduct services in institutions such as convalescent homes, jails, missions.
13. Encourage children to invite adults they know.
14. Suggest that church members enclose church bulletins or flyers when they write letters to friends and relatives. Also suggest they invite the persons to whom they are writing to visit your church when in your city.
15. Ask children, youth and adults in your church to watch for moving vans in their neighborhoods and give the addresses of new families to the church office or visitation committee chairman.
16. Maintain an active Cradle Roll visitation program.
17. Conduct an active Home Department. Ask Home Department members to give you names and addresses of people who need to be reached for Christ.
18. Conduct a community religious census by means of the telephone.
19. Offer to conduct brief devotional services in industrial plants in your community.[6]

A special churchwide "Operation Friendship" visitation ministry has been conducted for several years by an Illinois church. It includes visiting prospects (such as church visitors or other persons new in the community), hospitalized church members, adult Sunday school absentees, etc.[7]

Churches should be careful not to overlook the need for seeking to contact adults in new building complexes, such as high-rise apartments and mobile trailer parks.

Identifying absentees is a relatively simple process, requiring a workable record system and faithful recording secretaries. In some churches visitation workers meet weekly for a meal or refreshments, receive assignments, go out from the church to make contacts, and return to report their successes. A less structured approach leaves the visitation to each department and, in some instances, to each teacher. The key to either approach is to find faithful workers and set up some system of reporting assignments that will locate visitation breakdowns. Whatever the plan, these efforts pay off in long-term benefits when consistently followed over the years.

REACHING ADULTS THROUGH VACATION BIBLE SCHOOL

One of the excellent values of vacation Bible school is its ability to provide contact with unchurched parents through the VBS children. One summer a large Midwestern church added several dozen *new* unchurched families to its prospect list through children in the community who attended vacation Bible school. As a result several adults came to know the Lord and also joined the church.

A church in Racine, Wisconsin, conducted several neighborhood backyard vacation Bible schools all across the city. On the closing Friday *morning*, a total of more than two hundred mothers *and* fathers—most of them non-Christians—attended the demonstration programs held in the backyards where their children had attended.

In Nebraska an evening family VBS has attracted entire families, including nonchristian parents. A vacation Bible school "mothers' club" held at the same time as the children's VBS program has given women in an Illinois church on unusual opportunity to invite friends in their neighborhoods to Bible study and other sessions of interest to today's women.[8]

REACHING ADULTS THROUGH HOME BIBLE CLASSES

In recent years many churches have found that home Bible classes are providing fantastic opportunities for reaching and winning adults to Christ. Many adults will consider attending a Bible study group in a home long before they will agree to attend a church. Consequently, pastors are keenly enthusiastic about the evangelistic outreach potential of home Bible classes. According to an unpublished research project, 33.0 percent of 1,405 pastors stated that their churches sponsored home Bible classes or that individuals in their churches conduct such classes. An additional 46.3 percent reported that they would *like* to have such classes. Of the pastors whose churches have had or now have home Bible classes, it is significant that 86.3 percent feel that they are highly effective.[9]

In one church, for example, "it was found that over a six-month period 30 adults had made profession of Christ. Of these, the pastor was directly responsible for four. The rest resulted from the witness and work of others in the church—largely through home Bible classes."[10]

Wollen suggests three kinds of home Bible classes: (1) for regular church attenders (for the training of leaders for the other two kinds of home classes), (2) for the unlearned and new converts, and (3) for the unsaved.[11] Whereas the concern of this chapter is evangelism, another chapter discusses the role of home Bible classes for instruction of Christians.*

A home Bible class can be started by encouraging an interested Christian couple to invite neighbors in for a weekly evening of Bible study. There may also be daytime studies for women or for retired persons. In a home Bible class program the director or other person responsible enlists host couples and secures teachers/leaders and lesson materials, under the guidance of the church. (The host or hostess need not be the teacher/leader also.)†

As its name implies, a home Bible class should study primarily the *Bible*. But study materials can be helpful, as long as they help in the study of the Bible rather than replace it.[12] For classes of unsaved adults, it may be well to study Bible books such as John, Mark or Romans.[13]

REACHING ADULTS THROUGH SPECIAL DAYS

Many non-Christians who do not attend church regularly *will* attend a special day program. These may include a Christmas program, an Easter service, a New Year's Eve program, a service on Mother's Day, etc. A Midwestern church discovered that unsaved parents of Sunday school children attended on Sunday nights when their children were taking part in a special ten-minute departmental program in the evening church service.

REACHING ADULTS THROUGH OTHER EDUCATIONAL ACTIVITIES

Camping programs that include unchurched and disadvantaged children can give a church an open door to their unchurched parents. The concern of a Sunday school teacher for the child of unsaved parents goes a long way in influencing that mother and father for Christ. Departmental parent-teacher meetings and mothers' teas have been used by many churches to demonstrate their interest in parents and their children. Father-son or mother-daughter banquets or recreation nights, sponsored by the church's weekday club leaders, are a sure way of getting non-christian parents to hear the gospel. Men's fellowship activities are excellent means of outreach to unsaved men.‡ Though geared mainly to young people, a coffee-house ministry sponsored by a church can also win adults to Christ.[14]

WINNING ADULTS

Sharing Christ with adults and winning them to Him should be a concern of every educational activity in the church—and of every Christian.

*See chap. 11, "Adult Education Beyond the Sunday School."
† Qualifications for home Bible class leaders are discussed in Wollen, pp. 16-20.
‡ See chap. 12, "Men's and Women's Organizations in the Church."

While it is true that conversion is one experience occurring at a given time, evangelism is the use of every Biblical means to bring one to conversion and discipleship. . . . While the moment of the new birth is the critical point of evangelistic purposes, it is preceded and should be followed by other important events which, as a whole, constitute the totality of evangelism. It is in this setting that the ministry of Christian teaching can be seen as a dynamic factor, in some cases the most dynamic factor in evangelism.[15]

The dynamic of person-to-person relations is important in winning adults to Christ. In this day of social change, people are saying, "Don't talk to me of an impersonal Christianity or shout from your lofty perch that you love my soul. If you love an invisible part of me, you must accept what you see of me; you may not approve of me but you must accept me." In other words, we should seek to win a person to Christ because he is of intrinsic worth, not because we need more stars in our crown or wish to soothe a conscience troubled by the minister's reminders that the vast majority of all Christians—perhaps 95 percent—have never led a soul to Christ. Manipulation of people for one's own purposes is not the objective of evangelism.

The most important aspect in winning adults to Christ is the work of the Holy Spirit in relation to the Word of God.[16] No church or individual believer can succeed spiritually when depending exclusively on his own resources. Every church that places a higher premium on its *own* efforts than it places on the work of the Holy Spirit will become a spiritually lifeless church.

Who has not looked with amazement at the sad spectre of a hyperactive church that seemed to be vitally alive until people began to drop out from exhaustion or sheer boredom? The reason is that activity is not the sign of spiritual vitality. The enlightened body of Christ will bear active groups, but the sure sign of spiritual vitality in a church are: (1) the birth of new sons and daughters into the Kingdom of God; (2) growth in the Christian graces, and (3) increasing evidence of the fruit of the Spirit in the lives of believers. Activity based on any other motive, no matter how dynamic, is a prelude to ultimate spiritual death.[17]

Lois LeBar calls attention to the danger of self-centeredness which dishonors the Holy Spirit and hinders effective evangelism.

The greatest competitor of devotion to Jesus is service for Him. How often we start a project in our love for Him, with the purest of motives. But as the process becomes complicated and personalities grate upon each other, persons tend unconsciously to protect their egos and defend their own rights, with the result that Christ is pushed off center by the pressure of the work itself. When the Spirit of God is grieved because Christ deserves preeminence in all things, the work drags and people grow discouraged.

If Christ is truly real to us, everything else is less real. If we abide in Him as the branch abides in the vine, fruit is the natural consequence. In order to bear more fruit upward, our roots have to go deeper down in the Lord. More than servants to work for Him, the Lord seeks sons to fellowship with Him. Concentration on the work produces barrenness. Our chief work is to reflect Christ. The Spirit jealously guards the centrality of Christ unless His ministry is quenched.[18]

TRAINING ADULTS TO WIN ADULTS

Not every Christian automatically feels competent or qualified to witness to others about their need of salvation. As Orlando Harms wrote,

> Most Christians find themselves petrified when they see the opportunity to [witness for Christ]. One reason is that most of us have withdrawn from God's world into our own little church world where we never have real contact, fellowship, or closeness with any one other than with our own. And when the opportunity comes to share our faith, we don't know how to move and we blanch and become speechless. In so doing, we deprive many of their opportunity to hear the Gospel, and we stifle ourselves spiritually.[19]

However, this is not to say that adults do not *want* to witness for Christ. As one writer put it, "Many laymen are ready to act if only they knew precisely how [to] share the Gospel."[20]

Therefore Christian adults need help in how to evangelize; they need training in the techniques of evangelism. Several denominational and independent publishing houses publish study materials for lay courses on evangelism.[21] Correspondence courses are also available from several sources.[22] Another concept—evangelism through films—is explained in a filmstrip by the Moody Institute of Science.*

Training courses on evangelism—whether conducted for Christian adults in a single church or on a communitywide basis—have helped many adults become better equipped to share their faith in Christ with others and to be effective soul-winners.

Perhaps no evangelistic tool has proved more effective in helping reach adults for Christ than the *Four Spiritual Laws* booklet published by Campus Crusade for Christ. Many churches have conducted training classes to help adults learn how to use this tool effectively. Results have been unusual in terms of the number of Christians who have begun shar-

---

*See the filmstrip listed in the "For Further Reading" section at the end of this chapter.

ing their faith and in the number of adults who have professed Jesus Christ as personal Saviour.

However, no training course alone nor any single evangelistic "tool" can substitute for the individual believer's dedication to Christ and love for souls. Orlando Harms has stated this well:

> . . . sharing our faith does not require eloquence or special ability which most of us may not have; it simply means that no matter who we are, or where we are, if Jesus Christ has done something for us which He can do for others—it is up to us to tell it like it is. Someone has said, "Witnessing is simply taking a good look at the Lord, and then going out and telling people what you saw." God does not want us to work for Him—He wants to do His work in and through us. As D. T. Niles puts it, witnessing is "One beggar telling another beggar where to find bread."[23]

Surely as more Christian adults are trained and mobilized as effective witnesses for Christ, churches today can begin to reach and win more adults to the Saviour.

NOTES

1. Bureau of the Census, *Statistical Abstract of the United States: 1958* (Washington, D.C.: US Department of Commerce, 1958), p. 25; and Bureau of the Census, *Statistical Abstract of the United States: 1968* (Washington, D.C.: US Dept. of Commerce, 1968), p. 10.
2. Elmer Towns, "Faces of Evangelism," *Christian Life*, 30 (Nov., 1968):80.
3. Elton Trueblood, *The Incendiary Fellowship* (New York: Harper & Row, 1967), p. 28.
4. Paulus Scharpff, *History of Evangelism* (Grand Rapids: Eerdmans, 1964), p. 313.
5. Ibid., p. 187.
6. Adapted from *Reaching the Unchurched* (Kansas City: Nazarene, 1966), pp. 7-8.
7. For a detailed explanation of this program, see Lawrence O. Richards, *The Pastor and His Visitation Program.* Christian Educ. Monograph, Pastors' Series, No. 13 (Glen Ellyn, Ill.: Scripture Press, 1967).
8. Roy B. Zuck, "The Church's Summer Witness," *Christianity Today*, 13 (June 20, 1969):37.
9. "Research Report on Home Bible Classes." Unpublished report (Glen Ellyn, Ill.: Scripture Press, 1968).
10. Albert J. Wollen, *How to Conduct Home Bible Classes* (Wheaton, Ill.: Scripture Press, 1969), p. 5.
11. Ibid., pp. 11-15.
12. Study materials useful with unsaved adults have been published by several groups, including the following: Billy Graham Evangelistic Association, 1300 Harmon Place, Minneapolis, Minnesota 55403; Campus Crusade for Christ, Arrowhead Springs, San Bernardino, California 92403; Keith L. Brooks Bible Study Series, Moody Press, 820 N. LaSalle St., Chicago, Illinois 60610; and The Navigators, Box 1659, Colorado Springs, Colorado 80901.
13. For additional information on home Bible classes as a means of evangelism, see the following sources: Joe Bayly, "Who Me . . . Lead a Bible Study?" *Moody Monthly*, 64 (Feb., 1963):20-22, 60-61; Richard Bohrer, "We're Bringing Them in Through the Living Room," *Moody Monthly*, 63 (Mar., 1969):32-34, 81; "Church-related Home Bible Classes." *Link*, 17 (Apr., 1969):3-7, 14; Robert Flood, "The Growing Quest for a First-Century Church," *Moody Monthly*, 69 (Oct., 1968):16-18; Howard G. Hendricks, *The Pastor and Home Bible Classes.* Christian Educ. Monograph, Pastors' Series, No. 19. (Glen Ellyn, Ill.: Scripture Press, 1967); "How to Start a Neighborhood Bible Study" (Dobbs Ferry, N.Y.:

Neighborhood Bible Studies, Box 222, n.d); Ron Rendleman, "The First Step," *CBMC Impact* (July, 1968), pp. 3, 12; Albert J. Wollen; *How to Conduct Home Bible Classes* (Wheaton, Ill.: Scripture Press, 1969).

14. The following books give information on this unusual contemporary means of youth and adult evangelism: Lyman Coleman, *The Coffee House Itch* (Newton, Pa.: The Halfway House, n.d.); and John D. Perry, Jr., *The Coffee House Ministry* (Richmond, Va.: John Knox, 1966). For information on how to start and conduct evangelical coffee houses, write Coffee House Ministries, 313 N. Blanchard, Wheaton, Illinois 60187, or Coffee House Information Service, 300 E. 44th St., New York, New York 10017.

15. Donald S. Aultman, *The Ministry of Christian Teaching* (Cleveland, Tenn.: Pathway, 1966), p. 99.

16. For a detailed study of the work of the Holy Spirit in relation to Christian teaching, see *The Holy Spirit in Your Teaching* by Roy B. Zuck (Wheaton, Ill.: Scripture Press, 1963).

17. Donald S. Aultman, *Contemporary Christian Education* (Cleveland, Tenn.: Pathway, 1968), pp. 121-22.

18. Lois E. LeBar, *Education That Is Christian* (Westwood, N.J.: Revell, 1958), p. 239.

19. Orlando Harms, "Tell It Like It Is," *The Christian Leader*, 32 (May 20, 1969): 24.

20. Elmer A. Martens, *Church Outreach: What Is Involved* (Fresno, Calif.: United States Conference, Mennonite Brethren Churches, 1967), p. 3.

21. The following is a selected list of materials on lay evangelism training:
    Evangelism. New York: Christian Education Office, Home Department, Christian & Missionary Alliance, n.d.
    Margaret Graham, *Personal Evangelism* (Leader's guide to accompany the textbook *How To Win Souls*). 2d ed. Wheaton, Ill.: Scripture Press, 1961.
    Craig Massey, *Effective Visitation* (Leader's guide to accompany the textbook *How To Do Effective Visitation*). 2d ed. Wheaton, Ill.: Scripture Press, 1963.
    Lawrence F. Swanson, *Evangelism Through the Local Church.* Chicago: Harvest, 1968.
    Studies in Christian Living. Colorado Springs, Colo.: The Navigators, 1964. (Book 6 is "Growing in Service.")
    Ten Basic Steps Toward Christian Maturity. Arrowhead Springs, Calif.: Campus Crusade for Christ, 1964. (Book 7 is "The Christian and Witnessing.")

22. For example, Back to the Bible Broadcast, P.O. Box 233, Lincoln, Nebraska 68501; Emmaus Bible School, 156 N. Oak Park Ave., Oak Park, Illinois 60301; Moody Bible Institute Correspondence School, 820 North LaSalle St., Chicago, Illinois 60610.

23. Harms, p. 24.

FOR FURTHER READING

Aultman, Donald S. *Contemporary Christian Education.* Cleveland, Tenn.: Pathway, 1968.

———. *The Ministry of Christian Teaching.* Cleveland, Tenn.: Pathway, 1966.

Barrett, E. P. *Sunday School Evangelism.* Rev. ed. Wheaton, Ill.: Evangelical Teacher Training Assn., 1966.

Chafin, Kenneth. *Help! I'm A Layman.* Waco, Tex.: Word, 1966.

Coleman, Robert E. *The Master Plan of Evangelism.* Westwood, N.J.: Revell, 1964.

Ford, Leighton. *The Christian Persuader.* New York: Harper & Row, 1966.

Hoglund, Gunnar. "All These Ways to Evangelize," *The Standard*, 58 (Dec. 16, 1968): 25-26.

"How They Reach the Unsaved," *Moody Monthly*, 69 (Oct., 1968): 19-21, 66.

Little, Paul E. *How to Give Away Your Faith.* Chicago: Inter-Varsity, 1966.

"Lunch-hour Bible Study Challenges Oil Company Workers," *Good News Broadcaster,* 26 (Dec., 1968): 38-41.

Monro, Clayton and Tagel, William S. *Witnessing Laymen Make Living Churches.* Waco, Tex.: Word, 1968.

Raines, Robert A. *New Life in the Church.* New York: Harper, 1961.

Reaching The Unchurched. Kansas City: Nazarene, 1966.

Richards, Lawrence O. *The Superintendent and Sunday School Growth.* Christian Education Monograph, Superintendents' Series, No. 5. Glen Ellyn, Ill.: Scripture Press, 1968.

Rinker, Rosalind. *You Can Witness With Confidence.* Grand Rapids: Zondervan, 1962.

Sisemore, John T. *Sunday School Ministry to Adults.* Nashville: Convention, 1959.

Swanson, Lawrence F. *Evangelism In Your Local Church.* Chicago: Harvest, 1968.

Trotman, Dawson. *Follow-Up.* Colorado Springs, Colo.: The Navigators, n.d.

Trueblood, Elton. *The Incendiary Fellowship.* New York: Harper & Row, 1967.

"Winning Women." *Moody Monthly,* 67 (Apr., 1967): 30-31.

Filmstrip: *Space Age Evangelism, A New Concept in Church Outreach.* Chicago: Moody Institute of Science. Color, 33⅓ rpm record.

8

THE LEARNING PROCESS FOR ADULTS

Milford F. Henkel

"You can't teach an old dog new tricks." With this adage many have assumed that adult education is not possible. But the axiom is not true. Adults not only *can* but *are* learning new things.

Many adults are engaged in education. In fact, adult education in the United States has grown from fifteen million adults in 1924; to twenty-two million in 1944; to thirty million in 1950; to fifty million in 1955; to sixty million in 1965. This growth of formal adult education is seen in the development of university extension departments, in classes offered by YMCA's and other social groups, in the increased interest of adults in learning foreign languages, and in the number of adults returning to college—either in day or evening school—to complete their education. Adults are so eager to learn that each year an estimated one in every three adults in the United States participates in some kind of educational enterprise.

Interestingly, local churches offer more formal educational courses for adults than any other educational institution. Over eighteen million adults are enrolled in the educational program of the church. However, the adult department is often the most neglected department in the Sunday school. Adults offer the Sunday school its greatest potential for growth. When the Sunday school enlists an adult, it often reaches an entire family.

Whereas many workers with children enjoy teaching boys and girls "because they are so responsive," many teachers of adults feel frustrated. It seems to them that the adults don't prepare or respond to the lesson. The teachers see little or no changes in the lives of their adult students. And many professing Christians appear to be defeated persons. But Christian adult teachers have the privilege of presenting Christ to their students as their Saviour and leading defeated persons to lives of victory in Christ.

The late MILFORD F. HENKEL, Ph.D., was Professor of Philosophy and History, Grand Rapids Baptist Seminary, Grand Rapids, Michigan.

By discovering how adults learn, a teacher can enter a new world of effectiveness. Too often, the Sunday school has ignored the principles of the learning process. But how do adults learn? Are there certain magic formulae which will open the doors of learning to the adult? Are there some laws or principles of learning which can be applied in order to help insure success? Is learning static or dynamic?

Educational psychologists are not agreed concerning the learning process. They debate the differing virtues of theories of learning. On an academic level this is informative and interesting, but it doesn't tell us *how* adults learn.[1] As a matter of fact, based on our present knowledge, the laws of learning cannot be stated absolutely. Such "laws," if they do exist, are not known. However, we can discuss profitably the general *principles* which influence learning. There is no quick and easy formula to develop effective learning; there is no secret principle we can apply and always be assured of success. Learning is not something which is static and fixed. Rather, it is dynamic and growing.

ADULT LEARNING AND CHILDHOOD LEARNING

One of the first questions to raise in discussing adult learning theory is, Do adults learn in ways significantly different from those of children? To phrase this in a different manner, Is the learning process the same for adults and children? Is the only difference scholastically between adults and children that the adults have larger bodies that cannot be crammed into the children's desks? Are the needs and the experiences of adults so different and varied from that of children that they need separate methods of instruction, facilities, curricula, teaching approaches, reading materials, audio-visuals and textbooks?

Certainly there are many differences between adults and children, and yet the best evidence we have today indicates that there is but a small difference between the adult and the child in the actual process of learning. Learning is not something that is easy for the child and difficult for the adult. At every age level, at every time of life, learning involves a degree of difficulty. Learning offers its own rewards and incentives. The adult can learn as easily as the child. In fact, there are certain factors that often make it easier for the adult to learn than the child.

If this is so, some might ask, "Why is it, then, that adults have more trouble than children in learning? After all, don't adults have more knowledge and experience than children? Is it not true that adults can more easily relate new experiences to previous ones, and can handle many ideas and concepts that a child can't?"

With so many things crowding into an adult's mind, it is often difficult to give undivided attention and concentration to the subject being studied.

Science refers to this as the "pro-active inhibitor" of memory or the factor of memory that may inhibit learning.

Many adults forget how difficult it was for them to learn to walk or talk. With the passing of time, it seems as if it was very easy to learn these skills. We know, however, that such skills were not easily learned. This can be seen in observing a child learning these skills. Adults often simplify the learning process concerning the things they know. It's easy to walk or talk *after* you know how, but not *while* you are learning how.

If an adult realizes that learning and the ability to learn do not stop at childhood but continue throughout life, he can develop an attitude of continuous learning. Furthermore, the techniques of teaching adults *will* be different from those used in teaching children because the teacher has a much wider spectrum of experience to build on in adult education than he has in the education of children.

There are also differences between children and adults in degrees of readiness. By readiness we mean the time when the individual is ready intellectually, emotionally and otherwise to learn a new truth or principle. In addition, there are also differences in the amount of desire to learn and in the extent of participation. The extent of participation will differ with the age level. The greater the degree of participation and involvement, the greater the degree of learning. Many adults, though they have the maturity and the experience to participate *actively* in the learning process, don't do so. Fear of embarrassment often turns potentially active participants and learners into passive ones.

Learning at the adult level is the natural tendency; it is the outgrowth of continuous learning. The old attitude that adult learning is only remedial has been disproven. Those who have this attitude show that they have not kept up with the times.

FALSE CONCEPTS ABOUT ADULT LEARNING

Kidd discusses seven myths concerning learning and classifies them under the following headings:

1. You can't change human nature.
2. You can't teach an old dog new tricks.
3. The "hole-in-the-head" theory of learning.
4. The intellectual notion of learning.
5. The bitter-sweet notion of learning.
6. The mental age of the average adult is twelve.
7. Continuous education is available only to those who have a high I.Q.[2]

If human nature cannot be changed, then there is no room for teaching Christianity. Those who argue that human nature cannot be changed advance the idea that man is unalterable. Obviously this is contrary to the Christian teaching on the new birth.

Some people accept the idea of the "hole-in-the-head" theory of learning. This view often stresses repetition and seems to assume that by some process facts can be forced, poured in, pressed or stamped into the brain. This view is expressed in the old saying, "Cram it in, jam it in—still there's more to follow." Learning under such a view is a simple process: organize your facts logically, and use repetition and reinforcement to make sure the facts are properly injected into the mind.

Closely related to the previous view is the logical-intellectual concept of learning. The teacher simply arranges the content of the course in a logical manner and presents it to the student. The student is expected to memorize the material and be able to present it back to the teacher. Under such a view of learning, the term *intellectual* has become synonymous to many people with the term *dull*.

Some have argued that all learning must be new, interesting and exciting, because pupils more easily learn that which is new, interesting and exciting. There are times, however, when learning is not of this nature. Instead, it is hard work and demands persistency. Some teachers have gone to the opposite view and held that we only learn what is hard or difficult. This is like the view that medicine is only good when it is harsh or bitter. We vividly remember some of our mistakes, but all learning is not of this kind.

Another mistake is to place the mental age of most adults at twelve years. During World War I, the United States Army introduced intelligence tests to thousands of men. For the first time, these tests could be applied to a large segment of the adult population. The average scores of the men in military service in 1917 corresponded to the average scores of school children of the ages twelve to fourteen.

Obviously, the level of education in America has greatly increased since 1917. I.Q. tests have been more carefully refined; even at best, intelligence cannot be equated with academic achievement in school, nor can it be equated with the I.Q. test that measures only the possible potential a person may have for academic achievement. Yet this view is repeated over and over again as an explanation for some of the "adult literature, adult magazines, and repetitious television programs." When the publishers or producers are asked why, they respond, "We are aiming our show to the average adult who has a 12-year-old intelligence."[3]

The view that continuous education should be restricted to adults of high ability is false. This is obvious by the fact that more than half this nation's adults are engaged in some form of continuous education. The adult is not just a larger child; physically, socially, intellectually and by experience, he is vastly different from the child.

WHAT IS ADULT LEARNING?

What then is adult learning? How may it be defined? J. R. Kidd defines education as planned learning. He states, "Learning is the active, not the passive, part of the process."[4] Stinnette says, "Learning is the fruit of an empathic and reciprocal participation between teacher and pupil."[5]

Learning may be defined in different ways. At the lowest level it is the *mastery of facts*, the learning of things that are to be memorized, for a short time, such as cramming for a test. The second stage of learning includes not only the acquisition of facts, but also the *retention* of them. This deals with how much is retained of that which was learned. A third level of learning is both the acquiring and retention of facts, and also the *ability to transfer knowledge* to new and different situations. This involves using that which is learned. At its highest level, learning results in changes of the pupil's actions. Such learning includes not only the acquisition and retention of facts and their application, but the actual changing of the individual. The Christian teacher must lead his pupils into changed lives. The theological term *repentance* means "to change," and thus true adult education leads to changed lives.

Not all learning stems from a direct conscious approach, however. Much of what one learns is either incidental or accidental. An adult faces new situations and new learning experiences every day. Often he may not realize that he is learning. And incidental learning can also take place in the classroom.

Further, Sohn states, "Neither teacher nor student is accustomed to concentrated learning. Optimum performance throughout a class would be too fatiguing for many students and teachers."[6] Some learning in the classroom is concentrated, some is direct but not so concentrated, and some is indirect.

WHAT IS CHRISTIAN ADULT LEARNING?

A Christian concept of learning rejects the evolutionary idea that man is an animal, and that the learning process can be studied solely on the animal level. God, in the creation of human life, established some similarities between animals and human beings, but also some differences. Psychology, science and theology give insights into factors of the learning process. Most certainly, the concept of how a man learns is closely related to one's general view of man. For some liberals, the rejection of theological principles has also resulted in their rejection of a biblical basis of learning.

Christianity demands a changed life. In fact, the idea of change in behavior and action is of *biblical* origin. The New Testament reveals this when it speaks of becoming "a new creature" in Christ Jesus, and insisting that "old things are passed away" (2 Co 5:17). Therefore, Christian educators are never satisfied with learning at the lowest levels, that is, merely acquiring and retaining facts.

The Christian hears the goal of learning in the exhortation, "Let us go on unto perfection" (Heb 6:1), that is, spiritual maturity. Paul gives the biblical basis of learning in his injunction, "I press toward the mark for the prize of the high calling of God in Christ Jesus" (Phil 3:14) and in his instructions, "I have not yet obtained, but seek after" (Phil 3:12, free trans.). This is a concept of continuous education and continuous learning.

In an article concerning school dropouts, it was stated that the real dropouts are not the teenagers but rather the adults who withdraw from learning opportunities and privileges. Being an adult dropout from education is the exact opposite of the goal of being a continuous learner. Only in recent years has education, both secular and Christian, with the help of modern studies in psychology, rediscovered this important truth. Too often, the educational program of the church and the learning theories used within the church have implied that learning is static and fixed rather than a changing, dynamic process.

THEORIES OF ADULT LEARNING

Which theory of learning should a Christian educator accept? Some theories can be rejected because they presuppose an anti-Christian basis. Psychological and educational research have developed several different theories of learning. At present there is no "one" universally accepted theory of knowledge. In this relatively new field with our limited amount of knowledge, it is impossible to say that one theory of learning is true and all others are false. It is perhaps better to state that some theories are more useful or helpful than others. At the same time, a Christian must avoid accepting or rejecting the latest theory of psychology just because it is the latest.

C. Ellis Nelson points out this problem very well when he states,

> Christian education has, since its inception as a field of study in the early twentieth century, usually taken its learning theory from whatever reigning psychologists said at the time was true. Thus, we find Christian education textbooks using the "laws of learning," "stimulus-response" or its revised version of "drive-cue-response-reward" as a proper understanding of learning that could be applied to the learning of the Christian faith.
>
> The Church, by uncritically taking over theories that were usually developed in a study of animal behavior in a laboratory and assumed to be applicable to human beings, forgot the uniqueness of the Church as a society of believers, and the nature of man as a creation of God.[7]

While Stinnette makes this point very forcefully, he doesn't give a complete Christian learning theory, nor could he, with the limited knowledge of today. A Christian must consider the various theories of learning and apply Christian principles to them.

The following are among the common theories of learning prevalent today:

    1. Contiguity theory of Guthrie
    2. Correctionist theories of Thorndike and Gates
    3. Insight theory of Wheeler and Perkins
    4. Cognitive theory of learning
    5. Programmed learning

Guthrie is closest to Watson's behaviorism. His basic principle paraphrased says, "If you do something in a given situation, the next time you are in that situation you will tend to do the same thing again."[8] He goes on to say that in "any situation if you want to find out what an individual will learn, look at what he does. What he does, right or wrong, is what he will learn."[9] Guthrie is called a "contiguity theorist" because he assumes that learning depends only on the continuity of stimulus and response. He avoids any reference to the concept of reinforcement.

Thorndike was a pioneer in experimental psychology using animals. From the study of these he concludes that learning comes neither from reasoning or instinct, but from "the gradual learning of the correct response."[10] Thorndike was a reinforcement theorist; his primary principle of learning was the principle of effect. If the stimulus which is followed by response leads to satisfaction, the stimulus response is strengthened.

Cognitive theories of learning come from Gestalt psychology and place an emphasis on "the whole," and on the concept of insight: "Often learning occurs suddenly with the feeling that no one really understands."[11] Tolman stresses that learning involves changes in cognitive reality from one's experiences with external reality. The insight theory of learning, developed by Wheeler and Perkins, stresses the use of insight rather than rote memorization on the part of the learner. The learner is to gain insight into the total learning situation.

Still another structure is programmed learning. B. F. Skinner, though not the originator, is its most famous advocate. He is a behaviorist but has rejected stimulus-response psychology for respondent-and-operant behavior. He stresses reinforcement in the learning process: this reinforcement may be either positive or negative. The learning process is so designed that the learner goes through a series of small steps. These steps are so graded that the learner rarely makes mistakes. These steps or frames are in sequence and so the style of programming is "linear."

Crowder is also an advocate of programmed learning, but he allows a student who has certain amounts of knowledge to skip certain sections of the program. Thus his approach is known as "branching" for it allows the individual to advance in different directions.

Though at the present time one cannot dogmatically accept a particular learning theory as being completely correct, certain aspects of truth may be gleaned from the various theories of learning.

As a Christian considers these learning theories, he must interpret them in the light of the Word of God. Science has not given us complete information concerning learning theory, but God has given us an objective standard (His written Word) by which to evaluate the different learning theories.

The Christian view of learning is a perceptive view; it includes within it both the idea of conversion and change. By a conversion experience one comes to know Christ as Saviour. This furnishes the motivation for Christian growth and maturity. By this means, a Christian life is always undergoing change.

Based on the present theories of knowledge, the Gestalt or cognitive approach to learning, or some pattern of an eclectic approach, is probably the best solution for the church worker. Stinnette uses the term "an integrated view of learning" and, in so doing, implies an eclectic or cognitive view.

Perhaps Allport best develops a reasonable view of the learning theories for the Christian teacher when he states, "The array of things learned is so vast that we ought not to expect any simple theory of learning to suffice."[12]

A Christian teacher of adults can benefit by considering some common conditions found in learning experiences. These elements include motivation, structure of learning, transfer of behavior, environment of learning, readiness to learn, fulfillment and evaluation.

MOTIVATION IN THE LEARNING PROCESS

Regardless of one's theory of learning, a major facet of it is always that of motivation. It is much easier to learn that which we want to learn than that which we don't want to learn.

Pupils will learn rapidly if they are motivated to learn. All pupils are motivated but not necessarily motivated to learn what the teacher wants them to learn.

> Mr. A is a good man, well respected in the community, hard working, but isn't interested in going to church. He sends his children to Sunday school but doesn't go himself. Sometimes he spends Sunday mornings in

bed. Is he motivated? Yes, he is motivated to do what he thinks is important. In this case, it's sleeping.

Mrs. J. is always in Sunday school. She never misses. She enjoys her Sunday school class and her teacher. It gives her such a good feeling to be in Sunday school. As soon as she gets to class, her mind begins to wander. She never hears what the teacher really says. Is she motivated? Yes, but not motivated to learn what the teacher wants her to learn.

Every successful teacher motivates his pupils to learn. In a sense every teacher, even the teacher of adults, must be a "salesman" of the product he is selling; that product is learning. Adult teachers more than any others often ignore the techniques of motivation. They often assume that adults will be self-motivated to learn, but this usually is not the case. A good teacher will want to establish in his pupils the desire to learn. Good motivation by the teacher can be defined in just that way—establishing in the pupil the desire to learn.

Motivation is both internal and external. Internal motivation is intrinsic or within, and external motivation is from without. Motivation from without never becomes effective until it passes from extrinsic to intrinsic or internal. As in the reinforcement of learning discussed earlier, motivation may also have either positive or negative connotations to it. Many students can remember a teacher who used fear as a basis for motivation—fear of failure, fear of punishment, or fear of losing one's job if one did not learn the required material. This is the lowest of motivation, and is certainly not suitable for adults (and it is doubtful if it is suitable for children).

The first step in motivation is to attract the student's interest. Some pupils are motivated to learn because it is expected of them. At least the teacher who doesn't expect anything of his pupils will receive very little. On a higher level, motivation is based on giving the student satisfying and pleasurable experiences. Students do better in learning experiences when they know it is expected that they will succeed. Again, motivation must appeal to the student's interest. From his interest comes the desire to learn. The highest level of motivation leads one to want or desire more about the subject matter. This level should be the goal of every Christian teacher; he longs to have his pupils become continuous students of the Word of God and to obey the claims of Christ willingly.

Learning isn't always easy and interesting. Sometimes it can be very difficult. Learning is gradual, and at times arduous and even tedious. This can often be seen in the efforts of a student to learn a new language or skill.

It wasn't curiosity that killed the cat but rather the teacher who killed curiosity. Many children are motivated by curiosity, but by the time they are young people or adults, this curiosity has been squelched. A curious person is one who wants to find answers and thus is motivated to learn. As a teacher of adults develops the attitude of curiosity within his students, he helps motivate them to learn.

Rewards are often used as a means of motivation. Behaviorists have especially noted that incentives can stimulate learning in both animal and human subjects. However, when people learn *only* for rewards, they often stop performing the desired task if the reward is withdrawn. Thus, the use of rewards is not as good a means of motivation as some others, but it can be used successfully in some circumstances. Some adults respond to the challenge of performing a difficult task. Perhaps the highest form of motivation is that which arouses the interest of the individual. A basic principle is that motivation is most effective when it relates to the pupil's needs and satisfies those needs as he perceives them.

It must be remembered that the action of the learner can only be fully understood from the learner's point of view. Many times a teacher is frustrated because his adults resist learning something new. This is why the teacher must always try to understand how the individual views the learning situation, and what it means to him. An adult is not resistant to learning something *if* the learning relates to one of his own goals. The secret of teaching new ideas to adults is to make the ideas purposeful to the learner.

A successful teacher will learn to motivate not just negatively but in a positive manner. We are all familiar with the student who, immediately following the completion of an assignment or an examination, does very little studying. As time goes on, he begins to increase in his frequency and intensity of study only as the time of the next assignment or examination approaches. In this case, the assignment or the examination is the motivating factor, and since it is negative or based on extrinsic devices in and of itself, it does not develop a continuous learning. If this is the only basis of motivation, there is little or no further study when the assignment or examination is removed.

Some psychologists argue that future goals do not strongly motivate individuals with reference to their present behavior. Edward J. Green states that "an account of a present action in terms of a future event is not permissible. We do not deny that behavior has characteristics that may be named purposive."[13]

Christian educators recognize some validity in what Edward Green has proposed, but they refuse to get caught on the "either-or" dilemma. It is not either present goals or future goals, but rather, "both-and."

Christianity definitely motivates an individual both with an immediate goal (a better, more complete and Christ-honoring life) and with a future goal (eternity with God). To some, the immediate goal may seem more significant. This is especially true of children and young people who often feel they have all the time in the world. The adult never loses sight of the immediate goal but also becomes more interested in the future goal. One might say the future goal becomes more vivid and immediate as the person becomes older.

With chronological growth, an adult's perception of time changes: the child's endless concept of time is changed and now he begins to recognize the brevity of life. Time is something valuable, something to be almost hoarded rather than to be spent. Adults who lack the Christian goal of a future life often fear growing old. Other adults use old age as an excuse to withdraw from the world. They use such expressions as "I am too old. If I were twenty years younger, I would do so and so." Therefore the Christian teacher recognizes the need to motivate adults by appealing to both immediate goals and future, eternal goals.

STRUCTURE OF LEARNING

Absence of structure leads to anxiety. Without a structural framework, many class members get upset and may complain that nothing is being accomplished. The class members will lack an awareness of the overall purpose of the learning activities.

Gordon Allport points out that learning is clearly a disposition to *form structures*. We do not learn things in isolation, but sooner or later we tend to group them in some sort of a structured relationship. It is much easier to memorize something you can relate to what you already know, than to memorize nonsensical, meaningless phrases.

Most adults in church prefer familiar, customary patterns, rather than change and innovation. They tend to cling to the old, the habitual, the status quo. Drastic changes are neither sought nor desired by most adults in the church. Adult learners are more set in their learning patterns and in the way they have structured their learning. A proposed new structure will often bring resistance. This is why so many adults oppose change in the Sunday school or church. Yet man does not think in a vacuum, nor is the mind always looking backward to the past. Instead, the mind is looking forward into the future. Jerome Brunner in *The Process of Education* stresses the role of structure; he discusses the need for helping students see relationships in learning. When adults discover new and significant relationships in the learning process, they are more open to change and growth. In other words, successful teaching goes beyond the imparting of facts to the establishment of meaningful structures and relationships.

Mrs. J. has been a member of a Sunday school class for forty years. During the last twenty years she has been the teacher of that class. Sunday after Sunday she faithfully tells her class the lesson. Is she teaching the lesson or only telling the lesson? Is there a difference?

Since learning involves structure and relationship, then the telling of the lesson is not teaching the lesson. Furthermore, telling cannot always be equated with learning. The learner may be told something, but this does not mean that he learns the material, even by rote memory.

Real learning takes place when a person relates the new knowledge to what is already known. Thus, learning isn't the passive listening to facts or even the reproduction of facts. These must be related to prior knowledge.

TRANSFER OF KNOWLEDGE

Learning at the highest level goes beyond the acquisition and retention of facts. Many church members never apply to daily living what they learn in church. This doesn't necessarily mean they are hypocrites, but rather that their learning is incomplete. They must learn to transfer that which they have learned in one situation to another situation. To some extent, adults are more able than children to make this kind of transfer. This is because adults have a broader base of knowledge; that is, they have many more experiences which they can use to relate to the current learning experience.

Some educational psychologists have taught that only *specific* things can be learned, and that when specific things are combined together they will gradually form general concepts. According to this view, a person would not apply general concepts to particular situations. For example, one could not transfer the general concept of honesty to specific situations. Instead, one is honest only in specific situations. Ernest Ligon has followed this approach in developing a liberal Sunday school curriculum.

Programmed learning stresses the necessity of teaching small bits of information in step-by-step procedure. Glaser, in arguing for programmed learning, points out that "learning sequences consisting of small steps are associated with significantly better immediate test performance, better retention, and fewer response errors in the course of learning."[14]

The Christian teacher must face these questions: Can one teach general ideas or only specific facts? Can general concepts furnish a framework and structure for specific facts? Can general concepts be transferred to specific situations?

While it is true that we must teach specific facts and break down many of the things to be learned into small units or steps, we can *also* teach principles, and students can learn to apply these principles to specific areas of life.

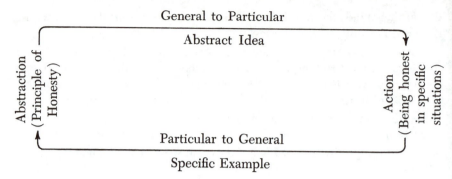

We may teach honesty as an abstraction, and we may also teach specific things about honesty. As these two are related to each other, an attitude of honesty develops both in the abstract and in the particular application of the abstract. To argue about the validity of teaching specific small steps instead of teaching principles is like arguing whether the chicken or the egg came first. There is room for both deductive reasoning (from the general to the particular) and inductive reasoning (from the particular to the general). A wise Christian teacher will recognize the place of both patterns in the learning process.

ENVIRONMENT FOR LEARNING

Is learning individual or social? In other words, can individuals learn in groups or only alone? Actually learning occurs *both* individually and in groups. One cannot learn for another person and in this sense the learning process is individual. Obviously the extent of learning varies with each individual, depending on his environment and innate capacities.

But learning is more than individually internal. If that were not so, there would be no group learning, group changes, nor any role for the teacher in the learning process. The self is never isolated; it is part of society and takes part in various social situations.

In adult Christian education, much learning is "social" in the sense that it takes place in groups such as the church in general, a Sunday school class, and other fellowship groups. In addition to many church-related groups, many Christian adults are also exposed to groups related to their business, their special interests and their communities.

People are attracted to a church group to the extent they accept the goal of the group, and to the extent they are accepted by the group. The goals of the group develop in cycle fashion. They reflect the mood of the group and also help establish the group's mood. Essentially, the goals become the generalized attitude of the group.

What then, is the teacher's responsibility in developing a favorable "environment for learning" in his adult class? As leader of the group he must give attention to ways to generate a sense of class unity and fellowship, and oneness of purpose.

READINESS FOR LEARNING

In general, an individual learns most easily when he is ready to learn. Readiness to learn is not always related to chronological age. One adult, thirty-five years of age, may have been a Christian for many years, whereas another adult of the same age may be a new convert and may have just started attending church. Because their needs are not identical, putting them into the same adult class does not recognize their differences in readiness and may not necessarily provide the best learning environment.

Readiness also means that learning is effective to the extent that the teacher begins with the present state of the pupil's knowledge and experience and seeks to guide him from the known to the unknown. If the teacher does not associate what he is teaching with his students' present experience and knowledge, the teacher may be inclined (1) to talk above the students' level of comprehension, thus making it difficult for them to understand readily what is being taught; (2) to present irrelevant and uninteresting material; and (3) to present material that is already known and therefore repetitiously boring. The idea that repetition or drill necessarily results in learning—especially with adults—has long since been disproved.

CHANGE IN THE LEARNING PROCESS

True learning involves the acquisition and retention of new concepts which lead to change in behavior. Effective learning is more than a passive acquiescence to material presented. Genuine learning, especially of Christian concepts, results in action or life response on the part of the student.

If teaching is merely telling, or if the gathering of facts is all there is to learning, then the lecture method is the zenith of teaching methodology. Of course, in Christian education there *is* content to be told, proclaimed, imparted. And it is for this reason that lecturing—telling and preaching—*is* a valid method of Christian instruction. However, the Christian educator does not assume that learning *automatically* takes place every time truth is proclaimed. Learning is complete only when the student acts on the truth, only when the truth brings changes to his life. In other words, learning includes but goes beyond the mastery of facts. Emerson illustrates this point as follows:

> A thing that has really been learned will be put to use in our daily activities or thinking. To say that a person has learned the importance of a nonstarch diet in remedying a certain health deficiency, and for him

then to continue to knowingly indulge in a diet predominantly starch is to say that he has not learned. *Knowing* right is not *learning* it until it has resulted in *doing* right.[15]

ACTION AND REACTION IN THE LEARNING PROCESS

As one humorist has said, education at the lowest level is transferring facts from the notebook of the teacher to the notebook of the student without going through the head of either one. But in a real learning situation, the material is presented to the student, the student reacts with the material, and this reaction produces a change in the student.

True learning involves the will and leads to volitional action. Both intellectual acceptance and volitional action are part of the complete learning process. If action and activity are stressed without intellectual guidance, this tends to lead to emotionalism or ignorant zeal. On the other hand, if the intellectual is stressed without an appeal to activity, this may lead to an impersonalization of facts and in some cases to hypocritical living.

CHOICE IN THE LEARNING PROCESS

Does one think his way into a pattern of action or act his way into a pattern of thinking? This age-old educational question cannot be answered with an "either-or." Rather it is a "both-and."

In the learning process, the student often has to make choices and judgments. Such judgment-making leads to commitment. Some choices are between good and evil. Other choices are between alternate "goods." In such cases, the decision becomes more difficult. For example, an adult may reason, "Should I take a second job to earn more money? If I do, I can support my family at a higher level and give more to the church. On the other hand, if I do, I will not be at home as much and the children need me at home." Choices like this confront every Christian.

By such choices the learner is encouraged to apply truths to his life. In allowing the student to make his own choices, it is implied that he must take the responsibility of his decisions. This sometimes places the teacher in a dilemma. While stressing the need of the student to make volitional choices, the teacher cannot forget that he has certain absolute truths and biblical standards to transmit to the student. As an absolutist and not a relativist, the evangelical teacher must ask himself, "How can I present the absolute truths of Christianity to my class in a meaningful way?"*

EVALUATION AND TESTING IN THE LEARNING PROCESS

Evaluation and testing are a vital part of learning. By such means both

*A relativist is one who believes that all truth is relative; an absolutist is one who believes that there are absolute or unchanging truths.

the student and the teacher become aware of what has and has not been learned. Testing also reinforces the learning experience. Sometimes adults may have a hazy idea about what is being taught. In response to a question they may respond, "I know the answer, but I just can't put it into words." Correctly interpreted this means, "I have an idea what it's all about, but I just don't have all the facts I need to explain it. I have a vague idea, but I haven't fully mastered the idea. I know something about it."

Evaluation may be done either by a test or examination, or by the question-and-answer method, or by a discussion in which the teacher listens intently to discover concepts the students have in mind.

Evaluation is not limited to the teacher. Students are continuously evaluating the teacher, the material presented, and the learning itself. Evaluation tells one where he is and what he has learned. After evaluation, one is able to determine where he wants to go and how to get there. This is planning. Teachers should encourage learners to engage in systematic appraisal of the learning being accomplished.

METHODS AND THE LEARNING PROCESS

As suggested earlier, an important aid to learning at the adult level is the use of good methods of teaching.

Adulthood is an ideal age with which to use visual and audio aids. But unfortunately most churches use visual aids only with children and seldom with adults.

The successful teacher gives the students opportunity to participate in the lessons, for he recognizes that every person in the group can contribute to the class. In the use of various teaching-learning methods, the successful teacher works to develop spontaneity, curiosity, initiative and resourcefulness within his students. He helps to shape the learning experiences of his pupils by the process of interaction.* Ideally, the students are taught to interact not only with the biblical subject matter, but also to come face to face with Jesus Christ, the Son of God. This is the ultimate objective of the learning process for Christian educators—to bring people, through knowledge of the Bible, to know the Lord personally.

NOTES

1. For helpful material on this problem, see chap. 7, "Theories of Learning," in J. R. Kidd, *How Adults Learn* (New York: Association, 1959), pp. 133-76.
2. Ibid., p. 21.
3. Ibid., p. 15.
4. Ibid.
5. Charles R. Stinnette, Jr., *Learning in Theological Perspective* (New York: Association, 1965), p. 9.

*Methods that facilitate interaction among adults are discussed in chap. 9, "Instructional Methodology for Adults."

6. David Sohn, *Programmed Instruction*, 1 (June, 1962): 4.
7. C. Ellis Nelson as cited by Stinnette, p. 5.
8. Winfred F. Hill, *Learning: A Survey of Psychological Interpretations* (San Francisco: Chandler, 1963), p. 42.
9. Ibid., p. 46.
10. Ibid., p. 58.
11. Ibid., p. 95.
12. Gordon Allport, *Pattern and Growth in Personality* (New York: Holt, Rinehart & Winston, 1961), p. 84.
13. Edward J. Green, *The Learning Process and Programmed Instruction* (New York: Holt, Rinehart & Winston, 1962), p. 80.
14. Arthur A. Lumsdaine and Robert Glaser, *Teaching Machines and Program Learning* (Washington, D.C.: National Educ. Assn., 1960).
15. Wallace Emerson, *Outline of Psychology: A Basic Psychology with Christian Implications* (Wheaton, Ill.: Van Kampen, 1953), p. 399.

FOR FURTHER READING

Birren, James E. "Adult Capacities to Learn," *Psychological Backgrounds of Adult Education*. Raymond G. Kuhlen, ed. Brookline, Mass.: Center for the Study of Liberal Educ. for Adults, 1963.

Caldwell, Irene Smith. *Adults Learn and Like It*. Anderson, Ind.: Warner, 1955.

———. *Responsible Adults in the Church School Program*. Anderson, Ind.: Gospel Trumpet, 1961.

Clemmons, Robert S. *Dynamics of Christian Adult Education*. Nashville: Abingdon, 1957.

Ford, LeRoy. "How Adults Learn," *The Sunday School Builder*, 49 (May, 1968): 16 and 49 (June, 1968): 16.

Fore, William F., et al. *Communication—Learning for Churchmen*. B. F. Jackson, Jr., ed. Nashville: Abingdon, 1968.

Green, Edward J. *The Learning Process and Programmed Instruction*. New York: Holt, Rinehart & Winston, 1962.

Jaarsma, Cornelius. *Human Development, Learning and Teaching*. Grand Rapids: Eerdmans, 1961.

Jahsmann, Allan Hart. *What's Lutheran in Education?* St. Louis: Concordia, 1960.

Journal of Educational Research, Vol. 60, No. 5 (Jan., 1967).

Kidd, J. R. *How Adults Learn*. New York: Association, 1959.

Knowles, Malcolm S. "A Theory of Christian Adult Education Methodology," *Wider Horizons in Christian Adult Education*. Lawrence C. Little, ed. Pittsburgh: U. Pittsburgh, 1962.

Koppe, William A. "Insights for Christian Education from Research in Adult Motivation," *Wider Horizons in Christian Adult Education*. Lawrence C. Little, ed. Pittsburgh: U. Pittsburgh, 1962.

LeFevre, Perry D., ed. *Philosophical Resources for Christian Thought*. New York: Abingdon, 1968.

———. *The Christian Teacher*. Nashville: Abingdon, 1958.

Margulies, Stuart and Eigen, Lewis D. *Applied Programmed Instruction*. New York: Wiley, 1962.

Miller, Harry L. *Teaching and Learning in Adult Education.* New York: Macmillan, 1964.

Morse, William C. and Wingo, G. Max. *Psychology and Teaching.* 2d ed. Glenview, Ill.: Scott, Foresman, 1962.

Proctor, Robert A. *Too Old to Learn?* Nashville: Broadman, 1967.

Stinnette, Charles R., Jr. *Learning in Theological Perspective.* New York: Association, 1965.

Ziegler, Jesse H. "How Adults Learn," *Presbyterian Action,* 9 (Oct., 1959): 12-13.

9

INSTRUCTIONAL METHODOLOGY FOR ADULTS

J. Omar Brubaker

You are there—in the city of Jerusalem. You listen intently as Stephen describes the qualifications and duties of a deacon. You sit with the council as he addresses them on "The Unbelief of Israel" (Ac 7). You see him stoned outside the city. You consider the implications of his life and death. You're in an adult Sunday school class!

The lesson lives and becomes vital because of the Holy Spirit's ministry through the Word *and* a variety of teaching methods used effectively by a teaching team. The methods include a colored slide projected on a screen; an interview—one teacher taking the part of Stephen and the other questioning him; "Stephen" reading his address, as given in Acts 7, from a modern-speech version of the New Testament while the class assumes the role of the council; an opportunity to share some reactions; and a series of frames from a filmstrip on the life of Stephen. This lesson was effective because the couple teaching the class believed that "Concern for the meaning of the lesson should be matched by concern for method in teaching it."[1]

CONSIDERING METHODOLOGY

There is no one best way to teach adults. Some methods are used more widely than others, and some teachers are able to use some methods better than others. But variety of method adds spice and effectiveness to most adult learning situations. Methods used to secure maximum class involvement and learning are best.

As a teacher or leader of adults considers instructional methodology, it is vital to remember that, in the final sense, only the Holy Spirit can do the work of God through the Word of God. LeBar stresses this fact as follows:

J. OMAR BRUBAKER, M.A., is Member of Faculty, Department of Christian Education, Moody Bible Institute, Chicago, Illinois.

It is the peculiar ministry of the Holy Spirit to make the Word of God an inner experience. . . . As God's active agent or method, the Spirit does subjectively within the pupil all that Christ has done objectively without. Educational method is simply finding out how the Spirit works and working with Him, rather than against Him, as we so often do even with the best of intentions. As the human teacher works with the divine Teacher, the Scriptural record becomes more than letters and sounds and words; it becomes the living voice of God speaking to the heart.[2]

Indeed, Christian education is "not by might [of excellent methods], nor by power [of polished techniques], but by my spirit, saith the LORD" (Zec 4:6).

We therefore look at the educational triad (teacher, lesson, pupil) from the perspective of the overshadowing divine Trinity. "Since the Creator-Redeemer is Lord of life, implicit throughout Scripture are His ways of working, as well as His thoughts. Action is always carried out by means of some method. If we aren't doing His work in the Spirit by His methods, we're doing it in the flesh by our own methods. The Lord's work done in the Lord's way will have the Lord's supply."[3]

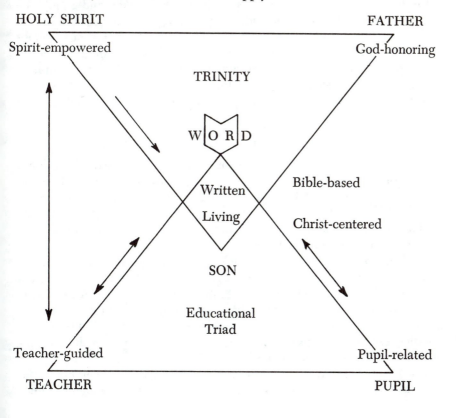

How did the Lord minister as a Teacher to adults when He was on the earth? The Scriptures were basic to His life and ministry. He embodied the truth. He was filled with the Spirit and lived in dependence on the Father, glorifying Him. He met people where they were, at their point of need, and ministered to them. After revealing to them the truth, Christ related it to them personally, resulting in changed lives. This is clearly illustrated in His ministry to the Samaritan woman in John 4. Basically, this is the essence of scriptural method.

Jesus, the master Teacher of adults, certainly employed numerous educational methods in His ministry. He lectured, asked questions, gave assignments, required reports, led His disciples in various projects, and "made use of the dramatic method quite a bit in His teaching either in a formal or informal fashion."[4] Christ chose these various techniques, which He used spontaneously and flexibly, on the basis of His purpose and His knowledge of His pupils. "If anyone would be a true Christian teacher, let him deny his own prejudices and take up Christ's methods, though they're not the easy ones, and follow the Master Teacher."[5]

Methods in themselves are essentially teaching tools and should be wisely chosen. They are not ends in themselves, but serve as means to ends. Yet they are vitally important because the *way* a lesson is taught determines, in part, *what* is learned or accomplished. "Method does teach in itself. And the method used has a great deal to do with the atmosphere of a group, with group interrelationships, and therefore is directly related to some of the intangible but basic learning and change that takes place in persons."[6]

CHOOSING METHODS

Because teaching is in a sense a cooperative art, the teacher should use teaching-learning tools in cooperation with his students. He will choose and use proper tools with pupils in mind, and he will use techniques in line with the objectives of the class or the purpose of the group. He, as well as the class, will need to understand the methods that are to be used —their advantages and limitations.

Methods must not be chosen arbitrarily, but rather for their appropriateness to the occasion. Because a technique is rated "best" on someone's list, that does not guarantee its success in another situation. "A method is 'best' *only* as it 'belongs' to that subject matter and that purpose which it can help to bring alive as it is used with wisdom by leaders."[7] Or as Zuck puts it, "The best method for any given occasion is the one that accomplishes the best results in the best way."[8]

The lesson will have to become meaningful to the teacher before he can choose the best methods to make it meaningful to his students. Other factors to consider in the choice of method are: the amount of time available to prepare and use the method, the adequacy of the facilities for using the method successfully, and the ability of the teacher or leader to use the method effectively. Not everyone can use every method with best effect. This is due to lack of familiarity with the method, or lack of confidence in using it. Sometimes the method does not fit or suit the personality of the teacher or leader, and he must be comfortable with the technique he is using in order to use it naturally. However, no adult teacher should fail to learn about and try new methods. Adults appreciate the use of a variety of methods for it enriches teaching.

SOME DIRECT-PRESENTATION METHODS

LECTURE

An old and reputable method, the lecture can be used very effectively in presenting the Word of God. Jesus, the master Teacher, often lectured. Though considered an easy method to use, it is "probably the most difficult of all to use to insure that learning will take place."[9] An adult may sit and listen, but that does not guarantee that he will learn. This method places a premium on listening, since it is a verbal presentation of lesson content.

Many teachers use the lecture method because it is the simplest way to cover a broad subject in a minimum of time. Many adults want the teacher to lecture, since it requires no verbal response from them. Without question, it is the most commonly used teacher-oriented method in teaching adults.

Criticism of the lecture method is justified for its overuse (often to the exclusion of other methods) and its misuse. It is not the ideal way to teach adults. "Even if your class members assure you that they got a great 'blessing' from your lecture," says Jacobsen, "they cannot have learned if they have not participated. . . . If lecturers would measure the results of their teaching in terms of changed attitudes and lives, perhaps many of them would revise downward their appraisal of their effectiveness."[10] Learning is more than listening, and good lecturing is more than just telling.

The good lecturer is well prepared, with material properly outlined so it can be communicated logically and clearly. He speaks with authority without being authoritarian. He can teach "out of life" and not just "off a book," for he believes what he teaches and shares it with conviction. The adult teacher will keep the pupils' attention with his attention—direct, friendly eye contact. He teaches with enthusiasm as an "animated audiovisual aid." Appropriate gestures, facial expression and voice inflection are all important.

Using the lecture method gives the teacher control of the teaching situation. It avoids wrong answers, difficult questions and sidetracking issues. Since more material can be presented in a given amount of time by this method, it is valuable for sharing information which otherwise would be difficult for the class to secure.

In presenting the lecture it is vital to use both verbal and visual illustrations. Verbal illustrations arouse interest, help clarify and drive home truths presented. Rhetorical questions can help stimulate thinking. Visual aids also help illustrate the subject, hold attention, assist learning and make it more lasting.

The lecture method can be one of a variety of methods used in a class period. It can be used to set the stage for a discussion, or it may be the best way to summarize a lesson. Edge says, "The lecture method is most effective when it is used along with some other methods. . . . It should be a relatively rare thing for the teacher to use the lecture method for the entire class session."[11]

SYMPOSIUM

This method is related to the lecture method, and it is more formal than the panel. The symposium is really a series of short speeches before an audience with a leader in charge. Each speaker presents his contribution in turn as a brief lecture. This method gives the class a wider range of information and viewpoints than is possible for one speaker. There is no discussion between the various members of a symposium. The speeches represent different aspects of a subject or varying viewpoints on it.

A symposium-forum is a symposium followed by audience or class participation by means of questions and dialogue with the speakers. Groups can create a kind of symposium. Small groups discuss an issue, then the leaders constitute a symposium and each presents his group's conclusions.

RESOURCE PERSONS

Individuals with certain information and experience—such as a church member who has traveled the Bible lands or a Christian schoolteacher—can be brought into a classroom to share with the class. A time for questions and discussion is helpful.

DEBATE

In a debate two or four speakers, for and against a proposition, alternately present their points of view. Rebuttals may or may not follow. Group members may question the debators following the debate, or the entire group may participate in an open discussion. A moderator or teacher in a debate introduces the proposition in positive terms. Regular debate teams have four members—two favoring the proposition and two opposing it. Following the introduction the first affirmative speaker speaks in support of the proposition. Then a person from the negative side gives arguments against the proposition. The second affirmative speaker then supports the proposition and the other negative speaker opposes it. If there is a rebuttal, there is usually a brief deliberation by the two teams before it begins. The order of speakers in the rebuttal is first negative, first positive, second negative, and second positive. The moderator should time the debators carefully. He should also be sensitive to emotional factors and make sure correct impressions are left with the group. "The purpose of a debate is to clarify, not to confuse; to crystallize, not to create more difficulty in understanding particular Bible truths."[12]

STORY-SHARING

A good example of the effectiveness of the story method is demonstrated by Nathan, the prophet. King David had sinned and had not repented. Nathan wisely used a story approach in his "lesson" to the king. He told the touching story about the wealthy sheep herder who robbed a poor man of his only lamb. (It is interesting to see how the Lord guides in the choice of methods as He surely did with this adult teacher.) David was so moved by the story that he passed judgment: "As the LORD liveth, the man that hath done this thing shall surely die" (2 Sa 12:5b). Thus David's heart was prepared as Nathan made the application, "Thou art the man." David learned his "lesson" and repented.

The story has been a means of teaching from earliest times. Jesus also knew the power of the story. Storytelling is not limited to teaching children; it serves well with youth and adults. A story's appeal knows no age limit. In teaching adults the story will usually take the form of an illustration, an incident or an experience. However, an occasional, well-told story can serve as a main method of communication with adults, as when Ethel Barrett told the story of D. L. Moody at a Moody Bible Institute Founder's Week service under the title "Dear Dad."

The story invites interest, as adults "perk up" to the teacher's words, "Let me illustrate." It leads to new insight and understanding. Someone has said that verbal illustrations are like windows to let in the light of truth. "As Moses lifted up the serpent in the wilderness" helped explain to Nicodemus a new lesson about the death of the Son of man (Jn 3:14).

The real life situation aids in problem-solving. A life situation brings in a "slice of life" for evaluation. It makes the lesson relevant, relating it in terms of the learners' experience. The life situation need not be true, but it must be realistic and plausible.[13]

To share a story effectively, it must be told with enthusiasm. But it must be done naturally and with good vocal expression. Appropriate gestures and facial expressions are in order. Using action verbs and descriptive phrases makes the story more vivid. The teacher must choose the right story for the occasion, outline the main points, practice telling it aloud, and let it live for him.

INTERACTION METHODS

QUESTION AND ANSWER

Adults should be challenged to think. Thought-provoking questions provide stimuli for learning, and can be one of the adult teacher's best aids in the teaching-learning process.

The master Teacher of adults set the pace in the art of asking and answering questions. In his treatment of Jesus' questions, Horne states, "Somehow at the beginning of this inquiry I sense that we are near the heart of the teaching methods of Jesus."[14] He reports that the gospels record more than one hundred different questions that Jesus asked.

Three basic kinds of questions used in teaching are the factual, thought-provoking and rhetorical. A factual question is basically seeking for factual information. Jesus asked, "How many loaves have ye?" (Mk 6:38) And they answered, "Five, and two fishes."

A thought question is one that is designed to provoke thinking. Jesus asked, "Philip, whence shall we buy bread, that these may eat?" (Jn 6:5*b*) Jesus asked this to test (prove) Philip.

Usually thought questions should be introduced with "How" or "Why." A rhetorical question is a thought question which does not expect an audible answer. Jesus didn't wait for a response to these questions; "Why reason ye, because ye have no bread? Perceive ye not yet, neither understand? Have ye your heart yet hardened? Having eyes, see ye not? and having ears, hear ye not? and do ye not remember?" (Mk 8:17-18)

The use of the question-and-answer method enables the teacher to focus on specific lesson points. It helps create interest and hold attention, as well as test knowledge and understanding. This method can be used effectively in conjunction with almost every other teaching method.

The recitation method, related to the question-and-answer method, is not used widely with adults, but should not be ruled out. Meaningful memorization should also be encouraged among adults, especially the memorization of certain biblical facts and Scripture verses. It was an adult who wrote, "Thy word have I hid in mine heart, that I might not sin against thee" (Ps 119:11).

FORUM

A forum is the audience asking questions after a speaker, film, symposium, interview, etc. Class reaction to one speaker's ideas is a lecture-forum. Reaction to more than one speaker's ideas is called a symposium-forum. Also representative individuals may answer questions asked by a group on a given subject.

GROUP DISCUSSION

"Through discussion a group of adults can explore a subject and find a level of working and talking that has meaning for them."[15] Opinions are exchanged, attitudes can be formed and decisions made. Though discussion may be thought of as "planned conversation," it is more than mere talk. It is possible that the person who talks the most may say the least! As an effective teaching method the discussion must focus on a genuine problem, question or topic, and be under the direction of a skilled leader or teacher. Informal and formal discussion as used for Bible study are explained helpfully in *Leading Dynamic Bible Study*.[16]

A good discussion is considered the most nearly ideal and effective of the major teaching methods for adults. This method has the potential of involving every group member in a meaningful learning experience. Every member may not contribute verbally, but all should be involved mentally and emotionally. In this kind of a discussion, what is said contributes to the subject at hand and adds to the participants' fund of knowledge in that area.

Edge points out that a discussion is a cooperative search for truth in seeking a solution to a problem. It is not a debate, and he carefully distinguishes the two.[17] It is certainly true that people are more convinced by the sharing of experience than by argument. How important, then, that discussion be seen as a cooperative effort in an atmosphere of caring and sharing, with the leader presiding over it with grace and skill.

Group discussion is not an "easy" method to use. It calls for more preparation, resourcefulness and ability on the part of the teacher or leader than many of the other methods. Profitable discussions take place when there is a thought-provoking issue or problem, and when the group members have sufficient background of experience and information to contribute intelligently.

For profitable discussion the group should be small enough for active participation by all—approximately ten to twenty members. Only one person should speak at a time, and all the others should actively listen. In larger classes some discussion is in order, provided each participant speaks loudly enough to be heard. Ideally the seating arrangement should be in a circle, with the leader appearing as one of the group members.

Apart from planning the discussion, the leader has three basic functions: start the discussion, keep it going on course, and summarize it. A variety of means can be used to launch a discussion, since a worthwhile one rarely "just happens." A thought-provoking question or situation, a brief lecture, or a film may serve as discussion starters. Jacobsen suggests "transition" methods or "lead-in" techniques such as Scripture search, brainstorming, question and answer, buzz groups, life situation, research and report, skit and role play.[18]

When a discussion lags, the teacher should throw in a question or two. Resource information may need to be given. If it wanders, he must bring it back with an appropriate comment or statement, and he should keep the group from going up "blind alleys." No member should be allowed to monopolize the discussion, every one should be encouraged to share, and each should respect the views and contributions of the others.

In concluding a discussion a good summary is important. It may be helpful to list on a chalkboard the main points that were made. The conclusion should be the one the group has reached, not a preconceived one concocted by the leader. When discussing the Word of God the conclusions should be in harmony with Scripture.

BUZZ GROUPS

Buzz groups are a method of group discussion by which everyone in a large group may participate simultaneously in smaller groups. This method may be used early in a class period to stimulate interest and participation, during a lesson to dig out meaning, or at the close of a session to consider implications and application. Each small group may simultaneously discuss the same or different subjects as assigned by the teacher. For example, a Bible study class of fifteen people may divide into three groups, each group discussing a different segment of the passage being studied, followed by a brief report from each group to the entire class. In certain instances, a teacher may have all three groups discussing the same passage.

The time spent in buzz groups may extend from five to fifteen minutes. The longer sessions take the form of study groups. Timing depends on the purpose of the assignment and the nature of the material being studied. The purpose of buzz groups is not to treat a topic exhaustively, but to get the members involved, thinking and sharing. This method helps create an atmosphere of informality.

Small group discussion and sharing usually allays fears of participating. It proves helpful to the individual as he participates, and helps group members become better acquainted. Often such a starter frees the hesitant student to participate later in the larger group. A formal leader is not required, but a leader should usually be appointed to guide the group, along with a reporter to take notes and share findings later.

TWO-BY-TWO DISCUSSION

"Neighbor-nudging" allows two people sitting next to each other to share or interact briefly in conversational style. In this way every member gets involved in a brief discussion of the problem or point under consideration. The teacher then suggests that ideas from these "two-somes" be shared with the larger group. This method is a miniature version of the buzz group.

GROUP CONVERSATION

In circular response the teacher makes a statement or asks a question and, beginning with the person to his right, each person in turn makes a comment on what has been said until all have participated.

Conversation between two people before an audience, as they informally discuss a topic before an audience, is another possible method. This may be called "dialogue discussion."

Group conversation is a good way to begin a session. The topic of such informal conversation should be in line with the lesson.[19]

PANEL DISCUSSION

This is an interesting variation of the discussion method. It is a somewhat structured discussion of a given subject. Generally three or four panelists are chosen to represent different points of view, and the teacher or leader serves as moderator. The panelists speak conversationally, contributing as they feel inclined. This method is especially adapted to the treatment of topical subjects. Unless it is an impromptu panel, panelists are selected in advance, with the understanding that they will make adequate preparation. The panel discussion should be introduced in such a way that the class knows how it fits into the overall course and goals of study. The moderator may interject questions or comments during the presentation, and at the end he should summarize the conclusions reached by the panel. It may be helpful to allow questions or comments from the class or audience after the panel has concluded, which would then be classified as a forum.

REACTION PANEL

This method allows individual class members to direct questions to a speaker for purposes of clarification and elaboration. Several approaches may be taken in using this technique. A teacher of adults may assign several students without previous notice at the beginning of a class hour to serve as a listening team during a twenty- or thirty-minute lecture, and then respond as a reaction panel the last part of the class hour.

Also, a panel may be assigned to listen and react to a visiting lecturer.

When using this approach, the speaker should be made aware of the fact that a special listening team will be evaluating the presentation in order to raise questions and make comments regarding the content that was presented. It is also helpful for the reaction panelists to meet the speaker prior to the session for a "warm-up" period.[20]

Whichever approach is used, it is important for the teacher or an appointed "listener" to summarize the ideas at the end of the hour.

METHODS STRESSING FIRSTHAND EXPERIENCE

RESEARCH AND REPORT

Assignments to do research may be made to individuals or groups. Some assignments may involve reading a book, magazine, newspapers, the Bible or biblical literature for the purpose of giving a report, review or summary. Reports may be given orally or presented in writing. A well-stocked church library is a real asset for this type of study. Other assignments may take the form of interviewing people, to learn their preferences, opinions and evaluations.

INTERVIEW

Interviews in class are interesting and informative. Used effectively they can add great resource and variety to the learning situation. They provide facts direct from the source of authority and experience. When dealing with a specialized subject, an interview with an expert in that field would be in order. These interviews can be done "live" or on tape. If done "live" in a class or group situation, the teacher or leader will take the lead in the interview. At times the class may lead in the interview and ask questions of interest to them. A class member may have the opportunity of bringing resource material to class via a taped interview he has conducted with a friend or resource person.

A teaching team can present an interview with Bible personalities, combining aspects of the role play. One member of the team would serve as the reporter or interviewer, and the other as the Bible character. Some suggested Bible personalities lending themselves to this type of presentation would be Joseph, Moses, King Saul, David, John the Baptist, John the apostle, Peter and Paul.

LISTENING TEAMS

Using this method involves dividing a class or group into two or more groups, assigning each to listen or look for specific ideas, problems or answers to questions during a lecture, film or story. After the presentation, reports are given by the teams and ideas shared. This method helps keep students alert and actively listening. Assignments can also be made to listen *outside* of class, instead of looking or reading.

TESTIMONY

Sometimes Bible truths or teaching points can best be illustrated by individuals from the class. Such a testimony demonstrates the workability of the point being taught and thus helps vitalize the lesson. Usually the individual who gives the testimony should be contacted in advance. The teacher can refer to such a testimony as he continues with the class study.

It is also very stimulating to a group of Christian adults to hear testimonies from individuals outside the group, particularly persons who have been led to Christ by the teacher or other members of the group. This method correlates particularly well with a lesson or series of lessons on evangelism.

WRITING AND TESTING

The class may be asked to write what the study has meant to them personally. They may participate in a written poll or survey. The survey may be a questionnaire, opinionnaire or some kind of reaction sheet. Responses need not always be signed. Individuals may be challenged to write their own paraphrase of some Scripture passage. Materials needed for written assignments in class should be kept on hand.

A lesson session could be built on reviewing answers to test questions which members filled out as preparation for the class period. Consideration should be given to the best answers in light of the passage being studied. A short quiz may stimulate interest at the beginning or end of a class session. Testing prior to a three-month unit of study, to discover what the students know, and quarterly achievement tests given at the end of a unit, should prove a challenge to adults.

It should be noted, however, that using tests and quizzes with adults in the church must be done cautiously and tactfully. Some adults may react negatively to being a participant due to a fear of doing poorly. The main value of the testing device in this kind of teaching-learning situation is to stimulate thinking. Therefore, some teachers prefer to let the group know that the quiz answers will not be collected but will be used in class discussion following the test.

SILENT THINKING

The silent-thinking method demands careful teacher direction and timing. The class is given a minute or two to *think* about a certain question or problem. Following the thinking period there may be an opportunity for responses from the group. This method is also known as reflection-response.[21] If the class members are asked to think and pray about the question or problem, this technique may be called reflection-prayer, but there would be no audible response.

METHODS USING PERSONAL CREATIVITY AND DRAMA

BRAINSTORMING

Brainstorming literally uses the brains, the thinking, of the group to "storm" a problem or situation. Brainstorming is "a conference technique by which a group attempts to find a solution to a specific problem by amassing all the ideas contributed spontaneously by its members."[22] Brainstorming is a pooling of everyone's ideas. Sometimes it is called "idea inventory." It is an exciting method and can be a helpful technique in adult Christian education. It requires the ability to share, value and accept every person's individual thinking. It will disclose the range of information, opinions, imagination and creativity in a given class or group. Brainstorming helps create an atmosphere of informality and openness.

In brainstorming, initial criticism of the ideas given is not permitted. Individuals should be free to share whatever idea comes to mind, whether or not it seems good at the moment. The point is to get as many ideas to work with as possible. Then after the ideas have been suggested, they should be evaluated, with the better ones being selected and an order of priority determined.

Careful attention should be given to details in using this method. It is especially important to have an individual or several individuals serve as recorders. In a large group, ideas will usually come rapidly, and it is essential to get each suggestion and comment written down as quickly as possible. It inhibits the process if ideas are withheld while a person is struggling to keep up with the recording process. Actually, the recording should be almost an unnoticeable aspect of the method.

OBSERVATION TRIP

An observation or field trip provides the opportunity to observe and gather information firsthand at some point outside the classroom. Careful planning is important. Objectives should correlate with the purpose of the study group. The group should be prepared for the occasion and know what to look for. Opportunity should be provided to evaluate and share what they saw, heard and did. For adults this kind of experience may range anywhere from a planned visit to a city ghetto to a tour of the Holy Land.

PROJECT

Edge defines the project as "an activity in which the class engages either to deepen or to express the learning which they have done."[23] It is on the giving, doing and serving side of Christian education. Stress should be placed on getting information and changing, developing or deepening certain attitudes, developing habits and rendering service. The project method should aid in learning and in the expression of spiritual ideals. This method does not exclude the use of other methods.

The teacher should cooperate closely with the students in using the project method. This method takes time. Projects should be carefully chosen and related to the course or group objective. Learning is made more meaningful, interesting and lasting through the project method. It helps greatly in developing leadership abilities.

CASE STUDY

In a case study the student learns through direct involvement in a situation he studies firsthand. The actual conditions of a given situation are seen as they actually are. This could be a problem situation involving an individual or a group. It could be a successful project or program that the group may want to study. It can be used individually or by any size group which is willing to become involved. Effort is required to go directly into a situation, to sources of various kinds, in seeking out information for a case study. Learning is effective because of such personal involvement.

An adult Sunday school class studying the Christian home may want to do some case studies of families who are conducting family worship successfully. Or a church group may want to investigate how another congregation started a branch work. It is possible to use this method in investigating some social problem in the community, seeking ways and means for solution.

The *case history* is similar to the case study but it is a *written* report. "The case history is a written report describing an event, incident, or situation that a learning group can profitably analyze, and discuss."[24] The case history can deal with the behavior of a person or a group. It may be based on an actual incident or an imaginary one. The group should read the case history before the time for discussion. It can then be discussed and analyzed through a group discussion, panel, symposium or buzz sessions.

ROLE-PLAYING

The method of role-playing is especially valuable in situations involving interpersonal relationships. "Role playing is accomplished when a person takes upon himself the life situation of another and attempts to see things from the inside."[25] It is "extemporaneous dramatization." It is not a skit, and does not involve the use of a script. It is helpful in observing various attitudes expressed as well as actions. It can provide a realistic situation in the classroom by which the learners may appraise their own actions toward others, and theirs toward them.

In a lesson on the Christian home the teacher may suggest in class a situation involving a parent-teen problem. (Complex situations should be avoided.) Class members could volunteer to assume the roles—a father and mother, and a teenage daughter. After briefing the actors and observers, the role play is presented. The characters are to give their spontaneous interpretations of the situation in action and word. As the scene is presented, the leader or teacher interrupts or "cuts" the action at the appropriate point, and then asks the class to evaluate the situation and set a learning goal. The participants may also share their reactions. It is also possible to stop the action at specific points for discussion and then let the role play continue. Sometimes a scene can be replayed using different characters and/or reversing roles.

Role-playing is helpful in stimulating discussion, gaining insights, and training in skills. It calls for a warm, accepting atmosphere in the group. The attitude of the leader is a key factor. He must not embarrass volunteers nor force individuals to participate.

Levit and Jennings give the following steps in the role-playing process: "Defining the problem; establishing a situation; casting the characters; briefing and warming up actors and observers; acting; cutting; discussing and analyzing the situation and behavior by actors and observers; and making plans for further testing of the insights gained or for practicing the new behavior implied."[26]

PLAY

A formal dramatic presentation, such as the play, has its place in adult Christian education. A script to be memorized is usually involved, as well as careful planning, proper staging and much practice. The Zion Passion Play, produced by the Christian Catholic [non-Roman] Church of Zion, Illinois, is a good illustration of how one church involves many adults, as well as young people, to share the gospel story. Recently, the narration has been recorded on tape and the actors use silent lip synchronization, thus enabling them to concentrate more on gestures and other actions. In another church the adults presented an Easter play for the congregation. This was an interesting change from the plays given on special days by children.

SKIT

A skit is a form of drama less formal and usually shorter than a play, though it generally has a written script. For example, as an approach to a lesson on husband-wife relationships several adults could present a skit that depicts some home problems to be discussed.

PAGEANT

In presenting a pageant, people go through certain actions related to a particular incident or activity. Costumes are often used and a narrator tells the story as the actors act it out. This is a valuable dramatic method for presenting missionary stories, character studies, Bible stories or other interesting incidents that help communicate spiritual truths.

TABLEAU AND PANTOMIME

In a tableau adults present a scene with little or no motion. This is an excellent way to stage the major Christmas scenes from the gospels for a Christmas program. When there is narration, the narrator is off stage. A pantomime is a scene acted out without narration.

DEMONSTRATION

What makes demonstration a valuable teaching procedure? Neufer suggests it is the visual impact and the conclusiveness of the demonstration.[27] Observers see the complete event. It can be repeated. Learners can ask specific questions. They can "see for themselves," and possibly try it themselves. Enough time must be allowed for the use of demonstration. It should be clear-cut and related to the lesson being studied. The demonstration must be well planned and should be rehearsed in advance.

INTERPRETIVE OR CREATIVE READING

Interpretive Scripture reading is a dramatic Bible reading in which individuals interpret the passage with special emphasis given to persons and unique situations. Class members may take the roles of certain characters as a passage is read. Variety in reading the Scripture should be stressed in the adult class. The teacher should carefully plan for this. Otherwise it tends to be the each-a-verse-around method every Sunday.

CHORAL READING

Choral reading involves a group in reading much as a choir is engaged in singing. Various parts are assigned to individuals and to subgroups within the group. Through such reading, interpretation and emphasis is given to the passage being presented. The psalms are readily adapted to this kind of treatment. It can bring variety into the reading of Scripture in the adult class, or it can be an effective part of an opening worship service for Sunday school, or a special program.

Teachers and leaders of adult groups can arrange such readings on their own, or a group or a committee from the group may prepare the choral reading. Some arrangements of choral readings may be purchased for use with adult groups. Many times they are included in materials provided for the adult class or group.

METHODS INVOLVING DIRECT BIBLE STUDY

The Scriptures may be studied in a ceremonial, mechanical, dull, now-we-are-in-Sunday-School manner. Or you—the teacher—and the class may study the Bible in a dynamic manner. You and your class may plumb the very depths of mind and heart, together, as you seek to know and do God's will through study of the written revelation. This spiritual experience together may be called *dynamic Bible study*.[28]

Pierce offers the following advice regarding the use of methods in direct Bible study:

Do not get tangled up in procedure so as to become mechanical and superficial. The group processes which we are considering are revealed to Christians by the Holy Spirit in order for them to achieve *reality* and *purposefulness* in Bible study. Make sure you use your teaching methods in a way to achieve these results.[29]

GROUP BIBLE STUDY

Henry Jacobsen writes:

This method is an adaptation of "Inductive Bible Study," sometimes referred to as "Direct Bible Study." Its objective is to help adults discover for themselves what a passage of Scripture *says* before they jump to conclusions about what they think it *means*. Questions by the leader should first focus attention on the context of the text; then he should ask questions of interpretation and of application.[30]

This method secures wide pupil participation. It aims at helping adults discover for themselves what the Bible says, and it develops their ability in personal Bible study, which is imperative to spiritual growth. It takes more time than merely telling what the Bible says and means. Group Bible study does not permit the teacher to cover as much content in a given lesson, but what is examined will be more meaningful, for the student has seen it for himself. Learning is more likely to take place because he was involved.

SCRIPTURE SEARCH

Using this method the teacher or Bible study leader will "focus on a pivotal question and then guide the pupils in finding, reading together, discussing the meaning of, and relating a series of passages of Scripture to each other."[31]

VERSE-BY-VERSE VS. SURVEY

The verse-by-verse method seeks to analyze, interpret and apply each verse one at a time. The verse-by-verse method is frequently overworked in teaching adults the Bible. Frequently this method leads to studying verses out of context.

In the survey approach, the Bible paragraph of several verses, not the verse, becomes the basic unit of study. It gives the broad general view without getting bogged down in an endless analysis of each verse. For this type of study a paragraphed edition of the Bible is helpful for reading and study.[32]

READ—THINK—SHARE

Margaret Hess tells of a method used by an English evangelist.[33] The main points are as follows:

1. Choose a passage of Scripture that lends itself to discussion.
2. Read silently a block of two or four verses (read at least twice).
3. As you read, look for God's message to you.
4. Ask for three or four volunteers to share briefly their insight, idea or question.
5. Assign each volunteer a number.
6. Encourage quiet ones to share their ideas.
7. Don't be afraid of the obvious. It may not be so obvious to someone else.
8. Proceed through the passage a few verses at a time.

AUDIO-VISUALS

"Looking in On Adults" is a disc recording, an audio aid—it can be heard. "St. Stephen's Gate" is a two-by-two colored slide, a projected visual—it can be seen. "Out on A Limb" is an adult-department sound filmstrip, an audio-visual—it can be heard and seen.

CHALKBOARD

This visual is a must in the adult classroom. It is an important visual aid, providing the adult teacher with a ready writing surface for planned or spontaneous writing or drawing during the lesson. Teachers should learn to use the chalkboard as a vital visual aid. It can easily be used along with the lecture or a variety of other methods. Care should be taken not to turn completely away from the class when using the board.

It can be used for words, phrases, snappy sketches or diagrams. The teacher may outline the lesson, diagram a Bible verse, illustrate the layout of the tabernacle, draw a line map of Palestine or chart the main points of an inductive Bible study in chart form. Or the teacher can write a thought-provoking question on the board before the class enters. This will get the class thinking at the beginning of a session. Also a class member may record ideas on the chalkboard as the class brainstorms a topic, or as reports are given from buzz groups.

MAPS

Maps are valuable tools in teaching the Word of God. The exodus and wilderness wanderings or Paul's missionary journeys are traced with greater meaning when using maps. Bible geography becomes alive— interest is stimulated, relationships are clarified and learning is reinforced. Use of maps provides for pupil participation as individuals point out lesson highlights on the map.

BULLETIN BOARD

An attractive, up-to-date bulletin board is an asset to the adult class-room, and in many other places in the church. Quotations, announcements, cartoons, lists, posters and pictures can be placed on the bulletin board from time to time. Themes, seasonal decorations and appropriate pictures add meaningful atmosphere to an adult classroom. Responsibility for keeping the board looking attractive may be just the kind of participation certain quiet, but talented adults in a Sunday school class need.

PICTURES

"One picture is worth a thousand words," goes the old Chinese proverb. Why not use *several* pictures in teaching adults. Why not use pictures regularly. They are easy to obtain. One women's Bible study class brought pictures they thought represented the women in the Bible whom they were studying. One beauty in curlers and a "facial mask" reminded them of Queen Esther—it took her a whole year to *get ready* to meet the king! A moving van in a country setting reminded them of Sarah—always on the move in the promised land.

A colored picture of a lily would illustrate our Lord's words, "Behold the lilies of the field." A picture of a beautiful snow scene could be shown when discussing the verse, "Hast thou entered into the treasures of the snow?" A picture of a stormy sea would illustrate the words of Isaiah, "The wicked are like the troubled sea when it cannot rest."

CHARTS

"A chart is a visual symbol which presents an idea and explains it."[34] This is the definition of a chart given by Ford, who also suggests a variety of charts: pinboard chart, sentence-holder chart, hinged chart, folded-word strip chart, embellished chart, strip chart, slip chart, inverted-flip chart, and the upright-flip chart. Getz adds organizational charts, Bible charts, and picture charts.[35]

FELT BOARD

Probably better known as the flannelboard, this visual aid is not limited to use with children. The creative adult teacher will want to make use of the felt board for displaying figures, felt-backed pictures and word strips, etc.

PROJECTED AUDIO-VISUALS

Projected visuals should be in use fairly regularly with adults because adults are used to television, motion pictures, filmstrips and the overhead projector.

"I Don't Want To Get Involved," a Family Films *16mm sound-motion film* on the subject of apathy, provided a challenging message along with a panel discussion in one church's adult department Sunday school hour. Moody Science films are being used widely in neighborhood evangelism, as well as in the military, public fairs and churches.

Numerous *filmstrips* are available to aid in teaching and training adults. The Moody Bible Institute filmstrip series on Bible survey is excellent. Series on the lives of Christ and Paul are available from several producers. The Scripture Press Royal Commission teacher-training filmstrips are excellent for training Christian education leaders, especially Sunday school teachers.

Good colored *slides* of Holy Land scenes can aid in Bible study, giving appreciation for Bible backgrounds and helping them understand Bible locations and customs. Nature scenes, pictures of people, animals, flowers and birds can all add interest and meaning to many Bible passages. A group of adults profited from such an illustrated portrayal of Job 38-41. A whole series of slides is not necessary for effective teaching. Individual slides of outstanding pictures and paintings make good picture studies. One slide or several can make an effective point in introducing, illustrating, applying or concluding a Bible lesson.

In recent years the *overhead projector* has been a regular tool used in many adult education classes. A Canadian Sunday school teacher, who didn't have room in the balcony of the church for a chalkboard, found that the overhead served as a practical and versatile visual tool. The screen hung beyond the confines of the balcony, where no chalkboard would stand!

Transparencies are being produced commercially, including Bible maps as well as other diagrams and charts for teaching the Bible and leadership training classes. More churches are purchasing overhead projectors and transparency producers. Pastors are using them for illustrating their sermons. A creative teacher will find ways to utilize this valuable, but not overly expensive, modern visual tool. It has advantages over the chalkboard but will not replace it.

Here are some tips for using the overhead projector effectively: (1) Keep the visual simple and uncluttered. (2) Concentrate on one point or one comparison. (3) Write or print in large letters. When typing use speech or primer typewriter. (4) Use color for variety and emphasis.[36]

For effective presentation, follow these tips: (1) Face your class or group. View the visual on the projector stage rather than on the screen. (2) Control class attention between you and the screen with the projector's on/off switch. (3) Turn off the projector when changing visuals to eliminate distraction. (4) Keep room lights on and be sure everyone can see the screen.[37]

Audio aids such as tape recordings and records (disc recordings) are being used more extensively in teaching situations. Bible studies, readings and stories are available on tapes and records for use in the home and the classroom. Moody Correspondence School has a variety of tapes which are correlated with a good number of its courses. The small cassette tape recorder, using small tape cartridges, is especially adaptable for classroom use.

The creative teacher will find many ways to use these convenient tools, and involve the class members as well. Interviews, reports, surveys, etc., can be made on tape. Resource persons can share in this way. Class members can share the class sessions and church services via tape with shut-ins and absentees. A taped incident or conversation may serve as an approach to a lesson or provide stimulus for a lively discussion.

Television may be useful from time to time in the adult program. Parts of a live program being aired during a class session could add interest to a study group. Possibly looking in on other religions or evaluating a religious program would be helpful. Closed-circuit television will serve in a variety of ways in some churches, as well as the video-tape recorder. Some are using it to evaluate teaching. Others record services and share them with shut-ins.

SUMMARY

Pierce advises, "You may be thinking how easy and natural all of these teaching procedures sound, but how hard it will be to use them with spiritual profit!"[38] The adult teacher and leader will need to study new methods and become fully conscious of what each one uniquely contributes. Practice will increase the ease with which he can teach or lead in a variety of stimulating ways. He should evaluate the use and effectiveness of the methods he uses.

Pierce suggests the following questions for evaluating a teaching method or procedure:

1. Did I *prepare* sufficiently in order to use this procedure to its best advantage?
2. Did I *use* this method in class in such a manner that it could work its best for the class?
3. Did the procedure actually *make its unique contribution* to class Bible study?
4. Did the procedure seem to *cause any change* in members toward the achieving of my larger teaching aim or subaim?[39]

Teaching methods are not toys nor gimmicks nor "tools of the trade." They are not ways to manipulate people, devoid of spirituality or concern. Instructional methodology is a most vital part of communication in the teaching-learning process. It is the *how* (the means) in the midst of the *who* (the teacher) and *what* (the content or the Word) and *whom* (the students or group members) in Christian education of adults.

What methods are used and *how* they are used is most vital to effective adult education in the church. The teacher (or leader) is still the key to a successful class (or group), granted the proper spiritual dynamic. Good methods do not replace the teacher or make up for a poor one. But good tools are most important to the skilled workman. "Be diligent to present yourself approved to God as a workman who does not need to be ashamed, handling accurately [and may we add—*presenting properly*] the word of truth" (2 Ti 2:15, NASB).

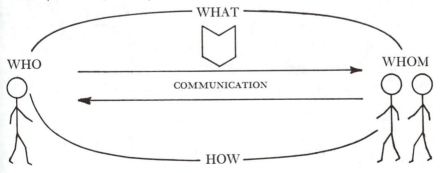

WHAT

WHO

COMMUNICATION

WHOM

HOW

NOTES

1. Gaines S. Dobbins, *Guiding Adults in Bible Study* (Nashville: Convention, 1960), p. 71.
2. Lois E. LeBar, *Education That Is Christian* (Westwood, N.J.: Revell, 1958), pp. 240-41.
3. Ibid., p. 50.
4. J. M. Price, *Jesus the Teacher* (Nashville: Convention, 1946), p. 95.
5. LeBar, p. 244.
6. Sara Little, *Learning Together in the Christian Fellowship* (Richmond, Va.: John Knox, 1956), p. 33.
7. Ibid., pp. 33-34.
8. Roy B. Zuck, *The Holy Spirit in Your Teaching* (Wheaton, Ill.: Scripture Press, 1963), p. 138.
9. Findley B. Edge, *Helping the Teacher* (Nashville: Broadman, 1959), p. 105.
10. Henry Jacobsen, *You Can Teach Adults More Effectively* (Wheaton, Ill.: Scripture Press, 1968), pp. 33-34.
11. Edge, p. 107.
12. Gene A. Getz, "Using Creative Methods," *Youth and the Church*, Roy G. Irving and Roy B. Zuck, eds. (Chicago: Moody, 1968), p. 382.
13. Jacobsen, p. 39.
14. Herman Harrell Horne, *Jesus The Master Teacher* (Grand Rapids: Kregel, 1964), p. 45.
15. *How to Lead Discussions* (Washington, D.C.: Adult Educ. Assn. of the U.S.A., 1955), p. 6.
16. Rice A. Pierce, *Leading Dynamic Bible Study* (Nashville: Broadman, 1969), pp. 67-77.
17. Edge, pp. 86-87.
18. Jacobsen, pp. 37-39.
19. Rachel D. Dubois and Mew Soong Li, *The Art of Group Conversation* (New York: Association, 1963), pp. 19 ff.
20. Harold D. Minor, ed., *Creative Procedures for Adult Groups* (Nashville: Abingdon, 1966), pp. 148-50.
21. Pierce, p. 45.
22. *Webster's Third New International Dictionary* (Springfield, Mass.: Merriam, 1961), p. 266.
23. Edge, p. 139.
24. Paul Bergevin, Dwight Morris and Robert M. Smith, *Adult Education Procedures* (New York: Seabury, 1966), p. 209.
25. Ibid., p. 41.
26. Grace Levit and Helen H. Jennings, *How to Use Role Playing* (Washington, D.C.: Adult Educ. Assn. of the U.S.A., 1956), p. 8. Also see Alan F. Klein, *How to Use Role Playing Effectively* (New York: Association, 1959).
27. Quoted in Minor, p. 152.
28. Pierce, p. 11.
29. Ibid., p. 50.
30. Jacobsen, p. 42. Also see these books on personal Bible study:
Joseph M. Gettys, *How to Enjoy Studying the Bible.* Richmond, Va.: John Knox, 1950; Irving L. Jensen, *Enjoy Your Bible.* Chicago: Moody, 1969; Lloyd M. Perry, and Walden Howard, *How to Study Your Bible.* Westwood, N.J.: Revell, 1958; Robert A. Traina, *Methodical Bible Study.* New York: Ganis & Harris, 1952; Howard F. Vos, *Effective Bible Study.* Grand Rapids: Zondervan, 1956; Oletta Wald, *The Joy of Discovery.* Minneapolis: Bible Banner, 1956.
31. Ray Rozell, *Talks on Sunday School Teaching* (Grand Rapids: Zondervan, 1956), p. 89.
32. For more on the values and limitations of verse-by-verse study and survey Bible study, see Jacobsen, p. 43.
33. Margaret Hess, "Discussion that Works," *Teach*, 9 (Winter, 1968): 10.
34. LeRoy Ford, *A Primer for Teachers and Leaders* (Nashville: Broadman, 1963), pp. 102-5.
35. Gene A. Getz, *Audio-Visuals in the Church* (Chicago: Moody, 1959).
36. *Creative Teaching* (St. Paul: 3M Educ. Press, 1966), p. 4.
37. Ibid., p. 5.

38. Pierce, p. 113.
39. Ibid., p. 117.

FOR FURTHER READING

Bergevin, Paul, and McKinley, John. *Design for Adult Education in the Church.* Greenwich, Conn.: Seabury, 1958.

Bergevin, Paul; Morris, Dwight and Smith, Robert M. *Adult Education Procedures.* Greenwich, Conn.: Seabury, 1966.

Bundy, Clarence E.; Holmes, Glenn E. and Morgan, Barton. *Methods in Adult Education.* Danville, Ill.: Interstate Printers & Publishers, 1963.

Caldwell, Irene Smith. *Adults Learn and Like It.* Anderson, Ind.: Warner, 1955.

———. *Teaching That Makes a Difference.* Anderson, Ind.: Warner, 1962.

Clemmons, Robert S. *Dynamics of Christian Adult Education.* Nashville: Abingdon, 1958.

———. *Young Adults in the Church.* Nashville: Abingdon, 1959.

Dobbins, Gaines S. *Guiding Adults in Bible Study.* Nashville: Convention, 1960.

Edge, Findley B. *Helping the Teacher.* Nashville: Broadman, 1959.

Ford, LeRoy. *A Primer for Teachers and Leaders.* Nashville: Broadman, 1963.

———. *Using the Lecture in Teaching and Training.* Nashville: Broadman, 1968.

Ford, Marjorie M. *Techniques for Better Teaching—A Leader's Guide for an Adult Study Course.* Wheaton, Ill.: Scripture Press, 1962.

Fore, William F., et al. *Communication—Learning for Churchmen.* B. F. Jackson, Jr., ed. Nashville: Abingdon, 1968.

Gangel, Kenneth O. *Understanding Teaching.* Wheaton, Ill.: Evangelical Teacher Training Assn., 1968.

Gresham, Charles R. *Training for Service in the Adult Department.* Cincinnati: Standard, 1966.

Getz, Gene A. *Audio-Visuals in the Church.* Chicago: Moody, 1959.

How to Lead Discussions; How to Teach Adults; Understanding How Groups Work; How to Use Role Playing. (Leadership Pamphlets Nos. 1, 4, 5, 6.) Washington, D.C.: Adult Educ. Assn. of the U.S.A., 1955.

Jacobs, J. Vernon. *Teaching Tools for Sunday Schools and How to Use Them.* Grand Rapids: Zondervan, 1963.

Jacobsen, Henry. *You Can Teach Adults More Effectively.* Wheaton, Ill.: Scripture Press, 1968.

Keys to Effective Teaching. Chicago: Moody Correspondence School, 1964.

Koenig, Robert B. *The Use of the Bible with Adults.* Philadelphia: Christian Educ. Press, 1959.

Knowles, Malcolm S. "A Theory of Christian Adult Education Methodology," *Wider Horizons in Christian Adult Education.* Lawrence C. Little, ed. Pittsburgh: U. Pittsburgh, 1962.

Kuhlen, Raymond G., ed. *Psychological Backgrounds of Adult Education.* Brookline, Mass.: Center for the Study of Liberal Educ. for Adults, 1963.

Leypoldt, Martha M. *40 Ways to Teach in Groups*. Valley Forge, Pa.: Judson, 1967.

Little, Sara. *Learning Together in the Christian Fellowship*. Richmond, Va.: John Knox, 1963.

Loth, Paul E. *Dear Jack, Letters to a New Teacher of Adults*. Wheaton, Ill.: Evangelical Teacher Training Assn., 1969.

McKinley, John. *Creative Methods for Adult Classes*. St. Louis: Bethany, 1960.

Minor, Harold D., ed. *Creative Procedures for Adult Groups*. Nashville: Abingdon, 1966.

Narramore, Clyde M. *Teaching Adults Successfully*. Glendale, Calif.: Gospel Light, 1962.

Pierce, Rice A. *Leading Dynamic Bible Study*. Nashville: Broadman, 1969.

Price, J. M. *Jesus the Teacher*. Nashville: Convention, 1946.

Rozell, Ray. *Talks on Sunday School Teaching*. Grand Rapids: Zondervan, 1956.

Salisbury, Hugh M. and Peabody, Larry D. *A Guide to Effective Bible Teaching*. Grand Rapids: Baker, 1966.

Snyder, Alton G. *Teaching Adults*. Valley Forge, Pa.: Judson, 1959.

Tested Ideas for Teachers of Older Youth and Adults. Elgin, Ill.: Cook, 1965.

Filmstrip: *Out on a Limb*. Wheaton, Ill.: Scripture Press. Color, 33⅓ rpm record, and discussion guide.

10

ADULTS IN THE SUNDAY SCHOOL

Ruth C. Haycock

Sunday school was not always for adults! During the first 110 years of its history this agency limited itself to the instruction of children and youth.

In 1890 and 1893 respectively the Baraca and Philathea Bible class organizations began to promote the establishment of men's and women's Bible classes, first in Syracuse, New York, and then more broadly.[1] Classes generally met in churches at the Sunday school hour. Though they were part of the Sunday schools, they were also independent groups receiving much of their direction from their parent groups, Baraca for men and Philathea for women, and from within each class.

Members of these Bible classes were aggressive in seeking out men or women as participants. Persons of any age or spiritual level were welcomed. Adult Bible study was made popular as they crossed denominational lines and promoted the establishment of classes in many kinds of churches. In many instances the classes grew to a size which made the lecture method the only feasible one, but lectures were generally more popular then than now, and the method seems not to have been a hindrance to the spread of the classes. They emphasized the necessity of class-member responsibility for the work of the class, with the teacher responsible for Bible teaching.

Though early manuals placed considerable stress on class cooperation with the church and Sunday school, as years passed and church activities broadened, classes tended to become more independent in spirit, often choosing curriculum materials, teachers, and missionary projects independently of the church. In time Sunday schools began to exercise a greater measure of control over their adult classes. More recently churches have seen that a Sunday school should be "the church organized for Bible

---

RUTH C. HAYCOCK, Ed.D., is Professor of Christian Education, Baptist Bible Seminary, Clarks Summit, Pa.

study," and have sought to corral their adult Bible classes and establish policy for them as part of their church-sponsored schools. Often the history of considerable independence has resulted in resistance to church control, and relics of the independent spirit remain.

REASONS FOR ADULT BIBLE STUDY

THE SCRIPTURES DEMAND BIBLE STUDY

Many Scripture passages teach the fact that believers are to study the Word. Perhaps the most familiar of these is 2 Timothy 2:15, where Paul instructs Timothy to give diligence that he may be approved by God, "a workman . . . rightly dividing the word of truth." Paul is aware of the fact that it takes diligent study to rightly understand God's Word, and he urges Timothy to engage himself in it. Later (in 2 Ti 3:16-17) Paul points out that because the Scriptures are inspired by God they are profitable for teaching and instruction.

New believers are encouraged to "desire the sincere milk of the word" in order to grow (1 Pe 2:2), and older Christians are reprimanded because they should have studied and learned more in order to be able to teach others (Heb 5:12-14).

In addition to direct statements enjoining the study of the Scriptures, there are others which describe what the Word of God does in lives. It brings great peace (Ps 119:165), cleansing (Ps 119:9), protection from sin (Ps 119:11), direction (Ps 119:105), prosperity (Jos 1:8), blessing (Rev. 1:3) and many other provisions. In each case it must be meditated on, or absorbed, or studied, if it is to be effective. Peter tells us that "all things that pertain unto life and godliness" have been given us through the knowledge of Him (2 Pe 1:3). But this knowledge of Him can come only through the study of the written Word, through the "great and precious promises" (v. 4) which permit us to appropriate His provisions.

Acceptance of the Scriptures as authority for faith and practice has as its essential corollary the study of the Bible by the individual. This fact was recognized by the leaders of the Protestant Reformation when their emphasis on the authority of the Bible and individual responsibility to God led to plans for distributing it and for setting up schools for its study. Both Luther and Calvin developed school systems so believers could be educated in order to study and understand God's Word.

THE PROBLEMS OF LIFE DEMAND BIBLE STUDY

God's thoughts are not man's thoughts. Since this truth applies to every area of life, only mature study of the Word can enable one to see God's answers to his problems.

Where but in Bible study can a husband and wife find all that their relationship should be as a picture of Christ and the church? Without a careful study of the Word, how would a believer know that God's concept of the employer-employee relationship is built on the fact that the Christian employee is actually serving Christ, even while working for another?

Man does not by nature go the second mile, or return good for evil, or turn the other cheek. His very nature is to retaliate. Neither does the unregenerate and untaught man sense that the way to life and freedom is through acknowledging himself a sinner and receiving Christ as his Saviour. Man does not of his own thinking arrive at God's answers to the problems of life. Apart from the study of the Bible, even the Christian is without the answers he needs.

God has established local churches as institutions for accomplishing His purposes in this age. But how are churches to know what to do and how to do it? Only through careful Bible study. The Bereans searched the Scriptures daily to be sure that what they were taught was from God (Ac 17:11). Only this kind of diligent attention to the Word can safeguard local groups of believers from falling into error and apostasy.

Believers who desire to be obedient to God and right in their relationships must make Bible study a regular part of their lives. An adult Sunday school department, meeting simultaneously with classes for other family members, furnishes an unusual opportunity for involving many adults in a study of the Scriptures.

GUIDELINES TO ADULT SUNDAY SCHOOL WORK

To be effective, an adult department or class must follow certain guidelines which grow out of the nature of adults and of the total church program.

THE TEACHER MUST BE ONE WHO HAS THE RESPECT OF THE CLASS IN BIBLE KNOWLEDGE, USE OF TEACHING METHODS, AND PERSONAL LIFE

Some adults continue attending a class when some of these qualities in the teacher are lacking, but those adults seldom invite others and are not enthusiastic about the class.

THE TEACHING MUST BE BIBLE-CENTERED, YET RELEVANT TO MODERN LIFE

It is a well-known fact that many adults who have long attended Bible-believing churches know little of the Bible. There are other agencies or meetings in which to teach nonbiblical subjects; the Sunday school hour should be preserved primarily for the Bible. Adults profit by consecutive studies in specific books of the Bible, surveys, studies of biblical topics and doctrine. Over a period of years there should be coverage of the entire Bible. Some provision should be made for different levels of study;

especially is there need for foundational courses in which new members untaught in the Word may enroll.

THE PROGRAM MUST PROVIDE BOTH INITIAL AND LONG-RANGE SATISFACTIONS
FOR EACH MEMBER

The adult who attends class even once ought to go home with certain favorable impressions: (1) that he was welcome and his attendance appreciated; (2) that he met people who will be his friends if he continues; (3) that he was believed if he said that he wanted to be a member of the class (Where but in Sunday school does an adult have to prove his sincerity by attending three times before he may be a member?); (4) that if he continues to attend he will understand the Bible better and will come to know the Lord.

Even a non-Christian should have these initial satisfactions, but these are not enough for an indefinite period. Long-range results ought to include (1) a personal relationship with Christ, (2) a recognition that one is growing in knowledge and understanding, (3) changes in one's own attitudes and actions, (4) friends who accept a person for what he is, and friends with whom he can have social fellowship, and (5) involvement in the membership and work of the church.

ADULTS MUST THEMSELVES BECOME INVOLVED IN THE STUDIES

Since the best in learning does not occur by mere exposure to or absorption of content, there is no substitute for involving the pupil. The involved adult usually retains more of what has been taught, more readily discusses his new-found learning with his friends, and is more ready for the Holy Spirit's application of the truth to his own life.

This involvement can take place in many ways: discussion, oral review, written quizzes, note-taking, home study, research in reference books, presentation of reports or of part of the lesson, asking questions. The use of visual materials often helps the student review and remember, or understand and apply.°

In order to permit student involvement, adult classes should be small enough so members can know one another and feel at ease in discussion or other participation. Small classes allow a teacher to use a variety of methods and visual materials. Room arrangement, as well as class size, can either encourage or discourage participation. When adults are seated around a table or in a circle or U-shape, more discussion is encouraged because they can see each other. But when adults are seated more formally in rows, they tend merely to listen to the teacher and answer his questions.

°For more on this subject, see chap. 9, "Instructional Methodology for Adults."

ADULTS MUST ALSO ACCEPT RESPONSIBILITY FOR THE WORK OF THE CLASS

The major effort in absentee follow-up, prospect contacts, and planning for activities and special events should be by class members, with the teacher as an adviser. It is in these kinds of activity that social needs are met; but more important, it is through involvement in reaching and winning people that adults grow in the Lord and in their ability to serve Him. As an adult class becomes larger, the students should recognize the need for dividing into two new classes as a privilege that comes with fruitful labor. The class is not an end in itself, and a teacher's responsibility is to teach the Word so that members will grow and eagerly serve the Lord in whatever place is most useful.

EACH CLASS MUST RECOGNIZE ITS RESPONSIBILITY AS PART OF LARGER GROUPS —THE ADULT DEPARTMENT, THE SUNDAY SCHOOL, AND THE CHURCH

Each class should recognize the ministry of other classes and see itself as one part of the total working force of the church.*

METHODS FOR ORGANIZING ADULT DEPARTMENTS

An adult department is generally organized in one of three ways, or in some combination of these ways.

TRADITIONAL METHOD

The oldest or traditional organizational pattern might be described as follows: One or more classes is provided without regard to age or marital status, and sometimes without regard to sex. A person enrolls in a class according to his preference for teacher, subject matter or classmates. A new class is formed whenever a group of sufficient size is able to obtain approval of the Sunday school superintendent or the board of Christian education. Members are permitted to shift their membership from one class to another if they so desire.

Though this plan of organization, or lack of it, has some advantages, in most churches the problems outweigh the values. Perhaps the outstanding arguments for it are (1) the lack of regimentation; (2) the ease of building up a strong class loyalty; and (3) the long-time enrollment within a given class, giving adults a sense of belonging to a stable group.

However, within this pattern of class organization certain problems seem to develop rather consistently: (1) the age range broadens over a period of years, as members invite their friends, until it often encompasses college-level students through senior citizens; (2) several classes compete for the enrollment of a member, thus making the individual's choice difficult; (3) resentment comes when a new class begins because in a sense each new group is a protest against existing ones; (4) classes tend to

*See chap. 11, "Adult Education Beyond the Sunday School."

develop cliquishness and an independent spirit because an inner core of members remains static over the years.

Some of these problems may be prevented by establishing departmental policies with which all classes comply, but in most cases other organizational patterns are more efficient.

GRADED DEPARTMENT

For many years the Southern Baptist Convention, as well as some other groups, has recommended age-graded, single-sex classes, several of which are organized into a department. A church may begin with men's and women's classes for young and older adults, with the break at age thirty-five or forty. As the membership increases, the number of classes is increased, with the age range narrowing, even to a one-year span. In a large church there may be several adult departments, each meeting for a departmental assembly before the Bible-study period. In some churches men and women meet in the same classes.

Following this pattern, many large adult departments have developed. Age grading narrows the span of interests and enables both the teaching and the social organization to fit the daily needs of pupils more effectively. It also provides a Bible-study program in which each person is automatically assigned to a particular class without choice on his part. This very rigidity however can also be a problem when the member's status or needs do not fit the age pattern.

One writer has raised the question, Where but in Sunday school is one assigned to a class on the basis of age? Are not interests, abilities and previous training of more consequence than age, or age and sex? Though it is true that some experiences are more common to one age group than to another, one may well ask whether age-grading which is narrowed down to one year, or even five, is realistic.

The concept of close age-grading probably grows out of experience with children and youth, but in adult life there is greater divergence of activity at a given age than among younger groups. Children are all in school and thus at age ten both boys and girls are likely to engage in approximately the same tasks and the same activities. But adulthood activities may vary from ditch-digging to managerial and professional tasks; the roles of men and women are often decidedly different; some adults are single while most are married; some are unsaved while others have matured spiritually over many years. Though it is true that the experiences of life change throughout the sixty or sixty-five years of adult life, it appears that classification in Sunday school merely by age, or by age and sex, fails somewhat to place adults in groups with similar needs.

THE ELECTIVE METHOD

Since the publication of Mavrodes' article,[2] many Bible-believing churches have experimented with the offering of adult elective courses. The method is simple. Several courses are offered each quarter (or semester), and each member enrolls in the course of his choice. Enrollment in each class continues only for the duration of that course.

Certain advantages are immediately apparent: (1) members choose courses in which they are interested and are therefore likely to be more serious in study than otherwise; (2) over a period of time an adult is taught by several teachers; (3) at the end of a quarter there is opportunity for shifting from one class to another without misunderstanding; (4) teachers may be recruited for a single course and are often willing to serve for a limited period; (5) courses may be repeated as often as needed.

The elective method requires careful planning, however, if it is to function well. In some way social needs must be met, whether by separate fellowship groups, by all-church activities, or by some combination of elective classes and some other organization. People seem to need to belong to a permanent group with which they can have fellowship in non-study activities and in which they can develop closer friendships.

Since class enrollments change each quarter with this method, members should be permanently enrolled in the Sunday school in addition to the short-term membership in a particular class. In addition to absentee follow-up during a course, there must be provision for contacting and registering all adults for each new quarter, lest some be lost at each change.

In a church where adults have had class missionary or service projects, a decision must be made whether each short-term class will have a project, whether projects will be departmental instead of by classes, or whether other adult groups or the church as a whole will be responsible for such activities.

Curriculum planning in an elective program also needs careful thought. This method cannot merely follow a publisher's adult curriculum of quarterly manuals, though some churches consistently use such a series as one elective each quarter. Courses should be chosen several quarters in advance in order to permit teachers to make proper preparation. It is well to require a textbook in most courses so students may be encouraged to study between classes.

Certain basic studies should be offered repeatedly and may be made prerequisite to others. Sequences may be set up with minimum requirements and a certificate given on completion. Such sequences encourage consistent enrollment in a meaningful series of studies. Assistance should be provided in the selection of courses so that a person chooses those for which he is prepared, and so that he receives a well-rounded Bible training. Some churches have three or four electives each quarter—one elective course each time for young Christians or beginning students, one course each quarter for teacher training, and one or two advanced courses on Bible study.

COMBINATION METHODS

It is evident from the preceding pages that no single adult organizational class plan holds all the advantages. Two methods have appeared which combine the values of age-grading with those of elective offerings. The first is more adaptable to a large church; the second does not require as many adults.

Adults may be divided by age into three departments: young, middle and older. Within each department several electives may be offered. In this way a church avoids narrow age divisions and is able to encourage departmentally planned social activities and projects. In a situation where it seems inadvisable to begin electives for all adults, the young adult department may start independently of the others.

A second method, described by Bunger, combines social groups with elective courses.[3] As a new member enrolls in the Sunday school, he becomes part of a social group based on his year of birth. These groups may be for men and women separately, or for mixed groups. The use of year of birth rather than age as the classification basis means that the group is kept homogeneous with respect to age without the necessity of yearly promotion of some members from each group. In other words, the group grows older together. These groups meet for fifteen minutes each Sunday to take attendance and an offering, to make announcements, and to introduce visitors. Elective study classes follow the opening session. In the church described by Bunger, six courses are offered each quarter, two in the New Testament, one in the Old Testament, one doctrinal and two topical. An adult superintendent and an adult council plan and coordinate the program.

A variation of this method has social group meetings confined to one evening a month, with the entire period each Sunday devoted to Bible study. Some churches provide a variety of social, recreational, and special interest groups, with membership optional. Agencies such as a career club (for single young adults), business and professional women, home builders, a bowling league, a mothers' club and a men's brotherhood meet social needs, with the adult Sunday school program designed for Bible study only.

Whatever method is used for setting up classes and departments, it is wise to be sure there is a suitable place in the adult Sunday school program for anyone who may wish to enroll—young or old, married or unmarried, saved or unsaved, taught or untaught, man or woman. Also it is wise to consider what objectives the adult classes are to fulfill. Are they to be social groups as well as Bible classes? Are they to have some missionary responsibility? Or is their purpose to reach out to the community and enroll adults in serious study of the Word of God?

OFFICERS FOR DEPARTMENTS AND CLASSES

The organizational plan determines to a great extent the officers or workers needed in the adult department and classes.

DEPARTMENTAL WORKERS

Every church which has more than two adult classes should have an adult superintendent or coordinator. His work will be similar to that of other departmental superintendents, except that in many cases he will not preside over an opening session. He will (1) see that classes carry out their responsibilities in relation to attendance and follow-up, (2) help recruit regular and substitute teachers (subject to approval of the board of Christian education), (3) work with his teachers and class officers in coordinating and improving the work of the department. Many churches also have an adult departmental secretary to whom adult class secretaries report. This office is particularly important if elective classes are held.

CLASS OFFICERS

The basic officers needed for a typical adult class are president, secretary and group leaders. Whether others are needed depends on the emphasis of the class.

Group leaders are suggested because a number of adult classes have found it helpful to assign each person in the class to one of several groups, headed by a leader. Louis Entzminger, who has been responsible for building up large Sunday schools, comments on these officers as follows:

> The modern . . . Bible class has gone to seed on social life. The primary work . . . is to teach the Word of God and win souls to Christ. When the chief emphasis is put on social life you can rest assured that there will be little spiritual life in the class. . . . An organized class needs, therefore, only the teacher, the president, the secretary, and the necessary number of group leaders. The group leader does everything a teacher does except teach. The group leaders enlist the members of their group in visitation. All new members should be visited [the following] week. A list of prospects should be on hand and absentees and prospects should be visited weekly by the group leader and those in the group he can enlist to help.[4]

When this system is followed, these officers, including the group leaders, can serve as an executive committee for the planning of class activities and assigning of other temporary responsibilities. If the missionary work of the church is done primarily through the Sunday school, each adult class needs a missionary chairman to promote this emphasis.

TEACHERS

Earlier in this chapter it was stated that adult teachers must be those who are respected for their knowledge of the Bible, their efficiency in teaching, and their personal dedication to Christ. They must be willing to study the Word and apply it to their own lives. They must be willing to experiment with various teaching methods and to involve their students. They recognize that responsible adults appreciate the opportunity to participate in meaningful class study.

Adult teachers should be approved by the board of Christian education (or by whatever group approves Sunday school teachers). They should be loyal to the church as well as to the Lord. Most church leaders believe that adult class teachers should be members of the local church so that they are subject to it and so that they exemplify what their students should be. They should be willing to work with the class officers in planning class functions and with other Sunday school staff members in matters pertaining to the entire school.

FEATURES OF THE ADULT CLASS IN ITS CHURCH RELATIONSHIP

It is important that the ministry of the adult Sunday school department be seen in relationship to the ministry of the entire Sunday school and the entire church program.

OBJECTIVES

Adult groups in the Sunday school should implement the church's objectives. Their activities should complement and not compete with those of the church as a whole. Adult classes can help develop leaders for service in other agencies.

An adult Sunday school class should not seek to do for its members what other agencies are set up to do. It is easy in an active church for each group to seek to do everything until none has a distinctive purpose. For example, in a church with missionary groups or an adult training hour, each of these, as well as the Sunday school, should have distinctive objectives that are clearly understood by all concerned.

LOYALTY

Adult classes, and especially their officers, should be loyal to their local church. Officers, or at least the president, should be members of the church. If persons chosen as officers are not in agreement with the church's doctrinal position and its program, that adult class may tend to become a seed-plot of discontent and criticism. A healthy adult class also promotes other agencies and activities of the church. Home visitors should seek to enroll members in other departments of the Sunday school as well as in their own.

CURRICULUM

The adult curriculum, whether uniform throughout the department or more varied, should be in agreement with the church's doctrine. To insure this agreement, course subjects and student textbooks should be approved by the board of Christian education, the adult council, or whatever group establishes the curriculum for other departments.

FINANCES

The financial system of the adult classes should reflect the fact that those classes are considered a part of the Sunday school and church, not separate entities in themselves. If there are class missionary projects, they should be church-approved. Classes should not want to support missions whose policies or doctrines are opposed to what their church teaches. Many church leaders feel that general class offerings should go to the church, through the Sunday school (with the expenses of the Sunday school included as part of the church budget). Some churches omit an offering in the study hour and stress the importance of everyone attending the church worship service and giving one offering at that time.

RECORDS

Since adults control the home and largely determine whether children and teenagers attend Sunday school, the record system used should be one which encourages reaching the family as a whole. One such system is known as the "Living File."[5] It provides for eliminating duplication of visits when several family members are absent, and has been unusually effective in many growing Sunday schools.

Several independent and denominational Sunday school publishing houses publish record systems. Many of them suggest the six-point record system for juniors (or primaries) through adults. This includes a weekly record of each member's attendance, offering, lesson preparation, Bible brought, church attendance, and punctuality. However, other adult classes prefer to record only individual attendance.

ADULT COUNCIL

If a church's adult classes are to operate as a department with some degree of coordination of policies, curriculum and activities, an adult council or committee is a necessity. This group may be made up of the president and teacher of each class, plus the adult departmental superintendent and secretary. In a church using elective courses, the social groups or the various age levels (instead of the actual classes) may be represented in such a council. Some churches broaden the adult council to include representation of all adult agencies. In either case the Sunday school superintendent and director of Christian education or pastor are generally ex officio participants on the adult council. The adult council can assist in setting up standards for class officers, working out curriculum details, planning for departmental activities, and recommending new classes to be formed.

CONCLUSION

Spiritual changes are dependent on the study of God's Word. Sunday school classes can reach more adults and teach more Bible than any other agency. To be effective they must be organized to present the Word at several levels, to get members personally involved in study and to lead adults in taking steps of obedience to the Lord. The details of organization of classes and departments must be constantly evaluated to determine if they are meeting the needs of the adults and accomplishing the church's objectives for the Sunday school.

NOTES

1. Marshall A. Hudson, "The Philathea Bible Class," *The Sunday School Times,* 1914, p. 11.
2. George I. Mavrodes, "Give Adults a Chance to Learn," *Moody Monthly,* 57 (May, 1957): 15-17.
3. Richard P. Bunger, "Six Keys to a Better Adult Department," *Teach,* 8 (Fall, 1966): 13-15.
4. Louis Entzminger, "Is Your Class Organized Efficiently?" *The Lookout* (Oct. 27, 1957). See also Louis Entzminger, "Studies in Sunday School Organization and Administration," *The Sunday School Times,* 1925.
5. Robert F. Richardson, *The Living File System* (Detroit: Living File Systems, 1957).

FOR FURTHER READING

Caldwell, Irene Smith. *Responsible Adults in the Church School Program.* Anderson, Ind.: Warner, 1961.

Dobbins, Gaines S. *Teaching Adults in the Sunday School.* Nashville: Convention, 1936.

Feucht, Oscar E. *Building Better Bible Classes.* St. Louis: Concordia, 1951.

Franklin, Lottie M. *So You Work with Young Adults.* Anderson, Ind.: Warner, 1960.

Gresham, Charles R. *Training for Service in the Adult Department.* Cincinnati: Standard, 1966.

Hanson, Joseph. *Our Church Plans for Adults.* Philadelphia: Judson, 1962.

Hatfield, J. C. "You Can Grade and Promote Adults," *The Sunday School Builder,* 37 (Apr., 1956):49.

Haycock, Ruth. *Survey of Adult Sunday School Work: A Paper Presented to the Commission on Research of the National Sunday School Association,* Oct. 6, 1958. Johnson City, N.Y.: Baptist Bible Seminary, 1958 (mimeographed).

Hudson, Marshall A. "Bible Class Work for Men," *The Development of the Sunday School, 1780-1905, Official Report of the 11th International Sunday School Convention* (Toronto, June 23-27, 1905), pp. 275-78.

———. "The Philathea Bible Class," *The Sunday School Times,* 1914.

Jacobsen, Henry. "Adults in the Sunday School," *Eternity,* 9 (Sept., 1958): 14-17.

———. *The How of Effective Lesson Preparation (for Adults).* Wheaton, Ill.: Scripture Press, 1958.

———. *How to Organize Adults.* Wheaton, Ill.: Scripture Press, 1963.

Leach, Joan. *How to Vitalize Young Adult Classes.* Cincinnati: Standard, 1965.

Leavitt, Guy P. *Building a Successful Men's Bible Class.* Cincinnati: Standard, 1963.

Lentz, Richard E. *Making the Adult Class Vital.* St. Louis: Bethany, 1954.

Mosier, Robert L. "Success of Age-Grading Adults," *Baptist Outlook,* 9 (Spring, 1958):6-8.

Narramore, Clyde M. *Teaching Adults Successfully.* Glendale, Calif.: Gospel Light, 1962.

Pearce, W. C. "The Adult Bible Class Movement," *The Development of the Sunday School, 1780-1905, Official Report of the 11th International Sunday School Convention* (Toronto: June 23-27, 1905), pp. 642-45.

Pentecost, Dorothy H. "We Select Our Own Sunday School Class," *Moody Monthly* 68 (Apr., 1968):51-54.

Phillips, William P. *Adults in the Sunday School.* Nashville: Sunday School Board of the Southern Baptist Convention, 1947.

Potts, Edwin J. "Sunday School Job Descriptions: Adult Department." Wheaton, Ill.: National Sunday School Assn.

Sixty-One Tips on How to Wake Up Your Adult Classes and Get Them Involved. Glendale, Calif.: Gospel Light, 1966.

Smith, G. Rogers. "How Adults Can Grow Up in Sunday School," *Eternity,* 20 (Nov., 1969):28-29.

Snyder, Alton G. *Teaching Adults.* Philadelphia: Judson, 1959.

Talbot, Gordon. "What Sunday Schools Say About Electives," *Moody Monthly,* 64 (Dec., 1963):30-34.

Thompson, Mary. "Trends in Adult Education," *The Baptist Bulletin,* 28 (Feb., 1962):25-27.

Tinley, Frederick G. "Let's Put More School in Sunday School," *Moody Monthly* 54 (Mar., 1954):12 ff.

Towns, Elmer. *The Single Adult and the Church.* Glendale, Calif.: Gospel Light, 1967.

Wells, Ernest R. "An Adult Class for Each Age Year," *The Sunday School Builder*, 37 (Apr., 1956):50.

Zeigler, Earl F. *Christian Education of Adults*. Philadelphia: Westminster, 1958.

Filmstrip: *Out on a Limb*. Wheaton, Ill.: Scripture Press. Color, 33⅓ rpm record, and discussion guide.

Record: *Meet Mr. and Mrs. John* by D. K. Reisinger and C. Leslie Miller. Glendale, Calif.: Gospel Light.

11

ADULT EDUCATION BEYOND THE SUNDAY SCHOOL

Edward D. and Frances F. Simpson

NEEDS DETERMINE OBJECTIVES

"Why didn't you watch where I was going?" Billy queried his dad as he balanced himself after a stumble. Adults might so question the leadership in some churches where a merry-go-round of activity bewilders even the most dedicated workers, or in other churches where dead routine beats out a funeral dirge.

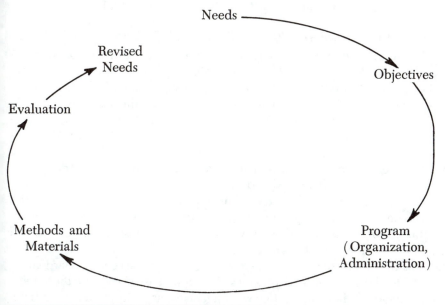

EDWARD D. SIMPSON, Th.D., is Chairman of the Division of Christian Ministries, Fort Wayne Bible College, Fort Wayne, Indiana. FRANCES F. SIMPSON, D.R.E., is Chairman of the Department of Christian Education, Fort Wayne Bible College, Fort Wayne, Indiana.

To provide an effective church program, the leadership of the local church should consider the needs of adults,* and then clearly state its objectives in terms of these needs. Only after objectives have been defined can a meaningful program be organized and administered, and proper materials and methods selected for implementing the program.

The following overall objectives for an adult church program are based on adult needs for evangelism, worship, teaching, training, service (outreach), and fellowship:

1. To challenge individuals to accept Christ as personal Saviour (Jn 3:16)
2. To elicit a spirit of worship toward God and a responsiveness to the direction of the Holy Spirit (Jn 16:13)
3. To provide opportunities for study of the Bible, challenging individuals to be conformed to the image of Christ (1 Co 3:18)
4. To encourage Christians to witness to the unsaved (Mk 1:17)
5. To emphasize complete commitment to Christ's service and provide training in the skills needed for such service (Eph 4:11-16)
6. To offer opportunities for Christian fellowship (Phil 1:9)

A FUNCTIONAL APPROACH CONTRIBUTES BALANCE

The total *task* of the church may be summarized in two words: evangelize and educate. Evangelism is reaching the lost; education is edifying the saved. This chapter is limited to a consideration of the educational program, divided into five *functions* which outline the scope of this task. These functions grow out of the objectives stated above: worship (objective 2), teaching (objective 3), service or outreach (objective 4), training (objective 5), and fellowship (objective 6).

To offer a balanced educational program, churches can provide several *agencies*, each of which majors in one of the above-mentioned functions. For example, the Sunday school majors in teaching, the training hour labels itself as providing training, men's and women's missionary organizations (and other agencies as well) provide opportunities for service, and the church services provide for worship.

Placing the leader of each of these agencies on a central board lends unity to the program and provides a comprehensive view of the educational work of the church. If several agencies major in the teaching function, a leader of one of them may be selected to serve on the board. Drawing the line of authority vertically, so that each leader represents his agency on the board, helps expedite proper administration and control.

*See chaps. 3-6.

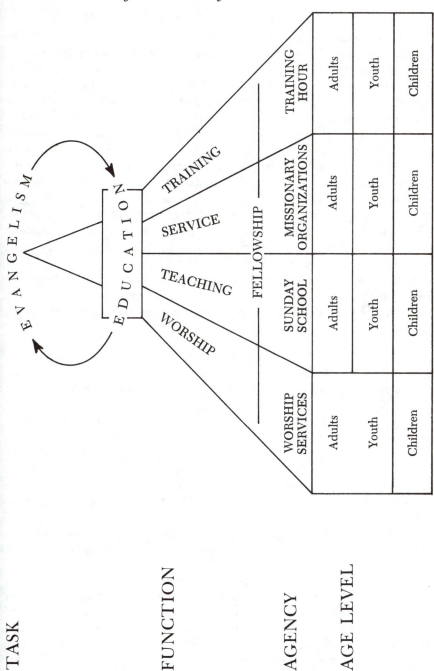

TASK

FUNCTION

AGENCY

AGE LEVEL

ADULT COUNCIL COORDINATES ADULT WORK

An adult council can help coordinate the work of the church with its adults. The leader of adults in each agency would serve on this council. For example, the council would include the superintendent of the adult department of the Sunday school, the leader of the adult training hour, presidents of the men's and women's missionary organizations, possibly the choir director (to represent worship), and perhaps a social chairman.

The purposes of this council may include the following: (1) evaluate the entire program for adults, (2) outline long-range and short-term goals, (3) devise overall plans for a program that will meet the varying interests, needs and abilities of the adults, (4) evaluate curriculum materials and library holdings to eliminate overlapping and overlooking of important emphases, (5) check the calendar to prevent conflicts in scheduling, (6) serve as personnel adviser to involve adults in service without overworking a few, and (7) plan seasonal activities, national family week, adult conferences, institutes and similar activities.

Such a council needs to be flexible, adapting itself to the adult constituency of the church. The structure of an adult program should be like the human body—able to make purposeful movements—rather than like a building, rigid and stationary.

WORSHIP

Worship is central to the nature of the church. Sometimes it has degenerated into mere ritual, but it *can* be an educational medium to the glory of God and the edification of believers.

In getting the mind and heart of the worshiper actively participating, the following ideas have been employed by some pastors: giving reading assignments to prepare for the sermon, printing the sermon outline in the church bulletin, scheduling small-group coffee-discussions of the practical applications of the sermon after the evening service. The goal in each case is to make worship meaningful and the response practical and God-honoring.

More pastors are recognizing the educational value of expository sermons that interpret scriptural passages and apply them to adult needs.

TEACHING

The teaching function of the church is carried on in a large measure by the Sunday school.* However, there are programs for adult groups which supplement the work of this agency, such as church-membership classes, vacation Bible school, home Bible classes, institutes or seminars, parent and teacher meetings, conferences and retreats. In addition, various other

*See chap. 10, "Adults in the Sunday School."

means can be used to minister to individuals, including guided reading, counseling, correspondence courses, etc.

CHURCH MEMBERSHIP CLASSES

Every church needs a plan for making the association of its members meaningful. General characteristics of such a plan might include these factors: (1) minimum of six successive one-hour sessions, (2) enrollment limited to fifteen persons, (3) pastor or church official serving as leader, (4) weekly Bible-reading assignments, (5) permissive atmosphere encouraging discussion, and (6) refreshments. Topics might cover the meaning of salvation, the work of the Holy Spirit, helps for an effective daily devotional life, the history and distinctives of the denomination, significance of the ordinances, the local church program, the importance of stewardship, and opportunities for Christian service. When such a program is required for new members, it makes them feel closer to the church, develops prayer life, provides a challenge to service, and deepens their understanding of and respect for the church.

VACATION BIBLE SCHOOL

Many churches are beginning to realize the values which accrue when classes for adults are included in vacation Bible school. These values include the opportunity for concentrated, short-term Bible study; training for new recruits who may later serve in some other agency of the church; evangelism of neighborhood families who may be willing to attend a short-term study program; involving parents of children who have been attending the club program or some other agency; promoting home Bible classes as a follow-up after vacation Bible school has closed. Possibly one of the most significant values is that of building family unity by providing a time for all members of the family to be involved in this educational endeavor. In this day when family life in America is being seriously threatened, providing an opportunity for the entire group to participate in Bible study builds family solidarity.

Adult VBS classes may be provided for parents, mothers, businessmen (or women), or single adults. The following subjects may be studied: Bible prophecy, Bible book studies, cults, Bible archaeology, missions today, science and the Bible, the spiritual life, doctrinal courses, etc. Some pastors find that VBS is an ideal opportunity for them to teach a class on family living (including family devotions, husband-wife relationships, spiritual responsibilities of parents, sex education for children, discipline in the home, etc.). Some churches have included classes on training for Christian service skills, such as teacher training, leadership development, evangelism, home visitation, song leading, etc.

Certain problems arise when adult classes are included in a vacation

Bible school. One is the need for additional teachers. Therefore, it will be necessary to find these or train them before the school begins. In some churches limited facilities make it difficult to consider an adult section in the VBS. To solve this problem, some churches have the children's VBS program in the mornings and the adult program in the evenings. Others have held morning adult classes in neighborhood homes or school buildings or even community halls. A third problem is that of scheduling the school at a time convenient to those who will be involved. Generally the evening hours are desirable if both men and women are to be reached, but women's classes may be held in the mornings.* However, this decision on timing will need to be made in light of the community the school serves.

HOME BIBLE CLASSES

This small homogeneous, informal group meeting for direct Bible study calls to mind New Testament references such as the house of Justus, Stephanus, Cornelius, Lydia, Nymphas, Titus, Aquila and Priscilla, and Apphia and Archippus. Certain principles are common to most home study groups: limited visible organization, friendly informality, limitation in size, open discussion, for learners not experts, direct but informal study of the Bible as the final authority, and church-relatedness. Some Bible classes in houses are designed for evangelism, whereas others are for Christians. Wollen writes about the benefits to Christians:

> There is an inner longing in the hearts of many of God's children today to share deep and intimate relationships with Christ in all the vicissitudes of daily activity, a longing to share the leading of the Holy Spirit in the more common elements of daily living. Christians are yearning for dialogue, not monologue. In the home Bible class these longings are met and shared. . . . Here, as Christians share together, spiritual reality becomes personal and exciting.[1]

Through home Bible classes many believers have grown in their knowledge of the Bible and their lives have been deepened and enriched spiritually.

Nyquist suggests the following advantages of studying the Bible in a group, especially for Christians:

1. It helps one establish a regular pattern of study.
2. Studying with a group enables one to check his own understanding of the text. It prevents reading between the lines as members check each other on the basis of the passage.
3. Each member of the group contributes his own experiences in life,

---

*According to a nationwide survey, 75.9 percent of the adult vacation Bible school classes were conducted in the evenings. *Research Report on Vacation Bible School Trends* (Glen Ellyn, Ill.: Scripture Press, 1969), p. 22.

with or without Christ, and his insights. The emphasis of the Holy
Spirit to him will increase the impact of the passage for each individual
present.

4. Joint consideration of the application of biblical truth will provide
   each individual with additional areas in which the truth of Scripture
   should affect his daily life. One person may see how a passage ex-
   horting care for other Christians applies to his relationship with his
   college roommate; another may see its impact in his own family; still
   another will share how it applies to his relationship with his employer.

5. Because of the interaction of different individuals in a group study,
   participants have a very natural setting in which to learn to know one
   another and to cultivate an honest, open relationship with others.
   This provides stimulus for prayer and many opportunities to help
   others as one learns of needs which would not ordinarily be shared.

6. A discussion study gives individuals an opportunity to learn to speak
   very naturally and freely of their own understanding of what the
   Scripture says. Participants become accustomed to speaking of their
   relationship to God so that in other settings they will more freely
   share with others what God means to them.

7. After attending and participating in inductive Bible studies for some
   time, the individual spontaneously begins to search the Scriptures for
   what they say before drawing hasty conclusions or making premature
   applications. This habit-pattern will remain throughout life and can
   be one of the most valuable products of such a group experience.[2]

Personnel needs for home Bible classes are simple. The host provides
the home, the host or an assistant serves refreshments, and the teacher
leads. Excellent suggestions on how to begin a Bible study group and
how to lead such a group in the inductive study of the Bible are given
in Nyquist's book.[3] There are many variations of this format, such as
men's groups in a YMCA building, factory or office; meetings of mothers,
parents, students in fraternities, or professional groups; groups meeting
at early morning, noon hour or evenings.*

INSTITUTES AND SEMINARS

In this plan a number of classes are held in the church or in homes
running simultaneously on the same night, covering a spectrum of subjects of interest to adults. Frequently such activities may be on a short-
term basis, continuing for six or eight weeks in the fall or spring.

PARENT-TEACHER MEETINGS

The Bible emphasizes that the spiritual training of children is primarily
the duty of parents (Deu 6:6-8; Eph 6:4), and most churches could serve

*For more details on home Bible classes (especially for evangelism), including
references to other publications on the subject, see chap. 7, "Reaching and Teaching
Adults."

such heads of homes well by establishing programs to train them in this ministry. The purposes of parent-teacher meetings are to help parents provide spiritual training for their children, to explain the church's educational program so that parents may cooperate intelligently, to show how curriculum materials may be used in the home to strengthen the work done in the church, and to provide opportunities for parents and teachers to discuss ways to work as a team for the spiritual growth of the children.

Programs will vary, but they should help parents see how to build spiritual foundations in a child's life as the church and home work in a dual role (not duel role!). Presentations may include lectures, skits, films, etc., followed with discussion. Refreshments may be served while parents visit with teachers.

Many values accrue from such meetings: parental interest increases, new teachers are recruited, curriculum use is enhanced, a sense of partnership develops, some parents are reached for Christ and grow in spiritual commitment, and children are reared more effectively for the glory of God.

CONFERENCES AND RETREATS

Sometimes a conference, like a camp, is an experience in out-of-doors Christian community living. However, a conference differs in emphasis from a camp. A camp provides more opportunity for recreation and emphasizes the "living together" of the community. A conference tends to major in study and discussions.

Various purposes may stimulate the planning of a conference, such as the development of spiritual life, planning for organizational activities, leadership training, missionary challenge, guidance in Christian parenthood and family life. Though most programs vary widely, many conferences for adults include a morning watch, breakfast, instruction period, snack, discussion or another instruction period. Lunch may be followed by a quiet hour, committee meetings, or recreation. After dinner there may be a fun-time, study period, vespers, and/or small prayer groups to close the day.

Adults have voiced the following benefits received from such conferences: experiencing a new dedication to God, receiving mental invigoration, enjoying physical rest or new social contacts, appreciating time with family or friends, learning the Bible better, growing in spiritual strength. From this summary it is obvious that conferences can minister to the whole man—spiritually, mentally, physically and socially.

Generally speaking, a retreat differs from a conference in that it may be more limited in time, more narrow in purpose, and may include a more homogeneous group. For example, some churches have conducted Saturday retreats for young married couples (called Couple Conferences) on marriage and family problems, and other churches have had retreats for their Sunday school teachers and/or other Christian education workers.

EDUCATIONAL MINISTRIES WITH INDIVIDUALS

Teaching on an individual basis must ever be a basic part of the work of the church. In a very small church, in fact, the growth of the work may depend on effectiveness in this area. But in every church, the ministry to individuals must be an essential consideration because each one has different needs and is at a different level in development. Two important ways of providing this assistance are guided reading and personal counseling.

Guided reading can be provided by (1) building a good library of books and periodicals, (2) publicizing library services, (3) making reading material readily available by bookmobiles, reading tables, etc., and (4) recommending materials of pertinent interest.

Counseling is also an educational means because it helps a person learn about himself and, as a result, initiates an educational reaction which enables him to grow. This ministry may be provided by the pastor or by mature Christians who know God and His Word and who can be the channel used by the Holy Spirit to bring healing to the mentally disturbed and solutions to the spiritually confused.

In addition to guided reading and counseling, churches can encourage adults to enroll in *correspondence classes*, attend some extension school or *night classes* of a Christian college, or enroll in a *radio Bible class*.

TRAINING

In considering the church's educational program for its adults, one significant phase is the training program—the purpose of this aspect of the work being that of helping them develop skills for service in the church. One agency which could be used more effectively in this task is the Sunday evening training hour. Too often this program is limited to the youth of the constituency. When planned and administered with the goal of leadership development in view, this can be an excellent training ground for churchmanship for adults. Further discussion of this function in the adult education program is given in another chapter.* Sunday evening (or weekday study groups) can also provide opportunity for adults to receive instruction and/or training in topics of special interest.

SERVICE

The function of service in the total educational program of adults is concerned with an outreach beyond the doors of the church. Visitation

*See chap. 13, "Recruiting and Training Adult Leaders."

and evangelism are two important aspects of service.* In addition, missionary organizations for home and foreign work can be considered a part of this element of outreach.† Since this function is adequately discussed in other parts of this book, it will not be developed further at this point.

FELLOWSHIP

In our fast-paced, technological age, many Christians sense the need for a closer bond of fellowship with other believers, for opportunities to share their problems and joys with a small number of concerned adults. This need accounts for the rise of small groups—for the purpose of Bible study, discussion and prayer—both within and apart from local church programs. More church leaders are recognizing the value of helping adults have opportunity for small-group encounters either at the church building or in homes. As Christians in "cells" of four to ten people have shared their burdens, discussed their problems, and prayed in genuine love for each other's needs, they have come to experience something of true Christian fellowship, the koinonia of the New Testament. Only through a small group Bible study have some adults begun to experience the joy of discovering scriptural truths for themselves. Frequently the observations of one's adult peers on the meaning of a Bible passage and its implications for daily living make more lasting impressions and have more life-changing effects than many sermons and Sunday school lessons.‡

Another form of Christian fellowship can be provided through social and recreational activities. These may be geared to a wide spectrum of people or to more homogeneous groups such as older or single adults.**

SUMMARY

The scope of activities and the age span in adult work is a reminder of the breadth of the task the church faces in its education program with adults. It is imperative that each undershepherd remind himself that although the spirit of inertia may seem mighty, the source of power to overcome this is almighty; although the ability of the apprentice may seem finite, the skill of the Craftsman is infinite; and although the picture the viewer sees is but a sketch, the pattern the Artist has outlined is, and in His time will be, perfect!

NOTES

1. Albert J. Wollen, *How to Conduct Home Bible Classes* (Wheaton, Ill.: Scripture Press, 1969), p. 6.

*See chap. 7, "Reaching and Winning Adults."
†See chap. 14, "Adults in Service Projects."
‡One organization which has promoted small group Bible study through the concept of Growth by Groups is Christian Outreach, Huntingdon Valley, Pennsylvania 19006.
**For more details, see chap. 15, "Church Recreation for Adults."

2. James F. Nyquist, *Leading Bible Discussions* (Chicago: Inter-Varsity, 1967),
   pp. 9-10.
3. Ibid. Also see J. Hills Cotterill and Michael Hews, *Know How to Lead Bible
   Study and Discussion Groups* (London: Scripture Union, 1962).

FOR FURTHER READING

Bergevin, Paul and McKinley, John. *Design for Adult Education in the Church.*
Greenwich, Conn.: Seabury, 1958.

Clark, M. Edward. "Evaluating Your Church's Ministry with Adults," *Baptist
Leader,* 29 (Oct., 1967):8-10.

Clemmons, Robert S. *Dynamics of Christian Adult Education.* New York:
Abingdon Press, 1958.

Ernsberger, David J. *Philosophy of Adult Christian Education.* Philadelphia:
Westminster, 1952.

Feucht, Oscar E., ed. *Helping Families Through the Church.* St. Louis: Concordia, 1957.

———. *Building Better Bible Classes.* St. Louis: Concordia, 1951.

Gray, Robert M. and Moberg, David O. *The Church and the Older Person.*
Grand Rapids: Eerdmans, 1962.

Gresham, Charles. *Training for Service in the Adult Department.* Cincinnati:
Standard, 1966.

Hanson, Joseph John. *Our Church Plans for Adults.* Valley Forge, Pa.: Judson,
1962.

Hugen, M. D. *The Church's Ministry to the Older Unmarried.* Grand Rapids:
Eerdmans, 1960.

Jacobsen, Marion. *Social Programs for Adult Classes.* Wheaton, Ill.: Scripture
Press, 1958.

Jones, Idris W. *Our Church Plans for Adult Education.* Philadelphia: Judson,
1959.

Khoobyar, Helen. *Facing Adult Problems in Christian Education.* Philadelphia:
Westminster, 1963.

Leach, Joan. *How to Vitalize Young Adult Classes.* Cincinnati: Standard, 1965.

Little, Lawrence C., ed. *The Future Course of Christian Adult Education.*
Pittsburgh: U. Pittsburgh, 1958.

Nelson, C. Ellis. "Criteria for Judging the Quality of Christian Education for
Adults," *Wider Horizons in Christian Adult Education.* Lawrence C. Little,
ed. Pittsburgh: U. Pittsburgh, 1962.

Raines, Robert. *New Life in the Church.* New York: Harper & Row, 1961.

Saffen, Wayne. *Young Married Couples in the Church.* St. Louis: Concordia,
1963.

Taylor, Marvin J., ed. *Religious Education: A Comprehensive Survey.* New
York: Abingdon, 1960.

Zeigler, Earl F. *Christian Education of Adults.* Philadelphia: Westminster,
1963.

Zuck, Roy B. *The Holy Spirit in Your Teaching.* Wheaton, Ill.: Scripture Press,
1963.

12

MEN'S AND WOMEN'S ORGANIZATIONS IN THE CHURCH

Lloyd D. Mattson

The time has come for a new appraisal of Christian education among adults. This will demand creativity and courage because many adults are notoriously resistant to change. Yet change must come if the church is to meet the challenges of this generation.

The challenges come from many directions. Not the least are the attacks of critics—friend and foe—who despair of the church's capacity to adjust to the world in revolution. This despair does not grow out of a lack of sympathy for the church, but from the church's historical intransigence.

Orthodox churches seem especially adverse to renewal. They have been accused of always being a generation behind. Some within the church accept this as a compliment, equating change with spiritual instability. There seems to be a subtle transferral of loyalty from the content of the gospel to its forms and methodology. Hence, when Sabbath schools were first proposed in England about two hundred years ago, dismay spread among the orthodox. Think of teaching street urchins on the holy day!

Typical of opinions expressed by contemporary writers who believe in the church is this one by Stagg:

> That the church needs to change the direction of its life from self-centered and cautious piety to costly love for the world to which it has been sent is obvious to growing numbers of informed Christians. The imperative confronting the church is to reverse the direction of its life; to be converted toward the world that it might there join Christ in his liberating work; to be transformed from the unholy worldliness of caution, fear, and retreat to the holy worldliness of boldness, courage, and sacrificial love for all sorts and conditions of men.[1]

LLOYD D. MATTSON, B.D., is Executive Secretary, Board of Men's Work, Baptist General Conference, Chicago.

Daniel D. Walker, a Methodist clergyman, states,

> There is a revolution in the church, and all of us should be aware of it. Creeds are crumbling and ecclesiastical systems are falling apart. What, then, is the layman to do? He must react to the revolution by becoming a revolutionist! If reform is in order, then he, like Luther, should be a reformer. If the organized church is too stuffy and tradition-bound to appeal to modern man, then like Wesley, the Christian layman should lead the exodus and head for the streets and open fields. If the temple needs cleansing, the churchman's place is beside the Christ who upset tables of tradition and drove out those who made the church indistinguishable from the society around it.[2]

These are discomforting ideas to those who defend the status quo, and the tendency will be to explore the theology of the writers rather than examine the validity of what they say. Somewhere near the heart of every call for change you will find a common voice: the voice of the layman who feels inadequate, uninvolved and uneasy as he looks out on a world in trouble.

A confirmation of this widespread sense of need among laymen is the response to writings that speak to this need. In 1967 Keith Miller wrote his spiritual biography *The Taste of New Wine.*[3] He did not write in the comfortable jargon of orthodoxy. He wrote out of despairing experience and he apparently touched a common nerve. More than 200,000 bought the book. Miller spoke for churchmen searching for vitality in Christian experience.

Another widely read author who speaks to the layman's need is Bruce Larson, executive director of Faith at Work and editor of a magazine bearing the same name. He writes, "Today every phase of man's life and endeavor is changing at an incomprehensible rate. Science, industry, world politics, social patterns, space exploration, communications, transportation, education, and many other areas are going through revolution. But nothing is more exciting than what is happening in the Christian Church in our time. God is raising up a lay ministry which is causing an upheaval in the church comparable to the Copernican revolution (when scientists discovered that the earth revolved around the sun, and not vice versa)."[4]

Larson's statement is of particular significance in that he suggests not only a need for change, but that, for many, change has come. The small-group movement associated with Faith at Work reports dramatic success in lifting Christian adults to new plateaus of spiritual vitality.

How can this vitality be gained by the church? What changes in concept and performance must be achieved in adult Christian education to bring about spiritual renewal, both for the church and its adults? Where do men's and women's organizations belong? The following pages suggest some answers to these questions.*

PROBLEMS IN ADULT CHRISTIAN EDUCATION

It must be acknowledged that Christian education has frequently been preoccupied with children and youth. In fact, in many minds youth work and Christian education are synonymous. However, the need for spiritual growth does not end when a person reaches twenty-five. It might be argued that in some respects the adult years are the most important, not only because there are more adult years than youth years, but because youth problems must ultimately be met by adults.

A major barrier to an effective adult Christian education program is organizational autonomy. A church may sponsor a men's group, women's missionary society, young adult fellowship, senior citizen's group, and several adult Sunday school classes. But each group exists largely to itself, with officers, calendar, and sometimes a budget of its own. Serious attention to distinctives or program correlation is uncommon, and a sense of competition is common.

Men's and women's organizations particularly tend toward independence. Probably no organizations of the church have received so little guidance by church leadership. Perhaps this is because men's and women's groups came into being through a slow historical process which differs from other organizations.

HISTORICAL HIGHLIGHTS IN MEN'S AND WOMEN'S WORK

No study of American church history can ignore the Ladies' Aid. In many frontier churches, and later in rural and small-town churches, the Aid was a very prominent force. Few male leaders, ordained or otherwise, were bold enough to spurn the Aid. It is unfortunate that the multitude of good deeds wrought by women has been overshadowed in legend by negative experiences.

Many reasons are put forth to account for the vigor of women's work. Social hunger created by the isolation of rural women made monthly meetings a welcome respite. Latent leadership talent among women found expression in the women's group. Certainly there were abundant needs, some of them brought on through masculine neglect, to which the Christian conscience of women could rally.

It is surely to the shame of the church at large and to men in particular that missionary concern has been traditionally identified with women's groups. In time, the broader objectives of the Ladies' Aid narrowed to

*For more on work among adult laymen, see chap. 16, "Adult Lay Movements and the Local Church."

the needs of missionaries, giving rise to the change in name. The women's missionary society became the ubiquitous standard-bearer for the Christian mission to the world.

The history of men's work is far less dramatic. For the most part it is the sad record of noble ideals and dull performance. None would debate the church's need for a vital male laity, but the brotherhoods that have achieved vitality have been rare.

Something of a guilt complex arose among men. If the women could muster such a force, why not the men? Were the men of inferior spiritual stuff? As a result of these questions, a variety of devices were tried to attract men. Under creative leadership some successes can be noted, but many men's groups could be described as a small gathering of discouraged men lamenting the absence of so many.

Whatever the reasons for the success of the women's groups and the failure of the men's groups, the contemporary church must reckon with new circumstances as it plans its ministry to people. Frontier and rural America are gone, and the stable population has gone with it. People are on the move. Urban and suburban America has generated forces that have changed the outlook of all people.

Leaders of today's women's groups continue a concern for missions, but their objectives extend to the whole world a woman encounters. The men's work that can hope for success today must be more than a drab monthly meeting with its warmed-over sermonette and cliché lunch.

It is proper to ask, in the light of social changes, if the need remains for separate men's and women's organizations. That question must be discussed in terms of the needs of people. Perhaps in the anxiety to perpetuate its forms of yesterday, the real purpose of the church has slipped from view.

The church is an instrument designed by God to serve the needs of people. The church and its forms are not ends in themselves, to be defended or perpetuated. The church *is* people; it exists for people. It would appear that this basic truth is sometimes forgotten.

The church program should be designed to lead people toward spiritual maturity so that they will fulfill the Great Commission both individually and collectively as church participants. How can men's or women's organizations contribute toward this end?

THE METHOD OF THE MASTER

It must be assumed that Jesus used the best methods in His ministry. He brought unlimited wisdom to the task. Every option lay before Him. No one could feel more keenly the agony of mankind, the brevity of time, the inadequacy of men, or the pressure of the multitudes. He chose to organize a small band of men. He spent most of His time with them, and directed most of His leadership energy toward equipping them to carry out His work.

It would be an error to think that Jesus selected the twelve merely to *use* them. There are many evidences of His love for each one, apart from any utilitarian service they might perform. The twelve had a unique call. Not every follower of Jesus was permitted to join the select band, though some requested permission. The point to be made is this: apparently there were primary values to be gained by working with an all-male group, values not to be found in a mixed group.

There was a small company of women also, knit together by a common love for Jesus. And the writer of Acts records a ladies' prayer group that met by a river (Ac 16:13).

It might be argued that social circumstances dictated the separation into groups of men and women. Yet Jesus was not adverse to changing social customs when His greater wisdom dictated the need. Throughout history one can trace the instinctive bond that knits together a group of men who have a common purpose. Can the absence of *men's* fellowships explain at least in part the evident femininity of the church?

Jesus' method, then, was *discipling*. Rather than beaming His message at random to the masses, He zeroed in on a small band of men. These, in turn, He sent out to do His work. The discipling principle must be present in a men's or women's work that would follow the Master's plan.

In the introduction to a collection of essays, D. Elton Trueblood states,

> Many of us are dedicated, but we do not know what to do to implement our dedication. We believe, with all our hearts, that Jesus Christ provides a firm center for our lives, but we do not know how to be His contemporary apostles. We realize that we are so badly outnumbered that any effort which we can make is likely to seem inconsequential. We want to raise our voices, but when we do they sound like voices crying in the wilderness. There is one tremendous answer to this problem: *we must help one another!*[5]

This is the strength of Christian camaraderie, and there is a mysterious quality found in the fellowship of men with men, and women with women, that does not exist in a mixed company. The force that holds the group to its purpose is *leadership*. This is always the case, regardless of the common cause.

LEADERSHIP FOR MEN'S AND WOMEN'S GROUPS

If adult Christian education is to participate in the overall renewal needed by the church, then a concern for *leadership* must be prominent. Programs do not build organizations, nor do constitutions or organizational charts. People are changed by people. Cultivating leadership is a major function of the church through Christian education.

A leader can serve effectively only when his objectives are clear. Here is where autonomy must yield to correlation in planning. The question was raised as to the need for men's and women's organizations in today's church. The answer was declared to lie in the needs of the people. The method Jesus employed was brought forth as a support for the small-group, one-sex approach to discipling. The apparently instinctive formation of all-men and all-women groups was referred to. Yet there is another, perhaps conclusive, line of reasoning. This relates to *distinctive goals.* And goals arise out of needs.

Some of the needs all Christians share are these: Bible study, prayer, worship, fellowship, service opportunities, training for service, missionary education, opportunities to give, motivation for spiritual growth. The church builds its program around these common needs.

Problems arise when each church organization attempts to become all things to all people. On the surface it would appear that a strong men's or women's program could be constructed by selecting at random three or four of these fundamental needs and striving to meet them.

Leadership comes into play when the church, out of concern for the spiritual growth of its people, views Christian education as an entity composed of parts, each with its assigned distinctives. This is quite different from viewing Christian education as an aggregate of several independent agencies, which may or may not report periodically to the church.

The logical distinctive of the Sunday school is Bible study. Many educators feel that there is little to defend the tradition for separate men's and women's Bible classes in Sunday school, or even classes divided by age. Many feel that course content should be given first consideration, with a variety of studies at various achievement levels.*

Prayer and worship opportunities form the core of the general church calendar. Certainly every church organizational meeting will include elements of worship and prayer. But of course each organization in the church will have specific prayer needs.

There are family fellowship activities and adult fellowship programs that relate to the whole church body. Some service opportunities flow out of the church at large. Training courses may be offered periodically for every church member. And surely missionary education cannot be viewed as the province of any one organization.

Giving is basic to Christian growth, and major financial matters belong to the overall church budget, not to separate organizations. Tithing is a

*For a detailed discussion on grouping adults by sex, age or content, see chap. 7, "Adults in the Sunday School."

personal and family matter, a significant part of one's motivation for spiritual growth.

What then remains for men's and women's groups? The following are some emphases that stem from adult needs:

INVOLVEMENT IN EVANGELISM

Planning should be deliberate, programs purposeful, to bring lost men to a personal confrontation with the gospel. Men have a greater opportunity to gain a sympathetic hearing from men than women or the church at large. Evangelistic men's activities aimed at reaching unchurched men whose homes are touched by the church through its youth program forms a worthy distinctive.

These activities may take many forms; frequently they will be informal, away from the church, and designed to create friendships. But the objective is clear—to win men to Christ.

The same objective belongs to women's groups. Specific evangelism, then, can be viewed as a distinctive for men's and women's groups.

LEADERSHIP FOR CHILDREN'S GROUPS

A second distinctive growing out of a need not met by any other church organization is represented by boys and girls. The growth of boys and girls clubs as Christian education agencies has provided the church with one of its greatest contemporary evangelistic and training opportunities. This calls for leadership.

Perhaps one of the most serious areas of neglect for which the modern church must accept guilt lies in the failure of Christian men to become heroes to boys. The church has fared somewhat better in retaining girls. But its record with boys is dismal. A major assigned distinctive for the church men's group is *the boys of the church*. For example, Christian Service Brigade, one of the interchurch Christian ministries for boys, offers a Brigademen program (for men).

The dominant influence in the life of an adolescent boy is another boy. But the next most important influence is a man. When Christian men accept the challenge of relating to boys and their interests, boys respond. They do not always respond enthusiastically to the typical adult-oriented program of the church, even though portions are declared to be for youth.

The impact of godly women on girls is equally vital. Giving leadership to boys and girls provides a clear distinctive for men's and women's groups.

While every church must provide leadership for family life and guard against destroying the family through the sheer weight of its calendar, both men and women admit to needs peculiar to their sex. A man's role as father and husband may create tensions. A men's group, under wise leadership, provides a forum for discussing such needs.

SERVICE PROJECTS

There are service projects best suited to men or women which may be assigned to these groups.* This will vary from church to church, but opportunities may be found for ministering in jails, detention homes, convalescent homes, missions, etc. Frequently a mixed group would be inappropriate.

Repair and maintenance of church or Bible-camp properties might be assigned to a men's group under the guidance of trustees. Women might have specific related duties as well. The fellowship of a work day has spiritual overtones of great significance.

Men's and women's groups might serve as a base for stimulating interest in good reading. Many Christian adults rarely read a book, even though books are more readily available than ever before. A serious effort with aggressive leadership can create reading habits that will vastly enrich the spiritual lives of dormant readers.

The goal of a men's program is to build men, not programs. The women's program is primarily concerned with building women. The details of organization and calendar should always be subordinate to that greater purpose.

BUILDING THE MEN'S AND WOMEN'S WORK CALENDAR

Too frequently, tradition is the dominant influence in program building. The day of the week, the topic of the month, the order of service, and the decor of the refreshment table are predetermined. If tradition does not fulfill assigned goals, then change should be guardedly instituted.

Little has been written, other than denominational handbooks, about either the philosophy or procedure for men's and women's organizations. A great deal has been written, and much recently, about the laity, but the term *laymen* refers not to sex but to all nonclergy. Men's groups in particular have not attracted the interest of writers.

One tradition that dies hard is the *monthly* meeting. It is felt that an organization that does not meet at least once a month is unworthy. A better rule of thumb would seem to be this: meet only as often as necessary to fulfill assigned objectives. The fact that the third Thursday is rolling around again is a poor excuse to plan a meeting. Of course this is not to suggest total irregularity in planning, but it is to suggest that each meeting should have a purpose more noble than the fact that "it is time again to meet."

*See chap. 14, "Adults in Service Projects."

The chief tool in program building is the church calendar. Since men's and women's work is one segment of a total ministry, every effort should be made to encourage members to gain the benefits of the total church program.

Again, women's groups tend to have traditions that dictate the calendar. Men's group leaders are usually desperate for ideas. Once the distinctive goals for the organization are determined, then the program committee is prepared to determine how these goals can best be met through correlated programming.

The following monthly activities are suggested as "idea starters" for a men's group. Adaptations can be made consistent with women's work goals.

January—Men's prayer breakfast, correlated with the church's annual prayer week observance.

February—Traditional boys' club month. Father-son dinner, or occasionally a father-daughter dinner.

March—Sweetheart dinner, with wives as guests of the men.

April—Men's missionary breakfast, with missionary guest who is participating in the all-church missionary conference.

May—Friendship evangelism outing—a recreational activity with unchurched men as guests.

June—Student recognition—men host graduating students, perhaps with other youths as guests. A cruise or outing.

July-August—Vacation months. Men and boys' campout, unchurched fathers of church boys invited.

September—Workday or men's retreat at Bible camp.

October—Men's prayer breakfast with guest evangelist, correlated with church evangelism campaign.

November—Community-interest month. Court or law enforcement official to discuss needs of community. Unchurched men invited.

December—A month usually overcrowded with activity. No meeting.

On examination of this suggested program some will protest that several activities include boys, young people, and even *women*. This is perfectly consistent with the assigned distinctives: a man's role as husband, father, and leader of boys. This is consistent too with the needed conservation of time. Correlation of activities spares the loyal church member from exhaustion while providing a measure of family-centered activity. To attempt monthly *men's* meeting, plus these other important activities, would demand many more evenings. And there is no law that demands monthly meetings.

ORGANIZATIONAL RELATIONSHIPS OF MEN'S AND WOMEN'S GROUPS

Men's and women's organizations form a part of the adult division of the church's Christian education ministry. They are responsible to the church, and, in turn, they are the responsibility of the church. Men's work is the church at work for God among men, meeting the needs peculiar to a man not being met through other church agencies.

The organization should be kept as simple as possible to accomplish its goals. Complex constitutions, membership procedures, budgets, and other traditional paraphernalia should be kept to the essential minimum. The church is the basic organization.

Involve as many reliable people as possible, and provide clear guidance as to their responsibilities. Grant authority to act without referral to a chain of committees.

The leaders of men's and women's organizations should be looked on as church officers. They should have the same resources as other leaders, the same dignity of office, and the same sense of responsibility to the church as a whole. The same high spiritual standards required for major church leaders should pertain to officers of men's and women's groups.

MEN'S AND WOMEN'S GROUPS AND RENEWAL

Adult organizations provide the church's best opportunity for discipling leaders to share the spirit of renewal described earlier in this chapter. Traditional meeting formats should be ruthlessly abandoned, providing for simple sharing by as many as possible.

This does not eliminate the need for careful planning; in fact, the need is strengthened. Topics difficult to treat through sermons may be introduced for discussion among the men or women. The helping-one-another concept may be explored in prayer-and-share sessions.

Will activities of this nature eliminate the less spiritually minded? Sometimes. But more often they will attract them. Nothing so repels the indifferent Christian as just another sermon or a rerun of an old film.

Christians may find opportunity to become acquainted, to learn the weaknesses and strengths of their fellow church members. They may find the courage to ask a question that is troubling many. They may return to their homes and to the larger church fellowship more confident in their spiritual lives for having met with a group of men or women.

Pastors may find a new rapport with their laymen, and the layman may come to understand better the burden his pastor bears. Women may gain new insights into the problems of the lady who lives in the parsonage. Leaders of men's and women's groups may find their work an exciting, rewarding spiritual adventure.

There was a men's group, a select company of ordinary individuals, led by a Carpenter. All of them were laymen. The Carpenter was no ordinary man; He was the God of heaven become flesh. He knew the needs of men, and how best to reach a world with His message.

It was He who organized a men's group. It is hard to imagine a better way.

NOTES

1. Paul L. Stagg, *The Unconverted Church* (Valley Forge, Pa.: Judson, 1967), p. 11.
2. Daniel D. Walker, *Enemy in the Pew?* (New York: Harper & Row, 1967), pp. 1-3.
3. Keith Miller, *The Taste of New Wine* (Waco, Tex.: Word, 1967).
4. Bruce Larson, *Setting Men Free* (Grand Rapids: Zondervan, 1967), p. 11.
5. D. Elton Trueblood, *Groups That Work: The Missing Ingredient* (Grand Rapids: Zondervan, 1967), p. 7.

FOR FURTHER READING

Anderson, Clifford V. *Worthy of the Calling.* Chicago: Harvest, 1968.

Ayres, Francis O. *The Ministry of the Laity.* Philadelphia: Westminster, 1962.

Chafin, Kenneth. *Help! I'm a Layman.* Waco, Tex.: Word, 1966.

Hakes, J. Edward, ed. *An Introduction to Evangelical Christian Education.* Chicago: Moody, 1964.

Halverson, Richard C. *Man to Man.* Grand Rapids: Zondervan, 1961.

Hill, Keith J. "Men in the Sunday School," *The Standard*, 59 (June 2, 1969): 25-26.

Howe, Reuel L. *The Creative Years.* Greenwich, Conn.: Seabury, 1964.

Jones, Richard M. *The Man for All Men.* Valley Forge, Pa.: Judson, 1965.

Larson, Bruce. *Dare to Live Now.* Grand Rapids: Zondervan, 1965.

———. *Living on the Growing Edge.* Grand Rapids: Zondervan, 1968.

———. *Setting Men Free.* Grand Rapids: Zondervan, 1967.

Mattson, Lloyd D. "Where Are the Men of the Church?" *Moody Monthly*, 67 (July-Aug., 1967): 43-44, 51-52.

Miller, Keith. *A Second Touch.* Waco, Tex.: Word, 1967.

———. *The Taste of New Wine.* Waco, Tex.: Word, 1965.

Sanders, Oswald J. *Spiritual Leadership.* Chicago: Moody, 1967.

Segley, Franklin M. *The Christian Layman.* Nashville: Broadman, 1964.

Shoemaker, Sam. *Extraordinary Living for Ordinary Men.* Grand Rapids: Zondervan, 1965.

Tournier, Paul. *The Meaning of Persons.* New York: Harper & Row, 1967.

Trueblood, Elton. *The Company of the Committed.* New York: Harper & Row, 1961.

Turner, Lee C. *Continuous Evangelism in the Local Church.* Des Plaines, Ill.: Regular Baptist, 1968.

Valentine, Foy. *The Cross in the Marketplace.* Waco, Tex.: Word, 1966.

Walker, Daniel D. *Enemy in the Pew?* New York: Harper & Row, 1967.

13

RECRUITING AND TRAINING ADULT LEADERS

Paul E. Loth

One of the greatest unresolved problems in the local church is the lack of prepared leaders. The need for lay leadership is further accentuated by the comparative dearth of vocational Christian workers. People's concerns have been so sharpened by the pressures of space-age living that already overburdened pastors can seldom do all they desire in serving their people. Personal counseling and interchurch involvements further restrict a pastor's time. If he is to accomplish his task he must multiply his outreach by lay leadership. He must train others to serve.

> Before the church can be effective, it must have trained teachers and officers to minister the Word of God to those who will respond. This is a realistic approach. Earnest evangelistic efforts should include, and in most cases be preceded by, a serious program to enlist and train every Christian to assume his teaching responsibility.[1]

While the entire church program often is dependent on lay leadership, the church's educational program particularly reveals this need. Broader concepts of the church's place in education for Christian living are emerging, calling for an expanded program. However, well-trained educational directors frequently are hampered in accomplishing this ministry by the lack of lay leaders. Furthermore, many churches today find themselves with good facilities in which to function, well-prepared materials to use, and talented overall supervision, but inadequate personnel to carry out the needed educational program.

The necessity of training lay leadership is not a discovery of this generation. It is the fulfillment of a basic program of God. To those specially endowed with spiritual gifts, He committed the responsibility of minister-

---

PAUL E. LOTH, Ed.D., is President, Evangelical Teacher Training Association, Wheaton, Illinois.

ing to others in leadership. "Go . . . and teach," He commanded (Mt 28:19). It is interesting to notice Paul's letter to Timothy, who was giving his entire time to serving the Lord. Paul encouraged him to multiply his witness for Christ by teaching others to teach. He urged Timothy to teacher-training activity when he wrote, "And the things that thou hast heard of me among many witnesses, the same commit thou to faithful men, who shall be able to teach others also" (2 Ti 2:2). Lois LeBar well emphasizes the benefits of obedience to this scriptural admonition:

> Our talent or ability is God's gift to us; the skillful use of that ability is our gift to Him. We'll never know the thrill of fulfilling the purpose for which we were born until we have developed our gift.[2]

To every believer is given the endowment of the Spirit of God, and from every believer is required the utilization of his spiritual gift or ability. Those capable of leadership must be recruited and trained to accomplish that which God has for them to do.

RECRUITING AND ENLISTING

The startling discovery of those who search for leaders usually is that within the church itself lies the potential for all the leadership a church needs. Learning of this potential can be accomplished in a number of ways. Many pastors use an annual talent-search sheet on which members can indicate past experiences, present interests and training desires.

A simple way to prepare a talent-search sheet is to list all places of service within a church program. These can be grouped by agencies of service. Before each position should be a place to check past service or to indicate years of experience. After each position there should be both a place to check interest and a place to indicate need for training. Some churches have found new Sunday school families a very profitable source of potential leadership. Personal interviews with those in church-membership preparation classes also reveal willing helpers capable of serving the Lord.

Potentiality is not enough, however. Those capable of leadership must be motivated to serve. As an individual comes face to face with Christ, he must also face the purposes and goals of Christ for his life. Often the believer's attitude is conditioned by the apparent value which the church itself places on service. An annual service of dedication, a well-spoken word of appreciation, recognition through a published list of those in lay leadership, or a banquet encourages those considering service to have high esteem for the work of the Lord.

Any service involves sacrifice. Along with public appeal from the pulpit there must be expression of the rewards of service for Christ and the happy result of witnessing for Him. The desire of true believers should be to please the Lord. They can be encouraged in fulfilling this desire by the attitude of others toward church ministry and service.

> If the attitude of administrators can be positive so that it is not "how can I best recruit and retain workers for this organization and make my load a little lighter?" but, instead, "how can we, as the Body of Christ, work most effectively in the cause of Christ, in the winning of individuals to a personal commitment to Jesus Christ?" then a church with this purpose and concern will display the kind of dynamic growth which is so urgently needed today.[3]

While some volunteer, others are hesitant to offer their services unless they are confident that they are fully needed. There may be strong attraction elsewhere. Worthwhile cultural and service organizations may compete with the church for capable leadership. As a result, the innate desire of Christians to minister, frequently finds expression outside the church. The opportunity for and challenge to church activity must clearly be presented.

Church needs can be made known by a church personnel committee (or individual) which continually works toward providing the church with the right leadership. This committee is able to see the entire personnel needs of the church and thus wisely assign the available talent. Such a committee can help avoid competition among church organizations for leadership. It is somewhat difficult for potential leaders to say no to an invitation which has been born of prayerful consideration and which is the consensus of an active church committee.

MOTIVATING AND ENLISTING TALENT	
Do	Don't
1. Use a talent-search sheet. 2. Have a church personnel committee. 3. Personally invite people to serve Christ. 4. Provide a job description. 5. Give opportunity for preliminary experience. 6. Recognize achievement.	1. Depend on general knowledge about people. 2. Have competition among church organizations for leadership. 3. Ask people to serve as a personal favor. 4. Assume people know what ministry is expected. 5. Be hasty in selecting leaders. 6. Criticize those who serve.

An invitation to serve in the church should be conveyed through a personal contact, preferably a visit.

There is no substitute for a personal interview. This is the most effective means of enlisting workers in any capacity. The best place to hold this conference is in the home. It is impossible to secure the desired results by telephone or casual conversation.[4]

A job description should be presented during the visit so that the prospective worker fully understands what his responsibility will be. Commitment is considerably easier to secure when the individual knows he is needed and what is expected of him.

Open doors of opportunity enlighten an individual to the possibility of contributing to the advancement of the cause of Christ. Parents who are involved in committees for social activities in the educational program become attached to the children with whom they work, and they appreciate their needs. In desiring the best for their own child, they desire also to see that his peers receive the same treatment. Others learn of the service potential of teaching by becoming an assistant teacher, or by caring for records or assisting in handwork. The youth counselor with a small group becomes experienced and enabled to lead a larger group. The person who just "goes along" finds the transition easy to "assisting" and then to "leadership itself."

Without recruitment and enlistment the best programs of leadership preparation often fail. Proper recruitment and enlistment challenge people with the opportunity, and encourage them in their dedication, but they also help direct them to the preparation they need to successfully fill that place to which God has called them.[5]

WAYS OF LEADERSHIP PREPARATION

Leadership preparation can be either a simplified or comprehensive program. Each church must discover for itself what is best. The director of leadership education has the responsibility of guiding this search for the best program and formulating specific plans for it. Before beginning a church training program, all the possible ways should be considered and selection made of those methods adaptable to the particular church situation.

GROUP METHODS

Group programs of training are imperative if there is to be the broadest utilization of training talent. Advantages and disadvantages of these various methods are presented on the charts on pages 184-185. All have a common characteristic. They utilize specialists and endeavor to learn from those who are trained and experienced. It should be remembered, however, that the contribution of the one in charge of the program is not the complete benefit. Participants should have opportunity to become involved through small discussion groups and reports. Another common characteristic of a successful group program of training is the careful utilization of varied teaching aids. Those in training learn how to use audio-visual materials properly as they experience a satisfying learning experience in a session in which visual materials are utilized effectively.

Group programs of training also must be directed toward applying what has been learned. Impersonalized presentation of factual content because of the size of a large group is ineffectual in preparing leaders. Each lesson to be learned should be immediately followed by the student's application of truths presented. Frequently a program of learning correlated with simultaneous service will challenge the student to search for answers to his problems and also provide opportunity for guided experimentation.

INDIVIDUALIZED TRAINING

Carefully organized, individualized training can be utilized equally well in either a large or small church. It is easily adaptable to immediate needs. A person can be quickly oriented to a place of leadership responsibility by a director of leadership education or other qualified individual personally guiding his preparation. This "counseling teacher" must practice the principles the potential leader or teacher is endeavoring to learn. Individualized training permits either acceleration or slower pacing to match an individual's needs and abilities. When built on a basic foundational program of group training, individualized training serves well for specialized preparation in various areas of leadership and training. It is equally beneficial when used to train in preparation for initial activity in one of the church educational agencies or as in-service enrichment after a period of experience.

DIRECTOR OF LEADERSHIP

A director of leadership education might be called the keystone in any church training program. While it is possible for the pastor, director of Christian education or Sunday school superintendent to serve in this capacity, it is often true that a separate individual whose main attention can be leadership preparation will serve best in leading the program. In some churches an assistant Sunday school superintendent is responsible for enlisting and training Sunday school personnel. This individual should have the responsibility of planning and coordinating various means of training. Teaching the training classes may not necessarily be part of his task, but he will expedite a program decided on by the Christian education board or committee of the church.

FOUNDATION COURSE

It is usually true that the various means of training can all be built on a

TYPES OF GROUP TRAINING			
Kind	*Description*	*Advantages*	*Cautions*
STAFF CONFERENCES	Regularly scheduled periods at which methods are presented and specialized instruction given.	Staff member has relevant matters presented which can be immediately applied in service.	Immediate needs can squeeze out the fuller enrichment program unless careful long-range plans are made.
CONVENTIONS (including workshops)	A gathering of all those interested in a similar endeavor for challenge and workshop problem-solving.	Rallies enthuse and challenge. Workshops permit a person to benefit by instruction from a specialist and to share the benefits of others' experiences.	Because of the emphasis on size and the many churches from which people come, specific help for a specific work is sometimes difficult.
LABORATORY SCHOOL	A school is conducted wherein a master teacher presents a lesson in an actual class situation. Observers are told why certain activities took place and discuss the situation. Students are also given opportunity to teach or lead.	The newly enlisted teacher or the worker with only a little experience has opportunity to observe correct methods. Guided experience can be gained.	The person leading or teaching must be careful to present methods which observing students can use.
CLINICS	Leaders or teachers meet together with specialists to present current problem situations and seek solutions.	Problems of leadership are often common to most in the same work. The teacher or leader has his problem considered and also learns in advance the problems he may face and their solutions.	Problems which are entirely personalized may not prove beneficial to the entire group. Those attending must be considerate in not pushing their particular situation as the only one to be solved.
COMMUNITY INSTITUTES	Community institutes may be sponsored by several churches or may be the extension or evening school of an institution of higher learning. Classes are presented in a number of subjects related to leadership education.	The more structured school atmosphere often provides an acceptance of solid course requirements. Regularly scheduled classes enable a student to complete a rounded program of leadership preparation.	There may be a tendency for subjects to go into more depth than leadership preparation requires. A community institute must be constantly alert to its objectives of lay leadership preparation.
FORMALIZED CHURCH CLASSES	The individual church trains its people for teaching and leadership through a series of regularly scheduled classes.	A church-sponsored program enables the church to correlate training with its educational program. The church also can orient the training to its particular needs and service its staff requirements.	Unless formalized church classes are coordinated with other means of leadership preparation and related to the actual church program, they may become competitive to other educational activities rather than serving them.
RETREATS (including seminars)	A church educational staff moves to a different location for an entire day or overnight. Here discussion groups and planning sessions center the attention of all on church ministry.	The concerted attention of all the staff, separated from other responsibilities and places of service, provides opportunity for enrichment and planning. This is usually a good means of building esprit de corps.	The absence of a member may cause him to lose an orientation to the year's work. Fellowship is important but a picnic attitude should not prevail.

common foundation, for all those in church leadership or teaching have certain common preparation needs. All should have an understanding of the Bible and all should have basic concepts of Christian education. A church desiring to develop its potential leadership will reach this goal more quickly if it weaves a foundational leadership training course into

TYPES OF INDIVIDUALIZED TRAINING			
Kind	*Description*	*Advantages*	*Cautions*
READING PROGRAM (books and magazines)	A guided program of reading in specific subject areas. Lists of suggested readings are followed. Guide questions may be given.	Permits the student to gain a wealth of specific information from many sources. The reader is enabled to establish his own rate of progress.	Meetings and other activities may disadvantage the reading program. The lack of teacher motivation and good selective lists of readings may hinder progress.
TAPES AND RECORDS	Tapes and records on training subjects present leadership and teaching themes. Tapes may also be made at conventions and workshops for personalized use.	The learner may set his own time for training and benefit by specialists' presentations. Life situations can be presented for vicarious experiences.	Since learning is dependent upon listening attention the learner must be careful not to allow home distractions to compete.
CORRESPONDENCE COURSES	A series of studies taken at the convenience of the learner. Questions guide the student in his study and enable the absentee teacher to discover a student's erroneous thinking and give correction and guidance.	Can be taken at a time and at the speed convenient to the student. A course presented by an academic institution usually incorporates the qualities of good education.	Verbal communication is abstract. Without the opportunity of interaction, students may become completely content-centered in their learning.
GUIDED PRACTICUM	Following a period of assigned reading and the observation of a master teacher or leader, the student serves under observation.	The learner receives personalized help and example. Guidance can be given either after direct observation of student activity or by planning with the student prior to service with subsequent joint evaluation.	Unless there has been sufficient foundation for the practicum, the learner may simply copy techniques without understanding the goals and objectives on which the methods are based.
IN-SERVICE COUNSELING TEACHER	One capable teacher serves as resource person for the teachers or leaders. This person visits actual class sessions, helps the teachers prepare lessons, serves as clinic consultant and encourages or guides to effective service.	The teacher or leader always has access to immediate help. Questions and answers are usually directly related to a specific situation. The counseling teacher can also serve in a direct teaching capacity.	The counseling teacher must be careful to guide the questioner to discovery rather than encourage dependency. Personal search for answers should eventuate from initial contacts with a counseling teacher.

its educational program for all adults. Such a program should include overview studies of the Bible so that there might be a comprehensive picture of the chronological thread which runs through the Scriptures. Training should also include an understanding of people and an understanding of the methods of communication with people. If the church's total educational program also can be presented it will help the individual see more clearly the part which he shares in communicating the gospel to others.

Courses of specialization can then be offered to those who have completed this foundational course. Departments in the Sunday school may wish to train workers specialized in their particular ministry. Youth leaders will want to have a program geared to counseling and advising young people. Workers in children's activity groups will also need guidance for the place of ministry they have. Those who serve in capacity as ushers and church officers will also find their preparation much easier if built on a common foundational course.*

IN-SERVICE ENRICHMENT

Added to initial preparation should be in-service enrichment. Too frequently this is only thought of as techniques and methodology. The development of one's personal devotional life, the continual expansion of Bible knowledge, the improvement of interpersonal relationships, as well as increased skill in the ministry in which the person is involved, are all part of in-service enrichment. The director of leadership education has a Herculean task in any size church. But the success of the educational program is his rewarding joy.

In-Service Enrichment

Experience and Guided Ministry

Specialized Training

Foundational Preparation for All Youth and Adults

STEPS TO SUCCESS IN SPIRITUAL SERVICE

DISCOVERING YOUR BEST PROGRAM

There is only one *best* leadership education program for any one church. There are at least four considerations that will help a church select the program it needs.

The first of these considerations is *the potential leadership* which exists within the church. The wealth of talent and background, and the depth of spiritual understanding is seldom realized without a survey or analysis. The excitement of knowing that it really is possible to have needed teachers and leaders can be sufficient stimulus to initiate a program of training. While many emerging leaders are exceedingly capable, these same individuals could be more useful with the preparation and training the church is able to give them.

The second consideration is the determination of *the church's capability to provide leadership preparation.* The director of leadership education must have an understanding of the needs and also an understanding of the potential within the church. He must further be able to provide a "trainer." This title probably best expresses the multiple responsibilities of the one who will be the teacher, the guide, the example and the "motivator" of those taking leadership preparation.

*For information on teacher-training courses offered by the Evangelical Teacher Training Association, see chap. 17, "Resources for Adult Christian Education."

The third consideration is *the urgency of the program.* If teachers are needed immediately or leaders must soon be selected, the extent of time involved in preparation must be considerably reduced. The active, functional church will be careful to have a long-range program looking forward to future leadership, but also a short-range program which will immediately provide the church with the leadership it needs. Every position should have a minimum preparation requirement which can be met by church education classes. Providing required training is an essential step to prepared leadership.

The fourth consideration is *the matter of facilities.* Effective retreats for leadership often require campgrounds; the showing of films requires available equipment; discussion groups require adequate classroom space. It should be noted, however, that capable leadership, preparing motivated students with a sense of urgency to accomplish the task God has committed to them, will often surmount facility restrictions.

Leadership education must be carefully integrated into the total church educational program. Plans should be made well in advance and widely promoted through posters, brochures, bulletin announcements, personal invitations and platform presentations. Participants need to clearly see the entire course and understand the purpose of each activity.

THE RESULT

Lay leadership is frequently the determining element in a church's vitality and service for Christ. A church multiplies its witness as it multiplies its leadership. Within the church are those placed there by God to serve. They are potential leaders and teachers. How well they serve reflects how well they have been trained. A consistent, continuous program of leadership preparation will help to provide a church with the leaders that church needs.

NOTES

1. D. K. Reisinger, "Teacher Training," *An Introduction to Evangelical Christian Education,* J. Edward Hakes, ed. (Chicago: Moody, 1964), p. 101.
2. Lois E. LeBar, *Education That Is Christian* (Westwood, N.J.: Revell, 1958), p. 22.
3. Robert K. Bower, *Administering Christian Education* (Grand Rapids: Eerdmans, 1964), pp. 129-30.
4. R. O. Woodworth, *How to Operate a Sunday School* (Grand Rapids: Zondervan, 1961), p. 145.
5. For more on enlistment and recruitment, see Roy B. Zuck, *The Superintendent and Teacher Enlistment.* Christian Educ. Monograph. Superintendents' Series, No. 3 (Glen Ellyn, Ill.: Scripture Press, 1968).

FOR FURTHER READING

Bower, Robert K. *Administering Christian Education.* Grand Rapids: Eerdmans, 1964. Chaps. 5-6.

Byrne, H. W. *Christian Education for the Local Church.* Grand Rapids: Zondervan, 1963. Chap. 3.

Eavey, C. B. *History of Christian Education.* Chicago: Moody, 1964. Chap. 14.

Edwards, Mary Alice Douty. *Leadership Development and the Workers' Conference.* Nashville: Abingdon, 1967.

Fidler, James E. *Our Church Plans for Leadership Education.* Valley Forge, Pa.: Judson, 1962.

Gable, Lee J. "Improving the Quality of Leadership in Christian Adult Education," *The Future Course of Christian Adult Education.* Lawrence C. Little, ed. Pittsburgh: U. Pittsburgh, 1959.

Gwynn, Price H., Jr. *Leadership Education in the Local Church.* Philadelphia: Westminster, 1952.

LeBar, Lois E. *Education That Is Christian.* Westwood, N.J.: Revell, 1958. Chap. 1.

Let's Look at Leadership. Philadelphia: Board of Christian Educ., United Presbyterian Church, U.S.A., n.d.

McKibben, Frank M. *Guiding Workers in Christian Education.* Nashville: Abingdon, 1953.

Milhouse, Paul W. *Enlisting and Developing Church Leaders.* Anderson, Ind.: Warner, 1946.

Reisinger, D. K. "Teacher Training," *An Introduction to Evangelical Christian Education.* J. Edward Hakes, ed. Chicago: Moody, 1964.

Syrstad, Ray. *The Superintendent and Teacher Training.* Christian Educ. Monograph, Superintendents' Series, No. 2. Glen Ellyn, Ill.: Scripture Press, 1968.

Taylor, Marvin J., ed. *Religious Education: A Comprehensive Survey.* Nashville: Abingdon, 1960. Chap. 25.

Thornton, W. Randolph. "Significant Recent Trends in Leadership Education for Adults," *The Future Course of Christian Adult Education.* Lawrence C. Little, ed. Pittsburgh: U. Pittsburgh, 1959.

Towner, Walter. *Guiding a Church School.* Nashville: Abingdon, 1963. Chap. 2.

Woodworth, R. O. *How to Operate a Sunday School.* Grand Rapids: Zondervan, 1961. Chap. 17.

Zuck, Roy B. *The Holy Spirit in Your Teaching.* Wheaton, Ill.: Scripture Press, 1963. Chap. 6.

———. *The Superintendent and Teacher Enlistment.* Christian Education Monograph, Superintendents' Series, No. 3. Glen Ellyn, Ill.: Scripture Press, 1968.

14

ADULTS IN SERVICE PROJECTS

Milford S. Sholund

The term *service projects* is not used freely in much of the literature on adult Christian education. Furthermore, the subject is seldom mentioned in the tables of contents and the indexes of standard works on Christian education. Among thirty volumes on Christian education generally found in libraries of seminaries and Bible colleges, only three give some description of the concept and function of service projects among adults.

In contrast to this paucity of references in Christian education literature, the term *service projects* is used frequently among professionals and laymen in Christian education. The Evangelical Press News Service in September, 1966, reported, "Some 6,000 volunteers took part in the 373 summer service projects conducted this year by the Board of National Missions of the United Presbyterian Church."[1] Ask a church worker, "Do you have service projects among the adults in your church?" and the answer will frequently be yes. But a few more questions on what these service projects are bring a confusing assortment of responses.

Obviously what seems to be generally accepted as an area of Christian education needs clarification if the term is to be used meaningfully and effectively. Thousands of churches have service projects for adults, but these activities need to be described, classified and validated for more effective use among adults.

THE MEANING OF SERVICE PROJECTS

The two words *service projects* used together or used separately have many meanings. This is not strange since most words have more than one meaning. The curious feature in trying to define these words is the fact that they are not used consistently with the definition given in Web-

---

MILFORD S. SHOLUND, Ed.M., D.D., is Director of Biblical and Educational Research, Gospel Light Publications, Inc., Glendale, Calif.

ster's unabridged dictionary,* nor is there a standard glossary in Christian education that defines them.. In a sense a person can make his own definition according to his concepts. On the other hand, since adult service projects are so common in Protestant churches, more attention should be given to defining and identifying their meaning.

A few years ago, ninety carefully selected leaders spent two weeks studying the subject of the future course of adult religious education. In the summary of objectives, there was no explicit mention of service projects. The nearest expression was a general goal worded as follows: "to help [adults] find for themselves the sense of mission which will focus [their] attention on something greater than [themselves] and thus release the hidden energies of [the] soul."[2] This is a general, vague statement of purpose. According to this recent view of adults in action, the expression of the energies of adults could take several forms, but not necessarily service projects.

Heim, in discussing the subject "Directing Service," maintains that the term *service* is that "element of the program in which pupils learn to contribute more fully to the welfare of others by performing acts of helpfulness."[3] In developing the subject, Heim thinks that *sharing* is a better word than *service*. He develops the idea of service projects more fully than the typical textbook writer for pastors, seminarians, and directors of Christian education.

McKibben maintained a generation ago that "church school workers are perhaps more lacking in appreciation of the general nature and significance of service training and expression than any other element in the total program."[4] His chapter entitled "Improving Service Training and Activity" contains helpful principles and ideas for service activities.

The term *service* is often equated with *activity* when used in the context of service projects. This exchange of terms means that service projects are often nothing more than activity. Some leaders warn against the tendency for such activities among adults becoming mere busy work.

In an effort to bring wholeness and wholesomeness into the concept of service, Thomson and Hough maintain that service in the local church is to be seen as the outcome of Christian worship and education.[5] They warn that Christian witness has much to fear from those who seek to escape in "church work."

THE PHILOSOPHY OF SERVICE PROJECTS

In recent years Protestant churches, especially in the United States, have sought to clarify the programs through which they can achieve the

---

*Webster gives these definitions: "Service: Performance of labor for the benefit of another," "Project: A planned undertaking."

goals of Christian education to the glory of Jesus Christ. Most authorities have classified the energies and expressions of Christian education in the four categories of worship, instruction, service and fellowship. Occasionally a fifth area, evangelism, is included. But most leaders today prefer to think of evangelism as inherent in all areas of Christian education. Service projects would be classified in the category of service in the program of Christian education.

In considering the biblical view of Christian education and service projects, Lentz suggests that the life and works of Christ constitute a foundation for service projects.[6] He cites the occasion when Jesus fed the five thousand (Mk 6:39-44). There were preparations for feeding, but the main purpose involved persons outside the group of the disciples. This benevolent action of Jesus and His disciples may be called a service project because they "projected" goodwill and good deeds to others. In this sense a group of adults in a local church should bear in mind that through service projects they are projecting Christ by showing and sharing His love.

Lentz also suggests that expressing Christ's love in practical ways contributes to spiritual growth. As Jesus trained the twelve, He stressed that what they learned from Him was to be shared with others. This is evident as He sent them into the cities to preach, to teach and to heal. He knew they would grow only as they put into practice what they learned from Him.

The idea of growing through serving is also a conviction of James Murch. In his pithy, pointed volume *Teach or Perish!* he contends that "projects should be considered as educational processes through which the pupil grows in stature."[7]

Undergirding the structure of service projects should be the love of Christ, the needs of others, and the values to the participants. If these three points are held in balance in service projects, the benefits will be more lasting. Unfortunately, this balance is not always maintained in adult work in local churches. The pendulum of extremism swings either toward pietism or toward social service. But Jesus Christ did not advocate this either-or approach. Christianity would be misrepresented if an indictment were to be passed on either tendency as if one were wrong and the other view were right. God wants us to learn in order to do. Both the learning and the doing are necessary and good.

THE KINDS OF SERVICE PROJECTS

Some service projects may be called introverted, whereas others may be considered extroverted. By "introverted projects" is meant those limited to more immediate interests of the adults within the church. "Extroverted projects" suggest those that extend to adults beyond the boundaries and buildings of the church.

The following group activities by adults in a Sunday school class or study group in a local church are examples of introverted projects: (1) preparing the classroom, (2) greeting strangers, (3) making name tags, (4) taking the offering, (5) mailing letters, (6) preparing news releases, (7) mailing notices, (8) ordering supplies, (9) playing the piano, (10) picking up hymnals.

Are these activities to be considered service projects? The answer is both no and yes. Those who say no recognize that these are maintenance jobs for group life in a typical church. These are jobs to be done. But those who say yes know that these ten activities and many more like them *are considered* service projects in many churches. The fact is that these ten items could be multiplied tenfold to a hundred and yet there would be work to do. There is no end to such tasks, but jobs are not necessarily service projects.

Arranging the chairs can hardly be considered a service project. There is good reason for believing at times that adult classes and groups in local churches are beating the air and wasting time when there is no greater meaning to service projects than maintenance tasks.

Extroverted service projects are often grouped in the familiar feminine interest of sewing projects and raising money for missions. The feminine feature of service projects has traditionally grown in American churches since women "have a heart" and they "have time." No one doubts that they have both of these qualities essential to service projects. But too much of the work in local churches reflects the agrarian setting of two generations ago. The capacities and interests of women in a technological era require more than repeating the old patterns of behavior. The sewing must be done; the raising of money is required for missions; but these activities cannot substitute for enlisting men and women of this generation to come to grips with the needs and problems in contemporary society.

For further lists of jobs and service projects, the compilations by Gable, Carlson and Schroeder and denominational leaflets will make more than five hundred possibilities available.[8] A few projects are listed below to suggest the wide range of possibilities:

> visiting the elderly
> visiting the ill in hospitals
> organizing used-clothing distribution
> welcoming new residents in the community
> visiting church or Sunday school prospects and absentees
> praying with the bereaved and sorrowful

reading to the blind

transporting college students or others to church

distributing Christian literature

helping construct a cabin or other building at a campsite

baking for a servicemen's center

participating in a rescue mission

improving the appearance of a Sunday school classroom

participating in a preaching service in a city or county jail

doing errands for shut-ins

arranging a picnic or excursion for underprivileged children or youth

sponsoring a teen coffee house or recreation center

Perceptive pastors and leaders will need to pray for wisdom when seeking to challenge their adults with service projects that reflect the love of Christ and grow out of a valid need and perform a beneficial service for others.

THE DEVELOPMENT OF SERVICE PROJECTS

Service projects are valid when they glorify Christ, serve the needs of others, and bring satisfaction to the participants. The development of service projects should follow an orderly fulfillment of these responsibilities and duties. Time is too valuable to be wasted on needless conversation and opinions; action is required.

In the adult division of the local church, service projects can be developed within the structure of any group such as Sunday school classes, Bible study groups, women's missionary fellowships and men's fellowship groups, etc.

The Southern Baptist denomination now offers men in their Brotherhood organization and women in their Women's Missionary Union a choice between the traditional weekly program and a new thrust centering on "action groups." In this new stepped-up program a person chooses a study group geared to a specific type of problem toward which the local church could marshal its resources. Following the study group the participants reorganize and continue as an "action group" to perform some service in an area of need. Areas for study and action suggested in Southern Baptist literature (which could be ordered and adapted for use by any church) include ministries to the economically disadvantaged; internationals; juvenile delinquents; the sick; persons in mission Sunday schools or Bible classes; and persons in prisons, hospitals, convalescent homes, etc.

The following principles should be considered by any group sponsoring a service project:

1. Encourage all members in the group to suggest ideas for service projects.
2. Encourage each member to vote when the opportunity is given to choose a service project.
3. Appoint or elect a leader for the service project. A leader can make or break the project.
4. Clearly state what the leader is expected to do.
5. Give the leader authority to act within the limits defined by the group.
6. Involve all members of the group in the project.
7. Let the group decide when the project begins and when it ends. Terminal dates are important.
8. Invoke God's blessing and guidance at all times.
9. Keep records of progress and problems to make the service project a learning experience for future guidance.
10. Evaluate the results, and report to the church what was achieved.

For further consideration, a helpful set of guiding principles is given in the *Encyclopedia for Church Group Leaders*.[9]

Service projects should be challenging, yet within reach; unifying to the group, yet diversified; competitive, but not at the expense of co-operation; consistent with the Christian conviction of the group, yet different enough to be interesting.

Service projects can be achievements of the groups that truly glorify God, meet a need, and satisfy the members. This happens when thought, time, energy and enthusiasm are combined to make the project successful.

THE VALUE OF SERVICE PROJECTS

Service projects have value for three reasons.

THE WORK OF CHRIST IS ACCOMPLISHED

Christ has no other hands, hearts and mind to do His work on earth than those committed to His will and work. If groups in local churches do not *act*, then much needed work goes undone. Adults who are spiritually motivated can make significant contributions to the cause of Jesus Christ in this generation.

Service projects should be worthy of the name of Christ. He taught that the sharing of a refreshing cup of cold water has special meaning if the giver provides it in Christ's name and for His sake.

MANY ADULTS CAN PARTICIPATE

The local church cannot demand the services of adults for many hours a week, but the collective efforts of several adults can accomplish much in a short time. Service projects provide the opportunity for adults to do something for Christ in a united effort which they could not do by themselves.

It is the feeling of being alone and not being able to do something significant for Christ that causes many church members to drift to other groups, clubs and societies. In the United States tens of thousands of organizations are designed to involve men and women in some kind of service projects. It is no sin for a local church to enlist the adults in service projects which can and should be more meaningful than the typical secular service organization. Unfortunately, too many churches fail to realize that adults want something to do together. Service projects that are wisely selected and carefully guided can fill a great need in adult Christian education.

ADULTS CAN MATURE IN CHRIST

The apostle Paul constantly taught that the ultimate goal in Christian life and experience is maturity in Christ. To the Ephesian believers he wrote, "For we are his workmanship, created in Christ Jesus unto good works, which God hath before ordained that we should walk in them. That we henceforth be no more children, tossed to and fro. . . . But speaking the truth in love, may grow up into him in all things, which is the head, even Christ" (Eph 2:10; 4:14-15). The "good works" of service projects can help adults mature spiritually.

The local church that thoughtfully and creatively involves adults in service projects is doing those adults a favor. One of the main reasons many adults are unable to cope with problems is their introspective view of life. They give too much attention to themselves without giving of themselves for the needs of others.

PROBLEMS IN SERVICE PROJECTS

Service projects are not exempt from problems. The following six are some of the problems to be avoided:

WORK WITHOUT WORSHIP

Service projects can easily become ends in themselves. Therefore one possible problem is the danger of emphasizing work for Christ without worship of Christ. Every occasion that calls a group of Christians to serve Christ should provoke the group to worship. The spiritual quality of service projects can be preserved when the leaders and members pause to praise and pray. Whatever the occasion and whenever the service project group meets, a moment of praise and prayer will do more to maintain spiritual vitality than any other effort or intention. The most wholesome efforts can quickly deteriorate for lack of vital worship of Jesus Christ as Lord and Leader.

THE RITUAL OF ROUTINE

Nothing devitalizes a group so quickly as routine. The surest way to kill a service project is to let it get boring. The most ambitious project can soon be wrecked if week in and week out there is the same deadening approach to the task.

Boredom can be avoided by changing pace. Variety of approaches and activities can stimulate interest and renewal. The members of the group should be encouraged to contribute their ideas on how to make the group project different and interesting. Don't hesitate to enlist the more unlikely members in a group to contribute ideas and ways of getting the job done.

SERVICE WITHOUT SATISFACTION

Satisfaction comes when the service project is well done according to plan and when the members of the group have a sense of personal achievement.

Jesus expected His disciples to rejoice in their work. When He gave the twelve and the seventy power to preach and to heal, He expected them to succeed.

Success need not be a sin. In fact, excellence should be expected in service projects. Too often mediocrity prevails in service projects of the local church. In an era known for technological wonders, members of the church should apply the finest skills and abilities when they are enlisted in service projects for Christ.

Unfortunately the law of transference of learning is seldom applied in church-related activities. An accountant may be an expert in his professional role, but he is expected to do wonders in the church with a shoddy accounting system. The skilled cabinet maker often is asked to nail two by fours together for a crude set of planks for use in seating the "kindergarten kids." No wonder he is disenchanted with service projects in the church.

Careful consideration should be given to selecting service projects that truly challenge the interests, capacities and skills of the members of the adult groups.

When adults are involved in service projects that truly motivate them to spiritual service, that stimulate their interest and enthusiasm, and that give them satisfaction, there will be unlimited possibilities for service projects that are worthy of Christ and His church.

FAILURE TO MEET A NEED

Noble aspirations are worthy of all Christians, but good intentions are not enough. Merely going through the motions of activity can be dangerous and deadening. When a group perpetuates a ceremony of bringing pennies to help the poor, there is the danger of self-deception. In a comparatively affluent society in the United States, church members cannot make gestures of goodwill which neither meet a need nor clear the Christian conscience.

The typical local church is almost certain to be caught in the trivia of some traditional practices that are outdated and outmoded. Pastors need to be perceptive and courageous in guiding their adult leaders into a critical and Christlike evaluation of the purposes of service projects. Christ was stern and devastating in His judgment of the waste in human energy, time and resources when they were misused. Service projects must be evaluated and reevaluated to learn if they really are necessary and meet a need.

INADEQUATE LEADERSHIP

The success of a service project is determined to a large extent by the leader. Many groups may tend to classify service projects as secondary in importance to other church functions. The church board, elders, deacons and comparable groups are composed of leaders whose ability and faithfulness have been proven. The next order of priority for leadership usually includes the established divisions, departments and organizations in the church organization. The Sunday school superintendent, the president of the women's society, the chairman of the missionary committee, etc., are considered important.

Where then does a leader of a service project come in priority? Obviously he is hardly known for his key position and responsibility. Yet he is called upon to apply himself to a task that often requires more skill, time, energy and management than the "preferred" positions in the church hierarchy.

Too often, then, service projects are second rate and are failures because the better leaders are seldom available.

If service projects are worth the purpose, the effort and value attributed to them, then the church must secure and train leaders to make them successful.

DUPLICATION OF EFFORT

Lack of communication among groups in churches is astonishing. The size of the church seems to make little difference. Groups in the local church can support missionaries, organizations and projects with little knowledge or understanding of what other groups are doing. The waste of money, energy and time is incalculable when all the more than 275,000 Protestant congregations in the United States are considered.

The results of service projects in the local church are often undiscovered and unknown. Few churches even know what service projects adult groups are sponsoring. Also, the loyalty within some adult groups to the programs is deeper than to the church itself. Thus there develops a conscious or unconscious protection of the interests of "my group" that defies control and supervision by the congregation. Such relationships often lead to jealousies and feelings that make service projects a "special project" rather than a Christlike cooperation for the good of others.

Obviously the correction of such distortion of effort by an adult group requires much prayer, patience and firmness of action. However, appropriate action directed by the Holy Spirit will be vindicated with blessing for the whole church.

THE OUTLOOK FOR SERVICE PROJECTS

Service projects, properly conceived and carefully supervised, can provide meaningful, satisfactory achievements for Christ and His church in this generation. The needs are great and the opportunities wide and varied. As Christian laymen engage in service projects, being "careful to maintain good works" (Titus 3:8), they manifest what James called pure and undefiled religion (Ja 1:27).

NOTES

1. Evangelical Press News Service, LaCanada, Calif. (Sept. 17, 1966).
2. Joy Elmer Morgan, "The Challenge of Our Times to Adult Education" in *Future Course of Christian Adult Education,* Lawrence C. Little, ed. (Pittsburgh: U. Pittsburgh, 1959), p. 10.
3. Ralph D. Heim, *Leading a Sunday Church School* (Philadelphia: Muhlenburg, 1950), p. 23.
4. Frank M. McKibben, *Improving Religious Education Through Supervision* (New York: Methodist Book Concern, 1931), p. 140.
5. R. W. Thomson and J. R. Hough, *The Service of Our Lives* (London: SCM, 1962), p. 22.
6. Richard E. Lentz, "A Role of Activities in Adult Groups," *Encyclopedia for Church Group Leaders,* Lee J. Gable, ed. (New York: Association, 1959), p. 363.
7. James DeForest Murch, *Teach or Perish!* (Grand Rapids: Eerdmans, 1961), p. 102.
8. Lee J. Gable, ed., *Encyclopedia for Church Group Leaders* (New York: Association, 1959), pp. 365-66; Violet Carlson, *The Christian Educator's File* (Chicago: Moody, 1954); George W. Schroeder, *The Brotherhood Guidebook* (Nashville: Broadman, 1950).
9. Gable, ed., p. 367.

FOR FURTHER READING

Bergevin, Paul. *Design for Adult Education in the Church.* Greenwich, Conn.: Seabury, 1958.

Clemmons, Robert S. *Dynamics of Christian Adult Education.* Nashville: Abingdon, 1958.

Eavey, C. B. *Principles of Teaching for Christian Teachers.* Grand Rapids: Zondervan, 1940.

Gable, Lee J., ed. *Encyclopedia for Church Group Leaders.* New York: Association, 1959.

Hakes, J. Edward, ed. *An Introduction to Evangelical Christian Education.* Chicago: Moody, 1964.

Heim, Ralph D. *Leading a Sunday Church School.* Philadelphia: Muhlenburg, 1950.

McKibben, Frank M. *Improving Religious Education Through Supervision.* New York: Methodist Book Concern, 1931.

Murch, James DeForest. *Teach or Perish!* Grand Rapids: Eerdmans, 1961.

Schroeder, George W. *The Brotherhood Guidebook.* Nashville: Broadman, 1950.

Taylor, Marvin J., ed. *Religious Education: A Comprehensive Survey.* Nashville: Abingdon, 1960.

Thomson, R. W. and Hough, J. R. *The Service of Our Lives.* London: SCM, 1962.

Wyckoff, D. Campbell. *How to Evaluate Your Christian Education Program.* Philadelphia: Westminster, 1962.

Zeigler, Earl F. *Christian Education of Adults.* Philadelphia: Westminster, 1958.

———. *Education for Churchmanship.* Nashville: Abingdon, 1966.

15

CHURCH RECREATION FOR ADULTS

Richard E. Troup

Jesus invited His disciples "to come apart" and rest awhile. Today also, as two thousand years ago, contemporary disciples must "come apart" for recreation lest they, in another sense, "come apart" emotionally under the strain of twentieth century living.

God built into the nature of man the need for work, worship, witness *and rest*. While the religious function of the weekly day of rest was fulfilled in Christ, according to the book of Hebrews, regular rest and respite from normal work continue as essential.

Are we saying then that the church needs to include secular recreational activities in its program? Not at all. Nothing secular belongs in the church. However, rest and recreation are not inherently secular. It is as possible to play spiritually as it is to pray in a secular manner. First Corinthians 10:31 and Colossians 3:17, 23 direct the Christian to do *every-thing* from a spiritual motivation. If fun can be to God's glory, it is spiritual and can be enjoyed by a believer. It is then part of a Spirit-led (and thus genuinely spiritual) life.

A church is under divine obligation not to overload any of its members with church-related work. Each member of a local congregation is a gift from God to that church to fulfill a role of Christian service. When too many tasks are placed on a minority of members, other believers are harmed because they are not given an opportunity to fulfill their responsibilities. Overloaded Christians may become spiritually empty.

A church must see that each member serves to the limit of his need but that none carries more than his share of the load. A church needs to arrange its program so that no one person is expected to try to take in all that the church offers. Regular worship, yes; definite work for Christ,

RICHARD E. TROUP, M.R.E., is Director of Leadership Development, Church Training Service, National Association of Free Will Baptists, Nashville, Tennessee.

certainly; faithful witness as an integral part of Christian living, surely; but regular periods of church-sponsored or church-directed and church-encouraged rest and relaxation are *also* a vital and necessary part of each Christian's life.

CHURCH RECREATION PAST AND PRESENT

Recreation for adults under church sponsorship is not new. After-service ice-cream socials in the summer, or "coffee and—" during the winter, all-day meeting with dinner-on-the-grounds, Sunday school picnics and basket suppers have long been a part of even the most conservative churches.

Recreational facilities within the church, however, have been limited. Printed materials on the subject have been few. And recreational leadership has seldom been a part of the training of either professional ministers or lay leaders.

However, each of these problems is being overcome in evangelical Christian circles today.

1. *Facilities.* It is not uncommon today to find conservative churches with gymnasiums, large dining rooms with kitchens, lounges with kitchenettes, fireplace rooms, game rooms, hobby and craft rooms, etc.

2. *Leadership.* National Sunday School Association workshops are conducted on the subjects of recreation, and several of its Sunday school encyclopedias include a few articles on the subject of recreation.*

A survey taken by the Accrediting Association of Bible Colleges reported that ten Bible institutes and colleges out of forty-four surveyed included courses on recreational leadership while eight included a course on arts and crafts.[1] The survey recommended that two-hour courses both in recreational leadership and arts and crafts be included in more schools as elective courses.[2] A recreational leadership course may be described as follows:

> This course is designed to show the relationship and contribution of recreational and social activities to the total education program of the church. Emphasis is placed on the development of competent leadership to plan and conduct the church's recreational and social function for all ages through activities such as games, parties, teas, banquets, dramatics, musical events, club work, hobbies, etc. A study is made of the acquisition and utilization of facilities and equipment required for an adequate program in churches of various sizes and types.[3]

3. *Literature.* Textbooks on Christian education in both liberal and evangelical circles show a definite trend toward more emphasis on recrea-

*E.g., vol. 12, published in 1965, includes "Recreation and Parties" by William R. Goetz, p. 122, and "The Total Church Recreation Program" by Carl W. Bunckley, p. 123.

tional leadership. *Religious Education: A Comprehensive Survey*, edited by Marvin J. Taylor and published in 1960 by Abingdon Press, includes no chapter on recreation nor even a reference in the index. Another, but newer, standard volume on Christian education in more liberal circles is *The Westminster Dictionary of Christian Education* published in 1963. In this book there is a three-column article on recreation that includes a shallow introduction to a philosophy of recreation and a few practical suggestions.[4]

In more conservative circles Peter P. Person's *An Introduction to Christian Education*, published in 1958, contains only a brief reference to recreation:

> Another area where techniques of Christian education are needed is in the field of recreation. Learning takes place not only in the classroom but on the playground as well. How may games and athletics come under the influence of Christian Education? How may the Spirit of Christ be brought into the social activities of our youth?[5]

However, *An Introduction to Evangelical Christian Education*, published by Moody Press in 1964, includes an excellent chapter on "Recreation" by Marion Leach Jacobsen.[6] *Youth and the Church*, published by Moody in 1968, contains a well-documented chapter filled with theological depth and practical suggestions, written by Edward L. Hayes.[7] Even a quick glance at the bibliography of any of these articles or chapters will show the reader that evangelical publishing houses are now in the business of providing more guidance to local churches in recreational leadership.

Church Recreation Magazine and the *Training Union Magazine*, published by the Sunday School Board of the Southern Baptist Convention, have provided in-depth help for recreational programs, not only of Southern Baptists but for many evangelical groups who draw upon these materials.

Our society is moving into increasing affluence, shorter workweeks, a tendency toward three-day weekends, and four-week or even longer vacations. Churches can guide Christians into a meaningful use of spare time with recreational activities that will build bodies, souls, minds and spirits to bring glory to the Lord Jesus Christ.

VALUES OF RECREATION

Recreation has a legitimate place in the life of an individual. When a person becomes a Christian, pleasure is not removed from his life but redirected into positive, Christ-honoring channels. However, many people wonder if the church should become involved in recreation. The cost involved, the time necessary, buildings to be erected, leadership to be invested—all these factors cause the church to ask carefully whether or not recreation belongs in its program for adults.

In a balanced church program, emphasis is placed on outreach, evangelism, fellowship and education. At first glance it does not appear that recreation fits into such a list. However, recreation is involved in *each* of these steps.

OUTREACH

It is easier to invite many unchurched persons to a recreational meeting than to a revival meeting. Informal get-togethers in a fellowship hall, backyard, recreation room or park provide a more natural invitation to persons who may feel ill at ease in a formal church setting.

EVANGELISM

A church reported to its denominational periodical that in a recent series of evangelistic meetings five persons received Jesus as Saviour. The article also stated that five members of the church's *baseball* team had accepted Christ during the season. As many had come to Christ through baseball as through a series of meetings! Church-sponsored camping consistently reports a higher percentage of participants accepting Jesus Christ as personal Saviour than any other major ministry.

FELLOWSHIP

The word *fellowship* has often been perverted to refer only to Friday night wiener roasts and Sunday night sandwich huddles. However, *koinonia* means sharing, having in common. It suggests a group of believers sharing common needs, burdens, blessings, victories. A very meaningful part of true fellowship is the integrating of new Christians into the genuine fellowship of a local body of Christ. Informal get-togethers enable fellow believers to "let their hair down," to admit that they are human, and to share together what it means in all situations to live for Christ.

EDUCATION

Teaching is frequently understood by the church to refer only to the academic impartation of factual Bible knowledge within a formal classroom. Although we are capable of producing persons with acceptable knowledge, many churches are deficient in producing desirable Christian attitudes and behavior patterns. However, what the world refers to as "learning the value of sportsmanship" provides for us an insight into an even deeper truth. On the basketball court, in the hobby room, on a hike, at the ping-pong table in the church basement—these places all offer opportunities for the development and expression of Christian ways of thinking and behaving in everyday situations.*

MAKING RECREATION CHRISTIAN

All that is done in the name of recreation obviously does not honor the Lord. To many non-Christians, *recreation* means only those activities which give a person a headache or a hangover—or vacations which require spending many dollars and traveling many miles. It is a joke in many offices that Mondays are needed to rest up from weekends, and that the week following a family's vacation is needed for them to recover from what is erroneously described as *recreation*.

On the other hand, dedicated Christians are concerned that their recreational activities be Christ-honoring. The following five factors are helpful guidelines for selecting and planning wholesome adult recreational programs in the church:

PERSONS

Fun should never in any way be destructive of another person, his reputation or his character. Stunts and skits should not introduce humor at the expense of race, language irregularities or physical handicaps.

PROPERTY

Recreation should never be damaging to property. A campsite, for example, should be left in good condition by Christians. In addition, recreation will not withdraw from the Christian's financial resources money that ought to be invested in savings, health or Christian work.

PURITY

In Christian recreation, jokes include no vulgar language or shady meanings. The places a Christian attends for recreation ought never to cause him to compromise his witness for Christ. Wearing apparel will be in good taste and yet modest.

In some communities bowling alleys and roller-skating rinks are clean and decent and therefore not objectionable to Christians. In other communities, however, bowling alleys are developed around a bar or have become hangouts for undesirable persons and thus rule out the Christian's participating in this activity while in those communities. Paul's refusal to eat meat in Corinth was based not on any inherent evil of a roast beef sandwich but on the local misunderstandings in Corinth.

*For more on the values of recreation for adults, and for families in particular, see chap. 26, "Encouraging Family Recreation."

PIETY

Though it cannot be proven from Scripture that any specific recreation on Sunday is improper, Christians must take care that their Sunday recreational activities in no way detract from their participation in Sunday church activities or their Christian witness.

Interestingly, some churches have included recreation in their Sunday programming. One aggressive church in Kentucky includes a Sunday afternoon junior softball league. To participate in the league, a boy must attend both Sunday school and the Sunday evening training hour.

Christians who have purchased weekend cottages or cabins and who spend Sundays in other than their home community can align themselves with churches in both areas where they are residents. Some families who live for an entire summer in a second community have, by their influence, brought new life to small rural communities.

A tent and trailer family camp near Birmingham, Alabama, operated by a Christian businessman, has included in its regular program an evangelistic Sunday morning worship service. It not only provides a place for camper Christians to make new friendships in the Lord but has been the means of unsaved campers finding Christ as personal Saviour.

PROPRIETY

While hearty laughter has a place in the Christian life, such humor should never be the cover-up of a fear of looking within. Not every "jolly Joe" is heehawing out of a guilty complex, but it is true that some Christians who seem to major in laughter do so only to avoid the consequences of what they would see if they were to examine their lives soberly. "Everything has a season," and to the Christian this includes humor at the proper time, at the proper place and in the proper manner. Sober moments of weeping and thinking, but also honest, intelligent healthy laughter, fun and recreational times are proper.

Words written to a situation far removed from recreation are relevant here: "Let all things be done decently and in order" (1 Co 14:40).

PLANNING FOR ADULT RECREATION

The wise church plans all its main events on an annual basis, incorporating them into an all-church schedule to avoid overlapping or omissions. This permanent schedule may be in the church office and can be printed on an annual basis. More frequently, however, it is released to the congregation month by month either with a mimeographed mailing or an all-church, bulletin board-type calendar.

A small church with one adult class may have a three-member social committee to plan social activities two months in advance. Coming activities could be announced in the Sunday school class for adults and in the adult services.

A larger church could have representatives from each adult organization (Sunday school, Sunday evening groups, men's and women's fellowships, etc.) who would serve as an all-adult social committee. This coordinated planning would assure or help prevent overlapping of activities by the various groups, would provide for all ages of adults, and meet all types of recreational interests.

One recreational activity each month would be a reasonable goal for even the smallest church. The adult class of an Illinois church with less than thirty members sponsored an annual social schedule similar to the following:

January—A New Year's Eve social sponsored by the adult class for all members of the family. This kept within the policy that once a quarter the adult-sponsored social activity would be a family event.

February—A sweetheart banquet.

March—A stunt and skit night, with each couple presenting a humorous song, drama, reading or skit.

April—A picnic, with a wiener roast and a miniature golf tournament.

May—Dinner for mothers at the church with the fathers providing the meal (spaghetti, meatballs, tossed salad, biscuits, etc.), and planning and presenting a program.

June—An all-church picnic, perhaps in conjunction with vacation Bible school or sponsored by the Sunday school. (This is the once-a-quarter, all-church, all-family social activity.)

July—Steaks barbequed over a charcoal fire, followed by a songtime and a Moody Institute of Science film. (This provided an ideal opportunity for Christians to invite nonchristian neighbors.)

August—A campfire, corn roast, watermelon feed or some other type of outdoor activity.

September—A back-to-school social with decorations, games, refreshments and devotions planned around the little-red-schoolhouse theme.

October—A Halloween adult masquerade party.

November—An all-church Thanksgiving dinner with games for all ages and a brief worship service. (This would be an ideal opportunity to bring contributions of food and clothing and to begin special emphases on the donation of "miscellaneous money" between Thanksgiving and Christmastime on behalf of the less fortunate in the community.)

December—Carol-singing at the homes of shut-ins.

Friday nights are preferred over Saturdays for adult socials because

Saturday evening activities may tend to prevent some adults from rising Sunday morning refreshed and in time to prepare leisurely for attendance at regular Sunday morning activities. Furthermore, recreational facilities in the church building on a Saturday night mean that the rooms must be straightened up in preparation for Sunday morning sessions.

Adult recreational activities appealing to parents of small children sometimes have the danger of creating unnecessary financial burdens on struggling young adults. Some churches have opened the nursery in the church building on evenings when adult recreational events were being held. Members of high school or college-age groups in the church have provided Christian service by manning the nursery at no charge.

The following features help make adult socials more interesting and worthwhile:

1. Plan each social around an interesting theme, with each phase of the evening coordinated into this theme.
2. Vary the time and place of the activity from month to month according to the season of the year and the theme selected.
3. Rotate the responsibility of social chairman. This will help assure new and fresh ideas.
4. Use a variety of promotional media such as postcards, brochures, bulletin boards, skits, etc.
5. Plan decorations that are not expensive but which relate creatively to the theme.
6. Use a variety of games, including opening ice-breaking games (with opportunities for persons to free themselves from the day's tensions and to learn the names of new persons present), more active games (perhaps of a partner or team variety), and transitional games of a quieter nature (perhaps while seated in a circle).
7. Have a brief devotional period while the group is still seated in the circle for the last game or while the persons are seated at tables or in easy chairs finishing off refreshments.
8. Relate refreshments to the theme. Also at each social have a different committee or person plan the refreshments in order to avoid having the same kind of refreshments repeatedly.
9. Be sure that clean-up responsibilities are delegated.
10. After the social, send invitations to the visitors who were present, encouraging them to attend other activities of the church.

A well-planned adult recreational program provides for adults of all ages. Young adults enjoy well-planned social events. In some parts of the country, churches plan regional social activities for single adults. Athletic leagues often minister significantly to unmarried young adults. Leadership involvement in recreational activities of boys, girls and youth can be a meaningful expression for a single adult.

Middle adults often feel they have outgrown the need for recreational activities involving physical participation. They believe they have put such "childish" activities beneath them. However, with middle age—called "the hurricane years" for the increase of heart attacks, ulcers and divorce, even in Christian circles—there is a vital need for an adequate recreational program. With less emphasis on strenuous physical activities and an adequate provision for the care of children, husbands and wives need the experience of an evening together apart from the normal routine of the home or business.

Senior adults, with earlier retirement and greater life expectancy, have an abundance of free time in their "sunset" years, and thus many of them welcome various recreational opportunities. Many widowed and other older single adults appreciate social contacts with others to help ward off loneliness. Many churches are realizing the wisdom in providing a well-rounded, meaningful recreational program for retired persons. Even camping for older adults is increasingly popular. The Salvation Army sponsors "golden ager" Monday-through-Friday camps during fall, winter and spring.

VARIETY IN ADULT RECREATION

Hayes lists a variety of recreational opportunities for young people, many of which can be utilized with adults also.[8] The following is an adaptation of that list, with several additional activities that would appeal to adults but not to teens. Some of these activities would interest adults of all ages whereas others would appeal more to younger adults and others to older adults. This partial list is given in order to suggest the wide range of opportunities for church-related adult recreation.

1. *Arts and crafts*

basketmaking	dyeing and coloring	photography
bead craft	embroidery	picture-framing
block printing	etching	pottery
bookbinding	gardening	radio-transmitting
cabinetmaking	hat-making	rug-making
candlemaking	knitting	sand-painting
carving	leatherwork	sculpturing
ceramics	marionettes	sketching
cooking	metalcraft	tin craft
costume design	model airplanes	toy-making
crocheting	model railroads	toy-repairing
drawing	painting	weaving
	petit point	wood carving

woodworking
writing
2. *Collecting*
   antiques
   books
   buttons
   coins
   furniture
   glassware
   guns
   Indian craft
   paintings
   ships
   stamps
3. *Drama*
   charades
   festivals
   impersonations
   making scenery
   marionettes
   mask-making
   masquerades
   pageants
   pantomimes
   parades
   play-reading
   puppetry
   stage craft
   storytelling
4. *Mental activities*
   book clubs
   debates
   discussion groups
   forums
   historical study
   lectures
   listening to music
   mental games
   public speaking
   puzzles
   reading
   study groups
   tricks
   television-watching
5. *Musical activities*
   bands

barbershop quartets
ensembles
glee clubs
orchestras
solo instruments
6. *Social activities*
   banquets
   basket suppers
   beach parties
   carnivals
   conversation
   dinners
   eating out
   family reunions
   field trips
   hobby shows
   parties
     birthday
     costume
     seasonal
   pencil and paper
     games
   picnicking
   potluck suppers
   treasure hunts
7. *Table games*
   anagrams
   caroms
   checkers
   chess
   crokinole
   dominoes
   Monopoly
   moon-trip
   parcheesi
   pickup sticks
   Ping-Pong
   skittles
   table-top golf
8. *Camping and out-
   door activities*
   bait and fly casting
   barbeques
   bird-watching
   boating
   camping

canoeing
corn roasts
clambakes
crafts from native ma-
   terials
fish fries
gardening
"helping holiday"
   construction parties
   (i.e., at campsites)
hiking
horseback riding
hosteling
mountain-climbing
nature study
   astronomy
   bee culture
   birdhouse-
     building
   caring for pets
   collecting
     animals
     birds
     bugs
     flowers
     minerals
     mosses
     rocks
   making nature trails
   rifle-shooting
   skiing
   snowshoeing
   snow-tracking
   tobogganing
   trap-shooting
   trapping
   walking
   wiener roasts
   visiting zoos
9. *Physical activities*
   croquet
   golf
   handball
   horseshoes
   ice-skating
   jogging

kite-flying
lacrosse
miniature golf
Ping-Pong
roller-skating
rope-skipping
rope-spinning
shinny
shuffleboard
soccer
softball
speedball
squash
stunts
tennis
tetherball
tours
track and field events
tumbling
volleyball
water polo
weight-lifting
wrestling

10. *Competitive sports*
archery
archery golf
badminton
bait and fly casting

baseball
basketball
  foul-shooting
  spot-shooting
  twenty-one
bowling
curling
distance-running—
  half-mile, mile,
  two-mile
relay races, baton-
  passing, shuttle
  hurdles
fencing
football
golf
gymnastics
handball
hockey
  ice
  field
horseshoes
hurdles
  high, low
jump events
  running high jump
  pole vault

running broad
  jump
running hop, step,
  jump
lacrosse
paddle tennis
Ping-Pong
riflery
rowing
shuffleboard
skeet
skiing
soccer
speedball
squash
swimming and diving
tennis
touch football
track and field events
trap and skeet
  shooting
volleyball
water polo
weight events
  shot put
  discus throw
  javelin throw
wrestling

FACILITIES FOR ADULT RECREATION

Even the smallest church can have at least one room specifically designated for recreational activities. Though a one-room church will find it difficult to have chili suppers in the same room in which it conducts worship, even this type of church building can be altered into two rooms by constructing an additional room or a basement. Many medium-sized and larger churches have a social hall in which recreational and hobby equipment is an integral part, constructed with a minimum of breakable contents. Before a church constructs a recreational building (or a room for multiple uses including recreation), it needs to be sure the congregation understands the philosophy and purpose of such a facility and is ready to plan and budget accordingly. In recent years an increasing number of churches have been erecting buildings to provide a variety of activities for the total needs of people within a Christian environment. Churches are also utilizing outdoor areas for recreation, thus providing for a wide range of activities from outdoor basketball, tennis, badminton, volleyball, horseshoes, etc., to picnic areas and even swimming pools. A church needs to plan such facilities in the light of (1) present and projected recreational facilities in its community and (2) anticipated population growth of various age-levels in the congregation and community.

Recreational equipment may be kept in a storage area with controlled access. Normally it should be available only when a designated person is in charge so that it can be checked out specifically to individuals. A greater initial investment in heavy-duty quality equipment is better in the long run than purchasing less expensive lighter equipment that is soon broken.

The church library can also assist the recreational programs of a church. In addition to books on adult recreation, the church library can include a file cabinet with folders and recreational magazines with ideas for skits, readings, games, parties, banquets, camps, crafts, etc.

CONCLUSION

As a part of a total ministry in the name of Christ the church has a responsibility to provide *adult Christian recreation—adult*, to meet the needs of persons who have passed beyond teenage development and are facing adult problems and pressures; *Christian*, to provide opportunity for genuine expression of the joy and peace and purposefulness of the Christ-centered life; and *recreation*, to truly re-create persons to be fully human as well as totally Christian by relating spare time to a Spirit-led life.

SOURCES OF MATERIALS

AUDIO-VISUALS

Let's Have a Party. Nashville: Broadman Films. Ten-minute color-animated sound motion picture.

ORGANIZATIONS

American Association for Health, Physical Education and Recreation (a department of the National Education Association), 1201 Sixteenth St. N.W., Washington, D.C. 20036. A membership organization, AAHPER provides periodicals, books and leaflets for all aspects of recreational programs in general.

Athletic Institute, 209 S. State St., Chicago, Illinois 60604.

Church Recreation Service, Baptist Sunday School Board, 127 Ninth Ave. N., Nashville, Tennessee 37203. Publishes *Church Recreation Magazine* and a wide variety of other helps, including films, books and booklets. A special recreation catalog and a booklet describing free helps are available.

National Recreation Association, 8 W. Eighth St., New York, New York 10011, publishes *Recreation Magazine*, books, booklets, and a wide variety of helps for a recreational program.

National Recreation and Park Association, 1700 Pennsylvania Ave., Washington, D.C. 20006. A service organization, publishing *Parks and Recreation Magazine* and a variety of publications and services especially in the area of outdoor recreational activity.

OTHER SOURCES

Banquet Aids, Grenada, Mississippi 38901. Catalogs list numerous decoration and program materials for all kinds of banquets.

Berea College, Berea, Kentucky 40403. Manufactures high quality table-top games. Catalog available.

Christian Service Brigade, Box 150, Wheaton, Illinois 60187; and Pioneer Girls, Box 92, Wheaton, Illinois 60187. Provide member boys' and girls' clubs with regular packets of game materials. Some of these materials may be adapted for adults.

Cooperative Recreation Service, Delaware, Ohio 43015. A variety of pocket-size kits of recreational and social activities as well as various types of games are available separately or in inclusive packages.

Jam Handy Organization, 2821 E. Grand Blvd., Detroit, Michigan 48211. A wide variety of printed and projected helps on all types of recreational activities.

Training Union Magazine, Training Union Department, The Sunday School Board of the Southern Baptist Convention, 127 Ninth Ave. N., Nashville, Tennessee 37203. Includes a monthly social for each age level, including young adult and adult.

FREE MATERIALS

The following is only a sampling of the free materials on recreation provided by numerous sources. Not all these items are from Christian sources and, therefore, not all their contents are usable by churches.

American Art Clay Company, Indianapolis, Indiana 46224. "An Eskimo Activity in Clay" describes how modeling clay may be used as a craft item.

AAHPER Free Materials, 1201 Sixteenth St. N.W., Washington, D.C. 20036. Single copies of booklets on health, physical education and welfare are free on request by title.

Best Foods Division, Corn Products Sales Company, 1437 W. Morris St., Indianapolis, Indiana 46206. The booklet "Thirty-two Ways to Make Merry with Color" describes many ways Rit may be used in a crafts program with inexpensive or free items.

Church Recreation Department, Sunday School Board of the Southern Baptist Convention, 127 Ninth Ave. N., Nashville, Tennessee 37203. "Free Helps for You" is a folder listing free booklets on many subjects for a church recreational program.

Coates and Clark, Inc., Educational Bureau, 430 Park Ave., New York, New York 10022. "Knitting Visual Aid Unit" available for introducing recreational programs on knitting.

Extension Service, University of (state in which you live). Provides wide variety of free literature including materials in health and recreational activities. Designed primarily for 4-H clubs and home use but can be easily adapted by churches.

Leather Industries of America, 411 Fifth Ave., New York, New York 10016. "Leather in Our Lives" explains background of leather products and introduces craft activities using leather.

Methodist General Board of Education, Division of the Local Church, Box 871, Nashville, Tennessee 37202. Provides bulletins and leaflets on a program of recreation and social activities for all age levels.

Office of Camping and Conference Program, Board of Christian Education, The Presbyterian Church in the U.S., Box 1176, Richmond, Virginia 23209. Leaflets on many aspects of the church's recreational program available primarily to Presbyterians but also to others who state the reason for their request.

Revell, 4223 Glencoe, Venice, California 90291. Booklets and leaflets showing how Revell models may be incorporated into a handcraft program.

Sun Life Assurance Company of Canada, 218 Sun Life Building, Montreal, Quebec, Canada or 1 North LaSalle St., Chicago, Illinois 60601. Booklets such as "New Horizons for Leisure Time" give specific suggestions for contemporary recreational activities.

Wheat Flour Institute, 309 W. Jackson Blvd., Chicago, Illinois 60606. Free booklet entitled "How to Make the Ten Best Sandwiches of the Year."

Women's Division, LBI, 155 E. 44th St., New York, N.Y. 10017. Although not all suggestions in the booklet "The Care and Feeding of Guests" apply to church situations, it gives many ideas for refreshments.

NOTES

1. S. A. Witmer, *Report: Preparing Bible College Students for Ministries in Christian Education* (Fort Wayne, Ind.: Accrediting Assn. of Bible Colleges, 1962), p. 98.
2. Ibid., p. 107.
3. Ibid.
4. Maurice D. Bone, "Recreation," *The Westminster Dictionary of Christian Education*, Kendig Brubaker Cully, ed. (Philadelphia: Westminster, 1963), pp. 560-66.

5. Peter P. Person, *An Introduction to Christian Education* (Grand Rapids: Eerdmans, 1958), p. 93.
6. Ibid., pp. 344-56.
7. Ibid., pp. 239-52.
8. Edward L. Hayes, "Recreational Activities," *Youth and the Church,* Roy G.
   Irving and Roy B. Zuck, eds. (Chicago: Moody, 1968), pp. 246-48.

FOR FURTHER READING

Bone, Maurice D. "Plan for Re-creation in Your Christian Education Program,"
The Christian Educator, 9 (Jan.-Mar., 1966):16-18.

Brewer, Jack A. *Fellowships from A to Z.* Nashville: Broadman, 1968.

Brubaker, Omar. "Fellowship—A Vital Element in the Christian Education Program of Adults," *Voice* 48 (June, 1969):15.

Carlson, Adelle. *Four Seasons Party and Banquet Book.* Nashville: Broadman,
1965.

Cassell, Sylvia. *Fun Together.* Nashville: Broadman, 1958.

Epp, Margaret. *Come to My Party.* Grand Rapids: Zondervan, 1964.

Ewart, David. "The Christian Use of Leisure," *United Evangelical Action,*
26 (July, 1967):15-16, 23.

Gaebelein, Frank. "The Christian Use of Leisure," *Christianity Today,* 9 (Jan.
31, 1964):9.

Handbook for Recreation. Washington, D.C.: U.S. Government Publishing
Office, 1960.

Harbin, E. O. *The Fun Encyclopedia.* Nashville: Abingdon, 1940.

Holbert, E. Joe. *Word Banquet and Party* Book. Waco, Tex.: Word, 1969.

"It Pays for the Church to Play," *Sunday School Leader,* 68 (Jan.-Mar., 1967):
47-48.

Jacobsen, Marion L. *Popcorn, Kites and Mistletoe.* Grand Rapids: Zondervan,
1969.

McGee, Cecil. *Drama for Fun.* Nashville: Broadman, 1969.

Mounce, Robert H. "A Christian Use of Leisure," *Christian Herald,* 91 (Sept.
15, 1968):8-9.

Parrott, Lora Lee. *Encyclopedia of Party Ideas for Adults.* Grand Rapids:
Zondervan, 1963.

Pylant, Agnes Durant. *Fun Plans for Church Recreation.* Nashville: Broadman,
1958.

Recreation for Churches: A Program Service Manual. Nashville: Convention,
1967.

Recreation Specials. Nashville: Broadman, 1968.

Stafford, Virginia and Eisenberg, Larry. *More Fun for Older Adults.* New York:
Association, 1966.

Turner, Allen R. "Christians and Their Free Time," *Christian Herald,* 91 (Sept.
15, 1968):6.

Williams, Arthur. *Recreation in the Senior Years.* New York: Association, 1962.

Wise, Donald and Margaret. *Planning Men's Banquets.* Chicago: Moody, 1967.

Wise, Margaret. *Planning Women's Banquets.* Chicago: Moody, 1964.

16

ADULT LAY MOVEMENTS AND THE LOCAL CHURCH

Joseph T. Bayly

The Protestant Reformation has been described as a "three-legged stool" because three New Testament doctrines were rediscovered and affirmed afresh by the Reformers.

The first of these doctrines was the sufficiency of Scripture as the sole authority for faith and life. Tradition must yield; the church must come into conformity with the Old and New Testaments.

The second doctrine was the necessity for faith alone as the condition of salvation. Christ by His finished work, not indulgences and other churchly works, is all that is needed for man's redemption. Faith in Him, faith that stands alone, satisfies the just demands of God.

The third doctrine was the universal priesthood of believers. The *cleros-laos* distinction is political and related to the early city-state, not religious nor a pattern for the Christian church. Mediation between God and man by a professional priest is pre-Christian; we have one Mediator between God and man, one High Priest, Jesus Christ our Lord. Laymen in the church may not have the same spiritual gifts as pastors, but this is a distinction of function, not essence.

John Calvin was a lawyer by training and background, not a priest or pastor. And since the Reformation, God has been speaking through lawyers and physicians, businessmen and engineers, teachers and homemakers, instead of confining Himself to professional priests.

Like the legs of a stool, these doctrines meet in the responsibility of all Christians—clergy and laity—for Bible study and Christian witness.

The Scriptures are perspicuous; they can be understood by laymen. Knowledge of Greek and Hebrew, and other formal training to which the

---

Joseph T. Bayly, B.D., is Managing Editor, David C. Cook Publishing Company, Elgin, Illinois.

professional has been exposed, are helpful but not essential for biblical study. Both clergy and laity can share the Holy Spirit's illumination; neither is preserved from the danger of private interpretation. Dr. Howard Kelly, a founder of Johns Hopkins Medical School and a world-renowned gynecologist, was an outstanding example of lay proficiency in biblical exegesis.

And evangelism can be carried on by laymen. In fact, it *must* be carried on by them, not merely by professional preachers, if the generations are to be evangelized. Dwight L. Moody was a successful shoe salesman, not a preacher, during the beginning years of his evangelistic ministry through the Sunday school he started above a market on Chicago's Near North side.

But the Reformation could not once for all restore these doctrines to the church. "The reformed church must be constantly reforming"; each generation of Christians has its own responsibility to preserve doctrinal integrity.

Perhaps the doctrine of universal priesthood has suffered more than the other two, because it was forgotten both by those who denied and those who affirmed the sole sufficiency of faith in Christ and biblical authority.

Professionals almost always look down on laymen, even resent them. "The man who is his own legal counsel has a fool for a lawyer." "My mother," said a medical student to me, "is a graduate of the Reader's Digest School of Medicine."

In common usage, the term *layman* is almost synonymous with ignorance. And this is so in every field except one: true Christianity. Here we are all the "people [laity] of God," "the household of faith," "a holy priesthood," "priests to God." The pastor who bypasses his laymen, arrogating total responsibility for Bible teaching and witnessing to himself, denies a biblical doctrine and returns to the pre-Reformation church. (One explanation of the sweeping reforms instituted in the contemporary Roman Catholic church is Pope John XXIII's observation of the worker-priest movement when he was papal nuncio to France, prior to his assumption of the papal office. This movement turned priests into laymen; the later Vatican Councils tended to turn laymen into priests.)

Today's pastor has a choice: He can be a one-man band, or the conductor of a symphony orchestra.

Failure to use lay instrumentation in the church is one reason lay movements exist outside the church. When laymen are used, it is often on a low plane compared to the level and challenge of their weekday vocations. Ushering and counting the offering will scarcely satisfy young executives who are involved in creative, diversified jobs—with authority—between Sundays.

RISE OF CONTEMPORARY LAY MOVEMENTS

If a pattern of modern evangelical lay movements outside the church can be traced, it began with the founding of Gideons International (present headquarters, Nashville, Tenn.) in 1899. This association of traveling men first placed Bibles in hotel rooms in 1908. The stated purpose of Gideons is to "win men and women to Christ in cooperation with all evangelical denominations; provide Christian fellowship among business men and women; and encourage extensive Scripture distribution. This distribution work is supported largely by local churches."[1]

It would be impossible to list all subsequent movements up to the present time in the brief scope of this chapter. The author has instead limited consideration to what seem to be trend-setting adult and young-adult organizations that have increased in strength since their founding. Another person's list would doubtless be different.

The purposes of peer-group fellowship and evangelism were also the occasion for the founding of Christian Business Men's Committee International (Glen Ellyn, Ill.) in 1930. A leader expresses the aim and relation to the local church in this way:

> Many pastors testify that men become more efficient church members and witnesses after contact with CBMC. We believe every man should find his own niche in his own local church and do his very best there. But CBMC is a plus effort and helps him win men to Christ whom he can bring into his church to be edified.[2]

Navigators—a lay movement like Gideons and Christian Business Men's Committee International—started on a small scale in 1933 as an informal ministry to men in the United States Navy. World War II increased the influence of this work among servicemen. Its goal is to "win men to Christ, train them as His disciples, and teach them to win and train others." Navigators (Colorado Springs, Colo.) attempts to "fulfill the Great Commission by helping recruit and develop laymen for effective Christian service." In fulfilling this purpose, Navigators "seeks to work in conjunction with established churches and mission agencies."[3]

Navigators is an example of a lay movement that has gone into a more general ministry than its first audience. Youth and campus ministries, general training of laymen, and follow-up programs for Billy Graham Crusades probably represent a greater part of current Navigator concentration than men in the United States Navy.

In 1939 Inter-Varsity Christian Fellowship (Chicago, Ill.) came to the United States from Canada, and before that, Great Britain. This is probably the prime example of a lay movement transplanted to the United States. The purpose is to "witness to students and lead them to Christ;

strengthen Christian students through prayer, Bible study, fellowship; present the call to foreign missions service and help students find their place of service at home or overseas; win international students to Christ."[4]

Youth For Christ International (Wheaton, Ill.) started in 1944. High school students, servicemen and young adults were the first audiences of this Saturday-night rally program on which Billy Graham cut his evangelistic teeth. Today's program is mainly concerned with evangelizing high school youth through Bible clubs. Sam Wolgemuth, YFC president, says, "We desire to cooperate with the church and channel believers into the church."[5]

Campus Crusade for Christ International (San Bernardino, Calif.) is the most recent major lay movement. Originally founded to evangelize college and university students, Campus Crusade "attempts to reach key leaders —athletes, student body officers, etc.," and its approach is based on the idea that "college students have a basic spiritual hunger and will respond if the claims of Christ are communicated simply by a spirit-controlled person."[6] Like Navigators, Campus Crusade has broadened out from its original audience—college students—to include a larger area of lay evangelism.

A recent increase in women's lay movements probably began with the organization of Christian Business and Professional Women of America (Kansas City, Mo.). Date of founding and other information about the purpose of this organization are lacking because to provide such information is "not in line with our policy which [the founder] has followed all these years."

Weekday Bible study groups, mainly held in homes, are a rather new development among laywomen. Neighborhood Bible Studies (Dobbs Ferry, N.Y.) was organized in 1960, and is typical of this movement.

Lay movements among professional people are represented by Christian Medical Society (Oak Park, Ill.), Christian Legal Society (no permanent headquarters as yet), Nurses Christian Fellowship (Madison, Wis.), and Officers Christian Union (East Lansing, Mich.). Christian fellowship and sharing Christian faith are dominant purposes of these movements; they have an added function of relating Christian doctrine to professional practices and ethics.

An emphasis on training laymen to function as Christian husbands and wives, fathers and mothers, neighbors and business/professional associates appears in such recent movements as Laity Lodge (Kerrville, Tex.) and Faith at Work (New York City). Both attempt to relate to local churches and pastors. These movements also reflect reaction against the increasing depersonalization of American life, including life in the church. Their members have been—in the main—supporters and leaders of the local church.

Although it is dangerous to generalize, the main type of lay movement that has been lacking among Evangelicals of this century is one of social concern. The social-gospel emphasis of theologically liberal Protestantism early in the century made such movements suspect; or perhaps, more accurately, cut the nerve that might have pained Evangelicals into action. The only exception that comes to mind is the Prohibition Party. Evangelical Protestants of this century have seemed to focus their social concern on alcohol and alcoholism.

Of course, some of these movements had social-action programs, such as Christian Medical Society's overseas drug and equipment distribution, now Medical Assistance Program (Wheaton, Ill.), as well as clinical work in inner-city rescue missions and medical work outside the United States.

But no modern parallel is found for the various evangelical laymen's movements with specific social concern of the nineteenth century (especially in such areas as abolition of slavery, child welfare and prison reform).

Nineteenth century United States laymen's movements still active today include the American Tract Society (Oradell, N.J.), which served the church; and the American Sunday School Union (Philadelphia), which founded Sunday schools, especially during the Westward expansion, which later became churches of various denominations. Both movements continue their basic ministries.

At various times in the past generation, laymen in main-line denominations have founded movements to protest theological liberalism in their denomination, and/or to combat the denomination's social-action pronouncements and programs.

A general characteristic of these modern laymen's movements is that their meetings and conventions have been held outside the church building. Homes, clubs, restaurants, hotels, convention centers, school and college classrooms have been used, as well as camps and conference centers built specifically for lay-group use. The total property investment represented by lay groups outside the church is doubtless many millions of dollars.

Most of the lay movements mentioned, as well as similar movements not mentioned, have a "basis of faith" or doctrinal platform similar to the Niagara Confession (authority of Scripture, deity of Christ, substitutionary atonement, bodily resurrection of Christ, the second coming). This has been helpful both in preserving doctrinal integrity and in avoiding denominational distinctives which could have fragmented the movements.

CONTRIBUTIONS OF LAY MOVEMENTS

What have been the positive contributions of these lay movements to the twentieth century church?

1. They have reaffirmed, by their very existence, the universal priesthood of believers.
2. They have been a third force in evangelism, along with churches and individual evangelists such as Gypsy Smith, Billy Sunday, Bob Jones, Sr., and Billy Graham. In the main, these lay movements have been cooperative rather than competitive toward the two other forces. Many people have been converted through a combination of these three influences.
3. They have doubtless added considerable numbers of new believers to the church, as well as preventing the dropout of many who have been raised in the church, especially teenagers and students.
4. In a period when theoretical ecumenism has been a key doctrine of liberal theological thought, evangelical lay movements have demonstrated the doctrine at work. No liberal ecclesiastical parallel exists to the denomination-arching activities and influence of Inter-Varsity Christian Fellowship and Campus Crusade for Christ among young adults, or of the Gideons and the Christian Medical Society.

   The identification of laymen with these interdenominational (a better description is "denominationally unrelated") movements reflects an innate Christian desire for oneness. It is possible that this desire has been a factor in the movements' growth, as ordinary grassroots Christians react against a narrow "we are the people" approach in some evangelical churches. This ecumenism is not imposed by an ecclesiastical hierarchy from the top down; it is (at least in origins and early growth) a true lay movement.

   At the risk of "chicken or egg" speculation, it is probable that (ecumenical) evangelical faith missions could not have developed to such an extent in the years since World War II without a prior and concomitant breakdown in insularity through laymen's movements. And it is worth noting that Billy Graham's world-enhancing ministry was formed in the matrix of such a movement, Youth for Christ.
5. They have provided a sounding board for and, in many instances, answers to moral and ethical problems that are not considered in most churches. This is true of high school and college movements; it is also true of such professional associations as Christian Medical

Society and Christian Legal Society (control of conception and abortion, for instance). In so doing they have freshly—and needfully —affirmed the relevance of Christian faith and doctrine to all areas of life.

6. They have provided individual Christians with the sort of small groups that seem necessary for spiritual growth, as well as emotional wholeness. Almost everyone needs a core of people by whom he is accepted, and to whom he can relate. It possible that the pattern of future churches is being developed in these lay groups.

7. The literature of these movements—periodicals, study guides, booklets, books—has been a significant contribution to the total Christian movement. It is conceivable that no single church denomination or group of churches would have had the evangelical resources for producing and distributing the literature which embodied the distinctive ideas of these movements.

8. In general, these movements seem to have arisen in response to an area of weakness or failure in the local church's ministry. This is particularly true of lay movements among young adults during the past two generations. In this way these movements have complemented and supplemented the churches' ministry and, in some instances, spurred them into action to develop their adult programs.

9. Through their regular programs and special training sessions (conferences, camps, conventions), these lay movements have been and continue to be a major force in adult education. This training is usually closely related to practical activity. Depth and quality of leadership—including creativity—are developed in these movements, partly because men and women are not working in the shadow of a professional (pastor or director of Christian education) as in the local church.

PROBLEMS OF LAY MOVEMENTS

But lay movements have also caused problems for the church, particularly the local church. These problems are frequently related to the movement's strengths.

1. They have siphoned off laymen's time from the church in whose program and activities it would otherwise be used. Frequently the most capable laymen—of various ages—are tied to activities outside the church.

2. They have taken money that would otherwise be available for the local church's program, including its missionary activities. This is a special point of friction in churches that teach "storehouse tithing."

3. By their specialized natures, these movements have contributed to gaps within the local church between the generations, the sexes, the educated and uneducated. The impression received, if not given by leaders of the movements, is one of inability to communicate outside the group. (Within the church the same problem is found, although at least a modicum of activity covers the spectrum of ages and conditions.)

   Another aspect of this increase in the generation gap is the time parents are away from home because of involvement in lay movements. But they would probably be gone for other reasons—including local church activities—even if there were no such movements. This is the nature of life today.

4. Some laymen have doubtless been spoiled for ordinary local church activity by their involvement in movements outside the church. When consideration doesn't have to be given to the other sex, children, the elderly, the unsophisticated, the poor; and when the extrachurch program can be maintained at a high degree of excitement, ordinary church services—even profound worship experiences—may lose their attraction.

IMPLICATIONS OF LAY MOVEMENTS FOR CHURCH LEADERS

What should be the attitude of the pastor, the director of Christian education, and other church workers toward these lay movements and the men and women who are involved?

1. Be open to lessons that may be learned from these movements. What is so attractive about the extrachurch program? Can methods be carried over, or can they be adapted to our particular church situation?

2. Rethink lay activities within the church. Perhaps there is not enough challenge—enough room for experiment and creativity—for a fresh approach, in the local situation.

3. Avoid any moves to try to control a particular lay movement outside the church. Instead, advise laymen who are part of the movement (but don't go beyond advice). Otherwise we may give an impression of feeling threatened and may alienate our laymen and the movement's leaders.

4. Cultivate an attitude of being "workers together" with lay movements in the Lord's work. The movement outside the church may plant, the church may water, but it is God who gives the increase.

5. Don't expect instant results from the attempts of laymen in these movements to evangelize their peers. It may be a year or more be-

fore people from neighborhood Bible studies or Christian business-men's meetings come to the church. Meanwhile, church leaders should try to be patient and should pray for their laymen who have established their own contact with the world outside the church. In time, the local church's own work will benefit. And immediately, the laymen are benefiting.

6. Be alert to the need laymen have to relate Bible knowledge and doctrine to their daily life. One professional man expressed his feelings this way: "The church never has anything to say about the problems and decisions I face in my work. There's nobody, no group of people, with whom I can talk things over—either there's a judg-mental attitude, or they give simplistic answers without trying to understand my real problems. That's why I'm so active in [the pro-fessional lay movement]."

Of course there are exceptions to the attitude expressed by this man, other compelling reasons that explain laymen's adherence to extrachurch movements. But this response should cause us to ex-amine attitudes and actions in the church.

7. Related to the former suggestion, church leaders should be sure that their churches provide the sort of small groups every adult needs. Laymen ought not to have to go outside the church to find a safe place, an accepting, concerned group.

From these seven observations it is clear that Christian educators are challenged by lay movements to reconsider the effectiveness of their own local church ministries to adults.

NOTES

1. "Gideons International," in *The Encyclopedia of Modern Christian Missions: The Agencies* (a publication of the faculty of Gordon Divinity School), Burton L. Goddard, ed. (Camden, N.J.: Nelson, 1967), p. 301.
2. *Business Men in Action* (Glen Ellyn, Ill.: Christian Business Men's Committee International).
3. George Sanchez, "Navigators," in *The Encyclopedia*, p. 468.
4. Eric S. Fife, "Inter-Varsity Christian Fellowship," in *The Encuclopedia*, p. 342.
5. Sam Wolgemuth, "Youth for Christ International," in *The Encyclopedia*, pp. 718-19.
6. "Campus Crusade for Christ," in *The Encyclopedia*, p. 106.

FOR FURTHER READING

Anderson, Clifford V. *Worthy of the Calling (The Layman's Vital Role)*. Chi-cago: Harvest, 1968.

Ayres, Francis O. *The Ministry of the Laity*. Philadelphia: Westminster, 1962.

Bestholf, Lloyd M. "Some Contemporary Lay Movements and Their Implica-tions for Adult Education in the Churches." In *Wider Horizons in Christian Adult Education*. Lawrence C. Little, ed. Pittsburgh: U. Pittsburgh, 1962.

Bow, Russell. *The Integrity of Church Membership.* Waco, Tex.: Word, 1968.

Chafin, Kenneth. *Help! I'm a Layman.* Waco, Tex.: Word, 1966.

Coiner, Harry G. "The Role of the Laity in the Church." In *Toward Adult Christian Education.* Donald L. Deffner, ed. River Forest, Ill.: Lutheran Educ. Assn., 1962.

Grimes, Howard. *The Rebirth of the Laity.* Nashville: Abingdon, 1962.

Kraemer, Hendrik. *A Theology of the Laity.* Philadelphia: Westminster, 1958.

Miller, Keith. *A Second Touch.* Waco, Tex.: Word, 1967.

————. *The Taste of New Wine.* Waco, Tex.: Word, 1965.

O'Connor, Elizabeth. *The Call to Commitment: The Story of the Church of the Saviour, Washington, D.C.* New York: Harper & Row, 1963.

Neill, Stephen Charles. *The Layman in Christian History.* Philadelphia: Westminster, 1963.

Raines, Robert A. *New Life in the Churches.* New York: Harper, 1961.

Roxburgh, Robert. "The Layman and His Church," *United Evangelical Action,* 26 (Jan., 1968):8-10 and 26 (Feb., 1968): 11-12.

Trueblood, Elton. *The Incendiary Fellowship.* New York: Harper & Row, 1967.

Walker, Daniel D. *Enemy in the Pew!* New York: Harper & Row, 1967.

Wentz, F. K. *The Layman's Role Today.* Nashville: Abingdon, 1963.

17

RESOURCES FOR ADULT CHRISTIAN EDUCATION

Richard E. Troup

It has been said that a good Sunday school curriculum is 90 percent teacher and 10 percent materials. Thus the most important "equipment" for a church Christian education program is adequately equipped teachers who are both dedicated to the Lord and trained in the skillful use of the Word of God.

However, this is not to suggest that materials and facilities are unimportant. While it is true that attractive curriculum materials and functional Christian education buildings will not "make" a good Sunday school, they can provide the plus factors that make a church program excel and be more effective for the Lord.

FACILITIES

PROVIDING DESIRABLE FEATURES IN AN ADULT CLASSROOM

Theorists in general education have discovered the qualities that make a room conducive to learning. The same factors that contribute to learning any subject apply to a facility dedicated to the study of the Word of God. What makes a room suitable for educational purposes? A graphically illustrated text, *A-V Instruction,* suggests the following seven criteria for evaluating a good classroom:[1]

Space. For presentations that are basically lectures, ten square feet per student has normally been considered adequate space. This means that a classroom twenty feet by thirty feet would be adequate for sixty adult students. However, sixty persons is normally considered too many for a class, unless for a given period of time it is possible to acquire a spe-

RICHARD E. TROUP, M.R.E., is Director of Leadership Development, Church Training Service, National Association of Free Will Baptists, Nashville, Tennessee.

cial teacher to benefit a larger number of adults than would usually be placed in one class. Also, to the degree that a teacher utilizes reports, discussions, panels, audio-visuals, etc., the requirements for square footage increase up to a possible maximum of eighteen square feet per student. A room twenty feet by twenty-five feet (450 square feet) has the right balance of width to length, provides sufficient space for a class of twenty-five or thirty students, makes possible the utilizing of class-participation methods, and also is large enough to accommodate a larger group if a special speaker is invited.

Light. A classroom for adults should be light enough so that books can be studied without eyestrain. The teacher should be able to control light without unnecessary confusion when a filmstrip or other projected visuals are required, with a light switch near him. The teacher should not be near an exposed light bulb, a window or a mirror, where a concentration of light might bother either himself or class members.

Color. Depending on the amount of light that enters the room through windows or is provided through artificial lighting, the colors of the room should be bright enough to be cheery without being garish, and should of course not be dull and depressing. The room should also be kept clean and neat.

Acoustics. Many church classrooms today are constructed with cement-block walls and concrete or wood floors and ceilings. Hence there is a distracting harshness of sound in the room. Proper acoustical treatment of a room can be provided through a soft tile on the floor and/or the ceiling, drapes at the windows and pegboard or bulletin-board material on the walls.

Ventilation. Because the temperature and air flow in an adult classroom may vary from that desired for children's facilities, it is best that the room contain its own control for heating, cooling and fresh air.

Storage and equipment facilities. Each adult classroom should be equipped with a screen for projected visuals, or a light, plain-color flat wall on which the films may be projected. There should be a file cabinet for extra copies of notes, outlines and manuals as well as basic visuals such as the maps and charts that will be used frequently in the room. There should also be tables or shelves for equipment such as projectors and tape recorders which will be frequently used, and basic resource materials such as Bible dictionaries, commentaries and concordances. It is not uncommon today for some class members to want to tape-record class periods, and there should be facilities for the tape recorders and microphones without creating a clutter in the front of the class.

Display space. Every adult classroom should include a chalkboard large enough so that the teacher can write drawings and outlines on the board in advance, and still have adequate space for additional writing. There should also be a bulletin board or two facing the class members either when they first enter the room or when they are leaving, or both. Upon this bulletin board the teacher can post up-to-date news announcements and items of information, or may place interest-producing bits of information that will promote discussions related to the subject under study. A portion of the wall may be also covered with pegboard, enabling not only pictures to be hung, but also shelves to be placed on which extra books can be displayed.

In addition to the above, there are other requirements for adult classrooms. Classrooms for adults should be conveniently located so they can be easily found by visiting adults. Directions to the rooms should be clearly printed on attractive signs. Classrooms for adults who are elderly or physically crippled, or classes that would include expectant mothers, should not require stairways, and should be on some floor that could be entered from the outside on a ground level. Restrooms should be conveniently located so adults will not be inconvenienced by long walks to poorly marked restrooms between Sunday school and church worship services. If classrooms for young married adults are in the general proximity of nursery rooms, parents can quickly find their way to their own classrooms, and also be more readily available if an emergency arises in the nursery.

Rooms for adults should be designated by number, not by the name of the teacher of the class or by the name of the class, or by any other technique which would tend to perpetuate this class's claim on the particular classroom. A card holder on the door could contain temporary attractive cards with the name of the course of study currently being taught in the room and the name of the teacher for the current quarter listed in small print underneath, as well as any further information that would be vital for courses currently meeting in that particular room.

Even if the Sunday school has a table at its main entrance for the greeting and registration of visitors, a small table inside each adult classroom could include a "welcome" sign, a guest-registration book, and copies of any current study materials for the use of guests. Hosts guide the visitor from the department entrance to his classroom and help him feel at home.

ADAPTING EXISTING FACILITIES

In many churches it is not possible for adults to occupy facilities specifically designed for classroom use by adults. Indeed, if any classroom in the church has to meet in rooms that are substandard, it should be the adult classes. Adults, more than children and youth, can readily overcome distraction caused by inadequate facilities. They are also the one group in the church that has the financial ability to do something about inadequate rooms. So, both out of necessity and design, it may be that adults will need to meet in other than ideal classrooms.

But what can be done to make these substandard facilities as serviceable as possible? In many churches adult "classrooms" consist of a section of a main auditorium or a large social hall. The first step toward improving that situation is to make the large room appear as much like a smaller classroom as possible. This can be done by temporary screens or curtains if these can be erected without distracting when the large room is used for fellowship or worship. It is also desirable to have the adult group face away from the larger room into a corner. Thus the space behind them will not be noticeable since their focus of attention is on a corner of a room or a wall immediately in front of them. In a social hall with a flat, smooth floor, it may be possible to divide the "classroom" from the remainder of the larger room by means of a piano or storage cabinets on rollers. Figures 1 and 2 suggest an ideal adult classroom and one way to adapt a portion of an auditorium for a class.

Although it is far from ideal to have more than one class meeting in the same room, some church auditoriums may be large enough so that more than one class will be forced to meet there. If so, strange as it may seem at first, three classes in the room will prove to be less distracting to one other than only two. If there are three classes, each teacher will not be directly competing with the voice of one other teacher, but rather with a constant hum of sound caused by two or more other voices.

It may be possible for some adult classes to use other rooms such as the church library, the lounge for wedding receptions, the choir room, the church office, etc. Even the church kitchen may serve as an adult classroom. It might also provide opportunity for the class to have a pot of coffee on hand, adding to an informal atmosphere for a discussion-type study.

EQUIPPING AN ADULT CLASSROOM

Chairs on which adults will be seated for forty-five- to sixty-minute class periods should be comfortable and sturdy. Some churches, rather than selecting folding chairs, are purchasing attractive plastic chairs that do not fold but can be stacked when it is necessary to move the chairs to the side and use the room for weekday clubs or adult social activities.

Adults seated around tables arranged in an L or T or U-fashion are not only encouraged to take notes, but also are stimulated by the informal room arrangement to participate more actively in the lessons. If tables are not possible, some class member who is handy with woodworking

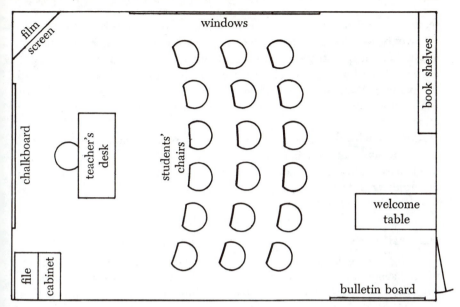

Fig. 1 *Adult Classroom*

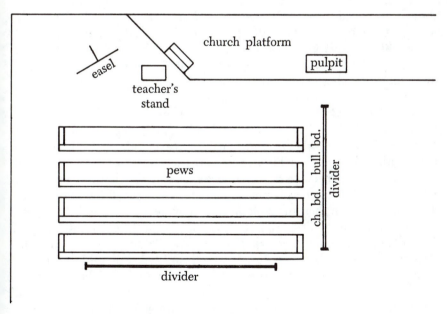

Fig. 2 *Adaptation of Part of Auditorium*

materials may cut extra pieces of masonite or plywood about twelve feet by twenty feet for class members to use as lapboards. Some teachers of adults keep a quantity of pencils on hand for persons who forget theirs. As an extra feature, some classes provide fine-point ball-point pens with the name of the class or church imprinted on them as not only a tool for Bible study but also a reminder of the thoughtfulness of your class and church.[2]

Ideally each adult classroom is furnished with a chalkboard and with easels or some other means for displaying maps and charts. If a class meets in a room that cannot be totally darkened, filmstrips and slides can be projected into a "rear projection screen."

STUDY MATERIALS

SELECT MATERIALS THAT MINISTER TO THE NEEDS OF YOUR ADULTS

Young adults—beginning with age twenty-one, or the cessation of their formal schooling, or marriage, or full-time employment or living away from their parents—have needs related to these important decisions in their life. Middle adults have problems related to establishing a permanent residence in a community, purchasing a house, securing permanent employment, training their children. Senior adults, beginning with their retirement from full-time employment, disablement because of health, or on becoming grandparents, have distinctive needs related to the latter years of their life. Adults also have needs based on their marital status (that is, whether they are single, married, separated, divorced or widowed). Study materials chosen for adult classes will be more effective if they are written with these various needs in mind.

Teach the Word of God to meet the needs of adults. Adults need intensive, direct Bible study. Adults need to be in learning situations where the open Bible brings them face to face with the truths of God and how these truths relate to their lives. Sometime during the church's schedule each week, adults need to be led into direct study of lesson-sized Bible passages. Adults also need opportunities to study the Bible with direct attention placed on their life situations. Thematic and survey Bible study meet real needs in adult lives, but these courses must be carefully taught so they do not become "mere opinion" studies. Adults also need the opportunity to choose between various levels and types of Bible study according to their level of maturity and past experience in Bible study.

ORGANIZE AN INTELLIGENT AND GRADED PROGRAM FOR ADULT BIBLE STUDY

A possible outline of quarterly opportunities for Bible study in a medium-sized church is as follows:

SCHEDULE	SUBJECT CONTENT Possible Quarterly Opportunities	TYPE OF COURSE
Sunday 9:30 A.M. (choose one)	Basic Steps in Christian Growth Old Testament Survey Ephesians Doctrine of Soteriology	For new converts For beginning Bible students For growing Bible students For advanced Bible students
Sunday 6:00 P.M. (choose one)	How to Teach History of Missions	For teachers For nonteachers
Wednesday 7:30 P.M.	Psalms	Devotional, for all
Thursday 10:30 A.M. (At a home)	John	Evangelistic—for women to bring unsaved friends

CHOOSE STUDY MATERIALS WISELY

The following is a listing of selected sources from which study materials for adults may be obtained. Brief annotations describe materials available from those sources.

Asbury Theological Seminary, Department of Evangelism, Wilmore, Kentucky 49390. Thematic Bible studies such as "Established by the Word of God," "Life in the Living Word," etc. Generous quantity discounts available, and special editions prepared for evangelists, churches and schools.

Back to the Bible Broadcast, Box 233, Lincoln, Nebraska 68501. Correspondence school courses include twelve- to fourteen-lesson courses such as "Foundation Studies in Christian Living," "Romans, Volume 1," "Romans, Volume 2." More compact three- to four-lesson booklets, such as "Russia's Doom Prophesied," "The Rise and Fall of the World Empires," "God's Program for the Church," "Living Without Worrying" are suitable for one-month courses, weekends, etc.

Baptist Publications, 2500 W. 2nd Ave., Denver, Colorado 80206. Courses designed for adult Sunday school classes are undated. Both teachers' and students' thirteen-study booklets on "Satan: Conflict of the Ages," "Science, Scripture and Salvation," "Family Talk—the Epistles of John," "Blueprint for Church Order—First Corinthians," etc. Program packets for Sunday evening "Training Union" programs adaptable for churches other than Baptist. Each set of thirteen programs based on the current copy of "Today's Living" magazine.

Berachah Church Publications and Tape Department, 5139 W. Alabama, Houston, Texas 77027. Sermons and Bible studies by Pastor Robert

Thieme are available in both tape and booklet form. Charts and diagrams are also available for many of the courses.

Bethel Lutheran Church, 312 Wisconsin Ave., Madison, Wisconsin 53703. "The Bethel Series," a series of Bible studies based on forty full-color paintings; depicts God's plan beginning with the creation. Widely used in Lutheran churches and adaptable to churches of other denominations.

The Bible for You, P.O. Box 15007, Atlanta, Georgia 30333. Taped Bible studies by Dr. Manford Gutzke on most books of the Bible plus tape-recorded studies on topics such as the Apostle's Creed, the Bible, Christ, Doctrines.

Christian Outreach, Huntingdon Valley, Pennsylvania 19006. Materials for "Growth by Groups" program include a basic manual and an initial ten-week direct Bible-study course. Additional Bible-study courses available.

Church Training Service, Box 1088, Nashville, Tennessee 37202. A quarterly magazine *Focus* contains monthly units on topics of Christian development. Each unit has a leader's guide loose-leaf packet and may be ordered in an undated format.

Crusaders' Bible Course, 4848 Northwest 10th, Oklahoma City, Oklahoma 73115. Four Bible-study courses cover the entire Bible with factual, true-false, and complete-the-blanks questions.

David C. Cook Publishing Company, 850 N. Grove Ave., Elgin, Illinois 60120. Undated, thirteen-lesson books designed for Sunday school elective courses; students' manuals and teachers' guide sets include "Basic Bible Truths," "Great Men of the Church," "Christian Family Living," "Christian Faith in Action," etc.

Emmaus Bible School, 156 N. Oak Park Ave., Oak Park, Illinois 60301. Correspondence school division of this Brethren Assemblies-related Bible institute offers a wide variety of courses usable by both individuals and groups.

Evangelical Teacher Training Association, Box 327, Wheaton, Illinois 60187. Prepared primarily for the training of Sunday school teachers, highly suitable for all of the leadership levels of the local church. Basic course program includes six subjects, three of which are a Bible survey covering the entire Bible, and three of which are of a practical nature. Advanced course program includes three content courses on various areas of Bible doctrine, as well as three methods courses. Students' manuals and a leader's guide are available for each course, and certificates are available for the completion of each six-course program.

Good News Publishers, 9825 W. Roosevelt Rd., Westchester, Illinois 60153. "One Evening Condensed Book Club" provides inexpensive editions of full-length books on a vast variety of subjects. Not prepared for Bible study as such, but desirable as discussion starters and supplemental readings. Topics include "Gems From the Psalms," "This Way to

Happiness," "How to Win Your Family to Christ," "Power and Peace in Prayer," etc.

Gospel Light Publications, 725 E. Colorado Blvd., Glendale, California 91209. Elective courses, designed for Sunday school but suitable for any adult group, include both quarterly style sets of students' and teachers' books, as well as an increasing variety of paperbacks, on subjects such as "Jesus the Revolutionary," "Christianity and the Cults," "God, Men and Missions," "Thirteen Men Who Changed the World."

"What the Bible Is All About" is a fifty-two-lesson, complete survey of the Bible adaptable for use by the teacher with a set of companion books ("A Look at the Old Testament," and "A Look at the New Testament") for student use.

Long-play records featuring Bible studies by Dr. Manford Gutzke, Dr. John Hunter, etc., for use as discussion basis; discussion questions and information on home Bible-study groups available with these records.

Higley Press, Butler, Indiana 46721. "Straight Through the Bible in Two Years" consists of eight study manuals, each with factual questions and self-grading programs enabling the student to check the accuracy of his own answers.

Inter-Varsity Press, 1024 Warren, Downers Grove, Illinois 60515. Open-Bible studies following idea-starter manuals prepared especially for college students, but highly adaptable for any group seeking mature Bible studies. Titles include "Look at Life with the Apostle Peter."

Moody Bible Institute, 820 N. La Salle St., Chicago, Illinois 60610. Correspondence courses available on several levels: Popular Bible, College Credit, Scofield Bible and an advanced study series. A great variety of courses on Bible books, Bible survey, church history, doctrine, marriage, prophecy, science, victorious living, etc.

Many paperback Moody books, although not specifically designed for study courses, are highly suitable either as supplementary reading to a regular course, or as the basis for a study course. Subjects include "Now That I Believe," "Methods of Bible Study," "The Perfect Will of God," etc.

Keith L. Brooks' Bible study courses now arranged in a "Teach Yourself the Bible" series, with attractive booklets on Bible books such as John, Galatians, and Romans as well as thematic studies "How to Live Forever," "Basic Bible Studies for New Christians," "Christian Character Course," "How to Pray," etc.

The Navigators, Inc., Colorado Springs, Colorado 80901. Basic plan for Bible study usable with any Bible passage plus several basic Bible studies for both new Christians and mature believers.

Neighborhood Bible Studies, 269 Broadway, Dobbs Ferry, New York 10522. Mimeographed study guides prepared especially for home Bible-study groups on Mark, Acts, Romans, Psalms and Proverbs.

Radio Bible Class, Box 22, Grand Rapids, Michigan 49501. Reprints of radio messages by Dr. M. R. DeHaan and Dr. Richard DeHaan, suitable for supplementary reading, parallel to regular courses, or as the bases for discussion-type courses. Includes a vast variety of subjects, each with four or five chapters, "Redemption by Blood," "Heaven," "Divine Healing," "The Holy Spirit," "Water Baptism," etc.

Scripture Press Publications, Inc., 1825 College Ave., Wheaton, Illinois 60187. Regular Sunday school students' manuals now in magazine form, entitled *Living Today*. The quarterly magazine *Fellowship* is suitable for home study or use by older adults and others in a Home Department.

Undated study guides based on well-known paperback Christian books, designed for use in Sunday evening training hour or other study groups. Includes "Personal Evangelism," "Christian Home," "How to be a Leader," "Church History Survey," "Bible Archaeology," "Mental Health for Christians," "Know Why You Believe," "The Bible and Tomorrow's News," etc.

Scripture Union, 239 Fairfield Ave., Upper Darby, Pennsylvania 19082. Basically a program for daily devotional Bible study. The quarterly "Bible Study Notes" are adaptable for group study by groups of persons, each of which joins the Scripture Union and receives the regular Bible study mailings.

Standard Publishing Company, 8100 Hamilton Ave., Cincinnati, Ohio 45231. Paperback study courses both on doctrinal subjects and practical areas of Christian living, with questions and answers at the end of each chapter. Teachers' guides available.

Taped Sermon Service, Tabernacle Book Room, Granby at Thole, Norfolk, Virginia 23505. Tape-recorded sermons and Bible studies of messages given by John Dunlap, Sidlow Baxter, Henry Brandt, Eric Fife, etc. On many Bible texts as well as topical studies such as Salvation, Women, Christian Education, etc.

Through the Bible Publishers, 4032 Swiss Ave., Dallas, Texas 75204. An undated series of "Do It Yourself" chapter-by-chapter study courses with twenty-four books of thirteen lessons each, covering the Bible from Genesis through Revelation.

Tyndale House, P.O. Box 80, Wheaton, Illinois 60187. Devotional books and supplemental reading books, especially featuring Scripture selections from the "Living" series, such as "Men Who Dared," a retelling of the lives of the major and minor prophets with Living Prophecies reprints of the prophets and additional interpretative commentary in paperback form.

Windward Press, Box 612, Elgin, Illinois 60122. "Conversations with Jesus Christ," a thirteen-lesson study on the gospel of John prepared especially for use in home Bible-study classes.

NOTES

1. James W. Brown, et al., *A-V Instruction* (New York: McGraw-Hill, 1964), p. 511.
2. "Quickey" pens, P.O. Box 276, Woodburn, Oregon 97071, are specially designed for marking Bibles without blotting through thin Bible paper.

FOR FURTHER READING

Brown, James W., et al. *A-V Instruction*. New York: McGraw-Hill, 1964.
The Church's Educational Ministry: A Curriculum Plan. St. Louis: Bethany, 1965.
Correlated Christian Education in the Local Church. Chicago: Harvest, 1962.
The Curriculum Guide, 1962-1963. Nashville: Convention, 1962.
Fore, William F., et al. *Communication—Learning for Churchmen*. B. F. Jackson, Jr., ed. Nashville: Abingdon, 1968.
Getz, Gene A. *Audio-Visuals in the Church*. Chicago: Moody, 1959.
A Guide for Curriculum in Christian Education. Chicago: National Council of the Churches of Christ in the U.S.A., 1955.
Wykoff, D. Campbell. *Theory and Design of Christian Education Curriculum*. Philadelphia: Westminster, 1961.

SELECTED EVANGELICAL PRODUCERS OF PROJECTED VISUALS

Cathedral Films, 2921 W. Alameda Ave., Burbank, California 91501
Concordia Films, 3558 S. Jefferson Ave., St. Louis, Missouri 63118
Family Films, 5823 Santa Monica Blvd., Hollywood, California 90038
Films for Christ, 1204 N. Elmwood, Peoria, Illinois 61606
Gospel Films, Box 455, Muskegon, Michigan 49443
Ken Anderson Films, Box 618, Winona Lake, Indiana 46590
Moody Institute of Science Films, 12000 E. Washington Blvd., Whittier, California 90606

Part II

HELPING FAMILIES

18

THE CHRISTIAN FAMILY IN TODAY'S WORLD

Oscar E. Feucht

In the past we tended to idealize the Christian home, where there were order and peace, love and service, daily devotions, loving parents and obedient children. But many church families did not live up to this ideal. And in the world of today with its hectic pace, the Christian home is even less effective. Living together in a Christian way is more than maintaining habits of worship and good routine. It deals mostly with the spirit in the home as reflected in interpersonal relationships that grow out of a common faith and a common purpose in life.

What does it mean for a family to be "Christian"? Families, as well as people, can be morally decent without being religious, or they can be religious without being Christian. The one-word difference between morality and religion is *God*. As soon as a person believes in a deity, we say he has a religion. The one-word difference between religion and Christianity is the acceptance of Christ as Saviour. But more particularly it means salvation by *grace*. Other religions teach salvation by works. All religions require some kind of faith. Christianity is a particular faith in Jesus Christ as Saviour and Lord.

The Christian faith is dynamic. It is a lively, life-giving, powerful thing. "It does not have to be told to do good works—it is already doing them," said Martin Luther. Essentially it is confession, repentance, and receiving Christ's forgiveness. The Christian family lives under grace, and it practices mutual forgiveness. We may speak of a certain rhythm of faith, love, trust and service in the Christian home. It's a style of life; not a certain way of doing some things, but a different way of doing all things.

OSCAR E. FEUCHT, D.D., served as Secretary of Adult Education for the Board of Parish Education of The Lutheran Church—Missouri Synod from 1946 through 1968.

In this chapter we shall deal with four aspects of the Christian family in today's world: the family in a changing culture, the home and Christian nurture, fathers and mothers as teachers, and family involvement by the church.

THE FAMILY IN A CHANGING CULTURE

SOME MAJOR FACTORS

There are many factors that have impinged upon the home and left some mark on family relations. Ten are especially significant.

Industrialization. Man has moved from the farm to the factory. In the process of social change from an agricultural civilization to life in small and large communities, the family has been affected. Sandals, clothing and all other physical needs were first provided in the home. In the industrial revolution this industry was transferred to factories, removing the father from the family (a clear break with patriarchalism), and frequently, the mother and children. Capitalism and the entire factory system is part of this movement.

> Production, marketing, and services to the consumer account for the occupational life of an increasing segment of our population. . . . All of this is made possible by a continuous development in communication and transportation, and as the speed of each of these increases, we might expect an even greater expansion in the industrial network.[1]

Urbanization. As people moved from the farm to the city, with part-time or full-time jobs, the number of farms decreased, becoming fewer and larger, and cities and metropolitan areas burgeoned to the point that we have metropolitan areas stretching from Boston to Washington, from Pittsburgh to Chicago, from San Francisco to San Diego, in what have been called "megalopolises." People are compressed into crowded cities.

Forty years ago 70 percent of the members of one church body lived in rural areas and 30 percent in cities. Now the very reverse is true. Between 1950 and 1964 the proportion of United States' population living in metropolitan areas increased from 59 percent to 67 percent. Demographers predict that it will be 75 percent by 1980 and 80 percent by 2000.

Technology. In the first decade of this century children in our families cleaned lamp chimneys, filled coal buckets, and chopped wood for the kitchen stove. Children today have fewer chores, and this is one of the problems we face. The machine age has come. Automation is here, and with it came some depersonalization. The factory worker turns out a piece on his machine which he knows only by number as U237. He may have little or no idea how it is going to be used in the finished product. Someone has said, "This has made human beings like player pianos." On the other hand the natural and physical sciences and the social and behavioral sciences have contributed immeasurably to the mental, physical and social well-being of individuals and families. Our horizons have been widened. Thousands of comforts and advantages have come into our world that have revolutionized living.

Consumer-oriented society. We live in a cash economy; we do not barter goods in exchange for goods. That day has passed. The family is no longer the producer; it is the consumer. Once we said every family needs one good wage earner and two wise spenders. Now, more and more, we need two good wage earners and two wise spenders in every family. We live in a day of many new household appliances: electric and gas stoves, refrigerators, washers, dryers, sweepers. The two-car family is here. Through television and radio even the family at some remote outpost keeps in touch with the whole outside world. Our standards of living have risen rapidly and we want to enjoy the good things of life. These marvelous new conveniences demand much more by way of annual financial income; and the sales pitch of modern advertising has put families under terrific pressures to have new things and keep up with the Joneses.

Services transferred out of the home. Formerly the family itself took care of much of the child's education in the home, tended its sick, and provided protective services. Now the schools have taken over the educational process. We send our sick to hospitals. Many kinds of services are offered for the welfare of citizens by the community, police and fire departments, etc. One of the biggest departments of the United States government is the Department of Health, Education, and Welfare. Education alone is a multibillion-dollar enterprise.

Religious influence has declined. Many a modern man is likely to give more attention to his car than he gives to his son and to the welfare of his family. He may be so concerned about his business that he has little time for church and religion. Personal and family religious concerns have decreased in many homes, including those where the members have church affiliation.

Until recently church membership had been steadily climbing. Now it is declining. We live in a day when money and goods (materialism), fun and pleasure (hedonism), self-service and gain (individualism) are on the increase in the lives of many people. On the other hand there is also developing a positive, moral consciousness, a new respect for people of another color or culture, and a disenchantment with war and destruction.

Part of this decline in religious influence is due to the transfer of Christian education from the family to the church.

> The abdication of the religious nurture function by the family, the inability of the public schools in a religiously pluralistic society to give

religious training, and the extremely limited time available to the church for formal religious education combine to leave a vacuum of religious illiteracy in America.[2]

Child-centeredness. There was a day when children had many home chores and were useful to the family as workers. Then came the time when child-labor laws focused on the rights of the child. Today the child is well protected from work, sometimes not too wisely. Pampering a child handicaps his progress toward maturity. Our society pushes the child toward the mother. He has been called "king of the ranch." One psychologist observes that we have become a society of child-watchers if not "child-worshipers." At the same time no previous generation has seen so much progress in the care and protection of children and given so much information to parents on child development.[3]

Woman's so-called inferiority has been exploded. Down through the centuries woman has been a second-rate citizen with second-rate status also in the home. Now civilization accords to her both legal and political status and almost equal position with man. She has entered almost every career and profession. Educationally she may be as well equipped, or better equipped, than her husband. Psychological studies have proved some differences but also many equalities between man and woman.

The knowledge explosion also influences the family. Much greater maturity on the part of everyone is demanded by the knowledge explosion. Higher education now claims a majority of our youth. New knowledge is coming to us so rapidly that only computers can tabulate it. Yet the human brain is a computer superior to any machine. Various estimates have been made regarding the proliferation of knowledge in our age of technological progress and research. One study estimates that all the knowledge man accumulated from the sixteenth to the twentieth century was doubled from 1900 to 1950; and that total was again doubled in a single decade, from 1950 to 1960![4]

Increased mobility. Rapid transportation and Tellstar communication have made the world one neighborhood. The auto and airplane have given us a mobility never dreamed of in another age. Americans are people on the move. In 1960 one in every six families lived in a county different from the one in which they lived in 1955. As we move from country to the city and from the city to the suburbs, from cottage to ranch house, we are moving up the economic and social ladders. This usually means separation from close relatives.

There are, however, advantages alongside the negative aspects. As some family relations are cut, new social connections must be developed. Schooling may be disrupted, but children may also enroll in a better school. Usually a job promotion and increased income is a result. Fortunately, telephones and airplanes make us only moments apart, but families must be strong enough to make the adjustments.

The industrial revolution of the seventeenth and eighteenth centuries was an extension of the human arm or brawn. The technological revolution of the twentieth century is an extension of the brain (cybernetics). It is in such a world that the modern family lives and moves and has its being. Our world is pleasure- and entertainment-oriented. In many respects it is not so different from the pagan world the apostles faced. In this world God wants Christian families to bear a testimony. God nowhere promised to keep it a simple rural world. On the contrary, at creation God assigned to man the task of subduing the earth (Gen 1:28), and we who live in the space age are seeing this fulfilled in a very marvelous manner.

OTHER AREAS OF CHANGE

This age has been characterized as the age of the sex revolution. Sex stimuli overwhelm child, youth, man and woman with an intensification perhaps never known before. Physical love particularly has been distorted.

> Love and sex have been equated. Satisfying one's sex drives and curiosities is made a positive good, whether this be within or outside of marriage. Sex becomes a sales medium in the business and entertainment worlds. With it all, however, is the concentration on biological, physical, bust-and-hips sex, ignoring or minimizing the emotional, psychological, and spiritual realities associated with sexual expression. The result is a stunted, immature view of sex in human life.[5]

Having said this, we need to add that the church is not guiltless. It has almost exclusively emphasized the negative side of sex. The old pietistic or puritanical view of sex was really not as biblical as we thought it was. It almost denied the doctrine of creation.

Other phenomena in our society are related to this reappraisal of sexuality. The average American family is smaller due to many circumstances, especially the more widespread practice of controls over reproduction. Couples believe they have a right to plan and space the births of children. The complementarian view of family authority is replacing a patriarchal pattern. The roles of both husband and wife, while not basically changed, reflect the fact that both have many and diverse responsibilities and tasks. Family roles are not as fixed and restricted as they were three generations ago. The authority pattern is changing, and not without some confusion. Divorce is accepted "as a realistic expedient for remedying a bad situation. It is preferred to the system of mistresses and paramours often found in lands where divorce is forbidden."[6]

With advances in diet and medical care, Americans are living longer. The number of older persons is increasing. In 1966 the United States Bureau of Census reported approximately 18,457,000 men and women aged sixty-five and over, or 9.4 percent of the total population as compared to 4.1 percent in 1900. It is estimated that this number will rise to some twenty-eight million by the year 2000. Women live longer than men. The big majority of older men (66.8 percent) and older women (62.9 percent) live in families. Only one in twenty-five lives in an institution. On the other hand, half of the present two hundred million United States citizens are under twenty-six years of age! Both facts are significant for the family ministry of the churches.[7]

Other generations have faced changes in their cultures, but never with the rapidity that we must deal with them today. It is easy to overgeneralize the negative aspects and fail to see the positive aspects. In many areas the gains outweigh the losses. On our part there should be no sentimental, nostalgic yearning for yesteryear. God has called us to live here and now for a purpose, to strengthen a society, which in three generations (and for some of us—in a single lifetime) has experienced the brutalizing ravages of three world-enveloping wars.

HOW IS THE FAMILY CHANGING?

The family has been under very close scrutiny in the last three decades by sociologists, psychologists and anthropologists; also by some churchmen, for instance, Derrick Sherwin Bailey and Otto Piper, who sought to find the biblical-theological dimensions of sex and marriage. One social scientist with a theological background, Dr. David R. Mace, in a 1968 conference of church leaders on sexuality, marriage and the family, summarized the current family scene. The following is a condensation of his significant summary:

How is the family changing? Marriage has been turned inside out. Similar values and traditions held the larger family together. Interpersonal relations were considered of a secondary nature. Now the very reverse is true. Today interpersonal factors are of primary value, and similar traditions are on the periphery. The hierarchical values of marriage have been reversed, which makes marriage much more difficult. The ancients avoided conflicts and asked the hierarchical structure to keep order; but with one divorce to every four marriages, the institution of marriage itself has been undermined.

Marriage has changed from an institution to a companionship arrangement. Now the companionship aspect is first and the institutional aspect second. Christian writers are pointing to the positive, theological dimensions of this companionship relation. Marriages cannot be held together today as formerly by external coercion. They must be held together by internal cohesion.

Marriage has moved from partners with fixed roles to partners with fluid roles. Many wives now have two roles, homemaker and wage earner, which roles they have a right to fill. Surveys show that many wives work an eight-hour day at the office and four more hours at home. The husband also, however, has two or more roles. Today both husband and wife play many roles as they meet the demands of our culture.

The extended family (consisting of a family nucleus and various near relatives) has been supplanted by the nuclear family (composed of father, mother and children). The extended family supported many family needs and supplied much assistance. We still have patterns of the extended family in the Soviet Union, in the African kraal (and in North America). The nuclear family tends to drive husband and wife more closely together but may restrict the good influence of the larger or "extended" family on the child.

Marriage has moved from being procreative-centered to being unitive-centered. Both of these goals are found in Scripture. History has emphasized the procreative; the population explosion deemphasizes it. The Hebrews permitted the man to put away a woman if children didn't come of the union. Today the pressure is in reverse.

Marriage has changed from a short-span institution to a long-span institution. The average wife is free of child-bearing before thirty and as early as twenty-six. By her early forties she virtually has completed her major preoccupation as a mother. Medical science has added years to the average life span which extends to the seventies. The parenthood task is completed earlier, so the period when husband and wife are alone again has been extended. This has affected the nature of modern marriage.

The family has moved from the one-vote system to the two-vote system. Formerly obedience and subservience to the husband-father was emphasized. The two-vote system is much more complex. Now married couples need to know how to manage good relationships, yet conflict remains an integral part of marriage, and a successful marriage lies in resolving conflicts. But this again requires much more by way of mature persons.

Marriages have moved from an in-group type of marriage to an out-group type of marriage. Mating and marriage were within the same nationality, social structures, religious belief. Now marriages are taking place across all frontiers, national, racial and religious, partly as a result of a more democratic society and more ecumenical thinking in the field of religion.

We are recovering in our time a more biblical view of sex—one that is more positive. For fifteen hundred years the church kept sex "in a tunnel" which reflected a negative view. In the old days marriage itself was considered sinful when sex relations were enjoyed, and celibacy was elevated far above it. There was a period of antisexual religion.[8]

❖ ❖ ❖

Man and wife are different. They serve each other in a complementary way. The husband provides the main income; his is an instrumental role. The wife supplies love and warmth to the household; hers is an expressive role. The modern wife fills a threefold role: as wife and mother, as companion and social arbiter, as partner in household management. While formerly the man may have been arbitrary in his headship, today the husband has become a president and his wife has become his executive secretary. True, in modern society the father's role is somewhat blunted, but he has not abdicated.

THE FAMILY REMAINS BASIC IN THE MIDST OF CHANGES

The family is here to stay. It has in the past, and it will in the future, adjust to cultural changes. And its stability is rooted in a heterosexual creation, that is, in the fact that God made the human being male and female. Paul in 1 Corinthians 11:11-12 (RSV) states this most clearly: "Nevertheless, in the Lord woman is not independent of man nor man of woman; for as woman was made from man, so man is now born of woman. And all things are from God." In Ephesians 5:21 (RSV), the same apostle says, "Be subject to one another out of reverence for Christ." A German authority translates the verse, "Fitting yourselves together in your proper place and order." First Peter 3:7 (RSV) speaks of the Christian husband and wife as "joint heirs of the grace of life."

Someone has put this very interestingly, saying that babies do not arrive at the shipping dock of some large factory. The family is basic because there is an attraction of man for woman and of woman for man. The result is marriage. Both have a desire for children, and as children come parents get the challenging task of nurturing them. As man and woman take up the tasks of their relationship to each other and their service to their children, they find the true fulfillment God had in mind when He created them man and woman.

Sociologists point to some real strengths in modern marriage, for instance, the equal importance of man and woman, the increased affectional relationship, the greater opportunity for leisure, the many helps which parents have available to them in the rearing of their children, better incomes for a majority of families, and better housing.

Our culture has given the individual man, woman and child more rights and respect. A false individualism, however, may develop, hindering family unity and harmony. The love relationship may have increased, yet parental concern may have decreased. The greater leisure can be great gain, but it also can be misused if we make pleasure a god. Psychology and education have contributed many helpful new insights which parents can use in the training of children, but without religious and moral training we also have an increase in delinquency. We have finer *houses*, more wonderfully equipped than the palaces of old, but materialism can keep these from becoming better *homes* for children, youth and adults.

Christian nurture means giving our youth spiritual values. Let us not look to science to supply such values. Science tells us *how* the world operates, but the Word of God tells us *why* the world operates and gives us the purposes behind life. These purposes are more effectively learned, as surveys have shown, from the home than from any other place.

Edith Hunter points out that religion, as a way of life, cannot possibly be taught in one hour a week; that people may profess the same creeds on Sunday but live by a different religion during the week. Then she issues the challenge:

> Unless the *churches* become more concerned with and aware of the day-by-day religion that its *member families* are living, they will play an ineffectual and trivial role.[9]

Fortunately, Christian adults are recovering their sense of vocation and also seeing their role in the family as part of God's calling. They see themselves as conveyors of the faith and not merely as people bent on the achievement of personal happiness. Edward and Harriet Dowdy, in their book *The Church Is Families*, put it this way:

> In the wisdom of God, the home is still the major training unit in every individual's experience, and, parents are still the first teachers. More education has taken place before a child enters school than will be possible in any other five years of his life. The mastery of a spoken language, for example, represents a tremendous educational feat. Even more dramatic is the development which takes place, to a very large degree, within the framework of the family.
>
> More than any other influence, the family determines the lifelong direction in which a person is going to develop. Although the most dramatic evidence of this influence is discernible in childhood, the family places its mark on every sphere of a person's experience. Like the watermark on stationery, every page of one's personal story is written against the background of his family.[10]

Marriage today must be strong enough to carry the additional demands which modern society places on it. The Christian family that looks on itself as a partnership, created by God, daily forgiven and renewed by the gospel, vitalized by the indwelling of the Holy Spirit, called to witness to Christ, is greatly needed in the changing culture of today's world.

One other fact needs to be faced by the churches. We shall not have less change in the future; society is never really at a standstill. The Christian family and the church must help to condition its members for ongoing change and to equip them to deal positively and redemptively as Christians with such changes.

THE HOME AND CHRISTIAN NURTURE

WHY IS THE FAMILY SO INFLUENTIAL?

At Cape Kennedy are found the launching pads from which rockets and space ships are projected into orbit. The mechanisms of the rocket must be properly set, because if a mistake is made, the rocket plunges into the sea.

Families are launching pads for human beings, children, youth and adults. Parents set the mechanisms of the soul as they supply the insight, the guidance and the teaching for radiant faith, dependability, honesty, the joy of work, and a happy outlook on life. Parents are not all authors of books, but they are all writing the lives of their children. No teacher has the high advantages of a Christian parent. Parents can enrich life or they can mar and scar a life, depending on the type of nurture they give, or the lack of it.

A survey of the Bible indicates that the family is considered the training school; it is the most influential factor in helping children and youth become the people of God. The church Fathers and the Reformers underscored this. This will not change, because again it is intimately and inseparably tied to the very nature of the man-woman, father-mother relationship and the concern of parents for their children.

Modern educators agree that for the transmission of our Christian heritage, the development of character and the improvement of society, the family is primary and basic.

Dr. William Kottmeyer, superintendent of schools of the city of St. Louis, in a letter to parents wrote:

> We live in times of tension and angry violence. Many of our youngsters are rebellious because they do not have the security and control of a stable home. The influence of the churches on young people seems to be growing weaker. Society appears to expect the schools alone to bear the responsibility of preparing children to live securely in tomorrow's uncertain world.
>
> Parents have always overestimated the effect the schools have on the training and education of children. From birth through high school a youngster with perfect school attendance spends about thirteen percent

of his waking hours in school. If the teachers have only that much time to teach, does it not seem reasonable that they be given a chance to do so? To operate a productive learning program, the teachers need the cooperation and support of the home. When the objective and purposes of the home are different from those of the school, there will be little learning done in the school.[11]

NONVERBAL, RELATIONAL TEACHING

There are three types of teaching which we frequently overlook. The first of these is *nonverbal or relational teaching*. This is not giving words and having them repeated and memorized. It is the kind of teaching we do by what we are, by what we do and by what we say. It refers to the moral and spiritual climate, or absence of such a climate, in a home. If God is not mentioned, how are children to gain a concept of their Maker and Redeemer? Parents are the ones that must show who God is. Parents must give love, confidence, praise, encouragement, a vision of excellence. Dorothy Nolte shows that much teaching takes place, frequently without words, simply by imitation:

If a child lives with criticism, he learns to condemn.
If a child lives with hostility, he learns to fight.
If a child lives with fear, he learns to be apprehensive.
If a child lives with pity, he learns to feel sorry for himself.
If a child lives with ridicule, he learns to be shy.
If a child lives with jealousy, he learns to hate.
If a child lives with shame, he learns to feel guilty.
If a child lives with encouragement, he learns to be confident.
If a child lives with tolerance, he learns to be patient.
If a child lives with praise, he learns to be appreciative.
If a child lives with acceptance, he learns to love.
If a child lives with approval, he learns to like himself.
If a child lives with recognition, he learns to have a goal.
If a child lives with sharing, he learns about generosity.
If a child lives with fairness, he learns justice.
If a child lives with honesty, he learns what truth is.
If a child lives with security, he learns to have faith in himself.
If a child lives with friendliness, he learns that the
    world is a nice place to live in.[12]

Children are an echo of their peers. If anger is shown, like an echo anger comes back. In whose image will your children be? In your image and your spouse's! In what other image could they be? What kind of an echo will they give? An echo of yourself! A Chinese proverb says, "A child is like a white piece of paper on which every passerby writes a little." This tells us how important our actions, our attitudes, our ordinary day-to-day living is, and how powerfully this relational teaching affects all members of the family.

SITUATIONAL TEACHING

Parents see all sides of the child, in many more ways than any teacher sees them. Parents are with their children at every developmental stage of life. They notice the progress the three-year-old makes as he approaches four, and that of the four-year-old as he approaches five. Moreover, they are present when the vase is broken, when the unkind word is spoken, when the accident happens on the street, when the story is brought back from the schoolroom. Thus parents are on the scene to use the teachable moments of life. In fact, the very incidents of everyday life are part of the curriculum. This situational teaching is presented forcefully for us in the words of Deuteronomy 6:7 (RSV): "When you sit in your house, and when you walk by the way, and when you lie down, and when you rise."

In a large musical family there were children of high school age and also a newborn baby. The older children were all taking piano lessons, and one day a daughter came to her father, saying, "Daddy, why can't we have a baby grand piano?" to which he replied, "Because we have a grand baby." It was just an incidental remark of a few words, but a whole philosophy of life was taught in a single sentence.

Elizabeth and John were farmed out to their grandparents while their father and mother were on a business-vacation trip. After grandfather read the devotions for the day he also made some comments, saying that our faith is a very powerful thing in holding people together in the family. Elizabeth, who was fifteen, was inquisitive and asked, "Well, did you and Grandmother ever have trouble?" Grandfather replied, "We don't talk about it very often, but there was a time when we were not getting along too well. And then one day I came in from the garden only to hear a voice upstairs. I went to the stairwell and heard Grandmother telling God what she could not persuade herself to tell me." Then the girl asked, "But, Grandfather, what did you do?" He replied, "I quietly walked up the stairs and knelt down beside her and told God my side of the story. And from that day to this we have never had a problem which we could not resolve by talking it over with each other and with God."

Practically every day we have such opportunities for Christian teaching and training. They come while we are washing the dishes, or looking at an album, or discussing a television program, or reading the newspaper, or when we are on a family vacation trip.

FORMAL AND INFORMAL TEACHING

The home has been rightly called a laboratory. The koinonia of the New Testament is best reflected in the Christian home where its members learn to bear one another's burdens and so fulfill the law of love. The most gifted serves the most, and the least gifted sometimes gets most. The home is the laboratory of Christian love, and a laboratory is where you learn by actual experience.[13]

The skills of Christian discipleship—prayer, worship, Bible reading, witnessing—can be learned only by doing them. No school can provide this sort of laboratory experience. Exhortation doesn't bring about what Bible-reading practice does. Unless parents help the child through the first prayers and help him day by day, he will probably not learn to pray freely. Thus, in family gatherings and in the person-to-person sharing around the supper table, the spiritual heritage of past generations and the current mission of Christ's people are shared, experienced, learned.

The home has to serve as a sort of blender that weaves together the varied currents that play upon the child in our complex world and helps to give children wholeness and meaning. In *Opening the Door for God*, H. L. Sweet says the family helps to make a pattern out of the jumble of influences. "It gives direction and purpose. It stimulates and guides growth. It interprets and demonstrates. That is why it is so important for parents to share as fully as possible the life of their children."[14]

All of this means that to be of much influence to the child the church must work through the home. One family-life educator indicates that society today is being "bleached" of its religious character, and mere religiosity is inadequate to meet the need. He suggests that responsibility must be returned to the family and the family equipped for its spiritual tasks.

FATHERS AND MOTHERS AS TEACHERS

THE ROLE OF THE FATHER

Much has been written about the absentee father. Present society keeps him out of the home more than in any other civilization, and it is likely that the club and the business, or even the church, may keep him from fulfilling to his satisfaction his role in the home.

Who is an ideal father? Someone who is more than a biological progenitor. He is one who gives of himself, of his spirit, and of his time to his children. He is one who loves as a father and is the source of strength to the family. He gives to the family its name and identity; he should give to it its purpose and integrity. He is to be a source of inner strength morally, psychologically and spiritually. The father encourages being as well as doing, that is, being a person who fulfills the Creator's intention and is a means of service to God, family and society. What father image does your child really get?

What is more, the father is also to be a teacher. He is an interpreter of the masculine, both to his daughter as well as to his son. He, more than the mother, is also an interpreter of the whole outside world—political, social, economic. He is a transmitter of norms and goals. He should be feeding the hunger of the mind and setting the sights of family members for their mission in life. He should teach orderliness and give responsibility, training his children for work, and induce management. He should develop trust and give confidence. Someone has well said, "Only he who trains a child is truly his father."

The father has not really vanished, and woman's desire is for his headship in her marriage. He is part of a new husband-wife team, to be sure. But he is also in a very special sense the father, the provider, who covers his family well with insurance, who spends time with the children in a meaningful way, who insists on a good education, but who, above all, gives to the family integrity and spiritual goals. It is, however, not the quantity of time he spends with the family, but the quality of it, that counts.

THE ROLE OF THE MOTHER

We have already indicated that the mother has a role as wife, as homemaker, as teacher, and as social arbiter for the family. She is endowed with a natural sensitivity to pain and the needs of others; she is the teacher of moral excellence and of religion. The author's own mother was his first seminary. The woman plays an increasingly important role in our society, not merely in the community, but especially also in the church. Her unselfish love and her service make her the conveyor of an *agape* type of ministry.

More women are in the labor force than at any point of our history, namely, 71 percent of our single women (January, 1968) and 50 percent of married women over twenty-five years of age (1966). Women have always worked on the family farm and garden beyond household tasks. What is different is the extent of the outside employment of women, which seems to be necessary in our economy. If all women stayed at home, the present economy of the world would fall apart. And this is not the first generation of which this could be said (see Pr 31). "In 1940 about 1.5 million mothers with children under 18 were in the U.S. labor force. Within the next decade this figure tripled so that in 1950 there were 4.6 million such working mothers. Between 1950 and 1964 this total doubled, and the figure stood at 9.5 million."[15] There is every indication that it will rise still higher.

The chief concern seems to be that while mothers are working, children are uncared for. Though a *vital* concern, this is an overgeneralization. The United States Children's Bureau reports that most working mothers provide for the care of their children through a father, a relative, a non-relative, another private home, a day-care center, and the like.[16] Less than 10 percent of the children, it was found, have no arrangements made for them (and these are mainly older children).

This is indeed a problem. But more than physical presence is needed. The personal character of the homemakers and the psychological conditions in the home should be the real focus of a positive approach. In many cases women have no other choice, if children are to be fed and clothed, and rents are to be paid.[17]

Today's woman has a longer life span and usefulness and is much better equipped to make contributions in many fields than any previous generation of women. This accounts for her broad perspective and her enlarged field of services. One active church woman gives this testimony:

> For the last two years I have been a working woman, albeit part time. In these two years I have done more personal, social, and spiritual growing than during any comparable previous period in my life—perhaps my beliefs and values were being put to the test by contact with real life. It's as if the Christian edge of my personality was being whetted by abrasion against suffering, against pettiness, against discontent. I am a nurse, and worked at a county hospital. I have now begun a new job, as a public health nurse, and expect to continue to grow in my understanding of what's needed by people and in my ability to serve them.[18]

We need to add that woman's highest service and her finest contributions are as wife and mother, in home, church and community. And churches particularly are deeply in debt to the Christian woman. It is in her role as a Christian that she finds her greatest fulfillment.

MUCH DEPENDS ON THE MARRIAGE

The marriage itself with all its intrafamily (relatives) and extrafamily (friends) relationships makes a lifelong impact on our children and their families. It has been said that "what the marriage is, the family becomes." This is one reason why so much attention is being given, also by the church, to premarital and postmarital counseling.

When the affectional relations between husband and wife are supported by a common faith and similar objectives in life, husband and wife become a team whose way of life is apparent in all that they do. Their unity and ideals are reflected in their whole style of life, in their concerns, interests, relationships. A balanced outlook on the world, fine character, mutual respect, and a high sense of responsibility are noticed at once by their children. If they also possess emotional maturity, self-giving love, and a sense of service, their very personalities are "the books their children read." Father and mother are the constantly operating visual aids of their children.

One area, by way of example, is sexuality. As Christian couples gain a positive, biblical view of sexuality, seeing sex as a gift of God and honorable, they are able to speak positively of the unitive as well as the procreative function of sex in marriage and radiate a warmth and fulfillment which a wholesome sex life provides. Such couples are equipped to give a Christian view of sex to their children and deal effectively with the so-called "sex revolution."

The daily exposure of children to balanced Christian living, not only in the parent-child relationship but also in the husband-wife relationship, is the best preparation for marriage. A successful marriage pattern is one of the best endowments we can give our children.

FAMILY INVOLVEMENT BY THE CHURCH

THE BIBLICAL CONCEPT OF NURTURE

According to the Old Testament pattern, it was through the parents that the child was to learn of God's love and care and so get a sense of security; to learn God's Word and truth and get a sense of authority; to learn right from wrong and so get a proper sense of morality; to learn how to commune with God and so get the highest privilege of which man is capable, worship.

There is no explicit mention of schools in Jewish life until after the exile.[19] The place of learning was the home in the earliest period. Instruction was in the hands of the parents, and teaching in the home continued to play an important part in family life. The Talmud speaks of the father's responsibility to inculcate the law, to teach a trade, and to get his son married.

In the New Testament there is a blending of instruction and discipline in the Greek concept *paideia,* the basic term for nurture. Arndt and Gingrich define the noun as "upbringing, training, instruction, . . . chiefly as it is attained by discipline, correction. . . ."[20] The apostolic injunctions concerning nurture are in practically every instance directed to the father, although not to the exclusion of the mother (Eph 6:1-4). While nurture is not restricted to the family, the home is always especially mentioned, also in the qualifications for bishops and deacons. The teaching, learning, correcting and guiding are closely associated with all interpersonal relationships in the Christian community (Col 3:12-25; Eph 5:21—6:4). Marriage and instruction were to be "in the Lord," that is, "in Christ," related to a grace-faith-love theology.

The spiritual lineage, like the familial lineage, was to remain unbroken as parents shared their faith and rehearsed God's great acts of salvation (Ps 78:1-8; Jos 4:1-7; Deu 6:1-9; 11:18-21).

When parents recognize that the everyday relationships of the home are part of the educational curriculum, then they begin to understand Christian nurture. William Barclay writes,

> The New Testament lays down no kind of curriculum of training for the child, knows nothing about religious education and nothing about schools; for the New Testament is certain that the only training which really matters is given within the home, and that there are no teachers so effective for good or evil as parents are. . . . As the church saw it, the school is at best an adjunct to the home. It is the parent who is responsible for bringing the child to God. The child is a gift of God to the parent, and the child must be a gift of the parent to God.[21]

It is plain then that nurture is more than a "schooling." To put it tritely: education does not happen in a school; it happens in a person!

Failure to grasp the fact that Scripture makes nurture the goal of Christian education and emphasizes personal discipleship is one of the basic causes why the modern church in practice so often bypasses the family. Christian education is much more than instruction in Christian doctrine, vital as that is. It is personal reconstruction and transformation by the gospel. It is much more than the acquiring of facts; it is the receiving of power. It is life-changing; it is making disciples of Jesus Christ.[22]

EDUCATIONAL PHILOSOPHY AND PRACTICE

The older the church gets, the greater is the accumulation of historical-theological data to be passed on to the next generation. The multiplication of knowledge has demanded schools and the extension of schooling. This has been a growing task since the synagogue schools were opened about 400 B.C. Public education (nursery through graduate school) has been mushrooming and becoming more and more specialized. The age-level approach and the isolation of developmental tasks by the psychologist-teacher, the departmentalization and classification of knowledge, the separation of home, school and church, have given us a highly structured, fully institutionalized educational system. As a result many parents have been led toward abdication of their teaching-nurture roles. "To a startling degree, American parents have handed child-raising to educational institutions that cannot or will not do the job," says a significant essay in *Time* magazine. "Parents never see the challenge; teaching a child integrity—the self-respect that makes for strong, kind men and women who can cope with life's temptations and who are willing to face the fact that life is a set of problems to be solved."[23] This requires warmly firm parents who admire each other and on whom the child can model himself; who provide opportunities for the child to prove his competence in work and love.

The point, however, is that churches likewise have formalized, structured, age-grouped, separated and institutionalized Christian education, have passed on the creeds and doctrines of Christendom, but have been weak on functional Christianity and the deeper dimensions of nurture through their divorce of church and family in their educational philosophy (partly) and in their operational practices (largely). This is the new challenge Christian educators must face.

FAMILY APPROACH BY THE CHURCH

Fortunately the behavioral scientists, the psychologists, and the greater concerns of the church for the well-being of the whole man have been pushing the church toward greater realism.

> Psychiatrists indicate that up to 90 percent of our behavior and attitudes are the result of the relationship environment under which we are raised. Even if it is less than this it still points up the importance of the parental role.
>
> Children have designed into their very nature a force that compels them to identify with an adult and through such identification pattern their lives. Again, this points up the importance of parents' lives in the formation of the lives of their children.
>
> Of all His creatures God has chosen to design the human child to be in a dependent role for a longer period of time. Animals mature in a very short time, some birds in a matter of weeks. Children remain in this position from infancy into their teens.[24]

Ernest M. Ligon in his character-research laboratory found "measurable evidence of effective character education only in situations in which the home has effectively participated."[25] "The primary role of parents in Christian education," says Donald R. Pichaske, "can also be supported on the basis of psychological insights. There is hardly a theory of personality development from Freud to Rogers that does not place strong emphasis on the critical nature of the bond between primary parent and infant in the child's development."[26]

Horace Bushnell in his famous book *Christian Nurture* (1847, reissued in 1947), Regina Wieman, Harry C. Munro, Samuel Hamilton, Wesner Fallaw, Randolph Crump Miller, Edith Hunter, these and many more, have called on the church to rethink its educational philosophy so as to embrace the home. They say that the home and the church must interpenetrate if nurture and education are to be combined effectively, because when views of home and church run counter to each other, generally the child adheres to the standards of the home. Religious integration does not come primarily from the child's idea of God but from a personal relationship with God, chiefly learned from a parent.[27]

One of the clearest calls to action comes from Edward and Harriet Dowdy:

> Earnest Christian education proponents have long since discovered that it is not a question of whether the home or the church shall religiously educate the children and youth, but how they may best work together.
>
> One major concern of most denominations is the adequate preparation of lesson and guidance materials. Curriculum, however, is far more than this. It is, more accurately, "the whole course that is to be run," the entire guided experience. In the final analysis, no denominational structure can devise the curriculum for your church. The climate of Christian concern by teachers, pastor, and congregation, plus local circumstances, prescribes the eventual form of the curriculum which you use.[28]

It is clear then that denominations need not only enunciate the family role in their educational philosophy but also follow through with operational policy, material and practice. Here the Presbyterian Church in the United States sets a good pattern:

> The most immediate and far-reaching form of Christian nurture which the church can provide takes place in the Christian household where persons live together intimately, expressing their faith to one another and absorbing the Christian faith from one another in both verbal and nonverbal ways. . . . Moreover the basic nurture of all church members, of whatever age, must necessarily be carried out in the household setting where the most elemental facts of life and death are met and the most intimate relationships established. Whatever is believed in the household is communicated to all members of the household. . . . Unless this basic sort of nurture in the Christian faith is done here, it is doubtful that it can be done at all effectively anywhere."[29]

This denomination is carrying through with a companion "Home and Family" educational program to articulate its philosophy.

Actually home and church dare not be separated. The church cannot function in a disordered world without the home, and the home cannot have spiritual fire on its altar unless it is part of the church. *What is more, home and church must have the same theology.* This makes Christian adult education *imperative!* The church needs to be much more supportive of the home than it now is. The church has neglected the home because it has been too concerned with its own survival and too absorbed in its own housekeeping chores.

INVOLVEMENT OF FAMILIES

We have seen some of the reasons why the church has not made more progress in family-life education, particularly in getting parent participation. Councils on Family Relations, The Child Study Association, a National Parent-Teacher Association, the decennial White House Conference, social agencies, and various departments of our universities have long been at work in this field. Why is there not greater interest in the church? We asked this question of ten leading Protestant educators. All agreed that parent involvement is dealing with the heart of the congregational task.

Dr. Paul Vieth replied, "Christian nurture grows out of the whole style of life of the home, and will not be achieved by simply devising curriculum plans which assume it." Then he added,

> In my present thinking, the most helpful element in the situation is the new emphasis on the lay ministry. Christian vocation includes Christian homemaking, and this is one of the most visible aspects of Christian vocation in the experience of most adults in the church. But as you are keenly aware, the understanding and practice of lay ministry depends on an effective program of adult education such as few churches have yet been able to achieve.[30]

Some fundamental rethinking is needed. More than two decades ago the writer helped a parish rethink its women's program, beginning with such basic questions as: What is a woman? For what should a church equip a wife? A mother? How prepare her for her basic mission? The outcome was ten neighborhood study-action circles with five parent-family topic studies and five missionary topics each year. Every woman was served in her own neighborhood. Ninety percent of the women of the parish were involved (a 300 percent increase). A viable service starts with the right questions!

The church must stop looking to the home as a *tool* for doing the work of the church (a fundamental mistake). The family must not be allowed to assume "the church can take over our responsibility for the education and nurture of our children." Home and church must realize their mutual interdependence.[31]

This in turn calls for a reorientation of pastors, teachers, directors of Christian education, Sunday school superintendents, teachers, church boards and officers. And the beginning is a recovery of the concept of Christian vocation as involving the whole style of life in the home, and a firmer stance by the church not to take over for parents.

The home can be linked to the church in many ways. Hopeful signs are the child-guidance questions of parents, the popular syndicated family columns in newspapers, the heavy focus on marriage and family in almost every magazine. Parents have *not* abdicated; most of them are really concerned. This is especially true of Christian parents.

The church should explore a number of approaches to parents: through the child to the parent, through the parent to the child, through the church's teaching agencies, through class mothers (one for every class), through parent-teacher meetings, through a parent-teacher approach to curriculum, through extant or awakened needs in parents, like the sex-education question. But all of these suggest some prime movers and a very human, helpful and realistic approach to families.

Among the viable contacts are: involving parents at the enrollment of every child, home contact and visitation on a regular basis, ongoing home-church relationship in the Sunday school no less than in the scouting program, quarterly parent-teacher conferences, involving parents in team-teaching with jointly planned projects, serving the many other needs of families (economic, physical, psychological, recreational, relational), courses for parents based on *their* curriculum, a church library well stocked with books for families, and adult involvement in the youth program.*

An assistant pastor looked for a more creative approach to the Christian education of children, in which theory and practice worked together. He recognized that personal commitment does not come with intelligent development, that "formation" of the whole person is of greater importance than "information," and that Christian fellowship or community does not necessarily grow out of an efficient organization.

The released-time program was failing. So he announced that there would be no further instruction until thirty parents volunteered to use their homes for classes of ten. This did away with "automatic religion where the parent had only to sign a card and forget about the whole thing." Grade-school children met after school once a week, junior highs on a weekday evening, all in their own neighborhoods. This eliminated transportation expense. This proved so successful that the next year 180 parent-teacher instructors and as many homes were enlisted to serve a parish of 1,600 members.

Two appeals motivated teacher recruitment and training: a personalized witness type of instruction and adult education for teacher growth. The small group permits person-to-person teaching and every group has its own learn-by-doing project each semester. This experiment suggests that Christian nurture cannot be isolated from the home, or separated from life, or confined to a building, nor ever be institutionalized. The leaders put it this way: "Religion is basically *not* a classroom subject; our

*Also see chap. 26, "Developing a Family-Centered Educational Program."

instruction must be alive, giving motivation for life today; love, not fear, must be the basis of our Christianity."[32]

If a pastor gives proper rating to his teaching-enabling ministry, regarding his office as more than preaching, pastoral calls, evangelism, and business administration, any church can develop an effective home-related ministry. The above-mentioned church, with 180 small cell groups in homes, operates with a staff of only two administrative secretaries who handle the mechanics. Hospitals and community organizations are using thousands of volunteers very effectively. Gray ladies, Red Cross and Community Chest workers are doing a magnificent job. Almost every church can find a director of volunteers òr a coordinator of Christian action who can assist with the details of a family ministry. Social welfare leaders have discovered the value of the "indigenous nonprofessional," a corps of lay workers who have the common touch. Needed are people who care; committed Christians who see the whole family, not just the child; who can demonstrate nurture as part of everyday living; who can host new families; who can listen for family needs and radiate a faith that works by love. Such leadership is to be found in almost every Christian community.

Parent involvement usually begins with teacher-leaders. What kind? Not those who are teaching merely to do the Sunday school superintendent a favor, or who think Christian teaching is merely telling a Bible-hero story or that drilling facts is equivalent to Christian nurture. But "visiting teachers" who have rapport with the family, can team up with parents, see the whole child, and are ready to "go the second mile."

What kind of theological stance is needed? One in which discipleship rather than mere church attendance or membership is the goal. One which sees faith, mutual forgiveness, love and service *in Christ* as the essence of Christianity. One that develops homes where God's grace flourishes; homes that are "a witnessing circle of believers" because Christ is in the daily lives of fathers and mothers.

Vance Packard, who discusses the spreading materialism of our day, dedicates his book *The Waste Makers*, "To my mother and father who have never confused possession of goods with the good life."[33] Hamilton says, "The young are not apt to learn religion or to be Christian unless their immediate environment, the home, is Christian in attitude and act more than in verbal expression."[34]

The family is a different structure than a school. It is an organism rather than an organization. It is a way of life rather than a succession of courses. The curriculum is what father and mother believe and live; it is an informal learning group. It serves as the hub of the wheel—the integrator and interpreter of life. The Duvalls have well summarized the significance of the home in these succinct words: "For the transmission of our Christian heritage, the development of character, and improvement of society the family is primary and basic."[35]

NOTES

1. Armin Grams, *Changes in Family Life* (St. Louis: Concordia, 1968), p. 27.
2. Carl F. Reuss, *The New Shape of the American Family* (Minneapolis: Commission on Research and Social Action, The American Lutheran Church), p. 7.
3. Grams, p. 44.
4. Ibid., p. 61.
5. Reuss, p. 2.
6. Ibid., p. 10.
7. *Facts About Older Americans* (1966); *Meeting the Challenge of the Later Years* (1967) (Washington, D.C.: U.S. Dept. of Health, Education, and Welfare); and Oscar E. Feucht, "Open Doors for Older Persons" (St. Louis: Board of Parish Education, The Lutheran Church—Missouri Synod, 1967).
8. A condensation of remarks by David Mace at a Lutheran Consultation on Sexuality, Marriage, and the Family (Nov., 1968). See his article "Family Change Is Healthy," *Lutheran Women* (May, 1969), Lutheran Church Women, 2900 Queen Lane, Philadelphia, Pa. 19129. For a more comprehensive summary of a biblical view of sex see *Sex and the Church*, Oscar E. Feucht, ed. (St. Louis: Concordia, 1961), pp. 213-36.
9. Edith Hunter, "The Family Lives Its Religion," *Religious Education*, 52 (Mar.-Apr., 1957): 94-97.
10. Edward and Harriet Dowdy, *The Church Is Families*, pp. 15-16.
11. William Kottmeyer, "Letter to Parents," *School and Home* (Dec., 1968).
12. Dorothy Law Nolte, "Children Learn What They Live," *Scouting Magazine* (Apr., 1964), p. 31.
13. Samuel L. Hamilton, "The Family the Center of Religious Education," *Religion in Life*, 18 (Summer, 1949): 421.
14. H. J. Sweet, *Opening the Door for God* (Philadelphia: Westminster, 1964), p. 117.
15. Grams, p. 67. For more specific data write to the U.S. Dept. of Labor, Washington, D.C., for such summary analyses as: "Who Are the Working Mothers?" (1968), "Why Women Work" (WB 68-190), "Fact Sheet on Changing Patterns of Women's Lives" (WB 68-157), "Working Wives—Their Contribution to Family Income" (WB 67-271).
16. Ibid., p. 70. *Child Care Arrangements of the Nation's Working Mothers, 1965: A Preliminary Report*, U.S. Dept. of Health, Education, and Welfare and the U.S. Dept. of Labor (Washington: U.S. Government Printing Office, 1965).
17. There are many other reasons why wives are working: to help put children through college, to help husband through graduate school, to meet the high cost of living, to escape from boredom, to provide luxuries, to attain a sense of independence, to achieve a greater sense of fulfillment, to serve the community. See Rudolph Norden, *Lutheran Woman's Quarterly*, 27 (Spring, 1969): 26.
18. Louise Robertson, *Lutheran Woman's Quarterly*, 27 (Spring, 1969): 2-7.
19. *Interpreter's Dictionary of the Bible* (Nashville: Abingdon, 1962), 4:478-80.
20. William F. Arndt and F. Wilbur Gingrich, *A Greek-English Lexicon of the New Testament* (Chicago: U. Chicago, 1957), p. 608. See also George Bertram, *"paideuo," Theologisches Wörterbuch zum Neuen Testament*, ed. Gerhard Kittel and V. Gerhard Friedrich (Stuttgart: W. Kohlhammer Verlag, 1954), pp. 596-624.
21. William Barclay, *Train Up a Child: Educational Ideals in the Ancient World* (Philadelphia: Westminster, 1959), pp. 236, 262.
22. Hamilton, p. 421.
23. "The Difficult Art of Being a Parent." *Time* magazine 91 (Dec. 15, 1967): 30-31, condensed in *Reader's Digest*, 92 (Mar., 1968): 58-59.
24. Paul Hinrichs, *Family Life Supplement* (St. Louis: Board of Parish Educ., The Lutheran Chuch—Missouri Synod, Sept., 1968).
25. Ernest M. Ligon, *Dimensions of Character* (New York: Macmillan, 1956).

26. Donald R. Pichaske, "Foundations for Curriculum: Theological and Educational." Unpublished paper (St. Louis: The Lutheran Intersynodical Parish Educ. Committee, 1965).
27. Randolph Crump Miller, *The Clue to Christian Education* (New York: Scribner, 1950), pp. 9-14.
28. Dowdy, p. 38.
29. "The Life of the Particular Church as the Context for the Educational Work of the Church," *Foundation Paper*, 6:9; "Principles for the Development of the Christian Family Life Aspect of Curriculum," *Curriculum Principles Paper* III (Richmond, Va.: Board of Christian Educ., Presbyterian Church in the United States), pp. 2-9.
30. Mimeographed Report on this Survey (St. Louis: Board of Parish Educ., The Lutheran Church—Missouri Synod).
31. Dowdy, p. 16.
32. "A New Method of Religious Education in the Parish," *Crosswinds* (Sept., 1968), published at 75 Champlain St., Albany, N.Y.
33. Vance Packard, *The Waste Makers* (New York: McKay, 1960).
34. Hamilton, p. 421.
35. Evelyn and Sylvanus Duvall, *Sex Ways—in Fact and Faith* (New York: Association, 1961), p. 7.

FOR FURTHER READING

The Family in Today's Society

Crook, Roger H. *The Changing American Family*. St. Louis: Bethany, 1960.

Duvall, Evelyn; Mace, David R. and Popenoe, Paul. *The Church Looks at Family Life*. Nashville: Broadman, 1964.

Fairchild, Roy W. and Wynn, John Charles. *Families in the Church: A Protestant Survey*. New York: Association, 1961.

Grams, Armin. *Changes in Family Life*. St. Louis: Concordia, 1968.

Family Life Education in the Church

Dowdy, Edward and Harriet. *The Church Is Families*. Valley Forge, Pa.: Judson, 1965.

Feucht, Oscar E., ed. *Helping Families Through the Church*. St. Louis: Concordia, 1957.

———. *Ministry to Families*. St. Louis: Concordia, 1963.

McIver, Malcolm C. *Principles for the Development of Christian Family Education: A Leader's Guide*. Richmond, Va.: CLC, 1963.

Smith, Leon and Staples, Edward D. *Family Ministry Through the Church*. Nashville: Cokesbury, 1967.

Marriage

Bracher, Marjory L. *Love Is No Luxury*. Rev. ed. Philadelphia: Fortress, 1968.

Evans, Louis H. *Your Marriage—Duel or Duet?* Westwood, N.J.: Revell, 1962.

Hulme, William E. *Building a Christian Marriage*. Englewood Cliffs, N.J.: Prentice-Hall, 1965.

Mace, David R. *Whom God Hath Joined*. Philadelphia: Westminster, 1951.

Nelson, Elof G. *Your Life Together*. Richmond, Va.: John Knox, 1967.

Trobisch, Walter. *I Loved a Girl*. New York: Harper & Row, 1965.

"The U.S. Family: How It's Changed!" *Life* 61 (Dec. 16, 1966):4.

Parent Education

Fairchild, Roy W. *Christians in Families.* Richmond, Va.: CLC, 1964.
Parent Guidance Series (14 books, 32 to 68 pages each). St. Louis: Concordia.
Sweet, Herman J. *Opening the Door for God.* Philadelphia: Westminster, 1964.

Sex Education

Bailey, Derrick Sherwin. *Sexual Relation in Christian Thought.* New York: Harper, 1959.
Concordia Sex Education Series. W. J. Fields, ed. St. Louis: Concordia, 1968.
Frey, Marguerite Kurth. *I Wonder, I Wonder* (for ages 5-8).
Hummel, Ruth. *Wonderfully Made* (for ages 9-11).
Bueltmann, A. J. *Take the High Road* (for ages 12-14).
Witt, Elmer N. *Life Can Be Sexual* (for ages 15 and up).
Kolb, Erwin J. *Parents' Guide to Christian Conversation About Sex* (for parents).
Wessler, Martin F. *Christian View of Sex Education* (for teachers and church leaders).
Feucht, Oscar E., ed. *Sex and the Church.* St. Louis: Concordia, 1961.
Piper, Otto A. *Biblical View of Sex and Marriage.* New York: Scribner, 1960.
Scanzoni, Letha. *Sex and the Single Eye.* Grand Rapids: Zondervan, 1968.

19

BIBLICAL PRINCIPLES FOR MARRIAGE AND THE HOME

Morris A. Inch

The home is ordained by God according to His wise purpose for man's welfare. The Bible offers guidance toward marital felicity. This chapter considers not only the theoretical nature of marriage and the home, but the application of biblical principles to practical situations.

ELIGIBILITY FOR MARRIAGE

Marriage is for *adults*, for mature individuals. "Therefore shall a man leave his father and his mother"—a dependency situation, "and shall cleave unto his wife"—a mature association (Gen 2:24a). Marriage should not be thought of as a means of achieving maturity, but as an opportunity for those already mature. "They shall be one flesh" (Gen 2:24b) is an expression of intimate relationship, one which requires the fusion of two different personalities. Stress is to be expected as a result, rather than thought of as an exception to the rule. The immature are not prepared for such a fundamental and profound interpersonal experience.

Wedlock normally eventuates in the birth and rearing of children. This responsibility must not be taken lightly. "Train up a child in the way he should go: and when he is old, he will not depart from it" (Pr 22:6). This text is a promise, but it also implies an obligation. Those who contract marriage are accountable for their parental responsibilities. Scripture does not advocate children raising children.

Marriage is an expression of God's providential care for all men, but it is meant for those who can accept mature responsibility. Apart from this ideal, the problems of the parents are multiplied in their children. A Christian's marriage is further circumscribed to the household of faith

---

MORRIS A. INCH, Ph.D., is Associate Professor of Biblical Studies, Wheaton College, Wheaton, Illinois.

(1 Co 7:39). His home is meant to build not only for time but for eternity.

MARRIAGE AS A RELATIONSHIP

Relationship implies nearness to another not enjoyed by others in general. The term is more general than the associated words *alliance* and *affinity*. *Alliance* implies a somewhat artificial relation, a tying together. Matrimony has not only been thought of as a means of alliance for two clans, but it is often represented as an alliance itself. We commonly speak of "tying the knot" of matrimony. *Affinity* is true rapport and mutuality, the goal of marriage. Insofar as a couple may be said to achieve the ideal, they express affinity. The marital relationship involves both alliance and affinity, the means by which the association is declared, and the movement by which it is realized.

The word characteristically associated with marriage is *love*. Isaac's servant searched out a wife of kindred spirit to that of his master. The fortuitous circumstances of God's leading were reported, Isaac then took Rebekah to be his wife, "and he loved her" (Gen 24:67b).

Another's effort to claim the girl of his choice met with greater difficulty. "Jacob loved Rachel" (Gen 29:18a) and offered to serve her father Laban for seven years for her hand in marriage. Laban deceived Jacob on his wedding night by substituting his elder daughter Leah. Jacob persisted in his love, pledging himself for another seven years for the reward of his first love. As the term *love* is used in this context, it at least suggests an earnest and pressing desire for one of the opposite sex. It generally implies an active and beneficent interest in the well-being of the other as well. However, the latter does not always seem to be the case. We have the story of Ammon who forced his sister over her protests, because he "loved her" (2 Sa 13:1b). His conquest was bitter, and his love turned to abhorrence—an experience often resulting from promiscuity.

While marriage in biblical times was usually contracted by the parents, it was customary to consider the interest of the young man, and on occasion the agreement of the girl (Gen 24: 57-58, 67). Woman's status in the ancient world was little better than that of the beast. However, in the Hebrew home—with its emphasis on human dignity and the task of the family in communicating divine truth and concern—the woman was more favored. Love played an importance commensurate with the religious ideals of the people.

Love has in our society reached a near cultic level. It is a mystical experience, without explanation or qualification. One "falls into love" quite inadvertently, and tumbles out of love as readily. Marriage becomes a pawn to vacillating emotion. The biblical picture is much more realistic and responsible. It depicts love as a natural emotion, and an important but not sole consideration to matrimony. Love attends an intimate and mature relationship between man and woman. It does not define our responsibility but requires it. Monogamy is not a physical or emotional necessity, but a moral ideal.

The Christian marriage has a spiritual dimension, and attendant features which make it unique. The relationship is more than, but not totally different from, another marriage. For our purposes we will observe the traditional distinction between cardinal virtues (those common to man) and spiritual virtues (those more peculiar to Christian experience). The cardinal virtues will be assumed as guidelines for the responsible marital relationship, and the theological virtues summarized for additional guidance for the Christian union. The matrimonial ideal is something to be achieved. The Scripture has wise counsel for all persons, and pointed instruction for the Christian in this regard.

WHEN $1+1=1$

Marital partners merge into a corporate identity. They become one. The cardinal virtues no doubt do not exhaust the nature of a responsible relationship, but they are certainly critical aspects of such an association. They are four in number: prudence, temperance, justice and fortitude.

PRUDENCE

A prudent wife is described as being God's gift (Pr 19:14). Prudence is practical common sense, taking the trouble to think about what we do. Religious people are peculiarly prone to suppose that goodness excuses one for being foolish. The Scriptures place no premium on such irresponsible pietism.

"The heart of the prudent gets knowledge; and the ear of the wise seeketh knowledge" (Pr 18:15). During the years that I did marital counseling, it was my custom to give the couple a series of questions relative to their intended marriage. They were then given opportunity to discuss the questions in private, and to invite my participation as it seemed advisable. Some couples handled this exercise in a perfunctory manner, but most became involved in the issues. Their prudence demonstrated itself in an effort to anticipate the nature of marital responsibility, and secure counsel as needed.

"The simple believeth every word: but the prudent man looketh well to his going" (Pr 14:15). The prudent man is not gullible. He does not believe every myth circulated about marriage. He discerns between truth and phantasy. His concern is not to achieve somehow, but well!

He forsees the pitfalls, and realistically guards himself against them (Pr 22:3).

Prudence accepts instruction graciously (Pr 15:5). The person who knows it all should spare a fellow human from living with such intolerable presumption. A loving reproof benefits the prudent, but a fool sulks, nursing his bleeding ego. Marriage is a give and take.

The virtue of prudence is not an end in itself. Pride is its own undoing. Jesus prayed: "I thank thee, O Father, Lord of heaven and earth, that thou hast hid these things from the wise and prudent, and hast revealed them unto babes" (Lk 10:21). The sincerity of the child engratiates, while the craft of the prudent degenerates. The man who makes prudence his god, ends up manipulating his associates. The person who makes prudence his servant, lives skillfully in his environment.

TEMPERANCE

Temperance is going the right length and no further. It is restraint, not abstinence. Temperance is an expression of life in the Spirit (Gal 5:23), a requirement for a bishop (Titus 1:8), and the peculiar admonition to elders in the light of the wisdom expected of long life (Titus 2:2).

"And every man that striveth for the mastery is temperate in all things" (1 Co 9:25a). Paul makes a point of the fact that this is true of all men, not Christians alone. One couple's marriage was threatened because of the time the husband spent with his circle of male friends. The solution was as obvious as illusive to them. While the young wife had to accept the fact that some separation was desirable, the husband had to see that these activities had to have some restriction as the result of marriage.

Temperance is singled out as protection against failure in the Christian life (2 Pe 1:6). It may be assumed that it is no less important as a guide to marital felicity. A danger signal to married couples is the failure to achieve rapport, evidenced in an obsession with some compensatory activity. The substitution may take the most praiseworthy forms, such as community or church activity. Nevertheless, a healthy marriage and home depend on a proper balance, an avoidance of extremes. It takes time to live.

JUSTICE

The biblical concept of justice includes the thought of honesty and equity. To receive a candid response is necessary to the liberation of the self. Justice builds a bridge between a couple, and to the world of reality about them. However, truth can be painful. One very successful couple had the practice of reminding one another each day of something in their partner which they appreciated. Such strong ties of confidence were built to allow for the occasional word of constructive criticism.

Justice will not tolerate wrong (1 Co 5). A problem ignored will fester, infecting the whole. A real or imagined wrong can turn the home into the scene of cold war. Justice removes the cause of difficulty, accepting the pain of appraisal, and the cost of reconciliation. "To do justice and judgment is more acceptable to the LORD [Jehovah] than sacrifice" (Pr 21:3).

FORTITUDE

Fortitude faces the task, and sticks until fruition. It is necessary to the realization of most worthwhile goals (Ja 5:7). The race is not won in one lap. The famed miler Gil Dodds was never known for a "fast kick," but had an incredible stamina which allowed him to cross the finish line in record time.

Offenses must come upon the marital scene. It is as inevitable, as man is prone to error. Fortitude provides the continuity between the glad days past and the good things to come. It enables the marriage to weather the storm, waiting until the adverse winds calm. Fortitude and justice work hand in hand. Justice discriminates between adversity resulting from wrong done and that which befalls the guiltless (1 Pe 2:20). Fortitude provides the stability to make amends or endure injustice as necessary.

The ideal of marriage held by most couples is patently unrealistic. Sooner or later the naïve concept collapses, but the marriage must go on. There are riches to marriage yet to be discovered, but these await those who diligently apply themselves. Fortitude is not making the best of a bad thing, but delving into the best of a good relationship.

We have considered the cardinal virtues as applied to the marriage relationship. Love is put into proper perspective as couples realize the need of prudence, temperance, justice and fortitude in the successful marriage. Matrimony is less a mystery than a mastery of responsible interpersonal relationships in the context of mutual care.

WHEN $1 + 1 = 3$

The Christian marriage involves two in the presence of the Almighty. It is life tuned to God's will. The theological virtues are taken as reflecting something of the Christian experience. It should be observed that every man has a more or less explicit idea of what is of ultimate concern to him. These ideals are of fundamental concern to any marriage. Therefore, we should not think of the nonchristian union as taking place in an ideological vacuum, but with a substitute for the value structure we shall discuss in connection with the Christian home. Further, there is no necessary reason to suppose that a given Christian home is better achieving its ideal than a nonchristian family is achieving its alternative goal. The spiritual virtues which we will now consider are faith, hope and love.

FAITH

Faith accepts as true, and holds on to what is embraced in spite of changing moods. Faith is not its own object. Christian faith is trust in God the Father of Jesus Christ, and the efficacious work of His Son. The good news is accepted as true and is appropriated (1 Co 15:1-4), but also exercised in the light of changing circumstances and personal moods (1 Co 16:13).

The Christian couple has the distinct advantage of guidance by the Scripture, and recourse to God in prayer. Their faith is an ideological and practical bond. The application of faith to marriage bears illustration. Tensions arise in a home, and feelings are estranged. It is most difficult to pray to God while angry with one's spouse (cf. Mt 5:23-24). "Let not the sun go down upon your wrath" (Eph 4:26) is a most useful guide to keep grievances from growing into hostilities.

> Christian marriage is a triangle with God at the apex. It is formed by partners who have experienced God's forgiveness in Christ, being born of the Holy Spirit. These relationships, to God and to one another, draw the sides of the triangle and realize a Christian marriage.[1]

Blessed is the couple whose marriage is begun and sustained in faith in the Lord.

HOPE

Hope sees man's fulfillment beyond time. It identifies an aspiration, a desire for which temporality holds no final gratification. While projecting into eternity, it provides zest and expectancy to life.

In a sense, hope is faith cast into the future. Its object is the same almighty God, who will subject all to the reign of His Son (cf. Phil 2:9-11). The peculiar ministry of hope as described in Scripture is its purging effect. Paul warned, "Denying ungodliness and worldly lusts, we should live soberly, righteously, and godly, in this present world; looking for that blessed hope, and the glorious appearing of the great God and our Saviour Jesus Christ" (Titus 2:12-13). And Peter admonished, "Seeing then that all these things shall be dissolved, what manner of persons ought ye to be in all holy conversation and godliness, looking for and hastening unto the coming of the day of God" (2 Pe 3:11-12a).

Practically speaking, hope contributes at least two elements to the marital relationship. First, it *directly* reminds the couple that they will give account of their deeds, and second, it *indirectly* encourages them to understand that God has His way of making all things right. To wish recognition is normal, to require commendation for every act is sickness, but to live in expectation of "well done, thou good and faithful servant" (Mt 25:21*a*) is hope. The couple whose horizon extends to this life alone loses not only eternal life but the abundant life as well. Blessed is the marriage where Christ is its hope.

LOVE

The love of which we have spoken earlier is *eros*, an ardent desire and generally an earnest concern for the well-being of one of the opposite sex. But the spiritual virtue of love is *agape*, a self-activating emotion. *Eros* responds to something in another. It may change to hate as with the case of Ammon and his sister Tamar. *Agape* requires no external encouragement and, indeed, asks for none. "God commendeth his love toward us, in that, while we were yet sinners, Christ died for us" (Ro 5:8). There was nothing desirable which solicited God's love, nor would man's rejection of Christ seem to encourage it. For all that, God still stands in the posture of love toward mankind.

God's love not only constrains us (2 Co 5:14), but motivates our lives (1 Jn 4:19). It is expressed toward God and fellowman. In fact, man's failure to love others casts the love of God in question (1 Jn 4:20-21). *Agape* joins faith and hope in cementing the Christian marriage. For example, a very troubled young lady approached me in connection with her marriage. She was considering divorce because she said she no longer loved her husband. He was apparently something of a clod, well meaning but uninteresting and uncreative. What she had felt earlier for him had vanished. She was troubled over the thought of a divorce because of her Christian convictions, but had despaired of rescuing anything from the marriage. She eventually posed a most pertinent question: "Can love return?" I assured her that it could, and often did. *Eros* might return to her, but realistically *agape* was all that held the relationship together at that point. In this case, the marriage was saved. The husband was helped to overcome some of his boorishness, and the wife surrendered the impossible ideal she had demanded of him. Affection did return as a result of the virtue of love being able to endure the temporary despair.

Marriage is an intimate and responsible relationship between a man and woman, while *Christian* marriage involves the principles and presence of God in that relationship. The Christian couple is in the enviable position to realize the wisdom and dynamic of life together with God.

Each partner regards the other as a person who is significant in God's plan, and who has infinite worth as a redeemed individual. The highest objective to which husband and wife are committed in their married life is that the love of Christ may find a glorious expression in their love for each other.[2]

Blessed is the home where such love is realized.

ROLES IN THE HOME

The success of a family depends not only on mature relationships, but on the carrying out of specific roles. God has given the husband a directive role and the wife a supportive part (Eph 5:22-23). This does not imply that one role is superior to the other, and certainly not that God is partisan in His affection. In Christ there is "neither male nor female" (Gal 3:28b). Both husband and wife are to treat each other with respect as persons created in God's image and subjects of Christ's redemption (Eph 5:21). The dominant role is not meant to be domineering, nor the supportive cast a secondary one.

In practice, we find that men and women are more or less capable of fulfilling these assigned roles. However, the American male is increasingly losing his manliness, the aggressive nature which enables him to play a dominant role in the family. The American female, perhaps out of necessity but sometimes due to competition, seems to be modifying her cast as well. An upturn in homosexuality is but one evident result of this trend.

What is to be done? There are three corrective alternatives: (1) attempt to enforce the biblical order without consideration to the person's ability to fulfill its demands, (2) reject the biblical order for some reconstruction of roles, or (3) recognize the biblical order as a goal toward which we may work from the contemporary experience. The last of these alternatives commends itself for reasons which seem obvious.

For example, a dominant woman might encourage her passive husband in decision-making, even when she feels that the decision could have been rendered more readily and/or with better success by herself. A husband, in turn, may not exercise his prerogative, but be sensitive to his wife's situation, and give himself for and to her in love (Eph 5:25). In the long run both man and wife are happiest when he "wears the pants in the family," when the biblical roles are accepted as a rewarding goal toward which to strive.

The advent of a child into the home introduces still further role needs. The parent is to be a teacher (Eph 6:4). It is his responsibility to direct the child in the way of God. Some tension is to be expected as a result of this kind of discipline. A home without growing pains is one where the parents have neglected their roles as instructors. However, direction should be given graciously, and with thoughtfulness for the child's feelings. When possible the rationale for an action should be explained.

Scripture expressly warns the parent against provoking the child to anger (Eph 6:4). Alienation defeats the purpose of instruction. The attitudes engendered are as critical as the concepts learned. The warning here is especially aimed at the parent who makes an issue of his authority, who competes with the child rather than seeks to motivate him to godliness.

The child's role is to be one of obedience (Eph 6:1-3). This is a natural role due to his dependency, and the parental responsibility for his instruction. However, it is not without its frustrations, particularly in the contemporary American culture with its strong peer conformism. The parent must take care to distinguish between that which is holy and that which is simply antique. The youth must not too readily dismiss his parent's code as old-fashioned. The Scriptures place great confidence in the wisdom derived from preceding generations.

The goal of childhood is maturation, outer guidelines giving way to inner controls. The parent and child, if each plays his role well, work together for responsible personality. The assignment of roles is meant to remove unnecessary competition and to allow for maximum cooperation toward the realization of a mutual ideal.

THE CHRISTIAN HOME IN FOCUS

We have outlined the scriptural requirements for marriage, the nature of the matrimonial bond, and roles assigned to the members of the family. We have considered the institution of the home in general and of the Christian home in particular. It remains to bring the Christian home more sharply into focus by stating the following propositions:

1. *The Christian marriage is consummated in response to the believed will of God.* To remain single is not an abnormality but, under certain circumstances, the ideal (1 Co 7:32-40). The household of faith defines the limits, not the availability of a marriage partner. If one should wed, and with whom, are matters of divine guidance. If a believer should err in marrying an unbeliever, the former is directed to make the best of the situation, confident of God's grace in the matter (1 Co 7:13-16).

2. *The Christian ideal may be conceived as the sanctity-of-persons-in-filial bond.* The home is meant to nurture personal growth in a committed and accepting atmosphere. One should realize that he is surrounded by reverent and available persons.

3. *The Christian standard is no less than the perfect will of God (Mt 5:48).* The thought of this is enough to crush man's spirit were it not for

God's grace. There is forgiveness to be sought and claimed (1 Jn 1:9). The abundant life opens before him as he experiences the grace of God in filial surroundings.

4. *The Christian method is not to sanctify an otherwise secular association with gimmicks such as a picture or symbol, although these may have some value.* The nature of Christian faith must be communicated in the caring relationships of persons within the family, and their individual and corporate communion with God.

5. *The Christian purpose is to disciple (Mt 28:19-20), and the home reflects this goal most adequately.* No institution has such an enviable opportunity to instill basic Christian values. The child "is amenable to the parent's design, the order soon becoming internalized. Allegiances may change, energies may be redirected, but one's basic personality tends to persist. The potentiality of the home as a teaching institution is staggering, and is the measure of the parent's responsibility."[3]

6. *The feeling tone of the Christian family is to be one of freedom and forgiveness (Jn 8:36).* Openness with one another is possible because of the sense of God's pardon, and the injunction to forgive others accordingly.

7. *The expectation of the Christian family is for the consummation of all things in Christ (Rev 22:20).* When the family circle is broken in death, there is the calm assurance of being reunited in God's presence. The Christian family is finally and only in perspective when it is understood as an eschatological phenomenon, life looking toward the glorious daybreak.

NOTES

1. Morris A. Inch, "The Home as an Educational Agency," *An Introduction to Evangelical Christian Education*, J. Edward Hakes, ed. (Chicago, Moody, 1964), p. 411.
2. Dwight H. Small, *Design for Christian Marriage* (Westwood, N.J.: Revell, 1959), pp. 70-71.
3. Inch, p. 406.

FOR FURTHER READING

Brandt, Henry R. and Dowdy, Homer E. *Building a Christian Home*. Wheaton, Ill.: Scripture Press, 1960.

Brown, Leslie and Brown, Winifred. *The Christian Family*. New York: Association, 1959.

Channels, Vera. *The Layman Builds a Christian Home*. St. Louis: Bethany, 1959.

Crouch, W. Perry. *Guidance for Christian Home Life*. Nashville: Convention, 1955.

DeJong, Alexander. *The Christian Family and Home*. Grand Rapids: Baker, 1959.

Duvall, Evelyn. *Family Development*. Philadelphia: Lippincott, 1962.

Evans, Louis. *Your Marriage—Duel or Duet?* Westwood, N.J.: Revell, 1962.

Eavey, Charles B. *Principles of Personality Building for Christian Parents.* Grand Rapids: Zondervan, 1952.

Fairchild, Roy and Wynn, John Charles. *Families in the Church: A Protestant Survey.* New York: Association, 1961.

Fallow, Wesner. "The Role of the Home in Religious Nurture," *Religious Education.* Marvin J. Taylor, ed. New York: Abingdon, 1960.

Feucht, Oscar E., ed. *Helping Families Through the Church.* St. Louis: Concordia, 1957.

Getz, Gene A. *The Christian Home.* Chicago: Moody, 1967.

Inch, Morris A. "The Home as an Educational Agency," *An Introduction to Evangelical Christian Education.* J. Edward Hakes, ed. Chicago: Moody, 1964.

Jacobsen, Margaret Bailey. *The Child in the Christian Home.* Wheaton, Ill.: Scripture Press, 1959.

Kerr, Clarence. *God's Pattern for the Home.* Los Angeles: Cowman, 1953.

Narramore, Clyde M. *How to Succeed in Family Living.* Glendale, Calif.: Gospel Light, 1968.

Price, John M., et al. *A Survey of Religious Education.* New York: Roland, 1959. Chaps. 2, 3, 19.

Riley, John. *This Holy Estate.* Anderson, Ind.: Warner, 1957.

Small, Dwight Hervey. *Design for Christian Marriage.* Westwood, N.J.: Revell, 1959.

Tyler, Wilfred and Tyler, Frances. *The Challenge of Christian Parenthood.* Nashville: Broadman, 1954.

Werner, Hazen. *Christian Family Living.* Nashville: Abingdon, 1958.

Wyckoff, D. Campbell. *The Task of Christian Education.* Philadelphia: Westminster, 1955.

Wynn, John Charles. *How Christian Parents Face Family Problems.* Philadelphia: Westminster, 1955.

20

PREPARING YOUNG PEOPLE FOR CHRISTIAN MARRIAGE

Howard G. and Jeanne Hendricks

Don and Sue were "madly in love." A crescendo of feeling began between them a year ago when Don's family first visited Central Church. They liked each other's looks, and they soon discovered they had common interests. Don declared that Sue was "what I've always been looking for." Both were professing Christians. Now at the party honoring Don's upcoming college graduation, they wanted to announce their engagement, and be married next Labor Day weekend.

"It just all seems so right," Sue said to her mother. "I can transfer and finish college while Don is in grad school. We can easily find a student apartment. Everybody does."

"Pastor, I've just flipped over this girl," Don confided to his minister. "I think I need a wife, and Sue's the one. She's gotta be. I've never felt this way about anybody else. I want to be with her all the time. I think about her constantly. She fills a real need in my life; and besides, she's in love with me. What else do you need?"

Thousands of Dons and Sues step up to the starting line of matrimony constantly. On their shoulders we have placed the privilege—and the responsibility—of choosing their own life mates. Most of them sincerely want to do what is right; they seek the approval of parents and pastors, and in America the choice is almost entirely their own. If marriage were exclusively an individual matter, affecting only two lives, conceivably the choice of a life partner could reasonably be committed to personal whim or family preference. Marriage, however, is also a public matter, a legal concern, an influential agreement affecting the lives of the entire

HOWARD G. HENDRICKS, Th.M., D.D., is Chairman of the Department of Christian Education, Dallas Theological Seminary, Dallas, Texas. His wife, Jeanne, is a free-lance writer.

society. We must reject the idea that the selection of a wife or a husband is anything less than paramount in importance.

How, then, can young people be prepared to make a wise and lasting choice? Clearly, if they themselves are to make the selection, they must be given a supply of tools and know-how for that unannounced instant of decision when yes or no is required.

> A successful marriage is not one in which two people, beautifully matched, find each other and get along happily ever after because of this initial matching. It is, instead, a system by means of which persons who are sinful and contentious are so caught by a dream bigger than themselves that they work throughout the years, in spite of repeated disappointment, to make the dream come true.[1]

The church's task is to help give substance to the dream—to aid in the struggle against the headwinds of a hostile society—to augment the deposit of divine law in young hearts—to dispense words of hope to despairing parents—to give hearty support to God's strategy of the husband-wife team effort to accomplish His purpose.

THE CRUCIAL NEED FOR PROPER MARRIAGE PREPARATION

Marriage is the rare vocation for which no previous training is considered necessary. The tendency is to act as if one instinctively knows how to adjust to a marriage partner, or how to manage specific problems that arise within this most personal of all relationships. In reality, every bride and groom who stand before an official third party to link their lives in the most intimate human fusion known, bring to that experience a lifetime of preparation. Any encounter through the early years relating to the complementary sex, every answer—or lack of one—to questions about marriage or reproduction of life, is direct education for marriage.

Often the grooming for wedded life may be inadequate or misdirected. A couple may arrive at the juncture of saying "I do" lost in an impenetrable wilderness of advice without proper routing. To many it is a sign of weakness to seek help. On the other hand, those who desire help often cannot find competent resource individuals. Amazingly, this most determinative area of life is the one faced with the least preparation. It is easier to get married than to join a lodge!

Several reasons build a convincing case for the need for marriage preparation.

THE CULTURAL MILIEU DISTORTS THE BIBLICAL CONCEPT OF MARRIAGE

Raining down on American youth is a deluge of distortion to blur their ideas about God's original intent for marriage. Regrettably, even some church-related young people have bought the deception that marriage is, at best, a temporary pursuit of happiness, that the physical union of the sexes is the zenith of all strivings, that marriage is a kind of half-serious brand of living, a laughing-gas balloon into which everyone should step at some time, even though the ascent may be brief and disastrous.

Children grow up breathing a polluted moral atmosphere. Even the protective filter of a Christian home fails to prevent their absorbing some of the poison. Marriages continue to disintegrate at an alarming rate. The result is that an increasingly loud and desperate call for help is being directed toward the church. The church, after all, claims to be the keeper of the keys to life's intangibles.

However, no ecclesiastic, educational, or any other institution, no matter how elevated its motives, can alone do the job of preparing young people for marriage. This preparation is a home-grown, individually crafted undertaking. The church finds its highest level of efficiency in helping the home. Said one church, "We guarantee to do nothing to your child without your help."

Building a life that is suitable for blending with another life in a productive and salutary span of years is no accident.

> To bring two young people to church and pronounce them man and wife may make a marriage in the legal sense; but it doesn't make the kind of creative, growing relationship that a true marriage ought to be. This requires a long, complex process of mutual adjustment—a process that may take years to accomplish.[2]

Planted in today's world, such a human construction project requires close cooperation, a complementary enterprise, of both home and church. The home is enriched by the collective strength of the church, and the church educates the family with a view to building permanent and fulfilling marriages.

THE HOME IS THE MOST DETERMINATIVE UNIT IN SOCIETY

> First impressions are strong impressions. Adults cannot help re-living in some fashion the kind of life they knew in childhood. The warmth and intimacy of the family group become synonymous with life itself.[3]

Like a flashing neon sign, the truth of the foregoing statement lights up consistently in marriage-counseling offices—and with good reasons. In the early years, life-influencing qualities are formed—the conscience and value system, the sense of discipline, the self-image, attitudes toward God and others.

Moral, spiritual and emotional habit patterns—basic essentials in marriage—are developed in the unstructured, informal interaction of the family. From the educational standpoint the on-the-spot learning, contextual in nature, is the most effective. Family life is interpretive, where meanings emerge immediately, inescapably, through the "alive" quality of the home. It is perceptive education in its purest form, encircled by the goals and climate of the family. Every experience is significant, leaving with the individual an insoluble sediment of impressions to mark his personality. It is true that a child may repudiate his background training, but a frame of reference is there in which subsequent imprints will be placed for evaluation.

> In the early years a basic underlayer is formed which guides and controls feelings and actions then and for life. If the opportunity to help in the development of this vital underpinning is neglected or mishandled by parents during these years, there is no way to make up for it later.[4]

MARRIAGE ENCOMPASSES MORE THAN FACTS

A mere accumulation of knowledge about marriage is not enough for marital success. Marriage partners must know *how* to succeed. Facts alone enable one only to sin more intelligently; interpretation must explain those facts for meaningful practice. Attitude and competency in skills related to dating, courtship, marriage and parenthood must be considered. Marriage includes, but certainly is much more than, home management and sex education. The danger is no longer a lack of intelligence, but a deficiency of skills. Marriage itself is not in trouble, but education for marriage has failed.

MARRIAGE AND THE FAMILY ARE OF GOD

Current in our country is a genuine secular concern about the downward trend of the home and marriage. Higher education "family life" courses make a real effort to explain individual worth in marital love. For example:

> Conjugal love with its stress on ego-needs is probably more important and more basic to the American culture than to almost any other culture of the world. To be unloved in the United States is to be more than unwanted; it is to lack importance in the eyes of a "significant other"; it is to be unchosen. This is often extremely upsetting in a culture in which being chosen is often equated with having social worth as a human being.[5]

This present attempt to emphasize love and personal worth over the physical, tangible or economic aspects of marriage merits commendation. It is a step in the right direction, but it lacks the spiritual dimension which recognizes that the institution of marriage originated with the divine Creator.

The church should be leading, not following, the vanguard. It should be asking penetrating questions, not merely providing superficial answers. Positive challenges should replace negative responses.

Mark the elevated level of marriage in Scripture:

> The willing subjection of the Church to Christ should be reproduced in the submission of wives to their husbands. But, remember, this means that the husband must give his wife the same sort of love that Christ gave to the Church, when he sacrificed himself for her (Eph 5:24-25, Phillips).

God Himself designed the marriage relationship; it is not the product of human perversion, but of divine perfection. The Bible touches the nerve of need in this area. It is indispensable to know what is right before we can correct what is wrong. To strengthen homes through the church's training program is the challenge. On the one hand we must provide education through specific and related training for prevention of problems; on the other hand, we must also provide planned and adequate therapy for the solving of marital problems.

MEETING THE NEED FOR MARRIAGE PREPARATION THROUGH THE HOME

Faced with what seems at times like an impossible tangle of home negatives, parents desperately need an objective, knowledgeable, and biblically oriented third party to sort out with them the major strands of their role. Parents are stamping a permanent tattoo on their children in terms of marriage readiness. They are the models whom their children will follow. In the long chain of marriage trainers, parents stand as the first link. The task of the church is (1) to awaken parents to their responsibility, (2) to sensitize them to self-understanding, and (3) to coach them in relating to and teaching the children at various levels of development.

ESTABLISHING INDEPENDENCE

The long-range goal of parental marriage preparation is the severing of the child's psychological umbilical cord from its parents. As Levy and Monroe have stated, "Falling out of love with parents is the first step toward falling in love with a mate and beginning a new family."[6] This idea was first stated by God Himself in Genesis 2:24: "Therefore shall a man *leave* his father and his mother, and shall *cleave* unto his wife: and they shall be one flesh." Significantly, it is repeated by both Christ and Paul. Parents have approximately twenty years in which to shape and nurture their children. To be successful, "independence day" must not be abrupt; instead, it must be a process of growth, of learning by trial and error to fly alone, to make rational decisions unaided. We want the product of maturity, namely, independence. But frequently we do not want the process, namely, conflict.

In adult life young people need a double *point d'appui* (foundation), including (1) well-defined personal convictions (communicated through attitudes and relationships), and (2) a model to follow (the "audio-visual" of their parents' marriage, or that of other significant persons). Torrance observes, "Children are going to achieve those things which are valued by the society in which they live."[7]

If the home—the immediate society of children—houses creative parents, then creative children will probably emerge; if it houses loving parents, loving children will emerge, etc. Improvement of the parents' marriage enhances the prospect of successful marriage for the children.

CLARIFYING SEX ROLES

A child looks for answers to the universal queries, Who am I? and, What am I supposed to be doing? Within the framework of his own culture he needs to place God's original purposes for the sexes. The Creator made Adam and gave him a job assignment, which he performed. However, man was incomplete and God pronounced that "it is not good that the man should be alone." The primary purpose for Eve's appearance was to be Adam's helper, divinely designed to fit Adam's need. Companionship, love and cooperation were to characterize the relationship. Because Adam was created first, and because of Eve's sin in allowing herself to be deceived by the serpent, the wife was later given a place of submission to her husband (1 Ti 2:11-15). This fact can never be diluted; and try as we do to circumvent its reality, the wife fulfills her role to the highest degree when she accepts the fact that she was made originally as a vital auxiliary to man, not as the primary leader, functioning in loving and willing submission to him.

> For both husband and wife this truth leads to glory and to humility. It is humbling to the woman to know that she was created for the man, but it is to her glory to know that she alone can complete him. Likewise, it is humbling to the man to know that he is incomplete without the woman, but it is to his glory to know that the woman was created for him![8]

No thinking person denies that modern society demands leadership from women, and that many men have abdicated their place of responsibility in the home. Nevertheless, all of Scripture tells a story of rugged masculinity for men, and a delicate, yet heroic, type of womanhood for the complementary sex. To build on God's blueprint is to know the secret of successful marriage in the context of twentieth century living.

COMMUNICATING BY RELATIONSHIPS

How does one communicate in an age when absolute values are being discarded? What wave length transmits to a generation that arrogantly asserts, "It may have been OK for you, Dad, but not for me!" Or, "What was right yesterday doesn't cut ice today!" The only answer lies in the quality of the parent-child relationship, that *rapport* built through mature understanding. It lines the nest of the fledgling youth with warm receptivity to counsel and advice. Readiness is vital. Whether the information is purely sex-oriented or a related subject, such as answering a normal question, like "Mommy, why did you marry Daddy instead of some other man?" there is a time when the child *wants* to hear. As the child grows from his toddler years through young adulthood, the wise parent is sensitive to identify and seize on these informal teaching opportunities.

ADAPTING TO THE AGE LEVEL

In talking with young children about marriage, be brief. Also, gauge the discussion to the child's mental level. When a ten-year-old girl asks her mother how babies get started inside of mothers, the girl should not be frightened with a detailed description of adult copulation. She is not emotionally prepared for a lengthy answer, and that is not what she really wants to know. Her informational need is simply the fact that a very tiny egg is produced by the mother on a monthly cycle, and that this egg is fertilized by the male sperm and begins to grow. The act can be illustrated by familiar creatures of nature, if need be. And to the Christian the fact of God's divine provision of human reproduction can be interwoven to produce a worshipful attitude on the part of youngsters. This divine perspective on the subject of reproduction will later help repudiate a degraded view of sex, to which children are so frequently subjected in their environment.

Many Christian parents manage well to communicate regarding marriage to their younger children, but the blunt, sometimes disrespectful, attitude of teens becomes a barrier. May we suggest that teens be met head on. When a seventeen-year-old blurts out at the dinner table that so-and-so is suspected of being a "homo" or that the local high school is abuzz with the scandal about the sophomore cheerleader who is dropping out because she is pregnant, most parents almost instinctively try to hush it up, especially if younger children are present. The teen reacts with a negative "So what!" He labels his parents "completely out of it" and the process of noncommunication is underway for the next item of this nature. Deviations from pure and moral sex life, which are common subjects of news and conversation today, need to be surfaced and discussed discreetly with a view to helping teens understand the dire results as well as the prevention of such tragedies. Parents' refusal to talk about sex and its problems simply causes youth to turn to much less qualified and more secularly oriented people outside the home.

The principle of listening, someone has said, is to develop a big ear rather than a big mouth. If parents will listen actively, wholeheartedly, sympathetically—whether the subject is distasteful or not—the chances of the youth then listening to the parents are greatly enhanced. The theory is simple, but the practice becomes difficult in our overfull lives. As much as possible, parents should avoid saying, "I'm too busy to listen now."

A perfectly normal "blackout" period occurs during adolescence. In his desperate search for independence the child legitimately goes through a time when he does not want to talk to his parents more than he has to, and he especially does not want to listen. If this attitude, admittedly illogical, can be met with friendly acceptance, it will be shortened and minimized. Parental love should be mature enough to absorb this phase of growing up.

FORMING ATTITUDES

An article in *Reader's Digest* proclaimed that the most important need of children is a healthy sense of self-esteem.[9] It is a key factor in adjusting to life and also in consummating a successful marriage. The Christian has more reason than most people for self-respect because he is worth so much to God that Christ died for him. Yet the enigma exists that often the most secure person spiritually is the most insecure emotionally.

Such spinelessness has its roots in incipient relationships with parents. It is no small task to rear a child who is convinced that he is worth everything to you as a parent, and to God who gave His Son for him—and therefore deserves his own highest respect. The seeds of healthy pride are sown in the way in which a parent handles a child. Is his body treated with care, kept clean and adequately clothed? Are his possessions and privacy respected and protected? Does he share a proper amount of attention, and receive praise and encouragement for his efforts? Are his ideas considered seriously? Are there sympathy and comfort when he needs them? Are there limits set for excessive behavior, so that he learns to act in the best interest of others? Is he loved with an intelligent love which looks ahead, projecting his present activities into the future?

Children emulate their parents. Therefore, to learn to be a man, a boy needs to relate positively to his father. If a boy does not have a father, he needs a father-figure, and the church has a terrifying responsibility to its fatherless boys to provide such a need. To learn to be a husband, a boy also needs to relate to his mother in a warm, loving dependency, but certainly *not* in a smothering relationship. From his mother he forms his concept of a wife, and through his ties with his mother he learns to relate to the complementary sex.

Similarly, little girls need to relate to their daddies. However, a father who is a "sugar daddy" to his daughter is growing a poor prospect for a wife. A girl needs the security of love and acceptance, but she also needs the balancing opportunity to assume responsibility and to achieve by her own efforts. Also it is important for her to observe her mother in a wise relationship to her father. The unfortunate girl—and there are many—who lives through separation and/or divorce of her parents, and who is assigned to the custody of a bitter mother, is often poisoned against men in general.

Attitudes are contagious. Therefore don't ask God to change your children; ask Him to change you. Proper attitudes of parents toward marriage are basic to proper attitudes of children toward marriage.

MEETING THE NEED FOR MARRIAGE PREPARATION THROUGH THE CHURCH

The organized fellowship of believers plays a role in every age-group, but in terms of marriage preparation the junior high through young-adult age is particularly the focus of our concern.

The intrusion of adolescence into a child's life inevitably brings the excitement of approaching adulthood and independence. The teen lives in a world of immediate reality, spinning dreams of grandeur and achievement. His home, up to now a primary factor in his environment, tends to recede to a supportive position, and the magnetism of the outside world draws him. Former strangers may become closer than family ties. Depending on his early conditioning, the path from his door will lead to the place where he is accepted and where he can explore his interests. If habit patterns of childhood have provided a positive link with the church, it is likely that he will be found there, where his associates are significant persons who agree with and support his home.

Figure 1 demonstrates the ideal home-church relationship. It must be kept in mind, however, that home training flows continuously, whereas the church provides a more sporadic vehicle where the young person "plugs in" at a given level.

Moreover, the dilemma for the church is further intensified by the lack

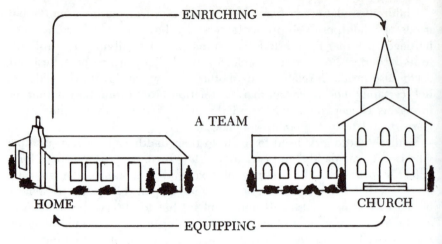

Figure 1

of a monolithic group of teens. Generally, four categories of young people are included in the average youth group: (1) members of Christian homes where biblical principles have been taught and practiced; (2) teens from homes where a profession of faith in Christ and the Bible is negated by secular living; (3) "good moral" young people from homes where no profession of faith is made; and (4) those from homes where neither training nor example emphasizes life's values. In all these brackets, deviations from normal family patterns commonly occur. The one-parent family, the stepchild relationship, and other departures from usual family life, present a peculiar challenge to marriage preparatory teaching.

Reaching young people through the church requires more than an intellectual presentation of scriptural truth. To teens, the church is the people who are there—the teachers, the youth sponsors, the officers, the pastor, etc. Through each of these individuals marriage preparation takes place, and this kind of readying for married living is a relational, as well as an intellectual, training experience.

TEACHERS AND YOUTH SPONSORS

A mixture of young lives is assembled in a church classroom. Facing them, an adult leader speaks. What happens to each of them as a result of this confrontation is determined more by what that leader is as a person than anything he (or she) can say. The feeling conveyed by his eyes, the attitudinal overtones of his voice, the reputation of his activities and life outside that room—all these weigh far more heavily toward his acceptance or rejection than the words he speaks. By his life, a teacher personifies and interprets marriage, even though he may not be teaching the subject directly. When called for, specifically definitive answers are required, but even more important is his confidence that Christianity has the answers.

One writer has well stated that "any program, no matter how charismatically planned and promoted, will succeed to the degree that the teachers are qualified to lead it."[10] The teacher must excel in example, in the organization of his thinking, and in the respect he commands from youth and parents alike.

The so-called generation gap is greatly diminished when the model adult makes himself available in the everyday reality of young lives. Understanding the enormity of problems facing young people, this unspoken message should come through with every contact: "I know there have been failures; I am aware that your immediate environment constitutes a threat to you; I realize that human weakness creates a formidable handicap in making decisions. *But*, I am confident that the resources of the Christian life, the power of the Holy Spirit, can redeem your situation; I have a firm commitment to God's Word for the enablement and direction you need."

CHURCH EDUCATIONAL ACTIVITIES

The searchlight of an intelligent analysis of current church family life needs to be focused on the policy-making in evangelical churches by Christian education boards and other pacesetters. Several key areas merit review:

The church must avoid an institutional narcissism, or self-centeredness, which ignores its societal context. With reference to marriage preparation, cultural orientation is imperative. Just as salvation is by personal faith in Christ, yet with revolutionary group implications, so marriage is a personal choice—but its outworking has far-reaching sociological reactions. The church cannot confine its teaching to personal interests only, else the ground gained will be lost in a rockslide of societal opposition. Teaching must be related to the world in which it is to be practiced.

The church must come to grips with human sexuality within a biblical framework. Stifled by an unscriptural repression of sex, the American populace is now captured and confused by the Playboy concept of "taking off the lid" and presenting sex in a sensual, relaxed and carefree atmosphere of luxury. A crucial need exists to speak out with a balanced, articulate communication of what God intends between men and women.

The church is culpable in fragmenting families. It has proliferated activities often to the degree that family members are too busy with church to live with each other. Wishful-thinking parents somehow feel the church is doing their job for them, but there is no substitute for home training. The church must augment the home so that *it*—the home —can do the training.

The agenda of educational activities in the church should lean heavily toward preventive more than therapeutic, corrective efforts. Adequate marriage preparatory training decreases the need for rehabilitation. In any case, corrective measures should not be so labeled, but woven integrally into the program. The following are only a few of the many possibilities:

1. Family-life needs and characteristics as a part of general teacher preparation.

2. A course of study in marriage and the family to a select group of leaders (who relate well to both youth and adults) so that they can share the counseling and educational load of the pastor.

3. Family-life committee included in the Christian education board to monitor this phase.

4. Elective courses in Sunday school, training hour, or adult vacation Bible school on family needs. Direct Bible study on key passages such as Genesis 2 and 3; Proverbs; 1 Corinthians 7:1-16; Ephesians 5:22-33; Colossians 3:18-21; 1 Peter 3:1-7.

5. Periodic parent-teacher encounters for the purpose of discussing child problems.

6. Family-life institutes or retreats for various age levels and interest groups, with resource individuals. (E.g., dating and courtship— for young and middle adolescents; the place of marriage—for later adolescents; problems of parents with small children, with adolescents, without partners; dilemmas of parents without children, or with grown children; mixed marriages; etc.).

7. Informal conversational groups in homes.

8. Library resources—books, films, tapes, records, pamphlets and periodicals with practical help for families, flexible enough to include new family problems which develop, and publicized with posters and brochures.

9. Development of a carefully structured means of referral to community resources (e.g., welfare agencies, Christian psychiatrists, etc.).

10. Annual family week to focus on the importance of the home.

THE PASTOR

So comprehensive is the role of the minister in the whole concept of marriage that only a skeleton of his responsibilities can be covered here. In the minds of his people, the pastor links marriage with the Lord and with the church. As spiritual leader of the local church, his influential functions include the following:

Premarital counseling. The pastor who unites a couple in Christian marriage is logically the one to instruct them concerning the significance and responsibilities of this union. For specific helps on this subject, it is suggested that pastors refer to the *Premarital Counseling Manual* listed at the end of the chapter.

Marriage and family counseling. For the couple, and for those close to them, an objective and spiritually oriented pastor is an invaluable help when problems arise. Again the ramifications of this function are extensive, and are best studied in more detailed information included in the bibliography.

Sermons. The doctrine of the family, as presented in Genesis 2 and 3 and Colossians 3, embraces more than empty or superficial platitudes. Touching the nerve of need, a brush with reality is needed to explain how to live the Christian life at home.

Frequent exposure to his young people. The informal setting where questions erupt, free of the threat of condemnation, should be sought. Brief, cursory words with an individual at the critical time often make a solid impact, and the pastor should be alert for these times of need and opportunity.

Classes for younger couples. Realistic training for the future can be realized in training classes on family government, finances, worship, recreation, sex education, etc.

His own family life. The busy pastor, constantly giving attention and consideration to others, may very easily tend to overlook his own family life. It is imperative that his own marriage be healthy if he hopes to affect other marriages positively. As Smucker wrote, "The call of the pastor is one of the singular calls of God. Yet the pastor is not God's angel. And while marriages may be made in heaven, they must be lived on earth."[11]

CONCLUSION

James A. Peterson, a veteran marriage counselor, concludes one of his texts with these words:

> Most families reach whatever degree of cohesion or happiness they achieve as a matter of chance. If husbands and wives gave only one tenth as much time to discussing and planning the future of their relationship as they do their business or even to their social life, their marriages would grow in meaning and cohesion. Many couples spend more time keeping their automobiles clean than in keeping their romance shining.[12]

In these violent crosscurrents of our modern cultural climate, Christians cannot afford to leave to chance the embryonic homes of the future. The key to this vigilance lies in the church's posture in reference to the home. Aloof parents must be aroused and prompted to constructive training of their children. Young people themselves need instruction that is sensitive to their requirements and tangent to life.

Boldly creative steps are necessary for the church to underscore the centrality of the home in its ministry. An unashamedly aggressive thrust to convince young people that dating, sex and marriage are more than interesting debate topics is long overdue. Lucidly written in the scriptural record are the orders for God's people: "Train up a child in the way he should go" (Pr 22:6). The need for marriage preparation is obvious; the means are at hand. The church must not let the home fail. Our obedience to teach the things we have learned to our children is undoubtedly the most valuable legacy we can leave for the Christian witness in tomorrow's world.

NOTES

1. Elton and Pauline Trueblood, *The Recovery of Family Life* (New York: Harper, 1953), pp. 56-57.
2. David R. Mace, *Youth Considers Marriage* (New York: Nelson, 1966), p. 76.
3. John Levy and Ruth Monroe, *The Happy Family* (New York: Knopf, 1967), p. 4.
4. Graham B. Blaine, Jr., *Youth and the Hazards of Affluence* (New York: Harper & Row, Colophon, 1966), p. 4.
5. Robert R. Bell, *Marriage and Family Interaction* (Homewood, Ill.: Dorsey, 1963), p. 103.
6. Levy and Monroe, p. 16.
7. E. Paul Torrance, "Developing Creative Thinking Through School Experience," *Source Book for Creative Thinking*, Sydney J. Parnes and Harold F. Harding, eds. (New York: Scribner, 1962), p. 33.
8. Dwight H. Small, *Design for Christian Marriage* (Westwood, N.J.: Revell, 1959), p. 32.
9. Floyd Miller, "What Every Child Needs Most," *Reader's Digest*, 48 (Jan., 1969): 149-52, reprinted from *The PTA Magazine* (Dec., 1968).
10. John H. Phillips, *Sex Education in Major Protestant Denominations* (New York: National Council of Churches of Christ in the U.S.A., Dept. of Educational Development, 1968), p. 14.
11. Ralph M. Smucker, "The Minister and His Wife," *Christianity Today*, 13 (June 20, 1969): 4.
12. James A. Peterson, *Education for Marriage* (New York: Scribner, 1964), p. 399.

FOR FURTHER READING

General Resources

Becker, Howard, and Hill, Reuben. *Family, Marriage and Parenthood*. Boston: Heath, 1955.

Bell, Robert R. *Marriage and Family Interaction*. Homewood, Ill.: Dorsey, 1963.

Bowman, Henry A. *Marriage for Moderns*. New York: McGraw-Hill, 1965.

Cavan, Ruth S. *Marriage and Family in the Modern World: A Book of Readings.* New York: Crowell, 1965.

Duvall, Evelyn and Hill, Reuben. *Being Married.* New York: Heath, 1967.

Landis, Judson T. and Landis, Mary G. *Building a Successful Marriage.* 4th ed. Englewood Cliffs, N.J.: Prentice-Hall, 1963.

———. *Personal Adjustment—Marriage and Family Living.* 3d ed. Englewood Cliffs, N.J.: Prentice-Hall, 1960.

Landis, Paul H. *Making the Most of Marriage.* New York: Appleton-Century-Crofts, 1965.

Levy, John and Monroe, Ruth. *The Happy Family.* New York: Knopf, 1967.

Ligon, Ernest Mayfield and Smith, Leona Jones. *The Marriage Climate.* St. Louis: Bethany, 1963.

Mace, David R. *Success in Marriage.* New York: Abingdon, 1958.

Peterson, James A. *Education for Marriage.* 2d ed. New York: Scribner, 1964.

———. *Toward a Successful Marriage.* New York: Scribner, 1960.

Popenoe, Paul. *Marriage Before and After.* New York: Funk, 1943.

———. *Marriage Is What You Make It.* New York: Macmillan, 1950.

Scanzoni, Letha. *Sex and the Single Eye.* Grand Rapids: Zondervan, 1968.

For Young People

Brandt, Henry R. *When a Teen Falls in Love.* Wheaton, Ill.: Scripture Press, 1965.

Califf, Stanley N. *Preparation for Marriage.* Philadelphia: Lutheran Church, 1967.

Capper, W. Melville and Williams, H. Morgan. *Toward Christian Marriage.* Chicago: Inter-Varsity, 1958.

Duvall, Evelyn Millis. *Love and the Facts of Life.* New York: Association, 1963.

———. *Why Wait Till Marriage?* New York: Association, 1965.

Duvall, Evelyn M. and Hill, Reuben. *When You Marry.* New York: Association, 1962.

Hulme, William E. *Youth Considers Sex.* New York: Nelson, 1965.

Mace, David R. *Youth Considers Marriage.* New York: Nelson, 1966.

Olford, Stephen F. and Lawes, Frank A. *The Sanctity of Sex.* Westwood, N.J.: Revell, 1963.

Miller, Randolph C. *Youth Considers Parents as People.* New York: Nelson, 1965.

Richards, Larry. *How Far Can I Go?* Chicago: Moody, 1969.

Shedd, Charlie W. *Letters to Karen: On Keeping Love in Marriage.* Nashville: Abingdon, 1965.

———. *Letters to Philip: On How to Treat a Woman.* Garden City, N.Y.: Doubleday, 1968.

Small, Dwight Hervey. *Design for Christian Marriage.* Westwood, N.J.: Revell, 1959.

For Parents

Blaine, Graham B., Jr. *Youth and the Hazards of Affluence.* New York: Harper & Row, 1966.
Brandt, Henry R. and Dowdy, Homer E. *Building a Christian Home.* Wheaton, Ill.: Scripture Press, 1960.
Evelyn, Louis. *Training Children for Maturity.* New York: Newman, 1967.
Fields, W. J. *Unity in Marriage.* St. Louis: Concordia, 1962.
Ginott, Haim G. *Between Parent and Child.* New York: Macmillan, 1965.
———. *Between Parent and Teen-Ager.* New York: Macmillan, 1969.
Jaeck, Gordon and Dorothea. *I Take Thee: The Art of Successful Marriage.* Grand Rapids: Zondervan, 1967.
McFarland, Robert and Burton, John. *Learning for Loving.* Grand Rapids: Zondervan, 1969.
Moser, Leslie E. and Moser, Ruth Small. *Guiding Your Son or Daughter Toward Successful Marriage.* Grand Rapids: Baker, 1967.
Renich, Jill. *Preparing Children for Marriage.* Grand Rapids: Zondervan, 1964.
Skousen, W. Cleon. *So You Want to Raise a Boy?* New York: Doubleday, 1962.

For Church Leaders

Belgum, David. *The Church and Sex Education.* Philadelphia: Lutheran Church, 1967.
Drakeford, John W. *The Great Sex Swindle.* Nashville: Broadman, 1966.
Duvall, Evelyn; Mace, David R. and Popenoe, Paul. *The Church Looks at Family Life.* Nashville: Broadman, 1964.
Feucht, Oscar E., ed. *Helping Families Through the Church.* St. Louis: Concordia, 1957.
———. *Ministry to Families.* St. Louis: Concordia, 1963.
———, ed. *Sex and the Church.* St. Louis: Concordia, 1961.
Hendricks, Howard G., ed. *Pre-Marital Counseling Manual.* Dallas: Seminary Book Room, 1969.
Mace, David R. *Whom God Hath Joined.* Philadelphia: Westminster, 1963.
Morris, J. Kenneth. *Premarital Counseling: A Manual for Ministers.* Englewood Cliffs, N.J.: Prentice-Hall, 1960.
———. *Marriage Counseling: A Manual for Ministers.* New York: Prentice-Hall, 1965.
Oates, Wayne E. *Premarital Pastoral Care and Counseling.* Nashville: Broadman, 1958.
Scudder, C. W. *The Family in Christian Perspective.* Nashville: Broadman, 1962.
Stewart, Charles William. *The Minister as Marriage Counselor.* New York: Abingdon, 1961.
Werner, Hazen G. *The Bible and the Family.* Nashville: Abingdon, 1966.
Wynn, John Charles. *Pastoral Ministry to Families.* Philadelphia: Westminster, 1957.

Zuck, Roy B., and Getz, Gene A. *Christian Youth: An In-Depth Study.* Chicago: Moody, 1968.

Additional Sources

American Institute of Family Relations, 5287 Sunset Blvd., Los Angeles, Calif. 90027. Pamphlets on sex and marriage for parents, counselors, the married, unmarried, young people, etc.
American Medical Association, 535 N. Dearborn St., Chicago, Ill., 60610. Sex Education Series: *Parents' Responsibility* (parents), *A Story About You* (grades 4, 5, 6), *Finding Yourself* (junior high), *Approaching Adulthood* (ages 16-20), *Facts Aren't Enough* (adults).
Concordia Sex Education Series. W. J. Fields, ed. St. Louis: Concordia, 1968.
    Frey, Marguerite Kurth. *I Wonder, I Wonder* (for ages 5-8).
    Hummel, Ruth. *Wonderfully Made* (for ages 9-11).
    Bueltmann, A. J. *Take the High Road* (for ages 12-14).
    Witt, Elmer N. *Life Can Be Sexual* (for ages 15 and up).
    Kolb, Erwin J. *Parents' Guide to Christian Conversation About Sex* (for parents).
    Wessler, Martin F. *Christian View of Sex Education* (for teachers and church leaders).
Family Life Publications, Inc., Box 6725, College Station, Durham, N.C. 27708.
Public Affairs Pamphlets, 381 Park Ave., S., New York, N.Y. 10016. Pamphlets on child development, mental health, family relations, etc.
Science Research Associates, 259 E. Erie St., Chicago, Ill. 60611. Better Living Booklets for Parents and Teachers (pamphlet list available). Junior Life Adjustment Pamphlets (for ages 10-14).

21

HELPING ADULTS MAINTAIN MARITAL UNITY

W. J. Fields

Premarital sessions with about-to-be-married young people should include the suggestion that they begin to change their use of personal pronouns from the singular to the plural, from "I" and "mine" to "we" and "ours." It is no longer "my" car but "our" car. Not "my" salary, but "our" salary. Not "my" parents and "your" parents, but "our" parents. The plural pronoun is an indication of what takes place in marriage. A union has been formed. Two individual and independent lives have been brought together and have been "pooled" to form a single life, a shared life—a single unit composed of two parts.

Marriage brings together two people who for a fifth or quarter of a century were in many cases unknown to each other. They were people from different family backgrounds, people with a completely different set of experiences, perhaps something of a different value system, people even with differing expectations of what marriage should be. Building a genuine unity into the newly established unit doesn't just happen. It demands conscious effort, genuine understanding, hard work, willing compromise, generous sacrifice, and unlimited forgiveness on the part of everyone. Problem areas that call for adjustments and unity include finances, sex, relations with in-laws, the working wife, where to live, etc.

To build and maintain marital unity a couple must overcome the many factors that make for disunity. And to overcome those factors they must first of all understand what some of them are.

EXPECTATIONS OF MARRIAGE

Each partner brings to the union his own expectations of what he would like the marriage to be. And these expectations are to a great extent

---

W. J. Fields, M.S., D.D., is pastor of the Memorial Lutheran Church, Ames, Iowa.

conditioned by the homes in which they were reared. It is there that they have learned to understand something of the dynamics of human relationships in the home—for better or for worse. They have seen the roles of father and mother, and husband and wife, in action. They may have agreed or disagreed with what they saw, and they may have formed their own opinions as to what these roles should be, but always they were formed within the framework of their own particular home environments. In addition, they have been emotionally oriented to their family structures, so that their attachment to the circumstances of their home-life was internalized to the point where they could hardly be objective.

Each of the marriage partners brings to the marriage his or her own ideas of what he expects to contribute and to receive in the relationship, and those expectations have been formed in the experiences of his own parental family. Sometimes those expectations are so different that the couple has hardly any common meeting ground.

One couple came for help (fortunately before they were married) when they were having problems of this nature. The young man had come from a home where the male and female roles had been clearly defined and distinguished. The men automatically assumed the responsibility for care of the basement of the home, the garage, and all of the outside garden and shrubbery work. The women of the household took over all the home chores, dishwashing, cleaning, cooking, etc. The girl on the other hand came from a home where all of these activities were joint endeavors. The men in the house assisted in washing dishes, cleaning the home, etc., and the women assisted with tending the lawn and shrubbery and garden. Both of these young people, because of their conditioning, were expecting that the pattern of their own homelife be followed in the new home. Consequently each of them reacted violently to the new situation. The young man felt strongly that it was not a man's task to dry dishes, and the young lady felt that not working together in everything showed a lack of togetherness.

This couple had to be led to understand that their parents had worked out the patterns of fulfilling their roles according to their individual needs and desires and that they were therefore satisfactory and desirable to them. They were, however, two different people and, for them, neither of these patterns would be satisfactory. They would have to work out a third pattern that would be satisfactory to both of them. This would take conscious effort and perhaps painful compromise of opinions and desires in order to effect a solution. In their case, feelings were so strong that the marriage was wisely postponed until they could think through and work through this problem more fully.

The problem is even more difficult when couples do not understand the dynamics of the situation, when each comes to marriage with his own expectations and automatically assumes that the other partner will have the same expectation.

In counseling, a good way to get couples to begin to gain insights and understanding into the thinking and expectations of their marriage partners, is to ask them to write specific answers to two questions. First, "What do I expect of my wife or husband in our marriage?" In other words, "What do I expect to get out of marriage?" Second, "What do I expect to put into our marriage?" In other words, "What does my wife or husband have a right to expect from me in this marriage?" A comparison and discussion of the answers to these questions frequently reveals to the couple that they are on different wave lengths. Such a discussion helps the couple gain insights and find solutions to their problems.

PERSONALITY DIFFERENCES

Another area of potential discord in marriage lies in the fact that sometimes husbands and wives don't understand each other as people, as men and women. Men and women are often referred to as opposite sexes. In the creative wisdom of God this is not the case at all. Men and women are not opposites, but complementary sexes. They do not "oppose" each other; they "complete" each other.

Each, however, has characteristics of his own, different from the other. Sometimes difficulties arise in a marriage when one of the partners expects the other to think and respond to situations in the same way he or she does. This is impossible because the sexes differ from each other psychologically.

In a series of "Committed Couples" sessions that the author conducted for engaged couples, one discussion centered around "Understanding Each Other as Persons." As the discussion moved along, one of the young men said rather critically of his fiancée, "Why do they have to go into all the details? When I call her and she has to be late for an appointment, why does she have to tell me all the little reasons? I don't care about the details."

This was the opportunity to begin the discussion of an extremely important aspect of happy married life, namely, understanding and accepting the differences between the sexes rather than criticizing and judging the other because of the differences. This young man was expecting his fiancée to think like he thought and react like he reacted. Not being interested in details, he expected that his future wife should not be either. He forgot that his attitude, carried into marriage, would make him a poor husband in at least this one regard.

One of the so-called "feminine" traits in our culture is the inclination to grasp details, and sometimes not being able to distinguish between what is important and what is unimportant because the details take on so much significance. One of the so-called "masculine" traits, on the other hand, is to be more wholistic in thinking, more inclined to see the total perspective than to focus on the minute details. They should not criticize each other for not being a carbon copy of what they would like each other to be. Rather, they should understand each other and realize how they complement each other.

It is said too that often the masculine characteristic is to be more logical while the feminine trait is to be more intuitive. The man may say, "I think this is so." The woman is more inclined to say, "I *feel* this is so." The man may make his decisions only after carefully weighing all of the factors in the situation, and the wife cannot understand why it takes him so long to make up his mind. On the other hand, he has difficulty at times understanding her reasoning. This does not mean that she is illogical. It means only that her logic is different from his.

Another characteristic in which men differ from women is in self-assurance. Perhaps because of our culture, the man is accustomed to making decisions more frequently and must live with his decisions. Whatever the reason, this accounts for the wife often seeking her husband's opinion even in seemingly insignificant and unimportant details. She may ask, for example, whether he thinks she should do a particular task today or tomorrow. The question comes in part from lack of self-assurance. He does her no favor by telling her that it doesn't matter and that she should do what she wants to. His opinion tells her that he is interested in her. And she wants to have him tell her, even though she may decide to do the opposite of what he suggested. This action helps her to determine in her own mind what she wants to do, even though the husband might then wonder why she asked him in the first place.

The Cana Manual, used by the Roman Catholic Church for their Cana Conferences (parish programs for married couples) lists some characteristic personality differences. One might not agree with all of them, but a discussion of them between husband and wife, or as a topic for a couple's group in the church should be very fruitful and enriching.

Masculine	*Feminine*
physically stronger	physically weaker
more realistic	more idealistic
logical	intuitive
more emotionally stable	more emotionally volatile
objective	subjective
more factual	more fanciful

slow judgment	quick judgment
literal	tangential
seeks love	wants love
self-assured	less self-assured
wholistic thinking	grasps details
less adaptable	more adaptable
less possessive	more possessive

SENSE OF VALUES

Every marriage counselor will be quick to point out that one of the tension areas in many marriages is the handling and spending of money. Who should handle the money and how it should be spent is determined, in part at least, by attitudes that have developed in their childhood homes. The entire process involves a great deal more than establishing a budget and living within it. Money and its use is symbolic of something more. It says something about the couple's sense of values and, therefore, something about the people themselves. Some people's outlook toward life is very much oriented around money and the things it will buy. They need material comforts to be happy, in part perhaps, because they have always been accustomed to them or perhaps even have been deprived of them. Others need very little of the material things to be happy. They find their happiness elsewhere. In all marriages couples need to strike a balance, to compromise their sense of wants and needs. If two people from the extreme ends of the curve become married, a good deal of adjusting of thinking and reshifting of values needs to be made.

The problems show themselves not only in the overall pattern of attitudes, but also in the specifics of everyday living. Because of earlier conditioning, what one considers a luxury might seem like a necessity to the other. The wife may not "have anything to wear" and the husband thinks he sees half a dozen dresses hanging in the closet and can't understand why one of them isn't good enough. The husband wants a new motor for his boat. To the wife that is a luxury that represents a complete waste of money. The husband thinks of it as a necessity. Or the wife thinks a new refrigerator is a necessity. The husband thinks a new car ought to come first.

Thus in marriage varying points of view are constantly in tension (not necessarily in conflict) with one another, and decisions and compromises must constantly be made. The individual viewpoints will be a reflection of the value system that each has and in which they must begin to grow together in order to develop and keep a unity in their marriage. This again takes conscious effort. It means constantly attempting to understand the other person's ideas (which is a part of Christian love) and to make decisions after taking all points of view into consideration.

VERBAL CONCEPTS

Another potential tension area lies in verbal communication. Words have meanings far beyond their dictionary definition. Words are but symbols for concepts that lie behind them. They are therefore emotionally loaded for the person who uses them or hears them. The concept that one person has in mind when he uses a given word may be entirely different from the concept the listener of that word envisions when he hears it. This is one reason why couples can so easily talk past one another. One marriage partner often reads meanings into words that the other never intended to convey. The connotations of any word depend on the individual's spectrum of beautiful, positive experiences. To another person the same word may recall a series of revolting, negative experiences. Thus, though the same word may have been used, it really was not the same "word" at all. It certainly did not convey the same meaning.

Consider this principle in terms of everyday communication. The word *love*, for example, is loaded with what our experience with it has been. To one it might mean something merely physical, because that is all that was ever associated with it. To another it might mean warmth and security and understanding. The word *sex* to one might have beautiful connotations because of wholesome attitudes communicated in the home environment; to the other the word might be repulsive because of unfortunate childhood experiences. The word *swim* will recall entirely different reactions from the man who has just won the free style from the girl who nearly drowned once and has been desperately afraid of water ever since. The word *father* to one person symbolizes strength and security and love. To another it recalls an entire syndrome of cruelty, desertion, drunkenness and irresponsibility. Even the word *Christ* means something more to the person in whose home the name was devoutly revered than to the person in whose home the word was hardly more than a curse word.

Words are loaded. To hear what the other person is saying does not necessarily mean to understand what he is saying. We interpret what others say by our own concepts of what the words mean. It is therefore vitally important that couples get beyond the spoken words to the concepts that the speaker means to convey. Every Christian spouse should be liberal with questions like, "What do you mean?" "How do you feel?" so that he understands the meaning behind a statement before he reacts to it.

FORGIVENESS

This chapter has been limited to problems of interpersonal communication. There may be many other problems that disrupt family unity, but usually they too involve a lack of understanding and communication with one another.

It is at this point that Christianity makes its unique contribution to marriage. The golden thread of Christian marriage is forgiveness and acceptance. Forgiveness means a great deal more than doing the other the favor of forgetting an isolated mistake, a hasty word, an irresponsible act. The Christian knows that God has for Christ's sake forgiven him all his sins. He lives under the umbrella of God's total forgiveness. Because of Christ the Christian lives under the constant forgiveness of God. So Christians now live in relationship with one another; they forgive as they have been forgiven. This means living in an attitude of forgiveness toward one another.

This is a reminder that all Christians need constantly. Because of humanness and sin, everybody is constantly in the position where he needs to be forgiven. To illustrate, suppose that there are two things that could be done or should be done at a given moment. A long overdue letter should be written home to parents who are most anxious to hear. At the same time the growing little child should be read to and played with. To do the one thing that should be done means not doing the other thing that should be done. As long as people are making decisions about what they are going to do they will have to be living under forgiveness.

This is true also in relationships between husband and wife. The husband should spend the evening with the family, but work is piling up at the office and simply must be taken care of in order for him to meet an obligation on his job. Something must be neglected. He needs to live under the forgiveness of his family for neglecting the one to do the other. A sick neighbor is in dire circumstances and needs help during her illness. Mother spends most of her time there for the week, but in doing so she neglects some of the things at home that she normally would do as wife and mother. She needs to live under forgiveness for not being everything to her family that she should be that week. Because of the constant limitations to good relationships that their day-by-day behavior poses, families need constantly to live under forgiveness with one another.

ACCEPTANCE

Forgiving one another in Christ means also accepting one another, fully and totally, in Christ. In the home, members of a family often judge one another and criticize one another instead of unqualifiedly accepting one another. Each thinks the others ought to think as he thinks, or be more what he should like them to be. Whenever people do not freely accept the human beings with whom they live for what they are, they are living in judgment of them.

Ephesians 5 illustrates well what is implied here. "Husbands, love your wives, as Christ loved the church and gave himself up for her, that he might sanctify her, having cleansed her by the washing of water with the word, that he might present the church to himself in splendor, without spot or wrinkle or any such thing, that she might be holy and without blemish" (Eph 5:25-27, RSV). For many years I could not understand why the latter portion of this passage, which deals with Christ's redemptive work, should be inserted in a section that speaks about the relationship of husbands and wives to each other. Actually, it is saying much. The church is accepted, blemishes and all. Covered with the righteousness of Christ, it appears holy and without blemish before God.

It is this kind of total acceptance that members of a Christian family are to share with one another. Those who bear the forgiveness and acceptance of Christ are to share that forgiveness and acceptance with one another. This type of forgiveness and acceptance grows out of Christian love. Love is an outgoing concern *for the other person*. It is an understanding of the other person for what he is, what makes him think the way he thinks, and act or react the way he reacts. Christian love is not an emotion as much as it is an attitude—an attitude that reaches out beyond oneself to the object of the love.

Accepting and enjoying each other physically and sexually are dependent on an accepting attitude that already binds the couple together spiritually, mentally and emotionally.*

When such love and understanding form the basis of family unity, parents are creating an atmosphere of warmth and unity and love into which to bring their children. Parents begin to establish a home for their children long before the children arrive. Children very seldom create a unity in the parents that was not there before. In fact, the very opposite is often true. Children pose a constellation of new problems as well as new joys. New adjustments must be made; new sets of interpersonal relationships must be established; new patterns of family living, of spending money, of use of time must be set up. Differing values will show in the training and disciplining of children. Each will again have his own opinions from his own parental home.

One reason for developing marital unity is, of course, for home happiness. Without such unity marriage becomes merely a living together

*For a more detailed discussion on marital unity in these various areas, see W. J. Fields, *Unity in Marriage* (St. Louis: Concordia, 1962).

under the same roof without relationships that are fully satisfying. Another very real reason is that what homes are today has a very strong bearing on what the homes of tomorrow will become. Today's children will be the spouses of tomorrow, and today's homes are training those spouses.*

THE CHURCH AND MARITAL UNITY

This is why the church, through all her agencies, should be vitally concerned about ministering to families. Special emphases may be given at special times and with special programs from time to time. In addition, pastors can make themselves available for marital counseling. In fact, much of pastoral counseling for married couples most likely is concerned with helping them maintain unity.

It would seem, however, that the dynamics of Christian living in the home come from consistent Christian living. The characteristics that make for a good Christian life also make for a good spouse. Since every individual to whom the church ministers is a member of a family unit, it would seem that in all agencies and organizations of the church every application of the Word of God should be made with the family in mind. It is there that the Christian, whether husband or wife, parent or child, lives out his Christianity in closest and most meaningful relationships. Christian love is more than a definition. It is more than being able to recite 1 Corinthians 13. Christian love is more than proper attitudes too. Christian love is attitudes in action, and that action must begin in the home.

FOR FURTHER READING

Bell, A. Donald. *The Family in Dialogue*. Grand Rapids: Zondervan, 1968.
Bower, Robert K. *Solving Problems in Marriage: Guidelines for Christian Couples*. Grand Rapids: Eerdmans, 1970.
Brandt, Henry R. and Dowdy, Homer E. *Building a Christian Home*. Wheaton, Ill.: Scripture Press, 1960.
Brandt, Henry R. and Krutza, William J. *Balancing Your Marriage*. Wheaton, Ill.: Scripture Press, 1966.
Burke, Louis. *With This Ring*. New York: McGraw-Hill, 1958.
Bracher, Marjory. *Love Is No Luxury*. Rev. ed. Philadelphia: Fortress, 1961.
Capon, Robert. *Bed and Board*. New York: Simon & Schuster, 1965.
Duvall, Evelyn and Hill, Reuben. *Being Married*. New York: Association, 1960.
Evans, Louis. *Your Marriage—Duel or Duet?* Westwood, N.J.: Revell, 1962.
Fields, W. J. *Unity in Marriage*. St. Louis: Concordia, 1962.
Fritze, J. A. *The Essence of Marriage*. Grand Rapids: Zondervan, 1969.

*See chap. 20, "Preparing Young People for Christian Marriage."

Harrell, Irene Burk. *Good Marriages Grow.* Waco, Tex.: Word, 1968.

Hine, James. *Come Prepared to Stay Forever.* Danville, Ill.: Interstate, 1966.

Hulme, William. *Building a Christian Marriage.* Englewood Cliffs, N.J.: Prentice-Hall, 1965.

Jaeck, Gordon and Jaeck, Dorothea. *I Take Thee: The Art of Successful Marriage.* Grand Rapids: Zondervan, 1967.

Jonsson, G. and Jonsson, L. *Can Two Become One?* Philadelphia: Fortress, 1965.

LaHaye, Tim. *How to Be Happy Though Married.* Wheaton, Ill.: Tyndale, 1968.

Locke, Harvey J. *Predicting Adjustment in Marriage.* New York: Holt, 1951.

Miles, Herbert J. *Sexual Happiness in Marriage.* Grand Rapids: Zondervan, 1967.

Miller, Randolph. *Youth Considers Parents as People.* New York: Nelson, 1965.

Narramore, Clyde M. *Happiness in Marriage.* Grand Rapids: Zondervan, 1961.

Nelson, Elof G. *Your Life Together.* Richmond, Va.: John Knox, 1967.

Peterson, James A. *Married Love in the Middle Years.* New York: Association, 1968.

Renich, Jill. *How to Find Harmony in Marriage.* Grand Rapids: Zondervan, 1964.

Small, Dwight Hervey. *After You've Said I Do.* Westwood, N.J.: Revell, 1968.

———. *Design for Christian Marriage.* Westwood, N.J.: Revell, 1959.

Filmstrips: Hollywood, Calif.: Family Filmstrips. Each filmstrip in color, with 33⅓ rpm record, and discussion guide.

Facing Problems of Modern Marriage Series
Problems of Early Marriage
Marrying Outside Your Faith
Christians and Divorce
Problems of the Modern Mother
The Early Years of Marriage Series
Making the First Year Count
The First Baby
Marriage Counseling Kit Series
Marriage Makes a Difference
Marriage Requires Adjustments
The Intimacies of Marriage
Making Marriage Last

22

GUIDING PARENTS IN CHILD-TRAINING AND DISCIPLINE

Martin P. Simon

Perhaps one of the greatest problems parents face continually is how to train and discipline their children. The Bible instructs parents to "bring them [their children] up in the nurture and admonition of the Lord" (Eph 6:4), but many parents are puzzled to know *how* to do so.

The following suggestions are given as some of the basic principles that churches should carefully and systematically impart to parents.

PARENTS TEACH BY THEIR CONVERSATIONS

"Any one of you boys might be a minister," said the Sunday school teacher to her class of boys.

I'll be that boy, said little Oswald Smith to himself, and that, in part, is how the greatest missionary congregation of this century—The People's Church of Toronto—got its start. That was Christian education in the church!

❖   ❖   ❖

Oswald Smith's sister Hazel was very sick. She heard the doctor say that she probably would not get well. Hugging her mother, she sobbed, "I don't want to die yet!"

But before long her tired body yielded to the thought of death. "I can't play anymore here, Mama," she said, "but Miss Nethercott says there are lots of children in heaven. I'll be able to play up there."

Her brother Oswald asked her forgiveness for teasing and hurting her. She smiled as she gave it.

Later she folded her hands as she gazed heavenward. "Blessed Jesus, take me now," she prayed. For a few moments she rested, as if awaiting the coming of her angel guide and the final summons.

The late MARTIN P. SIMON, Ed.D., was editor of *The Christian Parent* magazine and pastor of the Olive Branch Lutheran Church, Okawville, Illinois.

Suddenly, in a strong, clear voice she cried, "Good-bye, Mama!" Those were her last words. That was Christian education in the home.[2]

* * *

Dr. R. A. Torrey came to Toronto to preach the gospel, and the papers carried long accounts of the meetings. Oswald and his brother, along with many other people at Embro, Ontario, read the accounts eagerly.

Oswald got his mother's permission to go to Toronto with his brother, to hear Torrey. "I often wonder what would have happened had she refused," said Oswald Smith later. "Toronto was ninety-five miles away!"[3] But the boys had an aunt in Toronto.

Through Torrey's preaching the boys became quite clear on what Jesus means to us, and they accepted Him openly as Saviour and Lord of their lives. Then Oswald started a Sunday school in his home with the help of his mother.[4] That was Christian education in the home and the church.

* * *

These fragments out of the life of a great man of God show Christian education not as something memorized out of a book—though indeed flowing out of God's Book—but the ordinary circumstances of life which became extraordinary.

Much of this was based on a fact often overlooked in child-training. It is the fact that conversation is education, that parents teach by their talk.

When Oswald Smith's mother talked with a sick child about God's ways, this was not "just talk." It was education. When Oswald and his brother discussed the preaching of the gospel as reported in the newspaper, this was education. When a teacher, in offhand conversation apart from the lesson, speaks for Christ and His cause, this, too, can be education of the most effective sort.

Conversation is education! Conversation sets the climate of the home. Conversation is how parents mostly make their influence—good or bad— felt. From conversation, from the tone of voice in conversation, children catch their parents' ways of looking at things, and attitudes are thus built. Jesus Himself said He will judge us by our conversation (Mt 12:36)!

People don't act according to what they *know*; they act according to how they *feel* about what they know. And the conversation in the home chiefly determines those feelings for most of us.

* * *

Mr. Smith comes home from church, where he heard a sermon about missions. He is angry.

"Another sermon about money! Money, money, money, that's all the preacher talks about! I have to work hard for my money, and if the people in India want the gospel, let them work for it too!"

The children hear him. He has said such things before and will again. What kind of church members come from that home?

*   *   *

Mr. Jones comes home with his family from the same church service.

"Mary," he says, "that sermon hangs in my mind. Those people in India live in shacks we wouldn't use for pigs. When a child is sick probably there isn't even a nurse within a hundred miles—and they know nothing of Christ or heaven! Could you and the children get along a few more months with our old car if we give the money for missions instead of for car payments?"

Mother nods her head. The children nod too. They have often heard their father talk about missions and helping the poor. They will wait for the car.

*   *   *

If there is friendly talk in the home—more praise than blame, more joy than anger—that is *a friendly home*. Conversation determines it. If there is constant scolding, quarreling and blaming, much angry talk, *the home is unhappy*. Conversation determines it.[5] This is what the Bible is emphasizing in these verses:

> Hear, O Israel: The LORD our God is one LORD: And thou shalt love the LORD thy God with all thine heart, and with all thy soul, and with all thy might. And these words, which I command thee this day, shall be in thine heart: And thou shalt teach them diligently unto thy children, and shalt *talk* of them when thou sittest in thine house, and when thou walkest by the way, and when thou liest down, and when thou risest up (Deu 6:4-7).

INDISCRIMINATE SCOLDING IS HARMFUL

The Bible class was discussing the problems a mother had with her thirteen-year-old son. She told how she had tried to set him right by talking and scolding.

Someone asked, "What did you do that a heathen mother could not do?"

She was taken aback, for she had, in fact, done nothing that a heathen mother could not do. Mainly she had scolded.

As soon as a parent sees the glimmer of sorrow in the child about the wrong he has done (and no apology should be a forced one), then the parent should talk lovingly about the forgiveness God promises us. Often one sees this sorrow before the scolding begins. The child has broken the pitcher and is waiting with worry for the parent's reaction. If he is sorry, truly repentant, why scold?

Perhaps the parent could ask him, "How can I help you be more careful?" Normally a child will respond to kind ways. This kind of incident also provides an opportunity to talk with a child about what he has now again noticed—how hard it is to do what is right.

"It's not easy always to do right, is it?" a parent might say. "I have my troubles too. Yesterday I blamed you for tracking mud on the porch, then I found out you didn't do it. That was wrong of me. I asked God to forgive me, and I hope you will forgive me too."

This is more than "just conversation." It is Christian education, conversation on a higher level than scolding.

Frequently scolding becomes a habit. Used indiscriminately, it helps very little. It is often a way for parents to "let off steam," a way of "blowing one's top" in the family circle. By contrast, a friendly sentence with understanding and firmness behind it is far more effective.

Perhaps one may talk of "righteous anger" or Paul's words, "Be ye angry, and sin not" (Eph 4:26). But parents must be careful not to use these scriptures to justify impatience. The angry parent is emotionally involved and often says things in that state of tension that he later regrets. Then, too, anger begets anger. Paul advises, "Fathers, provoke not your children to wrath" (Eph 6:4).

There are three times especially when a parent should avoid scolding if at all possible. The first is at mealtime. This should be a happy time, thus contributing to proper digestion. The second time is bedtime, a time which provides unusual opportunity to get close to children. A parent may wish to review the happenings of the day, including some negative ones, but should avoid creating an emotional situation. The third time is "in-between time." This may seem idealistic, but if a parent keeps these three exceptions in mind he will discover that "scolding" will not become a bad habit that may do more harm than good.

It is possible to get into the *habit* of scolding and, in self-defense, children get into the *habit* of not hearing it. Parents in the end accomplish very little that a firm, friendly sentence would not have accomplished.

PRAISE IS BETTER THAN CRITICISM

A child dries four glasses, three of them with lint and streaks showing, and one is *almost* good. It is easy for the *perfectionist* parent to scold about the three dirty glasses and to overlook the child's accomplishment in drying the one.

There is almost always something to praise, and our own character grows attractive with the habit of looking for the best. Usually parents can find a true reason for honest praise in what their child does.

CORRECTIVE DISCIPLINE IS BEST WHEN BEGUN EARLY
AND GIVEN LOVINGLY, FIRMLY AND CONSISTENTLY

God clearly wants parents to be in control. One of the first Bible stories a child should learn is that of Eli and his sons. God punished Eli because he did not make his sons stop sinning. On the basis of this story a parent can say to the child, "God wants us to see to it that you obey your parents, and that you do what God wants. God is sad when parents let their children do what is wrong. That's what parents are for, to teach children to do right." A child so instructed is not likely to say or think, "You spanked me because you hate me," provided, of course, that the Christian parent is careful to be fair to the child, not letting his anger control his actions.

The sharpest verse in the Bible on corporal punishment tells us, "He who spares his rod hates his son, but he who loves him is diligent to chasten him" (Pr 13:24, Berkeley). Does this verse say a parent must spank *often?* No, it says that if a parent knows that a spanking is what his child *really needs*, then to hold back is false love.

Spanking is an emergency measure. If the boat is upside down, it must be turned right side up. My father and mother used the flat hand for what spankings we got. It is a handy "rod," swift, not too harsh, and settles matters fast. A friend, who has very well-trained children, has a small switch above the mantel. He seldom uses it. Usually a reference to it or at most a step or two toward it will bring the child to terms.

A little-known Bible verse worth memorizing is, "Correct your son, and he will give you rest" (Pr 29:17, Berkeley). A parent should begin to teach obedience early, keeping firm but friendly control from the start. Such correction should be considerate and sensibly Christian.

Teaching obedience begins, oddly enough, with giving the very young child his food and other attention when he needs it. Letting a hungry baby cry ten minutes beyond feeding time, while the mother gossips on the telephone or finishes mopping the kitchen, is teaching a child to develop temper. Give him early what he really needs, and he will not have so much need of developing temper.

If parents must spank or punish *often*, there may be something wrong with the way they are training their children. It might be wise for them to invite a mature Christian couple to visit in their home and then be receptive to their suggestions. Talking things over with even-tempered and successful parents is helpful especially to young parents and to parents in trouble.

It should also be noted that, in rare instances, children suffer from brain damage, thus making them nervous, irritable and persistently incorrigible. In such cases it is wise to consult a competent psychologist who can administer appropriate tests to determine if this is the case and, if so, prescribe appropriate action to lessen the problem.

In most normal situations, however, Christian children can be remarkably cooperative. When my son Paul, at this writing a state Senator of Illinois, was four years old, he received a tricycle for his birthday at the end of November. One of the next days his mother told me on coming home that he had refused to obey her. It is the only time we remember that either of our sons refused obedience outright.

Paul was playing on the floor, and I asked him, "Paul, is that right? Is that what you said?"

He answered, "Yes."

"Don't you know God wants us to see to it that you obey your father and mother?" I asked again.

He answered, "Yes."

For a moment, I was puzzled as to how to proceed. Then I asked, "What do you think we should do to make sure it doesn't happen again?"

He answered, "I won't ride my tricycle till Christmas."

In retrospect now, I think we should have reduced that sentence to perhaps a week. But I said, "Push your tricycle into the junk room."

He did that. We did not lock the room, but he didn't get his tricycle until Christmas morning. That day he arose very early, ran to get his tricycle, and was a very happy boy.

Children in Christian homes can be remarkably cooperative if one begins the matter right, and firmness is not rudeness.

WISE RULES ARE MADE LOVINGLY AND SPARINGLY

The mother who sets down a rule in the heat of anger, is not likely to be fair and just. The father who suddenly blurts out a decision "from the top of his head" will not likely make a good decision. Wait for a time when the family is happy together—this is important—and then bring the rule up for discussion.

With older children it is often wise to discuss the anticipated rules with the children. This is often helpful because a parent cannot always see the full bearing of any rule in quite the same light as the child. Parents need not fear that a child will be easy on himself. In fact, parents may have to restrain their child from making a rule *too* strict. Many teenage codes have demonstrated this.

It is wise to make few rules and not to expand them unnecessarily. Also parents should give children more freedom as they become old enough to use it properly.

ATTITUDES ARE MORE ESSENTIAL THAN WORDS

Why a person does a thing is more important than *how* he does it. Anyone can make a child conform with a big stick, but is this what a Christian parent should want? Should not the aim be to help the child to *want* to behave? In other words, a parent should seek to build attitudes.

The dinner hour was near, and two girls were playing on the floor. Their Sunday school teacher was their guest. Mother opened the kitchen door and said, "Girls, I need your help."

The girls paid no attention. The Sunday school teacher asked them, "Girls, do you know a Bible verse that begins, *'Children, obey—'*?"

The girls jumped up, stood straight, and recited, "Children, obey your parents in the Lord: for this is right." Then they went back to playing and ignored their mother. They had learned a Bible verse, but it had not been a message from God to their hearts. The *words* they knew, but the *attitude* of wanting to do what the verse said was missing. True Christian education must reach the feelings and influence the attitudes, thus forming character and will.

A little girl on her mother's lap heard the story of Samuel, given to God before he was born.

"Mommie, you gave me to God too, before I was born, didn't you?" she asked her mother.

Her mother was embarrassed. "No, Honey, I'm afraid I didn't."

The girl was sad. Then a happy thought came. "Mommie, can't you still do it? Can't you do it now?"

So in a prayer the mother dedicated her girl to the Lord right there, and a smile came on the child's face.

If a Bible story can touch the feelings of a child, causing her to *want* to be given to the Lord, that is Christian education and proper child-training.

It is realized that no parent can fully live up to what this chapter says. Every parent makes many mistakes, but usually the mistakes are not fatal as long as true love is present.

Parents must take their mistakes to God, learn from them, then forget them. Sometimes mistakes can even be used to illustrate the gospel of forgiveness, as when a mother or father uses them to teach their children that their parents have repented.

WISE PARENTS COOPERATE WITH THEIR CHURCHES IN CHILD-TRAINING

The church services, the Sunday school, the Christian day school, the vacation Bible school, and other church agencies provide training for children. A parent should know what is taught and reinforce the teaching by taking an interest in the lessons.

Church leaders, however, should take the lead in providing opportunities for parents to learn how to be better fathers and mothers. Pastors should plan their sermon schedules so that messages are given periodically on various biblical portions that focus on the home.* Special sessions should be conducted for parents during Sunday evening training hour on topics related to child discipline and training.

Every church should also concentrate on providing opportunities for premarital counseling, to include special help on child-rearing. In addition, an up-to-date library with a good selection of books related to the home should be available to every parent in the church.

NOTES

1. Oswald J. Smith, *The Adventures of Andy McGinnis* (Grand Rapids: Zondervan, 1955), p. 65.
2. Ibid., pp. 50-53.
3. Smith, *The Greatest Event of My Life*, tract (Toronto: The People's Press, n.d.).
4. Smith, *The Adventures . . .*, pp. 88 ff.
5. For more on the power of Christian family conversation, see Doris C. Aldrich, *Musings of a Mother* (Chicago: Moody, 1949).

FOR FURTHER READING

Aldrich, Doris C. *Musings of a Mother.* Chicago: Moody, 1949.

Baruch, Dorothy W. *How to Discipline Your Children.* New York: Public Affairs Pamphlets, 1949.

Brandt, Henry R. *Build a Happy Home with Discipline.* Wheaton, Ill.: Scripture Press, 1965.

———, and Dowdy, Homer E. *Building a Christian Home.* Wheaton, Ill.: Scripture Press, 1960.

Carollo, Betty J. "Ten Ways to Good Discipline Without Spanking," *Parents' Magazine*, 38 (Apr., 1963):62, 106, 108.

Denton, Wallace. *What's Happening to Our Families?* Philadelphia: Westminster, 1963.

Dowdy, Edward and Dowdy, Harriet. *The Church Is Families.* Valley Forge, Pa.: Judson, 1965.

Feucht, Oscar E. *Ministry to Families.* St. Louis: Concordia, 1963.

Ginott, Haim G. *Between Parent and Child.* New York: Macmillan, 1965.

Grams, Armin. *Children and Their Parents.* Minneapolis: Dennison, 1963.

Jacobsen, Margaret Bailey. *The Child in the Christian Home.* Wheaton, Ill.: Scripture Press, 1959.

LeShan, Eda J. "You Have to Say No!" *Parents' Magazine*, 38 (Aug., 1963): 38, 85-87.

*Following are some suggested passages for biblical messages on the home: Gen 2:18-25; Ex 20:4-5; Deu 6:6-12; 1 Sa 1; Pr 22:6; 31:10-31; 1 Co 7; Eph 5:22-33; 2 Ti 3:15-17; Titus 2:3-5.

Narramore, Clyde M. *Discipline in the Christian Home.* Grand Rapids: Zondervan, 1961.

———. *How to Understand and Influence Children.* Grand Rapids: Zondervan, 1957.

Orr, William W. *Children Can Be Taught to Obey.* Wheaton, Ill.: Scripture Press, 1967.

Puner, Helen. "Discipline: Strict or Permissive?" *Parents' Magazine,* 35 (Sept., 1960):39, 116-18, 120.

Simon, Martin P. *Pointers for Parents.* St. Louis: Concordia, 1963.

Thomas, Rachele. "The Challenge of Fatherhood," *Parents' Magazine* 42 (June, 1967):41, 43, 106-7.

Filmstrips: *Parents of Preschoolers; Parents of School-agers; Parents of Young Teens; Parents of Older Teens* (Hollywood, Calif.: Family Filmstrips), Color, each filmstrip has a 33⅓ rpm record and discussion guide.

23

HELPING PARENTS TEACH CHRISTIAN STANDARDS

Jeannette Acrea

Much of our culture today promulgates *non*christian standards. Rebellion, violence, and sexual stimulation are rampant. Violence is an integral part of many television shows. In fact, a worried client of mine complained, "I don't even dare allow my children to watch the cartoons anymore!" The majority of movies today are indicative of our preoccupation with morbidity and sexual excesses. Marijuana and many other drugs and "pills" are being used by thousands of teenagers in our land.

How can our Christian youth escape the maelstrom of nonchristian forces and influences? How can parents help their children maintain Christian standards? How can we help youth "stand fast" while these tentacles are reaching out to pull them into the trap of worldliness?

Morris and Natalie Haimowitz have hypothesized that the so-called causes of crime (poverty, "bad" neighborhoods, movies, TV, comic books, radio, crime stories, race, neurosis, etc.) are not real "causes" but are "associated factors," because *most* people subjected to these factors do *not* become criminals.[1] However, research has indicated that an inadequate *home* environment *is* a contributor to delinquency. Martin and Lois Hoffman have discovered that delinquents come from homes that are more punitive, more neglectful, and more inconsistent, and less warm and affectionate than the homes of nondelinquents.[2]

Though the family is not the only factor causing difficulty for our youth today, it *is* a major vehicle for transmitting moral values. This is not to suggest, however, that the home is the source of *all* the trouble. For the home is part of a larger cultural setting and is often buffeted by forces it is incapable of controlling or modifying. Nevertheless, the home and the church are our major allies, provided they are geared to meet our children's basic needs. For, as Kanner affirms, the basic drive in all

JEANNETTE ACREA, M.A., Ph.D., is codirector of Christian Psychological Services, Glendale, California.

behavior is the struggle for gratification of needs.[3] *If our homes and churches are meeting the needs of our children and youth, worldliness will be less of a magnet to draw our children into its whirlpool of conflicting emotions.* If a child's needs are not gratified, irritability accumulates until he becomes hostile. As he is envenomed more and more by nongratification, he will find a means to transmit this hostility to the external world, or to withdraw and turn the hostility against himself.

Children learn by what adults say and do. But if our words and actions are not consonant, our conduct will largely outweigh what we say. Christian standards are transmitted through the attitudes and actions of the parents and other significant family members, with verbal teaching serving to make those standards more incisive. In other words, verbal instruction in Christian virtues without the proper exemplification of those virtues is inadequate. Jersild notes this discrepancy between the words and deeds of the parents as the most significant complication confronting a child in his moral development.[4]

ATMOSPHERE OF THE HOME

A warm, democratic atmosphere is essential to the proper emotional development of children and, consequently, for effective teaching of Christian standards. As put by Jersild, "Moral development is closely interrelated with a child's *emotional* development. His capacity for *affection* influences the way he will respond to the moral teaching of his elders."[5]

Janie came running into the house, breathless. She had found a four-leaf clover. Mother was busy preparing dinner for their eight-member family.

"Mother, Mother!" Janie called.

"What is it, dear?" Mother smiled.

"Oh, Mother, look! I've found a four-leaf clover!"

Mother quickly glanced at the food cooking on the stove, turned the heat down, then bent her head and concentrated fully on Janie's thrilling find. At that moment Father came in and the three of them talked about the wonder and beauty of it, how God enjoyed variety, and why He would create a four-leaf clover. Janie's mother was sufficiently mature to be able to concentrate on this "little event" in Janie's life, even during the preparation of dinner for her large family. Father, too, was interested and willing—in fact, eager—to share the moment with them.

Little event? Yes. But there were many in Janie's life, and their cumulative effect was to make Janie aware of the wonder of God's creation, to show her that her father and mother shared her interests and considered them important, to give her incentive to further develop her imaginativeness, creativity and initiative. Also, it was another expression of her parents' love. Janie felt secure: that she was loved, belonged, was valued as a contributing member of the family.

In addition, her mother suggested that Janie put the leaf on the dinner table and share it with the entire family. During dinner Janie's discovery was discussed and this led to further conversation about God's wonderful creation and the beauties of nature. Later, during devotions, various members of the family thanked God for His creativity, the delights of discovering the unique, and the enjoyment of the commonplace. No one razzed Janie, because they too had known similar experiences wherein their parents had indicated interest and respect. When there had been a tendency to razz, father or mother had asked questions which brought out their feelings and also made them aware of how their statement might cause Janie to feel. Thus they learned to understand themselves, to feel accepted even when their feelings were hostile, jealous or envious, and to develop a feeling of empathy.

This little story illustrates several factors important in creating a loving, happy, Christian atmosphere in the home:

1. A system of values centered on the emotional and spiritual well-being of the family members, rather than on meeting a schedule or on materialism.
2. Interest in momentarily important incidents in the child's life, and willingness to use them to illustrate spiritual truths and help the child become aware of God in all things.
3. Harmony between father and mother.*
4. Sharing between all members of the family.
5. Acceptance of negative as well as positive feelings and encouraging their expression.
6. Encouragement of empathy between members of the family.†
7. Making dinner time a happy, sharing experience.
8. Having family devotions, and praising and thanking God.

This experience was quite different from that of a girl by the name of Mary. Awaiting her dreaded report card, Mary felt her hands wet with perspiration. She knew her father and mother wanted her to make all A's, and she was fearful. Sure enough, there were C's and B's along with only one A.

What shall I do? she thought, as she slowly walked home. *I don't dare show it to them; they'll be mad at me. Mother will scold me and tell me how dumb I am, and Father will look disappointed.* As she walked

---

*Significantly correlated with emotional health.
†Empathy can only be engendered when the child feels liked by others important to him, and likes himself.

along, she noticed a storm drain. Impulsively she chucked the report card down the drain. Arriving home, she was burdened with a heavy sense of guilt. Later, during the rains, it was swept out of the drain and her brother found it and took it to their parents. Her parents asked no questions to gain understanding of her feelings; there was only condemnation and the razor strap.

Mary's father and mother demanded perfection. Unable to fulfill their expectations, she never achieved a sense of self-worth. Now Mary, a grown woman, is still burdened with this need to "be perfect so people will like me."

Home should be a place where one can feel he can be himself and "be loved anyway." Parents often face the predicament of trying to encourage their children to do their best without causing problems like Mary's. If parents genuinely accept their children and have no need to "relive their lives through them," or be pretentious, their genuine feelings will be evident. Research indicates children achieve better when praised and encouraged than when criticized and shamed.[6] Feeling loved, accepted and worthwhile is encouraging and promotes the flowering of inborn potentials.

A friend hearing the story of Janie said, "That sounds so ideal. I'd like to curl right up in that family. What does one do if he can't follow through on these suggested principles?" An incident related by another friend is appropriate to this question. Her daughter, eight-year-old Linda, came into the house from playing with her girl friend, Marilyn, and said sorrowfully, "Mother, why doesn't Marilyn's mother love her?" Mother carefully responded, "What makes you think she doesn't?" Linda replied, "She is always hollering at her and saying mean things." Mother thoughtfully responded, "Well, honey, don't I holler at you and say mean things too?" "Yes," replied Linda, "but Marilyn's mother never says she's wrong or that she's sorry."

Everyone makes mistakes and frequently has conflicting emotions. Even the apostle Paul exclaimed, "The good that I would I do not: but the evil which I would not, that I do" (Ro 7:19). So we needn't berate ourselves; instead we should be honest and realistic with our children by admitting our mistakes and faults and saying we are sorry. "But," you may counter, "what will my children think of me if I admit mistakes?" Children are perceptive and aware in a general way of our inner feelings anyway. Being open with them, provided that the purpose is child-oriented rather than self-punitive, tends to make them love us even more and to increase their feelings of self-confidence.

One way a parent can help a child feel loved, accepted and worthwhile is to help him communicate. This is especially important if there is indication of emotional conflict. Draw him out. Encourage him to talk. If he feels accepted, he will soon start talking about what bothers him. This is salutary from the time a child is able to talk through adulthood. This doesn't mean a parent should pry, but rather relax and arrange circumstances so that the child can feel free to express his perplexities and strong feelings. Allow the child to do most of the talking. Rather than give your opinion, it is generally better to indicate understanding so he will be encouraged to continue. For instance, if a child says, "I hate Jim," you might say, "You feel Jim isn't a friend." Avoid censure, and patiently help him express his feelings. Should advice appear essential, try to help him arrive at the correct solution through his own thinking processes. This is usually not difficult if questions are asked which stimulate his thinking. Should advice still seem necessary, point out the alternatives and allow him to make a choice. This encourages initiative and makes him feel less dependent and more worthwhile.

In addition to emotional development, the child needs spiritual guidance and development. Do the family members, especially the parents, walk with God in such a way that He is part of their total life? Do they talk over their problems with Him and look to Him for guidance? Do they abide by His decisions? Is the atmosphere of the home conducive to walking with Jesus? Would Jesus feel comfortable and at home there? Do the parents provide good music in the home, meaningful family and private devotions, and Christ-centered literature? Do they bring spiritual values into family conversations in a natural way and by a joyous demeanor?

Narramore suggests the following thirteen ways to help children grow spiritually:

1. Establish a good relationship with your child.
2. Tell your child about your own experiences with God.
3. Talk with your child alone about his relationship to Christ.
4. Be sure your child attends a Bible-believing Sunday school and church.
5. Teach the Bible to your child.
6. Explain and interpret daily events in the light of the Bible.
7. Be an example of godliness to your child.
8. Flood your child's mind and heart with Christian literature.
9. Utilize music to influence your child.
10. Help your child develop Christian friendships.
11. Don't overlook the influence of Christian schools.
12. Christian camps can help your child.
13. Show your child how to share his faith with others.[7]

TEACHING CHRISTIAN LOVE TO OUR CHILDREN

Christ gave two commandments that encompass all others: "Thou shalt love the Lord thy God with all thy heart, and with all thy soul, and with all thy mind. This is the first and great commandment. And the second is like it, Thou shalt love thy neighbour as thyself" (Mt 22:37-39).

God's standard of love is high. "Love is patient and kind; love is not jealous, or conceited, or proud; love is not ill-mannered, or selfish, or irritable; love does not keep a record of wrongs" (1 Co 13:4-5, TEV). This kind of love, which comes only from the Lord, can be evident in a Christian's life only to the extent that he is in constant touch with Jesus, giving Him first place in every area of conduct.

But how can we teach our *children* this kind of God-given love? By having God's love within our *own* souls, for love is caught rather than taught. Our love is expressed to our children by taking care of their needs—physical, emotional and spiritual. Children need to be hugged, talked to, listened to, appreciated, respected, encouraged, and told they are loved. Assurance of love leads to an ability to give love.

It is important that mothers recognize that their own emotional state strongly influences their infants' emotional development. To develop into a loving person, an infant needs to experience love.

From the moment of conception, love can be showered on the child through proper diet and health measures, for the state of the mother's health affects the child during its intrauterine existence.

> Jersild asserts that the effects of the psychological state of the mother may indirectly affect the child. For example, when a mother is emotionally excited or disturbed, the ductless glands may release secretions into her bloodstream which may reach the child through the fluid interchange.[8]

After birth, as Fahs succinctly affirms, "The baby craves a spontaneous love on an instinctive level of real feeling. . . . A mature love strives to support him by meeting his needs."[9] Watson asserts that the infant learns through the reinforcements it receives, especially via the mother with whom he is usually in continuous contact.[10] In this continuous contact she is communicating herself.

Spitz states, "Affective signals generated by maternal moods seem to become a form of communication with the infant. . . . This mode of communication between mother and child exerts a constant pressure which shapes the infantile psyche."[11] He stresses that individual traumatic events play but a small role in this development, rather it is the "affective climate" or the "totality of forces" which influences the infant's psychic development.[12] Unpleasurable affects, as well as pleasurable affects, play an important role in the child's affective development. Psychoanalysis—

and nature itself—indicates how important frustration is in learning and in the healthy development of the psyche. Spitz's thesis is that unimpeded progress in the establishment of object relations is essential for the normal development and functioning of the psyche.

> The depriving "bad mother" and the gratifying "good mother" become synthesized, and both his aggressive and libidinal drives will be focused on her, with the libidinal or "love" drive predominant as the "good mother" aspects outweigh the "bad mother" aspects. The point Spitz makes about the two extremes of child-feeding (rigid schedules vs. self-demand schedules) as both being harmful conforms to the Christian principle of moderation or temperance.[13]

In the first year of life Spitz posits that if the mother has personality disturbances they will be reflected in disorders in the child. Either improper or insufficient relations with the mother may cause damage to the child.

> Improper relations are noted as "primary overt rejection; primary anxious permissiveness, hostility in the guise of anxiety, oscillation between pampering and hostility, cyclical mood swings, hostility consciously compensated."[14]

Watson's purview of research findings confirms Spitz's conclusions: the infant's personality development is profoundly influenced by general maternal attitudes or the "overall climate."[15]

In view of these findings, if a child is to be emotionally receptive to Christian standards, his mother can help him during his first year of life by neither depriving nor indulging him; by enabling him to enjoy a preponderance of pleasurable experiences (e.g., cuddling, holding, talking); and if necessary, by dealing with her own hostile, anxious or insecure feelings. By the end of the first year, and even more so by the end of the second year, the child's emotional pattern of personality has become quite clearly outlined. To repeat, this emotional pattern will strongly influence his spiritual growth.

TEACHING CHILDREN HUMILITY, MEEKNESS, AND SURRENDER TO GOD

Webster defines "humility" as "freedom from pride and arrogance." Scripture tells us not to think of ourselves more highly than we ought to think (Ro 12:3).

Many people think they are humble because they feel inferior. Halverson points out that such an individual has capitulated to the worst kind of pride, what he calls "pride in reverse or the back side of conceit."[16]

He also states that self-contempt is blasphemous and impertinent as it overlooks the inestimable worth and dignity of one for whom Christ died.

Meekness may be defined as "absence of wrath and a consistent mildness of temper; patience under injuries; long-suffering."

Deprivation or frustration of our needs generates irritated energy. If this frustration continues, irritability accumulates to the point of hostility, anger or wrath. Many Christian people, attempting to abide by Christian standards as they understand them, suppress their wrathful feelings, hypocritically giving a false impression of meekness. Others have so successfully repressed their feelings of wrath that they have no conscious awareness of them. Instead their hostility is drained off into somatic ailments or anxiety feelings or attacks. But, of course, neither of these solutions is efficacious. The feelings must be faced.

In the life of a Christian, the Holy Spirit may be quenched by sin, but He refills us when we confess that sin, repent, and surrender to Him. This may be compared to marriage: it is a once-for-all surrender, and yet a continuous surrender or submission. Surely daily surrender to the Lord is a spiritual virtue that dedicated Christian parents will want to see in their children.

How can Christian parents instill meekness, humility, and surrender to God in their children?

First, parents need to set the example. Parents who would implant these standards into their offspring must abide by them themselves—not legalistically but as living realities in their lives. Kind words of admonition will be helpful *if* they are accompanied by consistent parental behavior, and if they are dropped as gentle rain in a thirsty land. It is well known that children learn what parents *live*. Parents who are meek, humble, and surrendered to God will find it much easier to instill those same virtues in their children than parents who are proud, ill-tempered and not submissive to the Lord.

Second, parents need to help their children develop a realistic sense of self-worth. As many authors have pointed out, the one most significant element that influences a child's religious growth is his emotional development. Three factors of utmost importance in a child's healthy emotional growth are a feeling of belonging, a sense of personal achievement, and opportunities to share experiences and privileges with his peers.

When a child's emotional and physical needs are met, he is less likely to become angry or proud. He can accept himself because he feels acceptable. Superiority feelings are generally a defense against inferiority feelings. If a child feels his parents' love and respect, if he has been given sufficient opportunities to achieve, and if he has learned to accept his limitations, the defense is unnecessary. Parents can help children accept their limitations by being acceptant of the limitations themselves and expressively grateful for their talents and abilities. As previously mentioned, anger is a result of frustration. If the child's normal needs are met and he still is overly hostile, he is probably attempting to satisfy neurotic or unrealistic wishes and desires.

Third, parents need to lead their children to receive Jesus Christ as their personal Saviour. We cannot expect a child to act like a Christian if he isn't one. When a child can understand the plan of salvation sufficiently to be saved and he is emotionally open, the parent should deal with him personally, leading him to a decision. Be definite. Ask him if he would like to invite Jesus into his heart. If he indicates willingness, pray with him. Be careful not to pressure, for the decision must be personal. After the decision is made, help him grow in Christ by discussing the matter with him and teaching him more Scripture about salvation. Teach him about the forgiveness of God so that when he makes mistakes he will go to the Lord for forgiveness (1 Jn 1:9). Teach him to seek the Lord for guidance.

In summary, in teaching our children the Christian standards of love, humility, meekness, and surrender to God, our portrayal of these standards in our own lives will be our greatest ally. As we express our love in practical ways to our children, they will gain a favorable self-image, the core of a healthy personality.

TEACHING MORALITY

Christian parents interested in inculcating biblically based moral principles in their children will want their children to possess chastity, honesty, loyalty, responsibility, courage, friendliness, service, self-control, sympathy and kindness.

The most important factors influencing morality and character-building are the family, the neighborhood, and school associates. To avoid undermining the child's budding character, the moral tone of all three factors should be in harmony.[17] Nevertheless, the most important factor is parental influence, for the impact of the culture is largely dependent on parental interpretation.[18]

Jersild affirms that moral and emotional development are closely correlated.[19] The child's conduct will be influenced by his capacity for affection, by anxiety, by his capacity for anger, by fear of punishment or of peer-group disapproval or of conflicting impulses. A child burdened with emotional problems is hindered in developing a sound morality. Primary and necessary factors in the production of mature moral character are parental warmth, trust, fairness and consistency.[20]

Various studies have supported the view that "ego strength" is the salient factor in moral conduct.[21] For a child to develop high ego strength, an important factor is marital harmony between father and mother, wherein both are emotionally acceptant of and assume their own sex roles. This ego-strength interpretation of moral conduct suggests that moral character develops gradually, and this gradualism should be taken in consideration in working with a child. The younger child judges acts in terms of their practical consequences (e.g., punishment), whereas the older child may learn to weigh them in the light of motives, intentions and extenuating circumstances.

The reward-punishment, pleasure-pain principle is a medium for character-building, and is biblical. Hell is pictured as most painful, and heaven as most pleasurable. Morality will be incorporated as the child's philosophy of life if disciplinary measures bring gratification—gratification which is a logical result of his behavior. Restrictions or punishments are "good" for children if they sense that those restrictions or punishments help make their lives more free and gratifying.[22]

Discipline is a security measure for children. It is an ingredient of love if not actually synonymous with it. To illustrate, a client protested, "I wish you'd punish me for what I did. My parents never punished me and it made me feel they didn't care." Children need to know their limits so they can feel secure and free within these limits. They also need to have confidence that their parents will maintain the limits regardless of their "testing," for they need to be able to trust and rely on their parents' strength. To discipline intelligently it is necessary to know how the conduct relates to (1) the child's needs, (2) his group values, and (3) the demands of the situation. In other words, the parent should seek to understand the child's situational wish or fear in his undesirable conduct.

A child does not build moral character by mere conformance to the demands of his elders. Instead he needs opportunities to make thoughtful choices and to live out these choices. Lane and Beauchamp tell of a young boy who, moved by the plight of the people in a settlement district, sent all his clothes to them except those on his back.[23] His mother, delighted with his magnaminity, replaced his gift with shiny new ones and something extra: cowboy boots. Delighted he surely was, but she actually robbed him. He was not given the opportunity to learn by living by his choices. The ideal in helping our children accept moral standards is stimulation of the child's own moral judgment and control of action. This means we must deal with the child at his present level of maturity or judgment, rather than above or below.[24]

In summary, morality relates to emotional development and is a gradual process. Parental warmth, trust, firmness and consistency, intelligent discipline, relating morality to gratification, and verbal instruction are important factors in teaching standards of morality.

TEACHING MORALITY DURING EARLY CHILDHOOD

Hurlock asserts that training begun in the second year of life must be continued throughout childhood and must apply to specific situations as the child cannot yet transfer the learnings to similar situations.[25] Emphasis on self-control in avoiding aggressiveness and in respecting the property rights of others may be emphasized during the third and fourth years. The young child needs to be taught how to act. Being mentally immature he doesn't understand the reasons behind desirable behavior. His habits of obedience should be well established by the end of the fifth year.

Studies of the efficacy of punishment during early childhood indicated only 14 percent of the children felt that punishment motivated them to do better or to feel sorry. A clue to this ineffectiveness may be the findings that more than 50 percent of the parents showed anger when disciplining and more than 33 percent gave no explanation of why they punished.[26] Cranford claims the bulk of emotional disorders of children is due to poor discipline.[27] Advocating a reinforcement of discipline wherein the child is rewarded for good behavior and given a modified form of corporal punishment for unacceptable behavior, he says it is practical and effective from two to twelve years of age. His method consists of immediate rewards for good behavior, and a light though stinging lick of the stick administered without anger for misbehavior. He calls it the "carrot and stick" method. The sole purpose of the lick is to associate pain with the undesirable act. It should sting sufficiently to be unpleasant, but not be injurious. If one lick is unsuccessful it should be supported by another lick. The rewards should also be meaningful and immediately given, for example, penny candies to small children, praise to the adolescent. The infant can be taught by a stinging whack on the seat accompanied by "No!" This method of corrective discipline is based on respect for authority. To be effective the child cannot be allowed to challenge it successfully. Cranford urges that within this framework of respect, children should be given all the freedom they can safely handle to avoid impediment in their psychological and physical growth.

TEACHING MORALITY DURING LATE CHILDHOOD

As a child grows older, his moral judgments are increasingly influenced by social relationships outside the home.[28] Inasmuch as high ego strength is correlated with moral character, what familial factors are efficacious in its development? A study by Peck indicates a positive correlation between high ego strength in children and a family life high in consistency and trust.[29] In addition to the general climate of the home, the older child's personality characteristics are strongly influenced by his emotional relationships, especially with his parents and siblings, and by the disciplinary practices to which he is subjected.[30]

Hurlock's review of literature on this subject indicated that the younger child is primarily fearful that his misbehavior will be discovered and punished, whereas the older child, desiring peer acceptance, is more deeply concerned on a personal level.[31] However, when caught he is more likely to feel shame than guilt, as it is unlikely that a preadolescent child will feel obliged to control his behavior unless punishment looms ahead. Thus, in late childhood, moral shame is potent in the development of moral behavior.

Disciplining an older child is more difficult. He no longer accepts unquestioningly the punishment meted out. His sense of fairness and justice has been well developed, and he doesn't hesitate to complain about punishment he feels is unfair or unjust. The older child strongly resents corporal punishment. Investigators consider praise and occasional rewards, privilege or pleasure deprivation, and isolation for a short time "to think it over" as more effective than corporal punishment.

During the latter years of childhood more emphasis should be placed on the educational aspect of discipline in terms of teaching the child to understand why he should act in certain ways and not in others. He should be taught to apply *specific* moral concepts to generalized concepts of right and wrong. For instance, a child may not cheat if he likes a teacher. This concept may be broadened to avoiding cheating in any situation because of the effect on him as a responsible individual and the effect on the group. Although the well-known Hartshorne and May studies indicate that moral training must be specific to the situation rather than of a general nature, Rogers points out that generalization and specificity serve as essential corollaries.[32] Transfer of a trait to another situation will only be possible when the relationship is perceived. Parents can help their children appraise the moral implications in learning experiences to develop a functional morality.

Becker, Peterson and others have investigated how the attitudes of fathers and mothers correlated with conduct and personality problems in their children.[33] The children with conduct problems generally had unreasonable, emotionally erratic parents. The mothers were active, high-strung, dominant individuals with a propensity for giving advice. But the major finding pertained to fathers. Where the fathers were harsh and coldly aggressive, the children tended to have both conduct problems and personality problems. It is interesting to note that although both fathers' and mothers' attitudes were related to maladjustment tendencies in their children, the attitudes of the fathers were more intimately related. This verifies the growing concern about the necessity for fathers to assume their proper role in the home and to take a more active part in the rearing of their children. This finding indicates that younger children especially need love and kindness from the father.

Summing up, during late childhood parents should lean more toward broadening the educational aspects of morality training. Warmth, consistency and trust are related to ego strength and hence to moral character. Parents should understand the child's social milieu and the teaching contained therein and help him integrate it with parental teachings. Training toward generalizing specific moral concepts may be undertaken at this level of growth.

TEACHING MORALITY DURING ADOLESCENCE

Although adolescence is a time of stress and strain, if the child has experienced gratification in abiding by firmly implanted moral standards, he will be able to adhere to them when he is an adolescent.

Parents need to modify their concepts of their child's abilities as he grows older—and to treat him accordingly. Conflict is less in this turbulent period when parents act in ways that enable the adolescent to perceive they understand him and his needs. In punishing an adolescent, parents should avoid causing him resentment over "infantile punishment." Resentment is also activated if he feels the parents are overly harsh or that others equally to blame are not punished.

Research on juvenile delinquency indicates the teen delinquent is usually motivated by feelings of resentment and hostility dating back to his early childhood. He feels rejected and hostile toward society. Back of most juvenile delinquency is cumulative resentment for treatment causing feelings of inadequacy and inferiority, and punishment considered unfair.[34]

Rogers notes the need for adult guidance during adolescence, especially in resolving moral conflict.[35] Competency in moral guidance with adolescents is dependent upon rapport and a sound philosophy of moral education. Teens need to learn the reasons for morality, not simply the rules.

In summary, the adolescent is still in need of moral guidance as his life pattern expands. Genuine respect for the adolescent, together with objectivity, will enable him to accept parental guidance more readily.

TEACHING OBEDIENCE

When Jesus said, "If a man love me, he will keep my words" (Jn 14:23), He clearly indicated that obedience is an evidence and outgrowth of love.

And so it is with children. They are more likely to obey their parents if they love them. The Bible says, "We love him, because he first loved us" (1 Jn 4:19). Similarly with children, they can learn to love God and others if they experience or feel their parents' love.

Hurlock affirms that the educational aspects of discipline should be emphasized from babyhood through adolescence. From two years up the child can be taught "what is right and what is wrong and be rewarded with approval and affection when he does what is right."[36] Punishment, physical or psychological, should be reserved for willful disobedience and kept at a minimum. Consistency is essential for the psychological health of the child at all ages but especially in the early years when moral habits are being established. This points up the necessity for parents to be in agreement and to insist on conformance with these principles by extra-family members and baby-sitters.

Parents who can honestly enforce discipline sympathetically will help the child relate to the act rather than to parental disapproval. This helps the child feel understood and accepted even though discipline is enforced.

Jersild differentiates between remedial and punitive punishment.[37] Remedial punishment is for the purpose of deterring the child from repeating a forbidden act, but punitive punishment is for the purpose of revenge. Frequently the latter endangers the relationship and causes feelings of hostility and bitterness. The only benefit, if any, of punitive punishment is in relieving strong feelings of both parent and child, that is, the anger feelings of the parent and the guilt feelings of the child. Research studies indicate that power-assertive techniques of discipline (physical punishment, yelling, shouting, forceful commands, and verbal threats) tend to promote disobedience, whereas love-oriented techniques (praise and reasoning) tend to promote cooperation.[38]

Summarizing, Christianity and psychological research studies coincide: love is the best activating agent for inculcating obedience in children. Love teaches by example and precept; love is ego-protecting; love is aware of the child's limitations and abilities; love allows children to be people.

TEACHING CHASTITY

Chastity, a special aspect of morality, deserves specific mention. It is related to sex education. Cheryl, a mother of three young children, fearful of her sexuality, said, "I'll let my husband teach them whatever they need to know when the time comes." However, she was already teaching them by her attitude. Sex education isn't a lecture; it's a process. It begins the first day the child is born—by the ministrations to its needs, by the affectional relationship with his parents. Later sex education is taught by the parents' naturalness (or lack of it) in things pertaining to sex, for example, toilet-training, affectional relationships, interest in the newborn, open and frank discussion of birth and how it all happened, unashamed answers to questions, acceptance of the child's innate curiosity about his body, lack of undue modesty. When appropriate, parents may refer to God's wonderful plan for sexual fulfillment. They may explain that when two people become one in marriage they join with God in His creativity through procreation and fellowship through sexual union. The child needs to accept favorably his sexuality and sexual role and not feel guilt or shame.

If a child indulges in sex play (a natural part of growing up) or unseemly sexual practices, the parent should be understanding and noncondemning. The child should be taught as little negativism as possible, for whatever teaching is emphasized is generally the attitude brought into the marriage. Cheryl's mother taught her chastity and she is chaste, but it was all negatively attuned. Her mother had a "sex is bad" attitude. Instead of enjoying the relationship as a blessed gift of God, she and her husband both suffer because of her frigidity and fear. Their children too are being influenced by this negativism, for children unconsciously absorb the attitudes and feelings of their parents.

When a child reaches early adolescence, parents should be more specific about teaching chastity because of the temptations confronting young people to engage in sexual relations. Both boys and girls should be informed about the advantages of restraining themselves until marriage, and the disadvantages of indulging, for example, hindrance to a good marital adjustment, and the possibility of venereal infection. God's way as directed toward their highest good and greatest happiness should be made plain. Fathers should discuss with their sons the fact that it takes more manliness and moral courage to resist than to experiment.

When teens begin to date, parents should discuss with their young people certain dangers involved in dating and how to avoid them. This should be done tactfully to avoid feelings of guilt or ridicule. In essence they should be reminded that their emotions are strong, that they have had little experience in handling them, and they may get out of control. Remaining in the company of other people obviates placing themselves in a compromising position.

In summary, young people are more likely to inculcate the Christian standard of chastity, provided they are emotionally acceptant of their sexuality and understand the advantages of remaining chaste.*

*For more on this subject, see chap. 20, "Preparing Young People for Marriage," and chap. 25, "Assisting Parents with Sex Education."

HOW THE CHURCH CAN HELP PARENTS TEACH
CHRISTIAN STANDARDS

Fathers and mothers often have differing attitudes about child care which cause a rift between them. Any rift, minor though it may seem, is absorbed by the child and lessens his sense of security and family solidarity.[39] Churches can help parents by planning study groups for both fathers and mothers. To interest the father, some churches have found it practical to ask several fathers to come prepared to speak on a subject pertaining to child guidance. They may share their own successful experiences, or talk on a topic of personal interest. Churches using this method find that when fathers as well as mothers are asked to take special phases of subjects pertaining to child guidance and develop them for ten or fifteen minutes, a lively discussion period ensues, often lasting far into the night.

A PTA group, having difficulty interesting the fathers, sent the following announcement to all the homes: Papers Will Be Read at Our Next Meeting Written by the Children on the Topic, "What I Like About My Father." Fathers attended in droves.

Churches have found that including the children in some manner is very effective. One large church organization has meetings for the entire family. After a short message on a topic of mutual interest, they split up into buzz groups. Later they reassemble and report on their conclusions. This has stimulated increasing interest, and the groups are well attended.

Family "therapy" groups are helpful. In such groups, feelings and attitudes are expressed about child-rearing problems. These meetings are helpful in a number of ways: (1) parents are reassured by discovering, "I'm not alone"; (2) feelings are ventilated, thus enabling greater objectivity; (3) parents' personality problems may be uncovered and possibly worked through;* (4) experience and knowledge are pooled; (5) successful handling of children is encouraged and motivation is increased; (6) lasting friendships are often established. These groups may be organized in several ways: parents and children together; fathers and mothers together; couples in separate groups; children in one group and parents in another.

Churches can also provide helpful literature for parents through the church library. Pastors can help parents teach Christian standards to their children through sermons that stress the scriptural principles of morality, the importance of parental example and consistency, and what the Bible teaches about the Spirit-filled life, holy living and child-training.

To sum up, churches can help parents teach Christian standards by dis-

*If the personality conflicts are severe, the leader of the group may privately suggest professional help.

seminating information and organizing study and discussion groups to enable both parents and children to participate and gain mutual understandings.

NOTES

1. Morris L. and Natalie R. Haimowitz, *Human Development* (New York: Crowell, 1966), p. 391.
2. Martin L. and Lois W. Hoffman, *Child Development Research* (New York: Russell Sage Foundation, 1964), p. 418.
3. Leo Kanner, *Child Psychiatry* (Springfield, Ill.: Thomas, 1962), p. 680.
4. Arthur T. Jersild, *Child Psychology* (Englewood Cliffs, N.J.: Prentice-Hall, 1960), p. 413.
5. Ibid., p. 411.
6. Clyde M. Narramore, *How to Understand and Influence Children* (Grand Rapids: Zondervan, 1957), p. 41.
7. Narramore, *How to Help Your Child Develop Faith in God* (Grand Rapids: Zondervan, 1969), pp. 5-31.
8. Arthur T. Jersild, *Child Psychology* (Englewood Cliffs, N.J.: Prentice-Hall, 1960), p. 35.
9. Sophia L. Fahs, *Today's Children and Yesterday's Heritage* (Boston: Beacon, 1967), p. 35.
10. Robert I. Watson, *Psychology of the Child* (New York: Wiley, 1965), pp. 199-200.
11. René A. Spitz, *The First Year of Life* (New York: International U., 1965), p. 138.
12. Ibid., p. 139.
13. Ibid., pp. 169-71.
14. Ibid., p. 208.
15. Watson, p. 205.
16. Richard C. Halverson, *Christian Maturity* (Los Angeles: Cowman, 1956), p. 122.
17. Howard Lane and Mary Beauchamp, *Understanding Human Development* (Englewood Cliffs, N.J.: Prentice-Hall, 1959), p. 172.
18. Dorothy Rogers, *The Psychology of Adolescence* (New York: Appleton-Century-Crofts, 1962), p. 238.
19. Jersild, pp. 411-12.
20. Hoffman and Hoffman, p. 394.
21. Ibid., pp. 390-92.
22. Lane and Beauchamp, pp. 173-74.
23. Ibid., p. 172.
24. Hoffman and Hoffman, p. 425.
25. Elizabeth B. Hurlock, *Developmental Psychology* (New York: McGraw-Hill, 1959), pp. 154-55.
26. Watson, p. 361.
27. Peter G. Cranford, *Disciplining Your Child the Practical Way* (Englewood Cliffs, N.J.: Prentice-Hall, 1963), pp. 11-12, 67-73, 91-112.
28. Jersild, p. 409.
29. R. F. Peck, "Family Patterns Correlated with Adolescent Personality Structure," *Journal of Abnormal Social Psychology*, 57 (1958):347-50.
30. Watson, p. 532.
31. Hurlock, pp. 197-99.
32. Rogers, p. 235.
33. W. C. Becker, D. R. Peterson, L. A. Hellmer, D. V. Shoemaker and H. C. Quay, "Factors in Parental Behavior in Children," *Journal of Consulting Psychology*, 23 (1959):107-18; and "Parental Attitudes and Child Adjustment," *Child Development*, 30 (1959):119-30; and D. R. Peterson, W. C. Becker, D. J. Shoemaker, Zelda Luria and L. A. Hellmer, "Child Behavior Development Problems and Parental Attitudes," *Child Development*, 32 (1961):151-62.
34. Hurlock, pp. 308-9, 358.
35. Rogers, pp. 231-34.
36. Hurlock, p. 109.
37. Jersild, p. 92.
38. Hoffman and Hoffman, p. 189.

39. Paul Tournier maintains children have a terrible sense of guilt when their parents are in conflict. See *Guilt and Grace* (New York: Harper & Row, 1962), p. 93.

FOR FURTHER READING

Bye, Beryl. *Teaching Our Children the Christian Faith.* Chicago: Moody, 1966.

Cranford, Peter G. *Disciplining Your Child the Practical Way.* Englewood Cliffs, N.J.: Prentice-Hall, 1963.

Fahs, Sophia L. *Today's Children and Yesterday's Heritage.* Boston: Beacon, 1967.

Fromm, Erich. *The Art of Loving.* New York: Harper & Row, 1956.

Gesell, Arnold. *The First Five Years of Life.* New York: Harper, 1946.

Gesell, Arnold and Ilg, Frances L. *The Child from Five to Ten.* New York: Harper, 1946.

Ginott, Haim G. *Between Parent and Child.* New York: Macmillan, 1965.

———. *Between Parent and Teen-ager.* New York: Macmillan, 1969.

Halverson, Richard C. *Christian Maturity.* Los Angeles: Cowman, 1956.

Hoffman, Martin L. and Hoffman, Lois W. *Child Development Research.* New York: Russell Sage, 1964.

Hurlock, Elizabeth B. *Developmental Psychology.* New York: McGraw-Hill, 1959.

Jenkins, Gladys Gardner; Shacter, Helen; and Bauer, William W. *These Are Your Children* (expanded ed.). Chicago: Scott, Foresman, 1953.

Jersild, Arthur T. *Child Psychology.* Englewood Cliffs, N.J.: Prentice-Hall, 1960.

Lane, Howard and Beauchamp, Mary. *Understanding Human Development.* Englewood Cliffs, N.J.: Prentice-Hall, 1959.

Manwell, Elizabeth M. and Fahs, Sophia L. *Consider the Children, How They Grow.* Boston: Beacon, 1940.

Mow, Anna B. "How to Love a Teen-ager," *Eternity,* 18 (Sept., 1967):13-15.

———. *Your Child, from Birth to Rebirth.* Grand Rapids: Zondervan, 1963.

Narramore, Clyde M. *Discipline in the Christian Home.* Grand Rapids: Zondervan, 1961.

———. *How to Help Your Child Develop Faith in God.* Grand Rapids: Zondervan, 1969.

———. *How to Tell Your Children About Sex.* Grand Rapids: Zondervan, 1958.

———. *How to Understand and Influence Children.* Grand Rapids: Zondervan, 1957.

Ottersen, Ottar. *Those Most Important Years.* Minneapolis: Augsburg, 1966.

Pentecost, Dorothy. "Teaching Children to Pray," *Moody Monthly,* 64 (Mar., 1964):77-79.

Peterson, James A. *Toward a Successful Marriage.* New York: Scribner, 1960.

Piaget, Jean. *Moral Judgment of the Child.* New York: Free Press, 1960.

Rogers, Dorothy. *The Psychology of Adolescence.* New York: Appleton-Century-Crofts, 1962.

Spitz, René A. *The First Year of Life.* New York: International U., 1965.

Watson, Robert I. *Psychology of the Child.* New York: Wiley, 1965.

24

HELPING FAMILIES WORSHIP

Alta M. Erb

Early in the recorded story of God and His people we see a family of eight souls at worship. God had told Noah to prepare an ark, and he obeyed. God shut Noah's family in, and they enjoyed safety from the flood for almost a year.

Then God said, "Go forth. The earth is dry." The family's gratitude to the Lord for their safety was expressed in a sacrifice of clean animals. God appreciated the sweet savour.

Praise is sweet to God. The psalmist cries, "Oh that men would praise the LORD for his goodness, and for his wonderful works to the children of men" (Ps 107:8, 15, 21, 31).

WHAT IS WORSHIP?

A boy gave a good definition of worship in these words: "When I worship I think about God, I feel good about Him, and I want to do something for Him." God appreciates and is glorified by such a heart response.

When Isaiah came into the presence of God, God's purity called him to cleansing. Cleansed, Isaiah wanted to go and speak for God. Worship is what we do when we become aware of His presence and His glory. Jesus went out of the garden of prayer committed to die for the world.

Genuine worship of the Lord is personal fellowship with and praise for Him, which sends us forth with a commitment to Him.

Worship is no doubt the most profound and personal experience the human soul can have. Man was created capable of this relationship with God: to know God, to appreciate His goodness, to adore Him, to communicate with Him, and to serve Him. "God is a Spirit: and they that worship him must worship him in spirit and in truth" (Jn 4:24).

ALTA M. ERB, M.A., is Coeditor of *Family Worship*, Herald Press, Scottdale, Pennsylvania.

WHAT IS FAMILY WORSHIP?

According to Lentz, "Family worship is the reverent presence of a family group before God, collectively remembering His goodness in grateful praise."[1] In family worship all members are aware of God and of each other. Family worship must begin with this awareness of belonging together. The problems of father in his business, the trials of James at junior high, the loss of Timmy's tricycle, fellowship with the new neighbors—these are family experiences that may relate the whole family to God. Any need of any member of the family sends the entire family to God, the source of their help. We are admonished, "In all thy ways acknowledge him, and he shall direct thy paths" (Pr 3:6).

Family worship is an expression of the family's trust in the Lord. It can also lead to a seeking of forgiveness from Him and each other. Reading the story of envy and jealousy among Joseph's eleven brothers may bring conviction to any family member with these same temptations. Considering these temptations together and seeking forgiveness one of another may be a climactic experience for the whole family. They not only draw closer to the Lord, but they also experience a new sense of family unity. Spiritual conversation becomes less difficult. As Edith Lovell Thomas says, "The closer we draw to one another in the home circle, the easier becomes companionship with our Father."[2]

VALUES OF FAMILY WORSHIP

Family worship symbolizes the presence of God in the home. This is true even for the very youngest, who can comprehend spiritual truth to only a limited degree. In genuine worship the greatest value accrued is getting acquainted with God. Worship is more than a family ritual, more than an attitude or an atmosphere. It is a genuine response of the human heart toward God.

Acquaintance with God is based on a knowledge of the will of God as disclosed in His Word. We worship around the Word. A true worshiper opens his whole being to hear God, to discover truth, however simple his understanding of that truth may be. "Let the word of Christ dwell in you richly" (Col 3:16). Timothy learned the Holy Scriptures which were "able to make . . . [him] wise unto salvation" (2 Ti 3:15). Since the foes of young and old are spiritual, our weapons must be spiritual. In family worship the godly example of the parents comes to be explained in terms of the divine words.

Prayer—communication with God—is learned in family worship. The bridge between a family and God is an experience of praise, intercession, confession, and quiet appreciation. Whatever the experience of any one day, prayer can bridge the family with God. Grace at the table, although formal at times, can help build easy communication between the children and God. The reason for thanks is evident at a spread table, and is understood and appreciated. "In every thing give thanks" (1 Th 5:18). "Praise ye the LORD" (Ps 148:1).

> In the family the fellowship side of prayer is highly important. It brings the family together before the throne of grace. It magnifies the sense of all for each and each for all. It identifies the need of each with the desire of all, and the common need with the desire of each.[3]

A family may also worship through singing Christian hymns. My richest childhood worship was my singing alone in the hammock. The hymns taught me about God, for good hymns are full of theology. Moreover, they can effectively express the soul's desires. One family occasionally sings the doxology as the prayer at mealtime.

Acquaintance with God, the practice of listening to God in His Word, and the spiritual enjoyment of singing praises, prepare each member of the family for worship at church. Expectation of spiritual experience in the one aids expectation in the other. Only one other experience can compare with these—that in which the individual comes alone into the presence of God.

Anna Mow discusses how to educate a child to be ready to worship God.[4] One essential is reverence, which we must have to be able to worship. To hear God speak at any place, at any time, one must learn to be quiet. This spiritual value can be encouraged in family worship. "In quietness and in confidence shall be your strength" (Is 30:15b).

Another value accrued from family worship is the strengthening of family unity. Even little ones come to call this "our best family times." Here the best of character-building takes place; here the Christian pattern of family living unfolds. Love for God and family members grows.

True family worship helps furnish a spiritual climate in the home. In this atmosphere, faith can grow and Christian character develop. It is in the happy Christian home that lasting spiritual values are learned and accepted.

PROBLEMS OF FAMILY WORSHIP

An honest appraisal of the Christian home readily discloses problems for family worship, but these can be resolved by the family that genuinely recognizes the values of worship. This family will find times to worship together and create ways that fit into their family situation. Patterns that once were used in many families effectively, may not be possible today.

The father whose vocation takes him away from the home early in the day is the head of the family and the rightful worship leader, but he may not be in the home at the crucial moment. One mother heard re-

quests for prayer and prayed with her hand-clasped circle of schoolchil-
dren before they went out to meet the bus. This was invaluable, but it
was no substitute for the complete family at worship. And these same
children, being in varied school and church activities, were not always
at home during the same evening hours. These difficulties did not take
away the children's anticipation for worship with father. They found
times to worship together, even though at irregular times.

Such expectancy testifies to the values of true family worship. When
worship is genuine, irregular time patterns may be highly significant.
We do adjust to many current situations in home living. Family worship
is not impossible today.

Our present living makes life too full of. activity. It is difficult to shut
out the anticipated ball game, the unprepared-for church activity, the
pressing duties of the next hours, the hurt of a quarrel with a family member. Many people plan the day so full that good living is almost impossible. The feeling of rush and the inability to meet our full schedules
make it difficult to maintain family worship on a regular schedule. Regarding this problem the Gebhards give good advice:

> The family that cannot find unhurried time needs to examine closely the
> schedules of its members, and see if they are allowing the requirements of
> making a living or pressures from the outside to rob them of abundant life.
> For life itself is always more important than the things which sustain it.[5]

Some like to kneel for prayer. Others think they can hear each other
better if they are face-to-face in prayer. One family joins hands around a
circle. A family I visited was reading each day a portion of the apostle
Paul's life and of the biography of John Wesley. Some families sing frequently, which can add significantly to the family worship experience.

In a certain Chinese Christian family the family members, guests and
farmhands stood before breakfast as they sang, repeated a psalm, and had
a brief prayer. In the winter when work was light, they studied the Bible
and learned hymns for one hour after supper.[6] However, each family
must create its own pattern for worship. Patterning some other family's
time or way of worship may defeat the purpose. To meet God is the goal
for blessing.

HOW CAN THE CHURCH HELP?

That each family should worship together is a goal that ought to motivate the whole work of the church. It is in family life, primarily, that
spiritual values are learned. Here souls are nurtured in Christ. The following are some suggestions of ways churches can assist families in this
important aspect of home nurture:

BY UNDERSTANDING WHAT FAMILY WORSHIP IS

Before a church can help its families in family worship, it must understand what true family worship is. This has been developed in the first part of this chapter. Lentz explains that group worship in the home has three elements:

> (1) Family fellowship—family worship begins in awareness of belonging together in a family fellowship; (2) focus of . . . attention on God; (3) family group response—family worship culminates in commitment: deepened love for God, improved family life, service to others, participation in the church, Christian witness.[7]

BY SUGGESTING GUIDELINES

Families who most need encouragement and help on the why and how of home worship may be the most sensitive to help offered. Yet these are the ones the church should desire to help. Family worship cannot be legislated, because any member of a family who would resent suggestions from the church might make the service very difficult. The church must be wise to reach that one member. Love can help without imposing.

Helping must proceed slowly. If routine grace at meals can be improved in spirit and method, this would be a good first step. J. C. Wynn writes:

> In thanking God for our daily bread we are doing more than affirming our good fortune in economics. We are recognizing the presence of Christ in our midst. Prayer at mealtime is a profound symbol of our place in the family of God.[8]

Family heads who have been nurtured at routine, rather cold family altars will need help, here a little and there a little, to warm up to a start, or perhaps a fresh start. Embarrassment must be eased for some, and leadership rewarded. Spiritual refreshment must be experienced, and each member must come to worship with some expectancy. All this takes time. Problems that loom up very easily may defeat even a trial.

A first family worship must be significant. It might be held (at the suggestion of the church) when Dick gets his driving license, or when Dorothy is chosen for the vocal ensemble at North High, or at the time of some sharp financial loss, or on mother's birthday. Awareness of these or other experiences may help bring them together for a first worship service. It may be short, but it must be real.

If a family's first worship experience or any successive one can be worked out by the family (perhaps with some help from the church), even though it is a very simple service, it will mean more, and therefore be more acceptable. This means that the church leaders must become aware of many different patterns—what to do first, what might be included in each service, what Scripture passages may be read, how to pray, where to have the service in the home, when to have it, how to get each member to participate, what kind of songs to sing, the kind of language children can understand. No pattern will be equally stimulating to every member at each service, but we must be aware of the danger of a dead monotony.

No two families are alike, so leaders should think of individual families when preparing helps or adapting prepared helps. Time and energy thus spent is well invested. Each family in the church is worthy of some individual-family consideration because each is a family on its own. "We do it our way and you do it your way," said one girl to her cousin, "because we are two different families." Both ways were effective. The church should desire to serve each family, rather than force them into a uniform pattern.

The helps given should make Bible reading, study and memorizing more meaningful, singing more enjoyable, prayer more real and effective. Most Christian families need help in these three areas. A variety of approaches to these activities is a must for stimulating worship in the family. And do not forget that families change continually. A family of preschoolers will soon need more meat in their worship diet.

BY PERSONAL INTEREST OF CHURCH WORKERS

The pastor carries a great responsibility and a great opportunity. He joys to see his "children walk in truth" (3 Jn 4). Since families look to him for leadership, this anticipation makes it easier to accept his concerns and suggestions, and to approach him with questions. In one home prayer was offered for the pastor before the family left for church. This was their only family worship activity. How wise for the pastor to have given to that family a request for their special prayer support. Here was the start of a family worship experience.

Others in the church who can become involved in promoting family worship are the director of Christian education, Sunday school teachers, visitation workers, the music director, the missionary education chairman, the leader of prayer circles, etc. In some churches the board or committee of Christian education includes a secretary of family life, who sets up objectives and correlates the workers in various contributions to the families.

The opportunities for helping to worship, as discussed below, are unlimited. In any one church there needs to be cooperation, especially with the pastor. Helping cannot be done mechanically, yet certain workers have unique opportunities which must be appreciated and understood.

No two churches will work out this kind of help in identical ways. But if each worker can appreciate the importance of family worship and accept his bit of service opportunity, much can be accomplished for Christ and the church.

BY OFFERING SPECIFIC SUGGESTIONS

Some pastors encourage newlyweds to start their devotional life together by giving them a devotional book, such as *In the Presence of God.*[9] This small book has a month of devotions, each one based on a phrase of the marriage ceremony.

Another first family worship experience may follow the birth of a child into the family. *Meditations for the New Mother* by Helen G. Brenneman has thirty devotions for both parents on such occasions.[10]

A death in the family, a wedding, a birthday, the baptism of a family member, the beginning of a school term, any family crisis or major experience—all these are among the opportune occasions to introduce family worship into a home. Anticipate coming events in the church families. Giving helps for the observance of special days such as Thanksgiving and Christmas may open to a family the pleasure of worship together.

Worship plans for many special occasions have been published, but those planned by the church for its own people may be more effective. Also suggestions for worship at home are occasionally given in children's Sunday school lesson manuals. These may make a good beginning, since they will be introduced by a child rather than an adult. Leaders may use members of families to help prepare worship service suggestions.

Reading materials to promote family worship may be offered for sale or loan by the church. Knowing its families, a church can select and recommend more wisely. Devotional leaflets, pamphlets and books (not all prepared for day-by-day reading) put on display in the church vestibule or publicized as available from the church library will often be picked up, purchased (or checked out) and read. A variety of books will be necessary to meet a variety of needs.

The church library should also contain some of the good devotional books written for children. Even Bible storybooks should be included for families who do not own them. Reading these together may be the start of regular family worship for some homes. Bibles in different versions and paraphrases are extremely helpful to many families in their family worship.

Several denominational and independent publishing houses provide family worship suggestions in a worship magazine or in a section of some church publication. Use of these should be encouraged, and suggestions may be given on how to adapt them for greater effectiveness. Some churches pay the cost of putting these materials into every home, especially those newly established.

Many children's Sunday school take-home papers have good material to read in family worship.

Prayer requests printed in church bulletins, or on special attractive prayer-request cards, to be picked up or to be distributed, may help some families start praying together. Some Sunday school teachers send home prayer requests with class members.

When a family is visited by its pastor, by missionaries, by church visitors or by teachers, a brief worship service may draw a family together before God. It may also suggest enriching features for family worship, or may afford the occasion for promoting the family worship idea.

The annual observance of national family week should include direct and indirect help for family worship. In a family-week church service, give a demonstration of family worship centered around the theme of family week for that year. Showing a film on family worship, followed perhaps by a discussion, may encourage some family to begin or improve family worship. Some churches may also wish to select hymns for families to use at home on special occasions.

Soliciting the services of every family in the outreach program of the church may call families to prayer. One family worshiped together for the first time when they dedicated the Christmas bundle they had prepared for foreign relief. A family (or two families together) might be asked to prepare a service for a Sunday evening at church or for a community rest home. Enjoying some spiritual activity as a family will encourage spiritual growth together.

Possibly the greatest service a church can give to help families in creative worship is to feed each one spiritually. Someone has said, "The greatest need of children is better parents to live with." Would this not be true also of church workers and leaders? All who teach and preach the Word must believe that the Word of God is the greatest power for tearing down the strongholds of Satan and for building up spiritual strength.

NOTES

1. Richard E. Lentz, *Christian Worship by Families* (St. Louis: Bethany, 1957), p. 8.
2. Edith Lovell Thomas, *Music in Christian Education* (New York: Abingdon, 1953), pp. 40-41.
3. Herman J. Sweet, *Opening the Door for God* (Philadelphia: Westminster, 1943), p. 83.
4. Anna B. Mow, *Your Child, from Birth to Rebirth* (Grand Rapids: Zondervan, 1963).
5. Anna and Edward Gebhard, *Guideposts to Creative Family Worship* (New York: Abingdon, 1953), p. 28.

6. Irma Highbaugh, *We Grow in the Family* (New York City: Agricultural Missions, 1953), p. 116.
7. Lentz, p. 56.
8. J. C. Wynn, *How Christian Parents Face Family Problems* (Philadelphia: Westminster Press, 1954), p. 71.
9. W. Toelke, *In the Presence of God* (St. Louis: Concordia, 1962).
10. Helen G. Brenneman, *Meditations for the New Mother* (Scottdale, Pa.: Herald, 1967).

FOR FURTHER READING

Anderson, Doris. *How to Raise a Christian Family.* Grand Rapids: Zondervan, 1960.

Bayles, Paul. "The Family Altar," *The King's Business,* 49 (Dec., 1959):41.

Brandt, Henry R., and Dowdy, Homer E. *Building a Christian Home.* Wheaton, Ill.: Scripture Press, 1960.

Bye, Beryl. *Teaching Our Children the Christian Faith.* Chicago: Moody, 1966.

Davis, Clifford. *Your Family and God.* Chicago: Moody, 1957.

Edens, David and Edens, Virginia. *Making the Most of Family Worship.* Nashville: Broadman, 1968.

Erb, Alta Mae. *Christian Education in the Home.* Scottdale, Pa.: Herald, 1963.

Feucht, Oscar E. *Building Family Altars in Your Parish.* St. Louis: Lutheran Church—Missouri Synod, n.d.

———. "Helping Families Worship," *Helping Families Through the Church.* Oscar E. Feucht, ed. St. Louis: Concordia, 1957.

Florence, Lee, et al. *When Children Worship.* Valley Forge, Pa.: Judson, 1963.

Klewin, Thomas W. "We Gave Up 'Family Devotions,'" *Christian Herald,* 91 (Mar., 1968):31-32, 69.

May, Edward C. *Family Worship Idea Book.* St. Louis: Concordia, 1965.

Narramore, Clyde M. *How to Begin and Improve Family Devotions.* Grand Rapids: Zondervan, 1961.

Orr, William. *Family Devotions, A Key to Happier Homes.* Wheaton, Ill.: Scripture Press, 1967.

Santinga, Timothy. "Family Worship Can Work," *Moody Monthly,* 68 (Sept., 1967):32-33.

Scanzoni, Letha. "Family Devotions: Good Riddance or Good Time?" *Eternity,* 20 (Feb., 1969):20-22.

Van Kooten, Tenis C. *Building the Family Altar.* Grand Rapids: Baker, 1969.

Wynn, John Charles. *How Christian Parents Face Family Problems.* Philadelphia: Westminster, 1954.

25

ASSISTING PARENTS WITH SEX EDUCATION

Keith A. Bell

It is inevitable that children will receive some kind of sex education. This is so because they are sexual beings, and sex is a part of their human nature and exerts a pervasive influence in their lives from infancy. The obvious bisexuality of human beings impresses itself on children in numerous ways, such as father and mother, brother and sister, girl and boy, husband and wife. Only an exceedingly dull child could escape observing these distinctions, even if he had never witnessed anatomical differences between the sexes. But the inevitability of a sex education also arises from the ready accessibility of a variety of information from modern communications media and from the open and free discussion of sex in today's world.

WHY IS THE HOME IMPORTANT IN SEX EDUCATION?

The question, then, is not, Will our children become informed concerning sex? but rather, What *kind* of sex education will they receive? Unless our children develop wholesome attitudes concerning sex and its significance in human relationships, in addition to an understanding of the physiological facts concerning sex, the outcome of their sexual experiences may be more painful than pleasurable and more destructive than constructive. It is well known to professional counselors and pastors that the mismanagement of sex underlies the difficulties of many disturbed people.

Parents, therefore, cannot and must not take a laissez-faire attitude toward the sex education of their children. This is particularly true for Christian parents, faced with the task of guiding their children's spiritual,

KEITH A. BELL, Ed.D., is Dean of Students and Professor of Psychology, Seattle Pacific College, Seattle, Washington.

moral and psychosexual development in today's sex-obsessed world. When young people are confronted with problems concerning sex, the attitudes and values they have acquired in the home will determine their actions.

The "Playboy philosophy," which views women as ornaments and artifacts of pleasure, will have less appeal for youth who have been nurtured in an examined faith and who have grown up in an atmosphere of love and respect for all human beings, male or female. Also if they have grown up in homes in which there has been an open discussion of relevant issues in contemporary society, including sex and its use and abuse, and where sexuality and sexual morality are based on understanding the psychosocial implications of sexual response and relationships, they are less likely to experience the deep sense of guilt which some young people associate with sexual interests and feelings.

Parents, then, should be the number one responsible source of sex education. To be sure, no one person or agency can assume full responsibility. The school and the church must and do contribute, but the parents are in a social position to make the deepest and most far-reaching impact on the psychosexual attitudes and values of their youth. And in the process of dealing with these intimate problems, the family itself is strengthened.

Dr. G. G. Wetherill of San Diego City Schools observes that the family which discusses personal problems lives better together. Often parents have found that informal sex education within the family has become one of their greatest opportunities for coming closer to their children, thereby strengthening family ties. Honesty, openness and responsiveness to children's questions and needs in this area strengthen trust and confidence and facilitate communication.[1]

WHAT PROBLEMS DO PARENTS FACE IN SEX EDUCATION?

Probably few parents need to be convinced that their role in the sex education of their children is of great importance, but knowing its importance to the healthy development of their children doesn't of itself make the task easy. Several problems frequently beset parents when they are confronted with the task of guiding their children in their sexual development.

UNEASINESS WHEN TALKING ABOUT SEX

The chief problem for some parents is the anxiety they experience when they are faced with a question or situation which calls for an explanation of sexual functioning or for a discussion of some aspect of sexual behavior. These anxieties may arise from a variety of sources or causes:

Parents may have inadequate information about sex. Some people feel very embarrassed or awkward about discussing sexual functioning or sexual behavior because they themselves are inadequately informed or have an inadequate vocabulary to describe or express what they know. We too easily assume that parents are well informed about sexual matters for the simple reason that they are married and are therefore sexually experienced. It does not follow, however, that one understands a phenomenon because he has observed it or experienced it. To be sure, most young parents today know the basic biological facts about coitus and the reproductive process, but many of these parents, when confronted with the necessity of explaining the process to a child, find themselves paralyzed with fear and at a loss to know how to begin.[2]

Young husbands and wives should begin immediately to develop a vocabulary which is frank and honest, yet clean and modest. They should use correct terms when speaking of their own genitals and sexual functioning. If in their intimate conversations with each other they will begin to use such words as *penis, vulva, vagina, testicle, erection, sperm, ovum* and *copulate*, they will be pleasantly surprised how they may desensitize each other to these terms. And in the process they will become more articulate in phrasing their knowledge and understanding of sexual physiology and sexual functioning. It is much less frightening to answer a child's questions about sex and reproduction when one already has a store of accurate phrases at his command to use at the opportune moment.

Sometimes a group of young parents can help each other overcome their embarrassment and fear. In a young parents' Sunday school class a series of open forum discussions on "Questions Which Our Children Ask About Sex and Reproduction" provided an excellent opportunity to bring these anxieties out in the open and to learn how other parents answer questions which are similar for most parents. This type of discussion can be particularly beneficial if sufficient confidence can be established within the class to encourage even the most timid to participate and thus begin to develop a greater sense of ease in articulating their explanations about sex.[3]

The group leader is the key person in such an endeavor, for he needs to be sensitive to the needs of individuals in the class and help them become involved in the group interaction. If a church can obtain a Christian leader skilled in group counseling, such a person may provide the best leadership for this kind of discussion, particularly if he has had experience in family counseling. Even if professional leadership is not available, small-group discussions may provide effective help for many young parents whose fears arise primarily from their own inadequate vocabulary or sex information, or from a lack of confidence in their ability to handle questions concerning sex.

Parents may have improper attitudes about sex. Some parents feel unable to talk about sex, reproduction, and ideals of sex behavior because they are emotionally blocked by their own attitudes toward sex, or they may be suffering from the "silent approach" which they received when they were children. For a variety of reasons some parents have guilt feelings about sex and think of it as an unclean and base drive. It is not strange, then, that even the normal curiosity which a child has about reproduction and his own sexual anatomy will create anxiety for such a parent.

The following are some experiences or factors which lead to uncomfortable, awkward and inhibited attitudes about sex:

First, some parents have grown up in homes in which discussion of body functioning, of sex and sexuality, and of reproduction was taboo. Body parts were considered extremely private, nakedness was indecent, and body functions were obscene and dirty. Sexual desire and responsiveness were held to be synonymous with lasciviousness. This author is not arguing in favor of casting off all restraint and modesty, nor does he underestimate the consequences which may follow when someone is preoccupied with sexual passion. But repression of curiosity about the body and of sexual desire is not a solution for these problems; rather, it may aggravate them and lead to aberrant behavior. It is altogether normal that a child should be curious about his body, about where babies come from, and about how and why girls are different from boys. Wise parents take advantage of this curiosity to teach their children reverence for the wonder of life, healthy attitudes toward themselves and their own sex roles, and respect for the interdependence of men and women.[4]

Second, some parents may have had unfortunate and guilt-arousing experiences of a sexual nature. Homosexual episodes or incidents, a struggle to control masturbation, and premarital or extramarital liaisons may cheapen and debase sexual relationships and give rise to anxieties and guilt feelings.

Third, other adults may have suffered intensely traumatic experiences of a sexual nature sometime during childhood. Because of the anxiety-inducing nature of these experiences, they have been repressed into the unconscious life of the adults. But the anxieties continue to operate, nonetheless, and handicap their bearers in their marital relationships as well as in their parent-child relationships.

Frequently parents who suffer from such anxieties may need special counseling assistance to overcome old attitudes and habits before they can become comfortable and competent sex educators of their children.

UNCERTAINTY ABOUT PROPER SEX STANDARDS AND BEHAVIOR

Many parents face a dilemma concerning sexual morality and appropriate sex standards. No longer may Christian parents assume that the preponderance of public opinion and the popular social and cultural norms support traditional Judeo-Christian teachings concerning sexual morality. Sex is exploited by the mass media as a prime mode for advertising everything from mouthwash to automobiles. Art, literature and the theater are increasingly and uncritically portraying modes of sexual expression which directly oppose Christian values and ideals. Some of the current radical youth movements equate sexual experience and love. In classes in marriage and the family which the writer has taught in Christian colleges, the question has occasionally been asked by professing Christian young people, Are the standards of sexual morality set forth in the Bible really relevant to our day?

This confusion concerning sexual morality arises also from views being advanced by some religious leaders. The cult of the "new morality" with its situation ethics "asserts its roots lie securely in the teachings of Western Christianity, with *agape*—unselfish, self-giving love—as its sole criterion. The situationist asserts that rules and laws may be superseded by the claims of love in a particular situation, and thus that premarital sex can at times be justified. The crucial elements for making a decision lie within the situation; 'even the most revered principles may be thrown aside if they conflict in any concrete case with love,' says Joseph Fletcher."[5]

An evidence of the confusion which parents are experiencing with respect to sexual morality may be drawn from an article in the *Woman's Day*, in which the authors asked two parents to respond to the question, Should I give my daughter contraceptives? One mother said no because she believed that sexual union is a total union and that sexual fulfillment cannot be found in temporary relationships. On the other hand, a father said yes. He stated that he didn't want his daughter to have affairs, but he believed that the current scene made premarital sexual encounters highly probable; therefore, he felt it was his responsibility to protect his daughter from pregnancy.[6]

What about premarital intercourse? Parents inevitably face the question, Do the biblical standards of sexual morality make sense in contemporary society? Are they relevant to our culture?

Is there any biblical, rational and empirical support for premarital continence? It is true, as the Bible proclaims, that love is the fundamental principle and underpinning of all other laws and rules which govern the Christian's conduct and interpersonal relationships. But love which is based in *agape* rather than in *eros* takes the long look and is more concerned about the long-range consequences of behavior than it is with the immediate response to an excited state which travels under the name of love. The ethic of love which is so vigorously presented in the New Testament cannot be adequately understood except in the light of the total biblical concept of God, man and the world. The ultimate context of every moral situation is that of God's will, involving creation, judgment and redemption. This provides the framework in which all human decision-making finds meaning. Even though man was created to be free, his freedom is circumscribed by God's kingdom in which He is not only Creator, but Lord and Judge. Any man who attempts to live life outside this framework will find the chastening of God to be inescapable.

The case for chastity may be argued from other than religious grounds. Many psychiatrists and psychologists, particularly those who work on college and university campuses, are pointing out that in our day of greater sexual freedom, sexual problems continue to abound; indeed, sexual inadequacy seems to be increasing. A symposium on premarital intercourse concluded that young men and women of this generation need help in rejecting the subtle, persuasive, fraudulent national propaganda of the new sex morality. "Four thousand years of Judeo-Christian wisdom cannot be dismissed lightly. There are still valid and urgent reasons for saving sex for the right time, place, and person, within the sanctions of a concerned society."[7]

Young people, as well as their parents, need to remember that sex is not an isolated, unrelated part of life, but is tied into a configuration of folkways, customs and mores. When something new is added to a culture, or when a significant change is made in one part of a culture, related changes take place in other segments. This is just as true for sexual relationships as it is for other aspects of the culture. Modern monogamous marriage in Western civilization represents a complex interdependent value system. It places great emphasis on interpersonal relationships, mutual satisfactions, and on feelings and attitudes involved in the assumption that love is its cornerstone. It also emphasizes mutuality and anticipated sharing, and an expectation of sexual exclusiveness. Love, trust, family unity, monogamy, respect for human personality, and the oneness of which husband and wife are the parts, are all tied together in this configuration of marriage which is the goal of most Christian young men and women.[8]

If premarital sexual freedom becomes the norm in this country, are we willing to accept the changes which will come with it? What happens to confidence and trust in this new freedom? What about sexual exclusiveness? Are we willing to accept sexual intercourse as a casual experience of the moment, disconnected from any permanent relationships and long-range goals? Sexual exclusiveness is not something which begins after the wedding. It is something which reflects a person's point of view concerning marriage, the quality of relationships he expects in marriage, and the meaning of life. If a person can rationalize the acceptability of premarital sexual relationships for himself, he must also accept these relationships in his future spouse. He must be willing to marry a nonvirgin; he must be willing to accept the first child, even though it may not be his own. What will eventually happen to the Christian family under these circumstances?

One's postmarital behavior and relationships are not unrelated to his premarital behavior. If casual liaisons are acceptable before marriage, what logic makes them unacceptable after marriage? Kinsey and his associates found that women who had had premarital intercourse were about twice as likely to have extramarital intercourse as were women who had not had premarital intercourse. Even if the premarital relationship is not promiscuous but takes place in a stable relationship in which the couple is planning marriage, the risks are great and the dangers are high. Many engagements do not result in marriage. Consequently, intercourse even within the context of a love relationship is lacking in permanency and protection, especially for the woman. The writer has counseled with numerous young people who entered into premarital sexual relationships under the impression of having established an abiding relationship, and later were handicapped by the experience.

Many other arguments favor premarital continence which a parent should have in mind when he talks with his children about the rationale for the Christian standard in sexual behavior. One of the best treatments of this problem is the book *A Christian Interpretation of Marriage* by Henry A. Bowman, especially chapters 1 and 3. Beyond all the usual arguments which one may offer for chastity, the one which seems to be most significant to Christian young people, who want to see their lives in perspective, is that their premarital behavior should contribute to their long-term goals. Most of them hope for a happy, wholesome marriage in which there is confidence, sharing, and mutual enrichment. They should be equally concerned for the future well-being of their dating partners. Exploitation of another person for one's own gratification is not only contrary to the fundamental Christian ethic; it also destroys human personality and produces attitudes which are not beneficial to the tender and protective feelings of love which are so rewarding in a marirage relationship.

What about petting? Another perplexing situation which besets parents and for which they want a reasonable and adequate answer concerns the problem of petting. We are living in a generation in which there is more freedom of contact between sexes than ever before. This freedom of physical contact makes it necessary for young men and women to discriminate between the degree of contact that is wise and beneficial and that which is unwise, dangerous, and emotionally destructive. The parent must find a way to help his youth apply intelligent, critical judgment to this aspect of their premarital activities and evaluate them in terms of the goal of successful marriage to which they aspire. Physical contact between the sexes may extend from holding hands to sexual intercourse. It is difficult to draw any arbitrary line separating desirable physical contacts from those which are not desirable. Individuals react differently to various degrees of stimulation. For this reason, each individual must evaluate his behavior in terms of what happens to him as a person, and the degree to which he finds himself becoming sexually excited and involved.

Perhaps the best approach which can be taken to this problem is for the parent to point out frankly and honestly that intense love-making, often known as petting, is usually unwise, risky and unhygienic when it is pursued as a pleasurable end in itself, when it has as its goal the heightening of sexual sensitivity and response, the stirring up of sexually colored emotions and tensions which can be relieved immediately only by coitus or some substitute for it. Prolonged petting is the prelude to sexual intercourse and, as such, must be considered as a part of the sex act. Intense kissing and fondling are sexually arousing, and prepare the bodies of the participants for copulation. When the resulting bodily changes have taken place, sexual emotions may become so strong that a couple will engage in sexual intercourse without weighing the potential consequences. Young women who encourage petting because they enjoy the power which this gives them over men may not understand the strength and urgency of the impulses they arouse. If they do understand the force of these drives and are successful in stopping short of intercourse, they must still deal with the unsatisfied sexual excitment which tends to persist for some time after the petting encounter, and provides a strong temptation to masturbate for physical relief from sexual tension. Young women who enjoy sexually teasing and titillating young men to gratify their own sense of power and self-aggrandizement should consider well the selfish cruelty of this exploitative behavior and not be surprised if some young men become very aggressive sexually.

Persons who pet as an end in itself are like a squirrel in a turning cylindrical cage—constantly becoming exercised, but going nowhere. The terminus is frustration or escape from the cage. The writer has known couples whose relationships were filled with tension and irritability because they spent too much time becoming sexually aroused with no prospect of adequate release. When they changed their dating habits and began to enjoy a variety of intellectual, aesthetic and recreational activities together, and kept their physical love-making in bounds, their relationships improved, and their respect for and appreciation of each other as persons were enhanced.[9]

Unfortunately, petting is every bit as much a problem for Christian young people as it is for persons outside the church. Some contend that it is an even greater problem, particularly in those churches in which there are prohibitions on many forms of social participation, but seemingly none on petting in the back seat of an automobile in some secluded lovers' lane. For many young people this philosophy smacks of hypocrisy. Christian parents, as well as teachers, must make an honest assessment of the problem and emphasize the behavior which best produces Christian personality and relationships.

INDEFINITENESS ABOUT WHAT CONSTITUTES SEX EDUCATION

One problem which parents seldom verbalize but which nonetheless is of concern to them, is: What constitutes an adequate sex education? During the past twenty years there has been a pious rush toward increasing the sex education of our children, but much of this sex education has had as its chief concern the so-called "facts of life," the anatomy and physiology of sex. Essentially it has been education about human reproduction.

But sex education is considerably more than this. An adequate sex education must deal with those problems which are the real worries of youth. The emotions surrounding sex constitute their central problem. What is a young person to do about his sexual desires? How is he to sort out the various emotions which accompany these desires, ranging from waves of delicate tenderness to upheavals of adolescent cruelty? Should the drive be reduced by satisfaction? Should it be controlled? Can it be sublimated? What is he to do with the fantastic fears, wishes and dreams that usually accompany sexual feelings? Many young men and women, confronted with these surging, imperious emotions, and feeling that their passions are somehow different from those of other people, are in desperate agony because of their sense of guilt, their frustrated loneliness, and their sense of shame and unworthiness. For them, sex increasingly becomes something of which to be ashamed, to be feared, to be loathed. Yet, there it is, persistently asserting itself, a recurring drive which cannot be ignored. It is these dilemmas, these emotions which the young people want to understand, and which they must be able to relate to their lives and express in socially acceptable ways.

The core of the problem, then, is not the biological facts of sex, but the subjective aspects of sexuality, worry about one's sexual development and adequacy, and concern for the meaning of sex in human relationships. It is the feelings and attitudes surrounding sex which matter. We need to help our youngsters understand their passions and attitudes and to cope with them and confront them without depressing shame and confusion, or retreat into infantile or aberrant perversities. We need to help them reach out for what they need, for acceptable expressions of their sexuality, with an understanding of the personal and social consequences of their behavior.

In a sense, sexuality is basic to civilized life. It is a fundamental aspect of a relationship between a man and a woman which goes much beyond a series of nervous explosions in orgasm, or of copulation for reproduction. It is a relationship which, to be most meaningful and enriching, involves not only sexual emotions, but feelings of confidence and trust, of tenderness and self-giving, of protectiveness and concern for the other's welfare, of shared excitement and discovery of communication and participation. It should be pointed out that those cultures in which there have been great achievements and advances in the arts, humane arrangements of everyday life, and where kindliness has been stressed, are usually cultures where romantic love and the private relationship between one man and one woman have been glorified. Where women are merely the physiological artifacts of men, civilization is usually very thin.

An adequate sex education, then, must deal with the questions of sexuality, as experienced by human beings, and consequently must deal with fundamental questions concerning man's nature and his responsibilities in relations with others. This brings us face to face with the moral uses of sex and with religious considerations of sexuality. Man must deal with "right" and "wrong" in sexual behavior, even as he must confront this problem in other areas of behavior. The moral implications of sex may be even more pervasive in that sex involves relationships which have potentially long-range consequences in the lives of others. It is a person's awareness of these potential consequences and his ability to exercise control over his behavior which furnish the grounds for sexual behavior as a moral act. From the social and psychological point of view, parents and the church are in the very best position to provide the kind of sex education that relates sexuality to the meaning and purpose of life.

IN WHAT WAYS CAN PARENTS PROVIDE SEX EDUCATION IN THE HOME?

It should be obvious that the kind of sex education we are talking about is not accomplished through having a few more or less formal talks with son or daughter concerning the facts of life. Rather, it is a prolonged process throughout childhood and youth in which numerous methods of communication may be used to mold the attitudes, values and feelings of the developing sexuality of the young men and women who will one day emerge from our homes to set up homes of their own.

SET AN EXAMPLE

One of the most important ways in which parents may foster a healthy sexuality in their children is to set a good example. Children are much more likely to copy their parents' behavior than they are to follow their parents' words. This is particularly true if parents are persons whom children love and respect. In homes where the parents' love for each other and their children is expressed in mutual thoughtfulness, kindness and respect, children have an opportunity to see love in action and to develop kindred attitudes and feelings in themselves. Parents who encourage their children to give physical expression to their love, who allow their children to fondle them, and play with them in contact games are fostering the child's ability to give love as well as to receive it. Parents are the first important models to their children, and the male and female roles of the home have a prolonged impact on the child's ability as a lover.[10]

KEEP THE CHANNELS OF COMMUNICATION OPEN

Parents who are too busy to talk with their children about matters which concern the children will find it difficult to get the ears of the children when they want to talk of things which concern the parents. Modern life is not always conducive to leisurely talk, but some of the best opportunities for sex education come about in those casual, unhurried conversations when adults and their children are just being their natural selves. Informal discussions of sex are most likely to emerge if the younger generation has discovered that it is easy to exchange ideas with mother and dad. If children have learned that parents always have time to talk about whatever is of interest to their children—whether puppies, the stars, last week's football game, or what friends are "going steady"—they are likely to feel free to talk about sex—providing, of course, that they have not been made to feel that such a discussion is taboo or embarrassing.

Parents who elicit from their children freedom to talk about any subject, including sex, are those who not only talk to their children, but who also listen to them. Conversation is a reciprocal activity, and parents who wish to keep the avenues of communication open must be as ready to listen as they are to talk.

MAKE USE OF LIFE EXPERIENCES AS THEY OCCUR

The following are just a few examples of life experiences which provide opportunity for sex education. The reader will be able to think of many more.

A new baby in the home or the neighborhood. Parents may encourage their children and other children to help care for the baby in a number of ways within the ranges of their abilities. Through these experiences children learn something of the loving care which a baby needs. They also may learn something of the anatomy of the other sex, if the baby's sex differs from theirs. Before and after the birth of the baby, parents may find numerous opportunities to discuss the baby's prenatal development and the process of bringing a new baby into the world.

Taking care of pets or farm animals. Children who grow up around animals make many observations of the sexual behavior of those animals. These provide opportune occasions for discussing sex, and for distinguishing between the sexual behavior of lower forms of life and of human beings.

Observing other people bathing or toileting. Preschool children usually have occasion to see other children, and occasionally adults, when they are undressed. It is very natural for them to comment on differences between males and females, and to ask questions. They accept these differences readily and easily if parents answer their questions in a simple, matter-of-fact way.

When children use "four-letter words" about sex. Children frequently bring home objectionable words related to sex and sexual functioning. With some children, using these words is a badge of belonging to the "gang," or may indicate a need for self-assertion. For other children, it is simply an evidence of a deficient vocabulary. Parents can usually handle such a problem without much dramatization by asking children to bring home all the new words they hear and to decide together which ones are all right to use and under what circumstances.

Marriage of an older brother or sister, or of someone else close to the family. Here is an opportunity for helping younger children learn something of the serious meaning of marriage and of establishing a home. The permanence of the relationship, the responsibilities of the bride and of the groom, and the importance of marriage and a home in an individual's life can be discussed easily and naturally under this circumstance.[11]

These are only a few of many circumstances which arise in everyday life in which parents may have the occasion to weave instruction on sex and sexuality naturally into the stream of the life of their children.

HOW CAN CHURCHES HELP PARENTS WITH SEX EDUCATION?

First, churches can help young and older adults develop and maintain a happy and fulfilling marriage. Every church should have marriage clinics and discussion groups to help its members handle their marriage problems and adjustments. This is the basic step in providing a healthy climate for the sex education of children.

Second, churches and Sunday schools can have group discussions which will help parents. This will enable the parents to become more comfortable and competent in the discussion of both the anatomy and the physiology of sex. For such discussions, a large Sunday school class probably should be broken up into several smaller groups. These subgroups, comprised of compatible couples, could meet in homes one night per week, across a four- to six-week period, to open up questions and problems which they are confronting in the sex education of their children. Each couple should be encouraged to list questions their children ask, situations which arise, their own sense of uneasiness or awkwardness concerning sex. Within the smaller groups, these problems should be ventilated and clarified, and the couples should be encouraged to attempt solutions for questions and problems. Each subgroup should have a recorder who writes down the questions and problems raised and the tentative solutions offered.

After the subgroups have met for a stipulated period of time, they probably should assemble again as a total class to bring together their questions and problems and proposed solutions. It would be well for someone to compile the questions and problems before the full class meeting or meetings take place. At these full class meetings some Christian expert in problems of sexuality should be present to field the questions, pull together solutions, and correct false concepts.

A similar technique may be employed in which teenagers discuss with parents their questions and concerns in the area of sex. Here the problem is more difficult and delicate, and a step-by-step building toward openness, confidence, respect and rapport will be necessary before any significant results can be achieved.

Third, churches can offer courses on marriage, the Christian family, and sex education in the home. These may be offered during the Sunday school hour or in an adult study group on Sunday evenings or week nights. For example, "How to Live with Teenagers" is a course subject that would provide opportunity for giving instruction on the how of sex education to youth in the home.

Fourth, churches can develop a sex-education center. In small communities where there are only a couple of churches (or perhaps only one), the church can set up a selected library of the best books in the field, and carefully chosen pamphlets and leaflets. To expand their resources these churches may obtain films from public libraries, from social hygiene clinics, or from educational libraries of colleges and universities. In larger communities, churches can pool their resources and create a sex-education center of their own, with a wider selection of materials, including their own films. They may also employ on at least a part-time basis some Christian leader who is an expert not only in the Christian view of sex, but also a competent discussion leader who can help individual churches with their programs.

Fifth, pastors can preach sermons on human sexuality in which sex is related biblically to the nature of man and the meaning of life. The Scriptures are much more frank in their treatment of sex and sexuality than is often true for many pastors. Why shouldn't the pastor use these scriptural resources to deal with a problem which the church can no longer ignore? The blessing and sanctity of sex can be observed on the one hand, and tragedies from the abuses of sex can be observed on the other.

Sixth, pastors and church leaders can build bridgeheads to youth. They should establish and maintain communication, and become a friend to whom youth turn easily when they are seeking guidance.

Seventh, parents should seek to broaden their own horizons and deepen their understanding. This can be done by reading the plethora of literature which is now available. At the conclusion of this chapter is a list of readings which should serve as a starting point. There are numerous other resources available, many of which are listed in bibliographies within textbooks. Most of them may be obtained from public libraries. In these days when situation ethics is popular, Christian parents need to be well informed concerning not only the biological facts about sex, but to have a clear understanding of what is meaningful and good in life, and the kinds of responses and commitments needed to achieve these goals.

NOTES

1. G. G. Wetherill, "Accepting Responsibility for Sex Education," *Journal of School Health*, 30 (Mar., 1960):107-10.
2. Lester A. Kirkendall and D. Calderwood, "Sex Education, 1966 Version," *Illinois Education*, 55 (Oct., 1966):71-74.
3. Ruth Strang and H. H. Comly, "Child's Questions About Sex: With Study Discussion Program," *Parent-Teachers Association Magazine*, 59 (Jan., 1965):7-9, 35.
4. Belle S. Mooney, *How Shall I Tell My Children?* (New York: Cadillac, 1944), p. 22.
5. Orville S. Walters, "Contraceptives and the Single Person," *Christianity Today*, 13 (Nov. 8, 1968):16-17.
6. Marion Mainwaring and Fradelle Maynard, "Should I Give My Daughter Contraceptives?" *Woman's Day*, 34 (Jan., 1968):44-45.
7. Mervyn S. Sanders, *Medical Aspects of Human Sexuality* as quoted in Walters, p. 17.
8. Henry A. Bowman, *Marriage for Moderns* (5th ed., New York: McGraw-Hill, 1965), pp. 134-66.
9. Ibid., pp. 122-27.

10. Marion O. Lerrigo and Helen Southard, *Facts Aren't Enough* (Chicago: American Medical Assn., 1962), p. 18.
11. Ibid., pp. 59-62.

FOR FURTHER READING

Anderson, Wayne J. *How to Understand Sex.* Minneapolis: Dennison, 1967.

Babbage, Stuart Barton. *Christianity and Sex.* Chicago: Inter-Varsity, 1963.

Baber, Ray E. *Marriage and the Family.* 2d ed. New York: McGraw-Hill, 1953. Chaps. 8-9.

Barclay, Oliver R., ed. *"A Time to Embrace . . ."* London: Inter-Varsity, 1964.

Beach, Waldo. *Conscience on Campus.* New York: Association, 1958. Chap. 9.

Bernard, Jessie; Buchanan, Helen and Smith, William M., Jr. *Dating, Mating, and Marriage.* Cleveland: Allen, 1958. Chaps. 2-4.

Bertocci, Peter A. *The Human Venture in Sex, Love, and Marriage.* New York: Association, 1949.

Blood, Robert O., Jr. *Marriage.* New York: Free Press of Glencoe, 1962.

Bowman, Henry A. *A Christian Interpretation of Marriage.* Philadelphia: Westminster, 1959.

———. *Marriage for Moderns.* 5th ed. New York: McGraw-Hill, 1965.

Brandt, Henry R. *When a Teen Falls in Love.* Wheaton, Ill.: Scripture Press, 1965.

Bro, Marguerite Harmon. *When Children Ask.* Rev. ed. New York: Harper & Row, 1956.

Christianson, Wayne. "Must the Church Be Silent on Sex?" *Moody Monthly,* 68 (Jan., 1968):17-18.

Cole, William Graham. *Sex and Love in the Bible.* New York: Association, 1959.

Concordia Sex Education Series. W. J. Fields, ed. St. Louis: Concordia, 1968.
   Frey, Marguerite Kurth. *I Wonder, I Wonder* (for ages 5-8).
   Hummel, Ruth. *Wonderfully Made* (for ages 9-11).
   Bueltmann, A. J. *Take the High Road* (for ages 12-14).
   Witt, Elmer N. *Life Can Be Sexual* (for ages 15 and up).
   Kolb, Erwin J. *Parents' Guide to Christian Conversation About Sex* (for parents).
   Wessler, Martin F. *Christian View of Sex Education* (for teachers and church leaders).

Duvall, Evelyn. *Why Wait Till Marriage?* New York: Association, 1965.

Duvall, Evelyn and Duvall, Sylvanus M. *Sex Ways in Fact and Faith; Bases for Christian Family Policy.* New York: Association, 1961.

Eckert, Ralph G. *Sex Attitudes in the Home.* New York: Association, 1956.

Fishbein, Morris and Burgess, Ernest W. *Successful Marriage.* Garden City, N.Y.: Doubleday, 1948. Chap. 4.

Gruenberg, Benjamin C. *How Can We Teach About Sex?* Public Affairs Pamphlet No. 122. New York: Public Affairs Committee, 1946.

Himelhoch, Jerome and Fova, Sylvia Fleis, eds. *Sexual Behavior in American Society.* New York: Norton, 1955.

Hymes, James L., Jr. *How to Tell Your Child About Sex.* Public Affairs Pamphlet No. 149. New York: Public Affairs Committee, 1949.

Kephart, William M. *The Family, Society, and the Individual.* Boston: Houghton Mifflin, 1961. Chaps. 10-13.

Kris, Marianne. *When Children Ask About Sex.* New York: Child Study Assn. of America, 1953.

Lerrigo, Marion O. and Southard, Helen. *The Dutton Series on Sex Education.* New York: Dutton, 1956. This series of booklets is designed for both parents and children. The titles in the series are as follows: *Parents' Privilege* (what parents should tell children 3 to 8 years of age); *A Story About You* (for children 9 to 12 years of age); *What's Happening to Me?* (for the teenager); *Learning About Love* (for young people 16 to 20); *Sex Facts and Attitudes* (for adults who have responsibility for the sex education of children or young people).

———. Sex Education Series, prepared by the Joint Committee on Health Problems in Educ. of the National Educ. Assn. and the American Medical Assn. Chicago: American Medical Assn., 1967. Booklets in the series are: *Parents' Responsibility; A Story About You; Finding Yourself; Approaching Adulthood;* and *Facts Aren't Enough.*

McPartland, John. *Sex in Our Changing World.* New York: Holt, Rinehart & Winston, 1947.

Narramore, Clyde M. *How to Tell Your Child About Sex.* Grand Rapids: Zondervan, 1958.

Reiss, Ira L. *Premarital Sexual Standards in America.* New York: Free Press of Glencoe, 1960.

Renich, Jill. *Developing a Wholesome Sex Attitude in Children.* Grand Rapids: Zondervan, 1964.

Richards, Larry. *How Far Can I Go?* Chicago: Moody, 1969.

Sattler, Henry V. *Parents, Children, and the Facts of Life.* Garden City, N.Y.: Doubleday, 1956.

Scanzoni, Letha. *Sex and the Single Eye.* Grand Rapids: Zondervan, 1968.

Schweizer, Edsen. *The Christian Parent Teaches About Sex.* Minneapolis: Augsburg, 1966.

Scorer, C. G. *The Bible and Sex Ethics Today.* London: Inter-Varsity, 1966.

Shedd, Charlie W. *Letters to Karen: On Keeping Love in Marriage.* Nashville, Abingdon, 1965.

———. *Letters to Philip: On How to Treat a Woman.* Garden City, N.Y.: Doubleday, 1968.

Vincent, Clark E. *Unmarried Mothers.* New York: Free Press of Glencoe, 1961.

Whitman, Howard. *Let's Tell the Truth About Sex.* New York: Farrar, Straus, 1948.

Young, Leontine R. *Out of Wedlock.* Rev. ed. New York: McGraw-Hill, 1963.

26

ENCOURAGING FAMILY RECREATION

Marion Leach Jacobsen

An educational seminar on family living scheduled a discussion of why parents are not more interested in family recreation—why they do not spend more time playing with their children.

These are some of the answers suggested: "Play is children's business; let them do it." "Parents are too busy; they have too much else to do [especially in the church]; they are too exhausted." "Parents think that directing play and providing materials for it are enough without personally participating in it." "When some parents themselves were children their parents [especially their fathers] didn't play with them, so they, in turn, don't expect to play with their children." "Parents don't realize that they have responsibility in the area of family recreation."

It is true that parents are so aware of their large responsibility to support their children financially, to train them physically, mentally, socially and spiritually, that serious consideration of a planned program of family recreation may simply be overlooked.

IMPORTANCE AND VALUES OF PLAY

There has been some reluctance, especially in the Christian culture, to recognize dignity in the words *play, fun* and *relaxation*. These terms may even be associated in some evangelical circles with self-indulgence, wasted time or unspirituality. But recreation is a valuable outlet—a safety valve—for excess vitality and accumulated tensions. It rests, relaxes and refurnishes for the business of life.

"All ages need relief from boredom, relaxation from tensions, and the self-fulfillment found in recreation. Through play, many of our most pleasant associations with other people take place. The change of pace from work and responsibility which we find in play may be as important to our health as rest."[1]

Marion Leach (Mrs. Henry) Jacobsen, B.D., is a housewife and author, Wheaton, Illinois.

Parents must recognize recreation as an important factor in moral as well as physical and social development. Some of life's lessons are better learned across a badminton net than at mother's knee. Play arouses emotions—feelings of pleasure, challenge, pride, ambition, acceptance—that help the learning process. It creates attitudes which, in turn, build character—that part of personality that involves moral qualities. Play may help develop courtesy, kindness, generosity, friendliness, unselfishness, courage, tolerance, democracy, fair play, self-control, ambition, perseverance, determination, self-sacrifice, forgiveness, self-reliance, ingenuity, loyalty, aggressiveness, thoroughness, enthusiasm, reliability, and leadership ability.

Specialists in recreation have come into a new awareness that even in play "we are always dealing with the *whole man* . . . working not principally for strong muscles, great skills, or smooth teamwork, or to reduce juvenile crime, or fill time with pleasant activity and banish boredom, or save the wonders of nature *in vacuo*. We are always concerned with these in relation to man, the whole man."[2]

BASIC NEEDS

The experience of recreation is one avenue through which the individual can realize the fulfillment of basic needs—needs for security, recognition, acceptance, creativity, adventure, achievement, and group associations. It "unlocks the door to self-discovery, to the joy of sharing mutual interests and experiences with others."[3]

In an individual's important but tenuous relation to other human beings, play serves to break down walls that keep people apart. This is true in many other interpersonal relationships, but this chapter is concerned particularly with recreation within the family circle. Recreation can ease and enrich the relationships between parents and children.

What are the walls that separate parent and child? The differences between them in size, in age, in interest and goals, in ability to perform, in authority, and in personal maturity, create a sizable obstacle. But playing together facilitates its removal, whether the activity takes the form of reading a book aloud or roughhousing on the floor.

Playing together creates a feeling of closeness that is not only enjoyable while children are small but that leads to understanding and communication in the later more difficult years of parent-teen relationships.

CHANGES IN FAMILY LIFE

Duvall declares that "families have changed more in recent generations than in any previous century in recorded history."[4] American families today are unsettled, repeatedly moving from a known past to an uncertain future.

In 1890, 64 percent of American families lived on farms where the family was held together largely by economic necessity. Children played a significant part in the operation of the farm, care of animals, raising of crops, and household chores. The family was cemented together by work.

Today only 8.7 percent of families live on farms. Employed parents work away from the family dwelling and are not at home during the day. Now, with increased leisure time, the family may well be more strongly tied together through play than through work.[5]

TRANSFER OF FAMILY ROLES

Traditional family roles such as schooling, moral and religious education, production, nursing, and care of the aged have been largely transferred to agencies outside the home—agencies such as the school, the church, the YMCA, the factory, the hospital, or retirement and nursing homes. In some instances this is a change for the better, but it does result in a measure of decentralization of the family because it strengthens ties outside the home.

EMPLOYED PARENTS

Although the employee's work week has been reduced from sixty-four hours to thirty-five or forty hours, little of the increased leisure time is spent in family recreation. Too often the individual member of the family is overinvolved in activities with his own peer group. The average American father spends less than seven minutes a day playing with his children.[6]

McCall's magazine's "Parents' Report Card" registered the response of nine thousand teenagers to an opportunity to rate what was most important to them about fathers.[7] They rated highest that "he spends time with us." Few fathers appreciate how special they are in the eyes of their children. Most mothers are always around, but it is really an occasion when Dad does something with "the kids."

In 1890 "seven out of every ten working women were single. Six out of every ten women now working are married, and three out of every ten married women are presently employed."[8] Although it may be right and even necessary for some mothers to work outside the home, in many instances what the children need most is not what greater income affords —better homes, nicer clothes, newer cars—but just more mother.

Not only may both parents be employed away from home, but moonlighting further reduces time and energy for family recreation. So materialism—the passion to possess more things—easily crowds out recreation that creates family unity and enriches home relationships.

OTHER WEAKENING INFLUENCES

Other weakening influences contribute to the disintegration of the home. Easy transportation facilitates the removal of family members to other homes and outside activities. Conflicts arise when the beliefs and standards of the home are questioned or opposed by society. The authority of parents is no longer so readily accepted by their children. Modern communication—radio, television, the printed page—enable the outside world to exert a greater influence on young people than the parents or the church. Easy divorce, even among Christians, threatens to destroy the very foundations and framework of the family.

"The family has lost much of its former stability because so many new threats and dangers have arisen. The family is no longer that coherent, integrated group, unified by bonds of loyalty, common interests, mutual understanding, and deep concern on the part of each member for the welfare of the others."[9]

FAMILY RECREATION

Toward the repair and control of this deteriorating situation, family recreation can make a large contribution. Playing with one's children is no longer merely a pleasant pastime; it assumes significant and even crucial importance.

Although other agencies (commercial, civic, religious) offer recreation programs, "yet the home remains its most important center, where life-long recreation interests, skills, and tastes can develop. The parents' responsibility for establishing good patterns for their children, then, is very great."[10] Because recreation is only one part of life, children must also be taught to make room in leisure time for other things, such as love, study, service, worship.

Many Christian parents find it necessary to prohibit some popular forms of recreation. In this situation a positive program for family fun helps compensate for these negatives. Because there are so many opportunities—good and bad—offered for the use of leisure, Christian parents must help their children learn to choose wisely. Delinquents often have never learned to use leisure time constructively.

Aware of the part recreation plays in developing the individual, in strengthening and revitalizing the family unit, and in resisting the secular world's threat to the Christian home and its young people, Christian parents should give careful attention to their responsibility for family recreation.

FAMILY RECREATION ACTIVITIES

A successful program of family recreation demands the investment of time and effort, and requires careful planning. Since fun by process of spontaneous combustion is only occasional and quite unreliable, parents should not wait to "find time" for family recreation. They must *take time* to play with their children. Providing the materials and direction for play cannot take the place of the parents' participating personally in play with the child, and both mother and father must share this responsibility.

Christian parents need to review and honestly reevaluate the recreational standards and practices that make up their individual family backgrounds. The patterns of the previous generation may or may not be worth keeping. Openness to new ideas for family recreation will help today's mothers and fathers do better than their own parents did. Magazines and books, lectures and libraries, and the experiences of other families can enrich such planning.

EVERYDAY FUN

It is probably normal when considering family recreation to think of such specific activities as games, picnics, hobbies and trips. But much of the fun and delight of living together can be incorporated into everyday routine performances, such as eating meals together, getting children ready for bed, and enjoying pets in the home.

Ella B. Robertson says that the three essentials for a good meal are a clean cloth, good bread, and a smiling face at the end of the table.[11] Mealtimes (especially the evening dinner hour when all the family is usually present) can, with some intention, innovation and loving planning, become a time of family enjoyment.[12] The table setting, the food, the conversation, the interest of each individual in the others present, can make it an occasion for fun and fellowship. This does not happen automatically in most households, but it is a goal toward which to work. Personal experiences are shared; individual interests are made family enthusiasms.

Putting children to bed need not be a chore; it can be a time for play and togetherness. Such play has limitless possibilities where there is even a little imagination or a willingness to use ideas from outside sources. Reading aloud together, telling true stories from personal experience, taking a short walk, playing a game (indoors or out), just roughhousing on the floor, singing, or making wall shadows—these ideas suggest the wide variety of possible activities.[13] The father who wants to win and keep the confidence and love of his children should himself put his children to bed, with playtime included, at least twice a week.

Family reading (aloud) will be most rewarding if the limited number of books that can be read jointly are of top quality—written with a touch of genius, loved by many readers, and recommended by schools or libraries.°

Pets in the home make a large contribution to family fun if parents share the children's enthusiasm and interest in the pet instead of merely tolerating it. In addition to the proverbial cats, dogs, birds and goldfish, there are delightful pets from the rodent family—mice, hamsters, guinea pigs, and the newer gerbil (cousin to the meadow mouse). Mothers who are too fastidious to welcome pets into the home should look down the years to the time when it won't matter at all how immaculate the house was, but it will matter terribly whether or not the children had a happy childhood.

The preface to an excellent "Family Recreation Scoresheet" says, "The best gift you can bequeath to your children is not money, or land, or insurance, but a happy childhood. Be honest. Is your house a home? Is it *fun* to belong to your family? Does your family enjoy living?"[14] One thing is sure, Christian parents who laugh and play with their children instead of being long-faced and solemn have a better prospect of enjoying a good personal relation with their offspring and a better chance of seeing them come to love and serve the Saviour their parents represent.

HOBBIES

Hobbies, collections and crafts offer delightful possibilities for family recreation, especially when the whole family enters into the spirit of each individual's project, whether it be collecting stamps, miniature animals, records, shells or butterflies; making woven pot-holders, model planes or plaster-of-paris figurines; bird-watching; finger-painting; or soap-carving.

Many recreational activities can be enjoyed only if skills are developed and pertinent knowledge acquired. Especially during the child's earlier years, parents can share and promote such special interests as knitting, skiing, coin collecting or photography. Reference books, encyclopedias and libraries offer excellent material for the developing and enriching of such hobbies.

SPECIAL OCCASIONS

Plans for weekends cannot always accommodate a special family recreational event, but planning a month ahead can insure the scheduling of some of that time for family fun. Too many parents spend their weekends "working around the place," shopping, playing on the golf course, entertaining friends and being entertained, with little thought of recreation except being *away* from the children! Children will be quick to sense

°Schools and librarians can supply printed lists of recommended books for children of various ages.

their importance or unimportance in the family unit by the way their parents invest their time.

Sunday afternoons offer a good opportunity for recreation for Christian families within whatever bounds they decide to set for activities on that day. Here again, parents will wisely reevaluate in the light of New Testament teaching the taboos with which they themselves grew up. Some they will want to keep, some revise. In any case, Sunday can be a time for family fellowship, and it hardly seems as though the Lord would be displeased if it were a happy one. Some families have adopted the practice of usually doing nothing that doesn't include the entire family on Sunday afternoon. However, too much rigidity in this area may defeat the very purpose of the policy.

FAMILY NIGHT

The scheduling of a weekly family night set aside for family recreation should ideally begin while the children are small. It should be scheduled ahead of time on whatever night is best in a particular week. That date must be held firm, not made available for other engagements. On this night the entire family may participate in one activity, or each member work on his own project, wherever the group congregates.

Playing games, modeling with clay, listening to records, reading aloud, cutting a Hallowe'en pumpkin, coloring Easter eggs, wrapping Christmas gifts, decorating the tree, can all be fitted into this happy occasion. A consistently successful family night must be planned. Set aside some materials that are used only on that occasion—colored construction or gummed papers, clay, certain paints or pastel chalks, a book in the process of being read aloud, a few games that temporarily will not be played at other times. Plan a family night around something your children are currently studying in school—insects, a foreign country, electricity.

Snacking is an important feature of family night—popping corn, cracking nuts, eating pizza, toasting marshmallows, sucking an orange with a hole in it, "sugaring-off" with maple syrup, etc.[15]

The weekly family "do" may sometimes be an activity away from home —a picnic, a trip to the local library with a sharing of interesting finds, a visit to an amusement park, open house at the local fire department or telephone company, a band concert in the park. Whatever the program, adequate preparation, kindly tolerance, and enthusiasm are essential.

Some parents, including the mother of John Wesley and his many siblings, have set aside one hour a week to spend individually with each child. Whether they make cookies, read together, walk, or just talk, the child has for that one hour that rare privilege—his parent's undivided attention. Such "hours" have to be scheduled in advance, and are popular with children. One father took each of his children on an annual all-day trip. He never told them in advance what the excursion would be, and it didn't matter too much because they had Daddy all to themselves for one glorious day.

Holidays like Thanksgiving, Christmas, April Fool's Day, Fourth of July and birthdays can be a long-remembered part of family good times. Christian parents may do well to spend less energy objecting to the pagan or commercial elements in a traditional Christmas and recognize it as an opportunity to honor the Saviour and enrich family living and loving. All such special days, observed with *early* and *loving* preparations, need not be a chore, and can become happy, treasured occasions.

OUTDOOR RECREATION

Fun in the backyard offers families a wide variety of activities—picnicking, gardening, swinging, wading or swimming, flying a kite, playing badminton, tetherball, volleyball, croquet, horseshoes.

Walks that put the whole family in motion can be in the immediate neighborhood or, after a quick trip in the family car, for exploring an unfamiliar area. Public parks and forest preserves with marked trails may be added to the itinerary. A walk after dark with Mother and Dad can be a big adventure for preschoolers.

Both active and spectator sports belong on the family recreation program. Softball, bowling, miniature golf, skating and sledding are not too strenuous for most parents while their children are young enough to appreciate their company. Other parents may tackle skiing, mountain-climbing, and cross-country bicycling. A tandem bike is a good addition to a family's recreation equipment—at least you don't ride it alone! And fishing makes room for much talk and companionship, even when the catch is small.

TRIPS

Trips can be both recreational and educational for the family. Parents will find invaluable a list of interesting places to go and things to do with the family in the area where they live. Schools, libraries, PTA's and civic centers will be able to supply good suggestions—zoos, museums, botanical gardens, boat trips, and tours of dairies, industrial plants, radio and television studios, airports, fairs, beaches, nature centers and pet cemeteries.

Car trips with children can be transformed by starting early enough to allow for necessary *and unnecessary* stops without fretting. Reading aloud and playing games en route make the miles seem fewer.

VACATIONS

Vacations open the door for long-to-be-remembered family recreation experiences. It is good to go back to the same spot summer after summer and build up nostalgic traditions of repeated associations and activities. On the other hand, going to new places sparks the excitement of exploration. One solution to the high cost of vacationing with the family is a temporary exchange of homes—perhaps a city family spending their vacation in the country home of a family who would love to investigate a metropolitan area. Such arrangements might be worked out through friends or the pastor of a church in another part of the country.

CAMPING

House trailers with some of the conveniences of home are popular with many vacationing families, but America is fast becoming a nation of campers. Fifty million people went camping last summer, and there are currently about ten thousand campgrounds in the United States. Every season makes more convenient portable camping equipment available, though it is wise to borrow or rent such equipment before purchasing it. The operation may seem more of a hurdle for Mother to get over, but it has been said that a second try at camping usually convinces even Mother.

Robert Charles reports, "What is so enjoyable about camping? For my family, it was the sum of many varied shared experiences; sometimes, just fleeting moments of laughter; strange predicaments, new acquaintances, new scenery; time to sit and talk around a campfire, time to think and listen. You may think you know each member of your family well, but when you return from a camping trip you will feel you know them much better."[16] Many families agree that camping is not only fun but that there is less family bickering while camping than at any other time. It is a welcome deliverance from neighborhood problems, and it demonstrates the remarkable inventiveness of children in using nature's raw materials for play. "With the family so intimately related spacewise and so cut off from the usual outside environment, it is no wonder that families feel closer in spirit while camping than at any other time."[17]

PARENTS' ATTITUDES

If parents are to succeed in a program of family recreation, they must undertake and perform with enthusiasm, putting their whole heart into the project. Picnics or parcheesi must be not something to be endured but a genuine delight, even when problems are involved. Such an attitude, coupled with a determination to enjoy one's children *as they are* (trusting the Lord for what they will one day become) may call for nothing less than the grace of God, but that is the Christian parent's practical resource.

Family recreational activities should not occupy all of a child's free time, crowding out good times with friends of his own age. And parents who promote family recreation must not forget that what their children really need from them is not a pal but a mother and a father. As the years come along, parents also should be ready to accept the fact that their young people will need increasingly less recreation with the family and more of it with their peers outside the home. The weekly family night will not any longer be so titled nor so regimented. But it will still be important, at least on occasion, to plan good times as a family.

THE CHURCH'S ROLE

Too often the church has, by overprogramming, made it almost impossible for the family unit to function properly. The Fairchild-Wynn interviews of Protestant parents reported, "No problem was as frequently and insistently voiced as the pressure of time and schedule upon our families."[18] In many evangelical churches the weekly schedule includes four meetings on Sunday, a visitation night, one or more prayer meetings and, in addition, women's meetings, board meetings, clubs and youth programs, and choir rehearsals. Programs are developed for each age-group until the family unit is eclipsed by demands on its individual members. A church-related family can hardly find one night when its members can all stay home together. This problem and its remedy are developed in the next chapter, but this busyness is mentioned here because it directly affects family recreation. "Hundreds of pastors have been disturbed by the fact that the church, in organizing its work, often has contributed to the dismemberment of the family."[19]

ENCOURAGING FAMILY RECREATION AT HOME

How can the church encourage its families to have recreation in the home? First, by seeing the family as a unit and then programming church activities so that time is left for families to be together at home. Some churches operate their organization on the basis of a weekly family night at the church. It is one evening that brings the entire family to the church for the variety of activities that in most churches occupy four or five different week nights.

The family night at church can begin with a family supper hour at 6:30 (employed, commuting members coming directly from work), followed by periods for visitation, Bible study, youth clubs, board and committee meetings, and choir rehearsal. Part of the genius of this arrangement is organization that avoids loading the individual church member with several jobs in the church. He can take care of his at-the-church responsibilities in one evening and, happily, on the same night that other members of his family meet theirs.

Some churches not only move in this direction but also designate a particular night of the week as family night at home, and announce it in the church bulletin. One pastor, whose church had planned such a night for family recreation in its homes, "decided to slip around and see what people were doing. Most of them were not doing anything different from what they did on other nights. Some were gone, some were watching television, some were sleeping, and some were reading."[20]

EDUCATING PARENTS FOR FAMILY RECREATION

So families need not only to have fewer nights at church and more evenings at home, but also to know *what to do* on a family night at home. Churches that feel they have more important things to do than run a three-ring social circus at the church, but who also recognize the undesirable character of much recreation offered outside the church and Christian home, will accept the responsibility to educate parents for family recreation.

This can be done in a Sunday school elective course; at mothers' clubs or other adult social gatherings (it is important to train fathers as well as mothers); at a series of parents' workshops or a weekend seminar or retreat; at Sunday school parent-teacher meetings; or in Sunday evening sessions on family living for parents during the youth-group hour.

Church libraries should make available to parents a good selection of both secular and Christian books on family recreation—games, arts, crafts, hobbies, camping.*

The church should not overlook opportunities to bring families together *at the church* for recreation *as families*. Some Christians remember with nostalgia the old "church social" attended by parents *and* children. Other occasions of this nature are a meet-your-children's-Sunday-school-teacher party; closing exercises of a vacation Bible school; the church missionary conference; a church library night; an evening of music; a family talent night; a hobby show; a showing of family slides (limit the number!); the social hour at the annual watch-night service; and mother-and-daughter and father-and-son banquets (father-and-daughter is a pleasant variation). The annual Sunday school picnic is usually not held at the church but is sponsored by it and, when properly planned, can be an outstanding family recreation event.

There is an indirect but even more important contribution the church must make in its work of encouraging family recreation. That is its spiritual outfitting of the individual members of the family to live and play comfortably and happily together. The quality of family recreation in any home depends to a great degree on the personal wholeness (physi-

*See suggested books at end of this chapter.

cal, emotional, spiritual) of its members, especially the parents. Too often there isn't much fun in a family circle because selfishness, self-centeredness, childishness, lack of self-control, and materialism corrupt it. Families need and are crying today for more down-to-earth preaching and teaching that reaches them right where they are in the midst of everyday life situations.

Much evangelical preaching and teaching is theological, only indirectly related to such practical matters as friction between husband and wife or parents and children, worry, jealousy, anger, disobedience to parents, hostility toward children. Most laymen long for help with personality problems, the frustrations of housekeeping, the pressure of competition and compromise in the business world, neighborhood problems, emotional disturbances, or the tensions of suburbia. Some pastors who faithfully give their people the Word of God sometimes apply its teachings only in the most glittering generalities, which the average listener often fails to relate to specific situations in his life.

Fathers and mothers can expect small success in family recreation attempts until through the transforming power of Jesus Christ they personally become men and women of moral integrity, spiritual strength, poise, confidence, self-control, patience, cheerfulness, selflessness.

"How much I enjoy my family, and more especially how much they enjoy me, depend not so much on what I do (in fun planning) as on what I am."[21] The church that tackles realistically the personal needs of its adherents as individuals and as families will be laying the foundations upon which successful family recreation must be laid.

NOTES

1. "Today's Health Guide," "Getting the Most out of Your Leisure Time," *Today's Health*, 43 (July, 1965):37.
2. Luther Gulick, "Challenge to Recreation Today," *Recreation*, 55 (Dec., 1962): 506.
3. Lillian Summers, "Values of Recreation," *Recreation*, 55 (Sept., 1962):332.
4. Evelyn Duvall, *Family Development* (2d ed., Philadelphia: Lippincott, 1962), p. 58.
5. *Today's Health*, pp. 37-39.
6. Don and Doris Mainprize, "Families Are for Fun," *Moody Monthly*, 64 (Apr., 1964):49.
7. Lenore Hershey, "Parents' Report Card," *McCall's*, 93 (May, 1966):64.
8. Duvall, p. 55.
9. Oscar E. Feucht, ed., *Helping Families Through the Church* (St. Louis: Concordia, 1957), p. 50.
10. *Today's Health*, p. 37.
11. Ella B Robertson, *The Fine Art of Motherhood* (Westwood, N.J.: Revell, 1930).
12. Marion L. Jacobsen, *Popcorn, Kites, and Mistletoe (More Good Times for the Family)* (Grand Rapids: Zondervan, 1969), pp. 30 ff.
13. Ibid., pp. 37 ff.
14. "Family Recreation Scoresheet," *Recreation*, 58 (Nov., 1965):447.
15. Jacobsen, *Good Times for God's People* (Grand Rapids: Zondervan, 1952), p. 211.

16. Robert Charles, "Let's Take a Family Camping Vacation!" *Parents' Magazine*, 40 (Apr., 1965):68.
17. Jacobsen, *Popcorn* . . . , p. 118.
18. Roy W. Fairchild and John Charles Wynn, *Families in the Church: A Protestant Survey* (New York: Association, 1961), p. 130.
19. Feucht, p. 52.
20. Clate A. Risley, "Let's End the Church/Home Tug of War," *Moody Monthly*, 62 (Jan., 1962):20.
21. Jacobsen, *Popcorn* . . . , p. 21.

FOR FURTHER READING

A Family Book of Games. New York: McGraw-Hill, 1960.

Brandt, Henry E. and Dowdy, Homer E. *Building a Christian Home*. Wheaton, Ill.: Scripture Press, 1960.

Coffey, Ernestine and Minton, Dorothy. *Designs for a Family Christmas*. New York: Hearthside, 1965.

Dow, Emily R. *Now What Shall We Do?* New York: Barrows, 1966.

Duvall, Evelyn. *Family Development*. Philadelphia: Lippincott, 1962.

Edgren, Harry D. *Fun for the Family*. Nashville: Abingdon, 1967.

Fairchild, Roy W. and Wynn, John Charles. *Families in the Church: A Protestant Survey*. New York: Association, 1961.

Feucht, Oscar E., ed. *Helping Families Through the Church*. St. Louis: Concordia, 1957.

Golden Book of Crafts and Hobbies. New York: Golden, 1957.

Golden Guide to Camping. New York: Golden, 1965.

Jacobsen, Marion L. *Good Times for God's People*. Grand Rapids: Zondervan, 1952.

———. *Popcorn, Kites, and Mistletoe (More Good Times for the Family)*. Grand Rapids: Zondervan, 1968.

Johnson, June. *The Outdoor-Indoor Fun Book*. New York: Harper, 1961.

———. *838 Ways to Amuse a Child*. New York: Harper, 1962.

Koonce, Ray F. *Growing With Your Children*. Nashville: Broadman, 1963.

Masters, Robert V. *The Family Game Book*. New York: Doubleday, 1967.

Millen, Nina. *Children's Games from Many Lands*. New York: Friendship, 1965.

Neugold, Bill N. *Guide to Modern Hobbies, Arts, and Crafts*. New York: McKay, 1960.

Robertson, Ella B. *The Fine Art of Motherhood*. Westwood, N.J.: Revell, 1930.

Siplock, Judith Ann. "Meeting the Needs of Today's Disintegrating Families Through the Church Program" (Unpublished master's thesis, Wheaton, Ill.: Wheaton College, 1966).

Tedford, Jack. *The Giant Book of Family Fun and Games*. New York: Watts, 1958.

The Family Book of Games and Sports. Chicago: Popular Mechanics, 1954.

Wells, George S. *The Fun of Family Camping*. Indianapolis: Bobbs-Merrill, 1962.

Wynn, John C. *How Christian Parents Face Family Problems*. Philadelphia: Westminster, 1955.

27

DEVELOPING A FAMILY-CENTERED
EDUCATIONAL PROGRAM

Lawrence O. Richards

It was a brisk evening. Children dashed through freshly fallen leaves toward homes where windows glowed warmly against darkening shadows. Walking by, you could hear the cheerful voices of children and their parents.

"Got a cookie, Mom?"

"Hey, Dad! Know what I did?"

"Close the screen door, Honey!"

Life in a typical Midwestern suburb—active, happy, and focused around the home.

But at 8:30 that particular evening, three conversations took place between members of Community Evangelical Church. Those conversations were focused, directly or indirectly, on the home.

✿ ✿ ✿

In the counseling room at Community Church the Christian education board was talking about the latest crisis.

"Harv, I don't see how we can start a boys' club now. Everyone willing to work already has two jobs as it is."

"I know it. But look—we lost the Johnsons—those folks visiting us last month—because they want a full program for their kids. Tom Johnson told me that their former church had a top club program that their boy really enjoyed, so they want a church with a club program. Let's face it. To be competitive today we just have to have a complete program."

"Well!" Sue Hanson interrupted. "We've got just about everything now

---

LAWRENCE O. RICHARDS, Th.M., is Assistant Professor of Christian Education, Wheaton College Graduate School of Theology, Wheaton, Illinois.

—children's choirs, plenty of youth activities. Why, it seems I'm out every night now, driving one of my kids to some meeting."

"Another thing, Harv. *Why* must we have such a full program? A smaller church can't have everything some big churches provide."

"That may be, but folks expect it. They feel the church is responsible to help their kids become growing Christians. I think it's our responsibility too. So let's get down to work on personnel for our boys' club. Who do you think can squeeze in another night?"

❋ ❋ ❋

In Mable Harris' car, four young wives from Community's Homebuilders Class were returning from a district Missionary Society meeting. Jan Young had been quiet most of the way home, but then she spoke up.

"You know, I wish I had asked the speaker what it was that made her want to be a missionary. She said it was in her childhood—"

"Oh, I suppose it was some missionary conference at church."

"No, I think she said something about her home. I wish I knew how to guide my two children into Christian service."

"Heavens, Jan!" laughed Mary Gillis. "They're just toddlers. Wait a few years before you ship them off overseas."

"Besides," added Mable, "they'll get lots of missions' emphasis in Sunday school. I know they do in my primary department."

"Well," said Mary, "I wish you'd get my Johnny straightened out in your department. He's getting to be a terror at home."

"Why don't you discipline him?"

"Beat him? Sometimes I'd like to. But his dad spoils him terribly."

"I'm not sure that's what discipline means."

"Well, Pete took some psychology courses in college, and he says we mustn't overcontrol our children. He thinks the Bible is a little old-fashioned on child-raising, with its physical-punishment approach."

"What do you think?"

"I don't know. But I'm afraid Pete's way with the boys isn't working out—"

❋ ❋ ❋

The phone rang in the home of Bob Hall, the junior department superintendent.

"Hello, Helen. What can I do for you tonight?"

"It's Sarah again, Bob. She isn't doing her work at all. She didn't touch her workbook or memorize her Bible verse again this week. I've tried everything I can think of."

"Have you talked to her folks, Helen?"

"I don't want to do that. I'd feel I was tattling on Sarah."

"I'd think her folks would want to know, though."

"Maybe, but I feel that it's *my* responsibility. I shouldn't go bothering them just because I'm not able to do my job."

"Helen! You're one of our best teachers. Don't give me that 'not able to do my job' bit! Maybe you can get Sarah alone and find out what's bothering her. Why don't you try that? I'll be praying for you."

"All right. Thanks, Bob. You're a good superintendent."

*   *   *

AREAS OF TENSION IN CHRISTIAN EDUCATION

What is the relationship of Christian education to the family? How important to a valid Christian education ministry is it to get the home in focus?

We can begin to see the crucial nature of this issue when we note the tensions that exist in three areas of Christian education, illustrated by Community's members: tension within the Christian home, tension between "individual ministries" in the church and parental ministry, and tension between the administration of Christian education in the church and the home.* Let's look at each area.

TENSION WITHIN THE CHRISTIAN HOME

The conversation in Mable's car raised several basic issues that the women sensed but did not spell out. Clearly their church had not helped them face these issues—questions such as the following:

1. What role *does* the home play in developing consecrated Christians?
2. How can parents guide their children in Christian growth—from toddler to teen years?
3. How much can parents expect from the church in Christian education?
4. What specifically *should* parents expect? Missions in Sunday school? Discipline in the primary department?
5. What biblical guidelines are there for parents like Pete and Mary with child-raising problems?
6. How can the biblical guidelines be communicated, so that parents understand them and can work together in Christian training?

One thing is certain. The Scriptures do *not* suggest that parents are released from the responsibility for child-rearing (expressed in such passages as Deu 6:6-8 and Eph 6:4). Yet it is also true that "the unforgiv-

*By "individual ministries" in this chapter we mean the work of an individual serving within a church agency, such as that of a Sunday school teacher within the framework of the Sunday school.

able error of the modern Protestant church is to ignore the home and throw the individual more and more on the care and keeping of agencies."[1]

In most churches the focal nature of the home in Christian nurture is ignored, and parents are left with no guidance as to their educational role. The tensions expressed in Mable's car will always exist when churches fail to define, and parents fail to understand, the role of the home in Christian education.

TENSION BETWEEN INDIVIDUAL MINISTRIES AND THE HOME

Helen's telephone conversation with her departmental superintendent indicated that *she* felt responsible for Sarah's religious training. For Helen to call Sarah's parents would, to her, be admitting that she couldn't do the job alone. And Helen wanted to do the job—alone.

Once we grant that the home is the focus of Christian education, and that parents have the primary responsibility, we can begin to see ministries like Helen's in proper perspective. And we can begin to understand the tensions that now exist—the questions that must be answered:

1. What is the relationship between what is taught in Sunday school, for example, and at-home religious training?
2. What responsibilities does a Sunday school teacher have toward parents and toward pupils?
3. How can parents help make their children's church training most meaningful?
4. How can parents and teachers support each other?

Somehow, individual church ministries must supplement home training, not attempt to replace it. If they are to supplement home training, these ministries must be coordinated with parental instruction.

TENSION BETWEEN ADMINISTRATION OF CHURCH EDUCATION AND THE HOME

In the board meeting Harv was representative of "the average congregation, functioning with a church-centered, instead of family-centered program, with the emphasis on service by the layman to the church."[2] To Harv the church is the focus of education, responsible to provide a "complete program" and "to help the kids become growing Christians." To make the program move, laymen must take on two or three responsibilities. Mothers like Sue Hanson fit in primarily as chauffeurs.

Glance over the conversation again. Note the tensions the others seemed to feel. Yet, again, the basic questions haven't been asked—questions like these:

1. Is the church really able, alone, to create growing Christians?
2. Why must the church struggle to present a complete program?
3. Should we encourage parents, like the Johnsons, to look to the church as educator and nightly entertainer?
4. Are we right to take an adult away from his family to serve in more than one church agency?
5. Is programming that fractures the family, taking a different member out each night of the week, really contributing to Christian growth?
6. How can we plan a church program that will support the home as the center of education, not hurt it?

These issues must be faced. Too often Christian education is out of focus, with the emphasis on church program rather than the home.

Yet, Christian education must focus on the home. The patterns of our church life must be developed with the home squarely in the center, with the home clearly the focal point of our educational thinking.

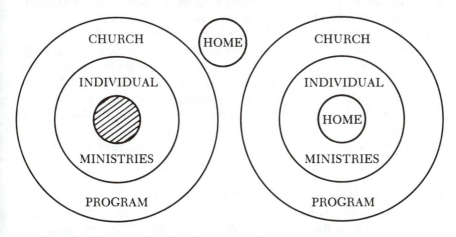

The home out of focus   **The home in focus**

When the home is out of focus (and too often today it is not even in the picture!), individual ministries become the sum and end of Christian education, and the church program is administered to support and develop a multitude of agencies.

What does "in focus" imply? First, that parents recognize their responsibility in Christian education, and are equipped to fulfill their ministry. Second, that individual ministries are viewed as supportive of and related to the parental ministry. Third, that the total church program is planned and designed to support the home as the center of Christian nurture.

BUILDING A FAMILY-CENTERED PROGRAM

How can a church develop a family-centered program? What is involved in making the home focal in Christian education?

The following are three basic principles:

We must train parents for their educative role. Actually, everything in homelife—parents' attitudes, conversations, examples—is educative. It is dangerous to consider Christian nurture simply as moments set aside for family prayer or Bible study. The whole pattern of homelife should reflect essential harmony with the faith we profess. It is dangerous for parents like Mary and Pete to seek everywhere for guidelines to discipline, except in their faith. When parental practices are out of harmony with God's Word, their formal instruction seems to have little impact.

We must relate individual church ministries to parental ministry. Certainly formal instruction in the church is helpful and important. Yet, too often it becomes a mere initiation into terms, divested of meaning by their separation from experience. So we must relate church ministries to the home; we must help parents guide their children in through-the-week living of Bible truths taught on Sundays.

We must administer our church program to help rather than hinder Christian training in the home. This means programming our activities to give families time together. It means limiting the leadership burden a parent is allowed to take, to give him time to minister to his family. And it means evaluating each agency, to see if its function might not be better fulfilled by the home; then encouraging and equipping the home to do that task.

What practical steps can the church take to implement these principles?

TRAINING PARENTS FOR THEIR EDUCATIVE ROLE

What needs of parents should be met by the church? We can summarize them as follows: To be effective in their Christian education ministry at home, parents need:

1. To take a biblical view of their responsibilities and roles.
2. To grow in personal use of the Bible.
3. To prepare for leadership in family devotions.
4. To understand the developmental needs of children and youth, and to learn how to meet them in a distinctively Christian way.
5. To develop scripturally based insight into crucial areas, such as discipline, sex education, training in responsibility and stewardship, etc.
6. To share with other Christian parents in the development of a

community of common family living standards, reflective of their faith.

7. To gain insight into the processes of moral and spiritual growth, and continually evaluate the quality of their homelife in this light.
8. To train for a creative use of family time.

Meeting such a wide range of needs clearly calls for a major effort on the part of the church. Yet, many avenues of education are currently available.* Often family-life education can be carried on through existing church groups, with no added programming to clutter the church calendar.

Clear pulpit exposition of the Bible's teaching on marital and family life is basic. This should be a major emphasis in a pastor's yearly preaching calendar.

A premarital counseling program is also important.

A continuing marriage counseling ministry that is preventative as well as corrective is also important. Family events (such as the birth of a child) and anniversaries provide occasions on which pastors may call. In some churches lay elders minister to families through a regular visitation of members in their charge.

Elective classes for parents may be offered through the Sunday school or evening program. These may cover a wide variety of topics, from general discussion of "The Christian Home" to specific problem areas, such as a course by a church in Texas on "How to Live with Your Teenager—and Like It!"

A family-life unit may be introduced in an adult Sunday school class curriculum. One Illinois class profitably spent a summer seeking biblical guidelines on "The Father's Role in the Christian Home," "Family Discipline," "Family Goals," etc.

Films and demonstrations can be scheduled during an evening service, with discussion to follow. A number of excellent films and filmstrips are available from Christian film distributors.†

Christian Family Week is part of the yearly calendar of many churches. During this week a variety of special speakers, classes, films, etc., may be scheduled.

Good books that cover a range of subjects make for year-round family training. When advertized effectively, and recommended in counseling, books in a church library play a vital role in a family-life educational program.

*For one of the best available discussions of these, see Oscar E. Feucht, ed., *Helping Families Through The Church* (St. Louis: Concordia, 1957).
†See chap. 17, "Resources for Adult Education," for a listing of Christian film distributors.

Informal discussion groups, formed for mothers or both parents, are often effective. Free discussion on child-raising or other practices should be encouraged, guided by a competent lay or professional leader. A variation of this plan is to discuss, chapter by chapter, a book to be read by each participant.

Family-life camps and retreats are being held by more and more churches. Many Christian camps and conference grounds sponsor family-life weeks or weekends, and supply competent professional leaders.

Training parents is a vital task of the church—and one that is certainly not impossible. Avenues of education exist within the framework of the average church today, and resources—books, films, courses, etc.—are available.

RELATING INDIVIDUAL MINISTRIES TO THE HOME

If individual church ministries are to be related to Christian education in the home, certain things are necessary.

1. Parents must be kept informed of what their church agencies are teaching.
2. Parents must support and sanction the teaching efforts of the church.
3. Parents must guide their children to see the relevance of what is taught in church to daily experience.
4. Parents must guide their children to be responsive to God when experiences arise in which Bible truths can be applied.
5. Parents and teachers must share insights into a child's spiritual growth and responsiveness.

While each of these necessities is stated in terms of the parent's responsibility, it is clear that the church must again take the initiative. The first step toward relating church ministries to the home might well be to lead teachers and other church workers to see that their responsibility begins with the child, but ends with the parents. No new teacher should be enlisted in the Sunday school, for example, until his limited-role idea of "child-teacher" has been replaced with a clearly understood "co-teacher with parents" concept. When teachers and superintendents have this new vision of their ministry, many practical steps can be taken to make the coteacher role a reality.

Parent-teacher meetings in a Sunday school department have long been used to help parents and teachers get acquainted. Broadened, these meetings can become occasions for demonstrating effective teaching methods, instructing in characteristics and needs of children in that age group, etc.

Quarterly curriculum previews should be extended to include parents. It is equally as important for parents as well as teachers to understand teaching goals.

Take-home materials provided by the publisher should be *used* at home. Story papers can serve as the basis for an evening's family devotions; pictures or handwork can become a topic of bedtime conversation. Large teaching pictures supplied for teachers can be purchased by parents, and each week the one related to the past Sunday's lesson can be displayed on a bedroom or kitchen wall.

Parent-information sheets should be prepared for parents each quarter by each Sunday school department. These sheets can contain copies of songs the children will learn, verses to memorize, etc. Songs can then be sung at home, and the whole family can learn the verses at the table.

Most important, a brief statement of the content and life-impact of each week's lesson should be included in these information sheets. Parents alone are in a position to guide the *daily* lives of their children and youth. The parents, not the teacher, are likely to have opportunities to relate a Sunday lesson to a weekday experience. To do this, parents *must* know what Bible content is taught, and the general trend of its application as suggested in the church.

Often a lesson for older pupils will close with a suggested follow-through activity. This too should be reproduced and passed on to parents. Mothers of preschoolers should be given copies of Bible-learning activities related to the services—activities they can guide at home.

Teacher-visits to the home now become opportunities to help parents understand their at-home teaching responsibilities, and to inform them of helps available.

Individual conferences between parents and teachers should be initiated by either of them whenever some need or problem is sensed. Obviously, such conferences will occur only when each has grown to trust and respect the other.

Guidance in reading is another ministry a church agency can fulfill. Teachers or leaders should be alert to recommend helpful articles in Christian education magazines or books from the church library.

Summed up, the church's primary role in relating individual ministries to the home is an informational one. A teacher or other leader can provide parents with needed tools, suggesting ways to use them. The parents must do the rest.

Yet, the responsibility for initiating such a program clearly rests on the church. And churches today have the framework in which to take those first important steps.

ADMINISTERING A FAMILY-CENTERED CHURCH PROGRAM

What we do in church programming is largely a matter of viewpoint. Too often in American churches the educational viewpoint is *church-centered*. Today the church-centered viewpoint is leading many churches to a proliferation of programming, and overinvolvement of laymen in church activities.

When church leaders come to a *family*-centered educational viewpoint, their goals change. And if reinforced by an intelligent appraisal of what family-centered Christian education involves, they often consider far-ranging changes in their present patterns of church life.

What steps will a family-centered viewpoint lead leaders to take? Three seem particularly clear:

Evaluate present agencies from a family-centered perspective. What is the purpose of each agency in the church? Is this a valid function of the church, or should it be performed by the home? How is the ministry of each agency related to that of the parents? What steps can be taken to make it related? Are the needs of parents being met through the present church program? Through what church agencies are parents being prepared for their educative roles? How can we best train parents within our present framework?

Even before a clear picture of the total educational ministry is seen, such an evaluation will lead to action. The Sunday school can be directed to take steps to relate its teaching to the parents' ministry. Elective classes for parents can be introduced.

When such an evaluative study is complete, basic changes in program patterns may be indicated. Some churches will eliminate several agencies and activities, and perhaps introduce new ones. The steps taken will vary from church to church, depending on the unique needs and ministries of each.

Program the activities to provide for maximum time for family life and minimum breakup of family units. Many churches today are clustering their activities.* In principle, clustering is simple: Put all church activities on one or two nights of the week so that mother, dad and children are all involved at the same time.

Clustering all activities on one week night is impossible for some churches, for this requires extensive facilities and additional leadership. Yet many churches have found that clustering is a practical way to eliminate several nights a month from a church calendar, and to free members for family life.

*For details, see Lawrence O. Richards, "Is Your Church Too Busy?" *Moody Monthly*, 67 (Jan., 1967):29-30, 50.

Establish a one-job-only personnel policy. When church leaders see that a member's primary educational responsibility is to his family, they will not overload him with church responsibilities.

Actually this policy leads, after some initial difficulties, to improved quality of church ministries. Most laymen with several church responsibilities are unable to do any of their jobs well.

Over a period of years a consistent family-centered educational viewpoint will slowly shift the pattern of church life and the quality of Christian education provided in a congregation. And ultimately the key to such change are leaders committed to a family-centered view, and effective in communicating it on every level of church life.

IS FAMILY-CENTERED EDUCATION POSSIBLE?

Can we develop family-centered Christian education within present church structures, or must we disband present agencies and begin again? The thesis of this chapter is that it *is* possible to move toward a family-centered Christian education within present church structures. This process of change in the local church may be a slow one, but it is within the capability of every congregation that catches vision of a family-centered program to begin to reconstruct their Christian education ministry.

But how about the outreach of the church? Doesn't family-centered education turn the church inward, away from the world of men Christ called us to reach? This chapter has examined only the educational program of the church, not its ministry of evangelism. Yet, to the author, family-centered education seems to be an *aid* to aggressive community penetration with the gospel.

A family-centered educational ministry need not mean eliminating "evangelistic" agencies such as vacation Bible school, which is very effective in its ability to reach homes untouched by other agencies. In fact, family-centered thinking leads to a reevaluation of the function of each church agency, and may well sharpen the focus of many on evangelistic outreach.

Perhaps the greatest implications of a family-centered emphasis for evangelistic outreach are also in terms of the family. Most churches today are *not* contacting the world by means of their church buildings and church-oriented programs. Yet Christians do come face to face with the world in a home surrounded by nonchristian neighbors. How foolish we have been to issue clarion calls to evangelism, and hustle our members to church—*away* from sinners who need the gospel! The adult released by a well-planned family-centered church ministry is freed, not only to educate his own children in vital Christian living, but also to build friendship bridges over which he can carry the gospel to a needy world.

NOTES

1. Wesner B. Fallaw, *The Modern Parent and the Teaching Church* (New York: Macmillan, 1946), p. 52.
2. John P. Uhlig, "A Parish Family Life Program" in *Helping Families Through the Church*, Oscar E. Feucht, ed. (St. Louis: Concordia, 1960), p. 246.

FOR FURTHER READING

Bell, A. Donald. *The Family in Dialogue.* Grand Rapids: Zondervan, 1968.

Fairchild, Roy W. and Wynn, John C. *Families in the Church: A Protestant Survey.* New York: Association, 1961.

Fallaw, Wesner B. *The Modern Parent and the Teaching Church.* New York: Macmillan, 1946.

Feucht, Oscar E., ed. *Helping Families Through the Church.* St. Louis: Concordia, 1960.

Hamlett, Bob. "The Family-Church Team and Its Goals," *The Standard,* 58 (Apr. 22, 1968):25-26.

Hart, W. Neill. *Home and Church Working Together.* Nashville: Abingdon, 1951.

Richards, Larry O. *The Key to Sunday School Achievement.* Chicago: Moody, 1964. Chap. 6.

———. *Tomorrow's Church Today.* Wheaton, Ill.: National Assn. of Evangelicals, 1968.

Risley, Clate A. "Let's End the Church/Home Tug of War," *Moody Monthly,* 62 (Jan., 1962):18-20.

"The Weakest Link in the Chain," *Interaction,* 7 (May, 1967):8-10.

Zuck, Roy B. "Churches Focus on the Family," *Moody Monthly,* 67 (July-Aug., 1967):32-33, 54-55.

———. *The Pastor and Family Life Education.* Christian Educ. Monograph, Pastors' Series, No. 15. Glen Ellyn, Ill.: Scripture Press, 1967.

INDEX